Urban Policy
Reconsidered

Urban Policy Reconsidered

Dialogues on the Problems and Prospects of American Cities

Charles C. Euchner
and Stephen J. McGovern

ROUTLEDGE
NEW YORK & LONDON

Published in 2003 by
Routledge
29 West 35th Street
New York, NY 10001

Published in Great Britain by
Routledge
11 New Fetter Lane
London EC4P 4EE

Routledge is an imprint of the Taylor and Francis Group.

Printed in the United Stated of America on acid-free paper.

10 9 8 7 6 5 4 3 2 1

Library of Congress Cataloging-In-Publication Data

Euchner, Charles C.
    Urban policy reconsidered: dialogues on the problems and prospects of American cities/ by Charles C. Euchner and Stephen J. McGovern.
        p. cm.
    Includes bibliographical references.
    ISBN 0-415-94470-8 (hc.: alk. paper) – ISBN 0-415-94471-6 (pbk.: alk. paper)
        1. Urban policy—United States. 2. Municipal Government—United States. 3. Cities and towns—United States. 4. Metropolitan areas—United States. 5. Urban renewal—United States. I. McGovern, Stephen J., 1959- II. Title.

HT123.E83 2003
307.76'0973—dc21

                                                            2002045467

This book is dedicated to
Nancy and Richard, James and Nancy,
Susan and Ramiro, and Claire and Michael,
and Lisa

Contents

Preface

For more than a generation, scholars have assayed the problems and prospects of American cities and reached depressing conclusions. Scholars of all ideological stripes—from Edward Banfield on the right to David Harvey on the left—have asserted that the decline of vibrant cities is virtually inevitable. Many popular commentators might agree with Barry Goldwater's infamous statement that the best thing the United States could do about New York is to saw it off and set it out to sea. The historian Theodore Hershberg put the matter this way: "All of America's cities are on greased skids. What differentiates one from another is the angle of descent. And unless there is a major shift in public policy, America will lose all of its major cities."[1]

The empirical basis for such a bleak view of the urban condition is abundant. Statistics documenting the loss of population and business, racial polarization, concentrated poverty, drug abuse, random and deadly violence, decrepit housing, crumbling schools, and distressed neighborhoods pervade the scholarly and journalistic literature and reinforce popular impressions of cities as being trapped in a state of perpetual crisis. A recent best-selling book entitled *A Prayer for the City* described Mayor Edward Rendell's desperate efforts to revive a struggling Philadelphia and implied that only divine intervention would suffice.[2]

On the other hand, the unrelenting wave of bad news about cities may be subsiding. The 2000 Census shows that the hemorrhaging of residents has slowed considerably in most urban areas. In some cases the process has even begun to reverse, as an influx of immigrants, young people, and empty nesters has brought renewed vitality to many cities. Marked improvements in a host of social and economic indicators during the 1990s—employment, poverty, home ownership, and, perhaps most dramatically, crime—have given urbanites reason to believe that the worst may be over and that brighter days lie ahead. Some respected commentators have even published books heralding the "comeback" of cities.[3]

As urbanists, we are heartened by the positive trends of the past decade and yet we know that we need to remain realistic about the immense challenges that persist. For instance, just how significant is the "back-to-the-cities" movement when the broad majority of Americans still prefer to live in the suburbs and exurbs? How impressive is it when some cities are experiencing a renaissance while many others continue to spiral downward? Or, in the case of cities that are flourishing, what do we make of the fact that prosperity is often confined to the downtown business district and a handful of nearby, gentrifying neighborhoods while so many other neighborhoods remain impoverished? Why have metropolitan areas become so divided along racial and class lines? Why are the more privileged members of society so eager to abandon the public realm within cities? What happens when the poor are left behind, marginalized and disempowered?

Even taking into account the recent good news about cities, one could conclude that urban America today is characterized by uneven development, fractured communities, and entrenched inequality.

This book investigates how and why U.S. cities arrived at their current situation and what their prospects are in the twenty-first century. Although a variety of social, cultural, and economic factors will be considered, we focus on public policy. An introductory chapter provides a brief historical overview of U.S. cities and the structural and political constraints that confront urban policy-makers today. The following five chapters then examine a series of issues that are especially critical for cities—poverty, economic development, housing, education, and crime. We aim to understand the impact of past policies of the federal, state, and local governments and how urban policy might be reconceived in ways that reinvigorate the public realm by promoting civic engagement and utilizing the potential of a reinvented government to bring about greater equality of opportunity. A short concluding chapter assesses the place of cities within our increasingly global society.

Two final points about the content and format of the book should be noted. First, we have limited ourselves to an analysis of urban policy and have thus chosen to minimize attention to the underlying politics associated with particular policy approaches. We understand that politics makes a big difference on a city's fortunes. We recognize the political impact of mayors such as Rudolph Giuliani in New York, Harold Washington and Richard Daley in Chicago, Dennis Archer in Detroit, Henry Cisneros in

San Antonio, Tom Bradley in Los Angeles, Federico Pena in Denver, Stephen Goldsmith in Indianapolis, Maynard Jackson in Atlanta, and many other mayors, as well as the influence of community-based organizations that press for change at the grass roots. We appreciate that political skills such as agenda-setting and coalition-building are crucial to the success of all political actors.

But we decided to keep our focus on policy, not politics. One reason for the decision is that we wanted to keep the book to a manageable size. We also recognize that others have already produced excellent works on urban politics. Dennis Judd's and Todd Swanstom's *City Politics*, for example, provides a thorough and readable tour through urban America's history, governmental and political systems, and political cycles. A sizable literature offers powerful portraits of particular mayors and numerous studies of the built-in political dilemmas of cities. Even though we try to focus on the policy dimension of urban affairs, addressing the political context sometimes becomes necessary. When we assess particular policy prescriptions—such as welfare reform, community policing, or school choice—we try to assess their political feasibility. We also suggest how even modest reforms may themselves engender a new politics of civic activism that will, in turn, prove to be conducive to further changes in policy—a virtuous cycle, if you will, of good politics and good policy.

Throughout the book, we use a dialogue format. We know this is an unorthodox stylistic device and deserves an explanation. Simply put, we thought that the dialogue format would stimulate critical thinking. We know from our teaching experience that there is nothing like the electricity generated by the give-and-take of lively classroom discussions and debate. All of us are challenged to question our own values and assumptions, consider alternative perspectives, think creatively about new possibilities, and anticipate the consequences of our ideas and arguments. We think of the Q&A format as like looking into a room through different windows: we know that a single question gives us a limited glimpse of our subject, but we hope that a series of questions coming from different angles offers the subject a certain depth. We also think the Q&A format is, well, fun. We were delighted when early reviewers told us that they were somewhat skeptical about the format at the beginning but soon found themselves immersed in the give-and-take that the format offers. We hope other readers agree.

Acknowledgments

Like cities, books are truly collective efforts. We have learned much about cities from working together. We have also benefited from the sustenance and feedback of colleagues. Early in the process, Dennis Judd and Susan Fainstein offered their encouragement and assured us that the topic and format would fill an important gap in the urban affairs literature. (That remains an empirical question.) Judd was also kind enough to read the manuscript and provide much constructive advice. Our colleagues at Harvard University and Haverford College help to make both institutions truly dynamic places of inquiry. Not a day goes by when colleagues such as Alan Altshuler, David Luberoff, and Paul Peterson at Harvard, Marissa Golden (Bryn Mawr College) and Cristina Beltran, Bethel Saler, Susan Liebell, Rob Mortimer, Susanna Wing, and Sid Waldman at Haverford do not spark a new idea or perspective for understanding a complex problem. For the environments and professional friendships that they supply, we say thanks.

Haverford College has furnished generous financial support while offering an ideal place for any scholar to teach, think, and write. A number of superb students at Haverford have served as research assistants and helped in particular with the chapters on poverty, economic development, and education. We are indebted to Michelle Coleman, Jennifer Constantino, Robert Donati, Vinny Indelicato, Rebecca Levy, and Colleen Owens for their thorough and accurate research.

Many thanks to our literary agent, Andrew Stuart, formerly with the Literary Group and now with the Stuart Group, for his enthusiasm throughout the project. A number of anonymous referees carefully read and commented on the manuscript, and we appreciate their perceptive critiques. We also owe a great debt to our thoughtful editor at Routledge, David McBride, whose intellectual range and curiosity helped us to realize our goals for the book. While we have benefited from the advice and counsel of many throughout this project, we, of course, acknowledge any and all errors as our own. Moreover, in the interest of accountability, it should be noted that chapters 1 and 2 were joint efforts. Steve McGovern is primarily responsible for chapters 3 and 5, and Charlie Euchner for chapters 4, 6, and 7.

Finally, Steve would like to say that this book would never have been completed without the unwavering support of his wife, Lisa Baglione, who has sacrificed much in both her professional and personal life in order to advance his career; now it's time for him to return the favor. Charlie would like to thank the many special people in his life, especially Mary Wissemann and the far-flung Euchner-Corzatt-Casarez-Giangrasso clan, for their support and inspiration.

Charles C. Euchner
Cambridge, Massachusetts

Stephen J. McGovern
Haverford, Pennsylvania

1
Cities and
the Life of the Nation

American cities have suffered immensely during the past half-century and yet they continue to capture people's imagination. Despite all the problems— poverty, crime, blight, traffic, poor services—cities still provide a source of energy and inspiration to the nation as a whole.

Think of all of the major symbols and landmarks of cities, and you get an idea of how vital cities are to the life of the nation. New York's Statue of Liberty, Times Square, and Central Park. San Francisco's spectacular Golden Gate Bridge. Boston's Freedom Trail. Chicago's Gold Coast. Miami's South Beach. Magnificent train stations in New York, Chicago, Boston, and elsewhere. San Antonio's Riverwalk. Seattle's Space Needle. The Arch of St. Louis. Philadelphia's Independence Hall. Downtown sports stadiums all over the nation. Cleveland's emerging waterfront district. Tampa's Ybor City. Nashville's Music Row. Washington's Mall, with its unique array of inspiring government buildings, museums, and monuments.

And beyond the awesome symbols and landmarks of urban America are the vital neighborhoods that make up a city. Some bear common names like Chinatown, the North End, Society Hill, and Shady Side, while others feature funky names like TriBeCa, SoBe, the Leather District, Haight Ashbury, Coney Island, and Bourbon Street. At their best, city neighborhoods are diverse, innovative, and dynamic, offering a rich and colorful environment that simply is not available anywhere else. The hearts and minds of even the greatest urban cynics are excited by these stirring images of cities.

1

Of course, cities are always looking for the best way to present their faces to the world. But underneath the glitter and intrigue, cities have to fulfill basic economic and social functions.

And they do. Cities have always occupied a central place in the economic, social, cultural, and political life of humanity. Time and again, individuals with specialized skills and varied backgrounds have come together in an urban milieu in search of opportunity and to pursue their destinies. The blending of people and talent in concentrated settings allows wonderful things: the exchange of ideas, the inspiration for scientific discovery, the creation of art, the struggle over political values, and the invention of new forms of social organization and physical development. The complexity of cities can be unnerving and chaotic to many, but that complexity provides an opportunity for people to regulate themselves and create a way of life that would be unthinkable in other settings. At their best, cities are places where civilization flourishes and community thrives.[1]

So what makes cities so functional? And how do the miracles of cities square with the problems of cities?

Cities offer complex and adaptive systems to organize all kinds of human activities. As the renowned planning critic Jane Jacobs notes, cities grow out of the infinite number of individual decisions that create an overall coherence that no one could design. Countless clusters of diverse people are connected with networks of roads, buildings, tunnels, and open spaces. We sometimes mistake the surface images of cities—the skyscrapers, the odd-looking bohemians, boisterous public events—for the dynamic processes that make these phenomena possible.[2]

The sidewalk and the street provide the connective tissue of the city—the way to gather, arrange, and link people, places, and activities. Like the neurotransmitters in a brain, they provide a system of regulation and feedback. The constant movement of information—and its organization in streets, blocks, neighborhoods, districts, and corridors—fosters constant adaptation and invention. The social theorist Steven Johnson writes:

> This knack for capturing information, and for bringing related packets of information together, defines how cities learn. Likeminded businesses cluster together because there are financial incentives to do so—what economists call economies of agglomeration—enabling craftsmen to share techniques and services that they wouldn't necessarily be able to enjoy on their own. That clustering becomes a self-perpetuating cycle: potential consumers and employees have an easier time finding the goods and jobs they're

looking for; the shared information makes the clustered businesses more competitive than the isolated ones.[3]

Order amid complexity makes cities cities.

One of the root problems of cities in recent decades has been the way these systems of order amid complexity have been broken. Cities have been so desperate for renewal that they have often wrecked the very qualities that give them life. To get suburbanites downtown, cities constructed great highways that slashed through vibrant neighborhoods. To house the cars, cities made room for large parking garages and lots that created desolate voids and exacerbated traffic congestion. To jump-start retail business, cities constructed huge malls that were cut off from the urban fabric. To attract tourists and create a "major league" image, cities erected large convention centers and stadiums that were even more remote. To house poor people apart from middle-class neighborhoods, cities designed grand housing projects that became synonymous with urban blight and crime.

Not all the news is bad—in fact, many cities are enjoying comebacks—but virtually every city in the United States faces the challenge of restoring the systems that made possible order among complexity. That is the job of the next generation.

The Rise and Decline of Cities

Americans have always looked on cities with a certain amount of fear and loathing, haven't they? Has that changed?

If you look at American society in the eighteenth century, you might assume that most citizens viewed cities as being utterly peripheral to their existence. After all, well over 90 percent of the population lived in rural areas working on farms. On the other hand, even farmers had an intimate relationship with urban places. Cities were commercial hubs where farmers journeyed in the springtime to purchase tools and supplies and returned at harvesttime to sell their produce. They interacted intensively with a merchant elite that operated out of coastal cites such as Baltimore, Boston, Charleston, New York, and Philadelphia and served as a vital link between America's vast hinterland and an Old World eager to obtain raw materials from America. Apart from their economic function, such cities became important centers of communications, as news from abroad arrived daily on tall ships. The most widely read newspapers were published in cities. The first libraries, colleges, and hospitals were built in cities. The administration of government occurred mostly in cities. Even for an overwhelmingly rural population, cities were indispensable to the young nation's vitality and even its survival.

The role of cities in American society only expanded during the nineteenth century with the advent of industrialization. The boom in the large-scale mechanized production of goods fueled an unprecedented upsurge in migration to cities, both from the surrounding countryside as well as from other nations. Millions of people flocked to cities in search of work and a fresh start in life. Cities doubled, tripled, and quadrupled in size in a matter of decades. The influx of humanity caused a myriad of problems for cities ill-equipped to cope with mounting congestion, poverty, disease, and crime. Yet urban life, nevertheless, remained alluring, an irresistible magnet pulling people of all kinds to seek their fortune. The nineteenth and early twentieth centuries were the golden age for cities.[4]

Not so for the latter part of the twentieth century. Cities in the United States fell upon hard times. Why?

Technological advances in transportation enabled more affluent residents to move from the congestion and grime of the central city to more tranquil neighborhoods on the outskirts and yet still be near enough to commute to their urban jobs. The so-called "streetcar suburbs" established an enduring American pattern: abandonment of the center and embrace of the periphery. The pace of suburbanization greatly accelerated after World War II with the rapid proliferation of automobiles and extensive construction of highways, all amid a postwar prosperity that made mass relocation to suburbia an affordable proposition for millions of urbanites. At the same time, jobs migrated from cities to suburbs, where real estate for industrial growth was cheaper. Immense factories that had provided employment for countless city dwellers for generations shut down and moved to the periphery.

This decentralization, a process aided and abetted by federal, state, and local policies, proved to be devastating for urban America. The urban tax base dwindled, public services were slashed, and the quality of life deteriorated. By the 1960s, urban neighborhoods were engulfed in riots. Politicians and scholars called for a bold response to the urban crisis.[5]

It seems as though the central aspect of the urban crisis is a breakdown of opportunity and order in communities. The natural response would be to try to find out how to bring those places back to life, right?

Many scholars and policy-makers argue that reviving cities requires nurturing the kinds of places where people want to live and work. If cities provide a strong foundation for individuals and groups to seek their own livelihoods, then a wide variety of urban problems can be solved. The problem of poverty is the paramount problem of the city—from poverty flow all kinds of other social problems, including education, public health, housing, and crime—and poverty itself results from the extreme isolation of certain groups from jobs and other opportunities. Advocates of a policy of place argue that the best approach to fostering equality of opportunity is to provide a robust public sphere—good common places where people can learn, play, work, and look after each other.

Thoughtful observers from Jane Jacobs to Robert Putnam worry that America is losing its common places and, in the process, isolating vulnerable populations from the fundamental opportunities they need to succeed. In the aptly named *Place Matters*, Peter Dreier, John Mollenkopf, and Todd Swanstrom write: "Today, growing spatial segregation means that economic, social, and political inequalities are piling on top of one another. As rich people gather in privileged places, they enhance their political power and social prestige. Poor and working people are stuck in places that society looks down on and that lack political clout."[6] William Julius Wilson's seminal analyses of American poverty argue that social and geographic isolation is the preeminent characteristic of poor people today.[7] Place not only matters but also acts as an independent force shaping the degrees of opportunity enjoyed by people of all walks of life.

Sounds like a powerful argument. But couldn't the causal arrows go the other way? Maybe the qualities that people bring to a community matter more than the particular characteristics of the place.

That is the argument of other theorists, ranging from the conservative Thomas Sowell to the radicals Samuel Bowles and Herbert Gintis. These theorists reason that a well-educated and motivated individual can prevail over even the most inhospitable environment. Where the right and left disagree is on the question of why certain individuals assume certain personal characteristics. Conservatives attribute individual character to culture, incentives, and even genetic makeup. Sowell's history of American immigrants, for example, shows that some groups (such as West Indian blacks) succeed in the same ghetto neighborhoods where others (American blacks) do not. The different success rates, Sowell argues, cannot stem from place if the groups share essentially the same kinds of place.[8] Liberals have a different kind of placeless explanation of urban fortunes. They tend to emphasize the importance of the class system, which empowers some people and disempowers others regardless of where they live.

Who is right?

Not to sound like a difference-splitter, but both sides of the argument are right. People's individual characteristics affect their social and economic mobility, and so do the kinds of institutions and groups within their midst. People and place are "constitutive" of each other. That is a social theorist's way of saying that no single factor exists outside other factors. A person's individual makeup results from the community setting—and that community setting, in turn, results from the individuals who live and work there. The question is how to use policy to make an impact on problems like poverty, education, and crime. Do you focus on changing individuals or changing communities?

Maybe the best way to understand the question is to try to determine what produces great turnarounds in social conditions. Malcolm Gladwell has popularized the notion of the "tipping point"—the stage at which enough elements of an issue change so that the whole character of the issue changes.[9] When do scattered incidents of crime snowball into a crime epidemic? When does the number of students succeeding or failing begin to affect the whole character of the school? When are there so many arsons in a neighborhood that everyone in the area seems to pick up and leave simultaneously? When are enough homes spiffed up that the area becomes popular and real estate values appreciate? Understanding these issues helps us to understand the relation between the part and the whole—the individual or group, on the one hand, and the larger community, on the other hand. Under a constitutive understanding of people and place, policy would work hard to create a larger environment that is conducive to human achievement and well-being—while at the same time trying to reach enough individuals so that they will create major change.

Let's get specific on the history of American urban policy. How has national policy attempted to respond to the urban crisis?

The federal government, under the leadership of President Lyndon B. Johnson, launched a "war on poverty," much of it targeted to the nation's cities, with the ambitious goal of constructing a "Great Society" grounded upon civil rights and economic security for all citizens. That effort was a peculiar mix of people- and place-oriented policies. Programs such as Model Cities and Community Action aimed to transform whole inner-city communities, but they did so by *targeting individuals* for change. Policies for job training, nutrition, counseling, legal aid—with programs concentrated in the most needy communities—would transform both individuals and communities. But before the Great Society could produce a tipping point for either the community or the people who lived there, the programs were cut or modified. No sooner had the war been launched than Washington began to backpedal, as the costs of war in Vietnam mounted and as popular resistance to an expanding welfare state and rising taxes spread. The election of Ronald Reagan to the White House in 1980 symbolized the federal government's retreat from urban issues.[10]

But Reaganism was just a sign of a larger trend in national politics. The Democratic administrations of Jimmy Carter and Bill Clinton and the Republican administrations of George H. W. Bush and George W. Bush were all reluctant to speak out forcefully on urban problems and how they might be addressed. During the 2000 presidential campaign, neither major party candidate made urban issues a priority. Cities, where millions of people still lived and worked, all but vanished from the public debate.

What accounts for the limited debate about urban policy at the national level?

After several decades of suburbanization, the locus of political power in the United States has shifted from cities to the suburbs. Public officials are now more responsive to the needs and interests of suburbanites. Bill Clinton, a particularly astute observer of the political scene, understood this very well and tailored his political rhetoric and policy initiatives to appeal mainly to middle-class residents of suburbia.[11]

But the limits of the debate about cities are deeper. There is a general perception that urban decline is the product of far-reaching societal forces and is thus inevitable. The public sector, even if it wanted to, cannot reverse sweeping trends that are beyond the control of any government. Widespread indifference to the urban condition also reflects an increasingly fragmented society in which the more privileged not only have moved away from cities but have erected all kinds of walls, figuratively and literally, around their suburban and exurban enclaves to separate themselves from the poor and dangerous left behind. Former Labor Secretary Robert Reich's oft-quoted phrase "the secession of the successful" captures the essence of a growing tendency among those with money and power to retreat from the public sphere into privatized spaces apart from the larger community.[12] In such a cultural context, cities and all of their problems are out of sight and out of mind, rendering the prospects for any sustained effort of urban revitalization bleak at best.

Is the situation really that grim for cities? Hasn't the last decade brought a turnaround in the fortunes of cities?

After several decades of uninterrupted decline, a number of important socioeconomic indicators improved during the 1990s, in some cases markedly so. Unemployment and poverty rates dropped. Crime rates plunged. Home ownership increased. Downtown business districts and many surrounding residential neighborhoods experienced a revival, aided by new investments in the arts, entertainment, sports, historic preservation, and waterfront development. In the political arena, cities witnessed advances in government administration, whether led by Democratic mayors such as Edward Rendell of Philadelphia or by Republican mayors such as Stephen Goldsmith of Indianapolis. As a result, the hemorrhaging of population in many cities slowed, with some even seeing unexpected increases in population thanks mainly to new waves of immigrants and empty nesters looking for a change in lifestyle after years of child rearing in the suburbs. A number of books hailed the "comeback" of cities.[13]

At the same time, many American cities, especially those in the Northeast and Midwest, did not experience a resurgence during the 1990s; their downward spirals persisted. Baltimore lost so much population that it used federal money to destroy thousands of units of housing. Many urban school systems were ravaged by dilapidated buildings, violence, and an inability to keep the best teachers. Even in cities that experienced a revival in downtowns, troubles persisted and worsened elsewhere. The downtown is its own enclave of energy and vibrancy, while the rest of the public realm may be run down and troubled. In Cleveland, for example, new sports arenas and museums improved the city's image nationwide but did not alleviate the city's basic problems. In Philadelphia, despite an impressive renewal of its Center City, neighborhoods to the north, west, and south continued to deteriorate and residents there continued to flee; Philadelphia lost more residents than any other U.S. city during the 1990s.[14]

This may sound callous, but why should Americans care so much about saving cities?

Start with moral considerations. In many urban communities, people are consigned to dangerous neighborhoods with few job prospects, poor schools, excessive health risks, and decaying or expensive housing. The American ideal of equality of opportunity meets its greatest challenge in the inner city. Even those who maintain that many individuals mired in inner-city poverty are there because of their own faults would have to acknowledge that many others—young children, to take just one obvious example—are innocent victims.

If moral arguments are inadequate to sway public opinion, advocates of urban revitalization might appeal to the self-interest of nonurbanites. You could make a case that cities are essential to the health of the nation. Economists talk about the benefits to be derived from agglomeration economies. Large settlements offer more advantages with respect to skills, productivity, and consumer access than small places. Urban businesses benefit by sharing an extensive labor market, a sizeable network of suppliers, and information that comes from frequent interaction with similar firms in the area. The creativity that comes from vibrant and diverse cities benefits the larger metropolis in the form of jobs, cultural and recreational opportunities, and incubators for new ideas.

At the same time, urban density helps to alleviate the costs of providing infrastructure and other public goods. It is much easier to supply transportation, energy, communications, education, and financial services in places where people are concentrated. The efficiencies of scale in cities reduce the overall costs of all kinds of activities. That is one reason why many planners and economists are concerned about the "sprawling" of America. Not only does the dispersal of development damage the environment, exacerbate traffic congestion, and make access to jobs difficult, but it also imposes high costs for basic infrastructure and services. As people move farther from the central city and inner suburbs, existing assets are left behind, essentially squandered. The quality of life for everyone declines in the sprawling metropolis.[15]

If popular support for urban revitalization remains tepid, then is there any hope for cities?

Some urge a more radical approach involving changes in governing structures. There are two schools of thought. One school—the decentralists—contends that government has become too centralized, that large, bureaucratic institutions have overwhelmed the ability of ordinary citizens to influence decisions that affect people on a day-to-day basis. People have come to feel disempowered and alienated from the political sphere. Power needs to be devolved from centralized, bureaucratic structures to local structures, perhaps at the neighborhood level. Such a decentralization of political authority will give ordinary people an incentive to engage in politics and government. Citizen empowerment will then spark the rejuvenation of cities.[16]

Another school of thought—the regionalists—takes the opposite approach. The regionalists insist that the governing structures of metropolitan areas are already too decentralized, with hundreds of units of government each pursuing their own separate agendas to the neglect of any common interests. The result is an inefficient use of resources and irrational public planning—and deep inequality across the region. The remedy, according to this perspective, is more centralization of political authority in the form of a stronger regional or metropolitan government.[17]

But if enacting public policy to benefit cities is such a tall order, it will be even more difficult to change the structure of government, right?

Precisely. Such changes typically require amendments to a state constitution or reforms of a city charter. Given the growing dominance of suburban interests in state legislatures—and the powerful lobbies for businesses, developers, home owners, and public-employee unions—it is hard to imagine major changes in the basic structure of local and regional governance. This does not mean that institutional changes are not worth pursuing but that the barriers to change are extremely formidable.

Is there any prospect for finding the right balance of centralized standards and resources on the one hand and local control of institutions on the other hand?

Maybe. Take the issue of public education. Most people agree that better schools provide one of the biggest attractions to suburban living. Urban school systems—with many notable exceptions—usually provide inferior education. City schools are too bureaucratic, beholden to union politics, unfocused academically, and overwhelmed by social problems that poor children bring to the classroom.

One approach to the urban schools problem might be to centralize and decentralize at the same time. If funding inequality is a major problem—with some suburban districts providing more than twice the per-pupil dollars as urban districts—then maybe school funding should be centralized. Maybe the state should pay most or all of the cost of public education, so that students in all districts enjoy equal opportunity. Michigan Governor John Engler in 1993 took a major step in this direction when he engineered a drastic cut in property taxes, the primary source of school funding, in exchange for a major increase in state funding of public schools. At the same time, if excessive bureaucracy is a problem in urban schools, maybe the actual operation of schools should be decentralized. Maybe the nation should reverse the century-long trend toward consolidation of districts and schools—as the nation's population has more than doubled, the number of districts has declined from 120,000 to 16,000—and allow schools to break off and run smaller operations. If the state established strong funding and clear expectations for education and then allowed schools and districts to meet those expectations in their own ways, maybe public education would enjoy the best of centralization and decentralization.

That seems to be a sound approach—but very difficult to realize in the real world of interest-group politics. Would suburban schools accept more equal funding? Would teacher unions accept a restructuring that reduced their bargaining power? Not without a fight. So where does that leave cities seeking creative reform?

In a democracy, reform requires winning the consent of the people, and so there is no choice but to find new ways to win public support. Somehow, the public and key constituency groups—from public-employee unions to developers to community advocates—need to be convinced that revitalizing cities is both desirable and possible.

The Communitarian Vision

So you're going to convince people to care about something besides their selfish interests? How could that happen?

To understand that issue, let us consider two different kinds of communities, one individualist, the other communitarian. Each exerts influence on the American political process. Each pulls the system in different directions.

First, consider a community in which people see the good life mainly as an individual endeavor, their success dependent solely on their own ability and effort. Such a community is deemed to function well when individuals pursue their own self-interest without interference from the government or other large institutions. The role of government is confined to maintaining a basic order so that individuals will be assured of the freedom and opportunity to seek their own agendas. It is assumed that the public interest—what is best for the community as a whole—will emerge out of the clash of myriad individual and group interests. The hallmarks of this individualist vision are individual autonomy, a limited public sphere, and a dynamic private sphere in which people robustly pursue their goals and desires. Individuals are asked only to respect the liberty of others and to perform certain minimal duties to keep the government functioning, such as periodic voting, payment of taxes, and obeying the law.[18]

How does such a vision of society and politics bear upon the status of cities?

In a community in which individualism flourishes, people focus their lives on family, workplace, and a small circle of friends. In such a community, people might see cities as being remote from their lives. If city dwellers wish to rebuild their community, that is fine—but the task is theirs alone. Even when critics appreciate the importance of cities to society at large, they often doubt whether the government can or should try to fix what ails cities. They see cities as products of powerful, private-sector forces that are immune from the efforts of public policy. The McGill Commission, appointed by President Jimmy Carter, argued that cities go through life cycles just as natural systems do and that policy-makers should not attempt to arrest the decline of industrial cities but should instead pay attention to the needs of people who happen to live in cities and towns.[19]

What is the alternative to the individualist vision of society and politics?

Consider a different kind of community where people see the good life as a collective enterprise. In this community, people believe that their interests are bound up with others living in the community. Rather than understanding society to be a collection of individuals, each operating independently, communitarians see society as the integration of individuals and groups into a common web of life. This collective mind-set cannot imagine living somewhere just as an individual. The creativity and joy of everyday life depends on the overlapping networks of people in jobs, schools, churches, political parties, advocacy groups, sports leagues, and other activities that bring people together. "We" is as important as "I" in this way of thinking. And—here's the importance of this mind-set—there is nothing that a "we" cannot do when people put their minds to it. Whether it is fighting a highway project, building a playground, running an insurgent political campaign, reviving a decayed business district, or fixing a local school, the "we" orientation has a power to make positive change in the city and beyond. Communitarians celebrate popular participation in the public realm and place considerable faith in the power of government to effect social change, including the revitalization of cities.[20]

Our society contains both individualists and communitarians, but aren't the individualists dominant?

It seems that way. Western European countries—Great Britain, France, Italy, Germany, Sweden, to name a handful—have embraced a wide range of more collective approaches to public policy. Each of those countries offers comprehensive health care, generous public assistance, free higher education, and vast public housing. Each of those countries also sets clear rules for public safety—gun control, for example—that free regional and local governments from having to take on major social policy challenges. The United States, on the other hand, has always been skeptical of a comprehensive policy for anything except national defense. American social policy develops in a scattered way across the states and localities. Even when the federal government gets involved, it is sure to provide leeway for states and localities; the federal government will set a basic standard or incentive for an issue—such as public assistance, health care, or public housing—and ask the states and localities to make adjustments that they consider appropriate for the people in their jurisdictions.

Americans seem much more comfortable with allowing the private market to determine the winners and then allowing for government to play only an ameliorative role in addressing social problems. A common refrain of Republican and Democratic politicians alike is that the "best social program is a job." Americans seem to believe at their core that private enterprise offers more people a chance to overcome their problems than any government program can. Government action is seen, by and large, as a necessary *response* to the concerns that are not addressed by the private sector rather than a structure to *establish* basic social opportunity.

You could argue that individualism has triumphed over communalism because it works better. It encourages people to be strivers, to work hard, invent, and build new things. Foreigners often envy America's sense of openness and possibility. Students come from all over the world to study at American universities. In the past generation, immigration has reached a new peak in the United States, particularly its cities. Immigrants and refugees come to the United States to find a better economic life; many countries, in fact, depend on the payments that family members send back to the native country from the United States.[21] Even some of the heartiest liberals in America agree that the room for individuals to strike out original paths for their lives is what makes America distinctive.

If there is a broad popular consensus in favor of individualism, then what is the problem?

People have increasing doubts about the kind of society that an individualistic system has produced. The emphasis on individual autonomy has had an atomizing effect. Individuals become so preoccupied with pursuing their own interests that they have trouble seeing themselves as members of any larger community with common bonds and goals. In the modern world, labor is increasingly divided into highly specialized jobs that individuals commute to by driving alone in their self-contained automobiles. Leisure time is spent sitting alone, watching television.

What are the economic consequences of this atomism?

In the economic realm, the acquisitive individualism of the Reagan and Clinton periods led to a widening of the gap between rich and poor. The United States has a more unequal distribution of income than it has had in more than a generation—by some measures, the most since the Wall Street Crash of 1929. The highest quintile (20 percent of the population) earned 50.0 percent of the nation's income in 2001, compared with 40.6 in 1969. The lowest quintile's share of the national income fell from 5.6 to 3.5 percent during that same period. The United States now has the highest ratio between the income shares of the top and bottom quintiles in the Western world: approximately 12 to 1, compared to 9 to 1 for France and Canada, 8 to 1 for Britain, 7 to 1 for Sweden and the Netherlands, and 4 to 1 for Japan. (The degree of inequality is larger and growing in Third World countries. It is not unusual to find ratios of 20 to 1 or even 30 to 1 in some poor, developing countries.) The share of the nation's wealth held by the top 0.5 percent of all households, the so-called "superrich," was 26.9 percent in 1983; as recently as 1976, that figure was 14.4 percent. The top strata of the system now hold more wealth and take home more money than ever before.[22]

The vulnerability of such an income distribution is underscored by the growing indebtedness of the lower quintiles of the population. Personal bankruptcies in recent years have reached historic highs. In the 1980s, total personal debt increased to $3 trillion in an economy that generated about $5 trillion a year. Annual borrowing increased from $394 billion in 1981 to $739 billion in 1986. Consumer debt passed $1 trillion in 1997, about $400 billion of which is credit-card debt. In 1997, there were more than 1.3 million bankruptcies, an increase of 63 percent from just ten years ago—at a time when the American economy was experiencing its greatest modern spurt of growth. Outstanding household debt was 101.5 percent of disposable income in 2001. Americans, who once saved 8 percent of their total income, now actually spend 1 percent more than they make. Monthly payments for personal debt—student loans, credit cards, and other short-term loans—now take 8 percent of a person's income.[23]

And when the rich and poor live in different worlds, it is hard to get the rich to care for the poor.

In a highly fractured society, the sense of mutual obligation becomes tenuous. Privileged groups do not have a sense of responsibility for the society at large. At the same time, individuals who are systematically ignored begin to feel aloof and alienated from the political system. Deep-seated alienation prompts the powerless to embrace modes of thought that legitimize separation from mainstream ideas and institutions.[24] Any thought of building diverse coalitions to advance common goals is dismissed as hopelessly naïve.

This fragmentation can be especially acute in big cities. Urban America at the turn of the twenty-first century is deeply fractured by race, class, and culture. Economic restructuring and social and technological transformations have driven people apart instead of bringing them together. Prosperous city centers characterized by shimmering, high-rise office buildings, luxury hotels, expensive new museums and aquariums, and gentrified historic districts are surrounded by vast stretches of struggling and impoverished neighborhoods. Inequality and segregation have become the defining features of the big city.

So at its extreme, an individualistic mind-set can prevent people from pooling their concerns into a larger common agenda. But American history is filled with examples of people coming together as communities to address common problems.

Individualism dominates American political philosophy, but communal sentiments lurk under the surface. The classic statement of this alternative outlook on politics is Alexis de Tocqueville's *Democracy in America*. A French aristocrat who toured the United States in the early nineteenth century, Tocqueville was amazed by the energy and common cause he found in

American communities. While Europeans tended to look to a centralized government to fix their problems, Americans tended to roll up their sleeves and fix problems themselves.[25] These communal values also emerged in periodic protest movements against entrenched interests.[26] The Populist movement of the late nineteenth century offered a vision of people coming together to create a community of equals in which the good of the community is given priority over the good of individuals and groups.[27] More recently, the civic outpouring that followed the September 11, 2001, terrorist attacks in New York City showed a deep desire of people to contribute to something bigger than themselves, especially in a time of crisis. But by and large it is safe to say that classical individualism has been the dominant public philosophy of America throughout the nation's history.

A desire for common cause—for people pulling together to solve problems as a community—bursts into the open episodically.

Right. Even as popular and academic support for individualism soared during the three decades following World War II, some scholars and commentators warned of the dangers of possessive individualism and the culture of narcissism that it spawned.[28] Individualism reached its peak in the1980s with the rise of Ronald Reagan and his unapologetic embrace of individual pursuit of self-interest. At that point, many thoughtful people began to reconsider communitarian ideals as an alternative to the extremes of individualism. In 1984, a group of scholars headed by Robert Bellah published the landmark work *Habits of the Heart,* which questioned just how deep the popular support was for extreme individualism. Bellah and his colleagues conducted hundreds of interviews with ordinary citizens and discovered that while Americans demonstrated an attachment to individual freedom, they also spoke movingly about community and their concern for the public interest.[29]

As Robert Putnam has pointed out, a nation of disconnected individuals not only creates a lonelier world but costs us in a wide range of practical ways as well. When neighbors do not know each other, for example, they are less likely to look after each other's homes. When people do not participate in rich social networks, they do not have access to the creativity and connections that make economic enterprises efficient and creative. When people lose their sense of commitment to the community, they are more likely to cheat on taxes or violate other laws. When people lose their "we" feelings, they are less committed to their jobs and even families.[30]

If individualism has its pitfalls, the communitarian approach surely does too. What are they?

Individualists contend that the enthusiasm for community inevitably leads to a slighting of the individual. Taken too far, some fear, the authoritarian impulses of a community could pressure individuals to conform to some amorphous conception of the general will. Others question the very notion of a common good and whether it is at all identifiable or achievable in a diverse society.[31]

And yet, despite these concerns, this communitarian approach has continued to attract adherents in recent years as a public philosophy that offers something valuable in a fragmented and divided society. Even as most Americans continue to respect individual autonomy, there seems to be a growing consensus that more attention needs to be given to community and the collective well-being of society. And there is no place in the country more in need of a revival of civic spirit than the American city.

What are the elements of a communitarian approach to politics, as opposed to an individualist approach?

The communitarian approach has three key elements: the engagement of people at all levels of the system, the marshaling of the power and resources of government to ensure a fair opportunity for all to pursue their goals, and the creation of public goods and spaces that all the members of the community can share. Each of these elements must be guided by not only a sense of entitlement but also a sense of responsibility for the community at large. Let us explore each of the three elements of a communitarian vision in turn.

First, the system has to *engage people at all levels of the system*. People need to be consulted about their needs on a regular basis. Elections provide a critical process for understanding how the public feels about common concerns, but voting is not enough. People also need to be brought into the public sphere to engage in political dialogue about community issues. There are literally dozens of ways to engage ordinary citizens in making policy. Residents can join political parties, neighborhood associations, boards of trade, special planning teams, nonprofit organizations, and advocacy organizations. They can petition elected representatives and government agencies. They can convene meetings and conventions, publish newspapers and pamphlets, and rally neighbors.

Second, the system has to *use the government* to provide basic equality of opportunity for all. Ultimately, to make things happen, people need resources. The government plays a critical role in providing resources such as job training programs, tax incentives to spur the production of affordable housing, and sophisticated technology for police to fight crime. Communitarians disagree among themselves about how much the government should engage in redistributive activities, but at the very least government should make sure that citizens enjoy the same basic goods and services wherever they live. States, for example, should provide roughly equal funding for schools. This does not mean that the government should try to determine economic outcomes, only that government should provide the same basic opportunities to all.

Third, the system should *provide a robust set of public goods and spaces for all.* At bottom, the city is a place that people share. For people to have a common sense of ownership—and the same opportunities to develop their talents and interests—they need to share that place with each other. That is why public facilities are not just "extras" but indispensable ingredients in the good city. Parks, playgrounds, pools and rinks, libraries, museums, universities, concert halls and theaters, plazas, galleries, cafés, waterfronts, community centers, houses of worship, bookstores, restaurants, and even sidewalks are all vital urban places. They provide open opportunities for people to pursue their interests as individuals, as groups, and as a larger community.

For a city to be a truly civic place, though, it needs to do more than provide these core benefits to its citizens. It also needs to find a way to demand something from citizens. Ordinary people need to have a spirit of commitment to something larger than their own interests. They need to feel a sense of responsibility for contributing to the well-being of the city. One of the frustrations of city leaders is the NIMBY (Not In My Back Yard) mentality that many neighborhood residents express when proposals for new housing and public facilities arise. In neighborhood after neighborhood, residents rise in protest against proposals for new housing, school buildings, ball fields, halfway houses, and public facilities. Concerned about property values, traffic patterns, and "undesirable" populations, residents often reject reasonable proposals—and politicians concerned about reelection bow to their concerns. But ultimately, the city must provide space for these kinds of facilities. While public officials should listen to residents' concerns, the residents in turn need to accept their role in supporting the many people and activities that make the city work. Benefit without responsibility is just selfishness.

Is it even plausible to believe that Americans, who have been so thoroughly entrenched in an individualist political culture, might view the political world through a communitarian lens and alter their political behavior accordingly?

There is no denying that fostering a broader sense of community and civic engagement is hard to do. But the potential is there.

Can you give an example of how public policy could help to revive the civic spirit—and, in turn, improve the political capacity of cities?

Let's take two basic areas of public policy—housing and crime. In each of those areas, mayors and other civic leaders realized that they did not have the capacity to turn things around themselves, so they adopted new strategies that required working with ordinary citizens in the community.

In response to federal cutbacks in housing programs, states and cities had to invent new ways of building and restoring housing. One way was to work with community development corporations (CDCs). CDCs are non-profit organizations that organize people in the neighborhoods to find appropriate sites, develop designs, and put together the financial and political backing for the creation of affordable housing. In New York, Chicago, Los Angeles, and other major cities, CDCs became the de facto housing development agencies of the city government. Although they could be criticized for increasing the development costs of housing, CDCs got the job done. They also engaged the community in the process, with hundreds of community meetings, job-training programs, and neighborhood picnics. When city governments turned to CDCs to work on housing policy, they got the side benefit of community engagement.

The same could be said for community policing. Just a decade ago, many American cities considered crime to be beyond their control. Drugs, guns, and gangs seemed too powerful for overworked police departments. But then police departments, one by one, adopted a wide range of new policies that engaged the communities in their own policing. Many police departments returned to the old beat systems, assigning cops to specific neighborhoods so that problems could be identified before they flared up. Simply getting cops out of squad cars sent a powerful message to residents: they are one of us. As cops got to know the neighborhoods at the street level, they began to spot problems better—and they could call on growing networks of churches, schools, and neighborhood groups to help maintain order. Neighborhood watches flourished in many cities as well. In once-desperate cities like Baltimore and New Orleans, community policing was supplemented by sophisticated new computer-based strategies to track and confront crime.

OK, so communities work together to build housing and maintain order on the streets. But what can the communitarian approach do for other problems?

The basic dynamics are the same for all policy areas. By creating a common ground with a broad commitment to investing in and improving that common ground, cities can address a wide range of other problems as well. Just for the purposes of illustration, let's consider two radically different policy areas—education and the natural environment.

Education is by many accounts the most pressing issue facing cities. If working- and middle-class families are to live in cities, they need more than affordable housing and safe streets. They need good schools. It is common in many urban neighborhoods for young families to stay in the city until their first child reaches the age of five or six, when children start kindergarten. Parents find themselves frustrated with rundown buildings, bureaucratic administrations, inadequate resources, and principals and teachers who are worn down by the everyday pressures and demands of the job. Parents look at standardized test scores and decide to go where schools have demonstrated higher levels of performance.[32]

A communitarian approach to education reform might dismantle the consolidated school district, with its command-and-control approach to running schools, and replace it with a flexible system that allows students to use government grants to attend whatever schools meet their needs. By letting "a hundred flowers bloom," this education reform would encourage schools to reach out to families and develop creative ways to address a whole host of difficult challenges. This approach rests on the basic finding of the effective schools literature: the best schools are those where principals, teachers, and families create their own distinctive community of learning. Rather than imposing cookie-cutter rules for communities of all kinds, this choice model would give everyone the resources—and the freedom—to build the best way for them.[33]

Might this more decentralized approach also permit the emergence of problematic schools too? What is to prevent a school from offering a curriculum based on some highly dubious pedagogical theory or limiting enrollment to students of a particular racial or economic background?

The shift away from a centralized, bureaucratic model of public education does not and should not require an abdication of public authority. At a minimum, all public schools would continue to be bound by certain basic standards, including civil rights laws, a core curriculum, and hiring standards for teachers. Exclusion of students on racial and economic grounds would not be tolerated. Indeed, a communitarian ethos would seek to reinforce the common school ideal, where all students would come together to learn regardless of their social, cultural, or economic background and where a genuine civic spirit would thrive.

What about the natural environment?

Increasingly, policy-makers realize that urban places are only as good as the natural environment of those places. People thrive in cities when they have access to a wide range of wholesome, natural spaces—parks, playgrounds, gardens, waterfronts, and so on. It is no accident that real-estate values increase near parks and other attractive open spaces. Even beyond providing important community amenities, the city needs a strong ecology to nurture its everyday business and neighborhood life. A well-tended environment can reduce the risks of flooding, moderate extreme temperatures, reduce pollution, use energy efficiently, process waste products, control invasive plant and animal species, define community spaces, and improve the health of young people.

So what is the best way to foster a healthful and vibrant natural environment?

By engaging people in the neighborhoods in their design, maintenance, and programming. In her classic work *The Granite Garden*, Ann Whiston Spirn calls on cities to develop comprehensive strategies to manage the urban ecosystem. By working with urban neighborhoods—schoolchildren, home owners, local businesses, parks advocates—cities can fashion a block-by-block revitalization of urban spaces. By caring for the city's natural environment, people can create the larger fabric of community life that makes the city "livable" and efficient for all. Spirn writes: "Only by viewing the entire urban natural environment as one interacting system can the value of nature in the city be fully appreciated. Only when the social values of natural processes are recognized can priorities be set, and conflicting and complementary values be resolved or married. Only then can urban form fully reflect the values inherent in nature as well as other social values."[34] Spirn and others have worked in cities across the United States to stimulate the kind of grassroots efforts that revive not only green spaces but whole neighborhoods.[35]

Constraints on Urban Policy-Making
The Question of Authority

In an age in which so much political decision-making occurs at the national level of government, what authority do cities possess to try and address their problems?

It is true that in some nations, cities possess no formal authority at all. For example, Great Britain has a unitary system of government where all formal power is vested within the central government; subunits of government exist, to be sure, but they have no autonomous authority. In contrast, the United States has a federal system of government. The Constitution established two separate and independent levels of government, one at the national level and the other at the state level. Neither level of government derives its power from the other; each exists autonomously.

So what is the constitutional foundation for local governments in the United States?

The Constitution leaves the governance of localities to the states. Of particular importance is the Tenth Amendment: "The powers not delegated to the United States by the Constitution, nor prohibited by it to the States, are reserved to the States respectively, or to the people." States have constitutional authority to create and dissolve local governments. Local governments, in fact, carry the legal status of public corporations—that is, artificial structures that are given distinct powers by the authorizing state government. Like private corporations, full membership in a town was originally restricted to people with an economic stake in the town. Many cities and towns were established with the specific purpose of undertaking business enterprises. Local governmental structures were considered necessary to create an environment where it would make sense to "settle Manufactures" in the area.

If local governments are essentially creatures of state governments, how much authority do local governments really have?

The controversy over "home rule" has dominated state and local politics for much of American history. State legislatures have carefully defined and restricted the power that city governments may exercise over law enforcement, education, health care, and other issues vital to urban residents. State control over local decision-making has long been a major source of conflict.

Why didn't urban interests simply seize control over state legislatures, particularly during those periods in U.S. history when the majority of many state populations resided in cities?

State legislative district lines were drawn so that rural districts with few voters got as much representation as urban districts with many more voters. The Maine state constitution of 1819 and a Louisiana statute in 1845 severely restricted the number of seats that could go to urban legislators. Such unequal representation ensured that state legislatures dominated by rural interests would continue to limit the powers of city governments. It was not until the 1960s, when the U.S. Supreme Court finally declared the practice of unequal representation unconstitutional in the cases of *Baker* v. *Carr* (1962) and *Reynolds* v. *Sims* (1964), that city governments began to enjoy the kind of representation they needed to influence state legislatures. But by then millions of residents were fleeing from urban centers and relocating in surrounding towns and villages, thus shifting the locus of political power away from the cities and toward the suburbs.

So how much legal authority do local governments have under the state governments?

For decades, Dillon's Rule provided the most influential statement of the principle of state authority over local governments. The jurist John

Forrest Dillon articulated the dependency of localities in 1867: "Municipal corporations owe their origin to, and derive their powers and rights wholly from, the legislature. It breathes into them the breath of life, without which they cannot exist. As it creates, so it may destroy. If it may destroy, so it may abridge and control. . . . They are, so to phrase it, the mere tenants at will of the legislature."[36] Even though Dillon sat on an Iowa Supreme Court, without authority over the federal judiciary, his doctrine gained wide acceptance nationally. Dillon's Rule gained influence through its breathtaking simplicity, not to mention the support of elite interests such as the federal judiciary, state legislative committees, and private corporations. For years, the rule was quoted as indisputable proof in court decisions, academic treatises, and everyday political debate. In *Trenton* v. *New Jersey* in 1923, for example, the Supreme Court agreed with the logic of Dillon's Rule when it called the municipality a mere "department" of the state.

In practice, the relation between state and local power is much more complex than Dillon's Rule. Even though political authority could be taken away from localities at any time, it almost never happens—usually just when the locality goes bankrupt (as Chelsea, Massachusetts, did in 1991). States have created literally thousands of local governments—cities and towns, counties, authorities, and special districts—and given them great authority to make decisions for their communities and constituencies. Once a local entity has been established, it is usually given the leeway to make policy as it sees fit, even if it often lacks the financial and political resources to implement the full range of programs and services that it might like. Until the twentieth century, states oversaw the founding of a multitude of new "whole" communities. Cities and towns were chartered to look after the health and welfare of their citizens; time after time, cities and towns merged to become larger cities and towns.

The apex of this annexation movement came in 1898 with the formation of New York City from the merger of the separate boroughs of Manhattan, Brooklyn, the Bronx, Queens, and Staten Island. The goal of such combinations was to amass greater capacity—more tax revenues, modern infrastructure, and seamless services. Annexations resulted from deals between the core urban community and outside suburban communities: in exchange for the tax capacity of the suburbs, the city would provide a wide range of infrastructure and services. As the twentieth century dawned, however, suburban communities began to resist annexation. The emergence of regional districts—for water, sewers, roads, bridges, schools, transit—reduced the attractiveness of a marriage with the city. Many suburban communities decided they could have their cake and eat it, too: they could have the full range of "urban" services but avoid having to become part of the more complex world of city politics.

So cities have limited authority in American life. How can they use the authority that they have to make delivery of services work better?

Some people think they cannot do it very well. Urban scholars such as David Rusk and Myron Orfield argue that the only way for cities to control their destiny is to link that destiny with the larger metropolitan areas.[37] Rusk and Orfield say that cities must form regional alliances—and merge with the suburbs, if they can—in order to have the capacity to develop adequate policies for education, housing, crime, transportation, the environment, and basic services. The logic is simple: only in larger places do the necessary resources exist to deal with common problems.

But other urbanists contest this view. Paul Grogan, who once served as the president of a national coalition of community groups called the Local Initiatives Support Corporation, says that cities contain most of the resources they need to rejuvenate their economies and neighborhoods. The key, Grogan says, is to pursue grassroots, flexible strategies that engage the people of the city in addressing their common concerns. The rise of community development corporations, Grogan says, offers a model for how the cities can be rebuilt. Rather than waiting for new revenues from higher levels of government or the greater capacity that a metropolitan government would bring, cities need to find new ways to build and rebuild with the resources already available. Cities possess an extraordinary built environment, with a breathtaking stock of buildings and roads and parks, all located on the edge of bustling downtowns, roads and transit networks, parks, waterfronts, museums, hospitals, and universities. The key to urban revitalization, Grogan says, is to exploit these advantages rather than waiting for the day when suburbs agree to share resources more equally.[38]

The role of public health centers is a case in point. Working with government grants and foundations and other resources, health clinics have become the center of community life in many urban neighborhoods. Nonprofit health centers work with housing nonprofits, schools, churches, and others to develop strategies for attacking not only medical ailments such as AIDS and infant mortality but also broader social ills such as street violence, drug abuse, and learning disabilities. One nonprofit organization in Boston, the Codman Square Health Center, opened a high-technology learning center and a charter school as a result of requests from its clients. In communities from New York to San Francisco, the health center's daily engagement with the lives of urban residents makes it an ideal vehicle for building "civic capital," which can in turn be used in confronting crime, fixing schools, providing job training, and restoring parks. When the capacity of the residents is combined with the other resources of the community, cities can be revived—block by block, neighborhood by neighborhood.

Ultimately, Grogan says, cities will thrive when they fix the things that ordinary people can fix in the neighborhoods. Surveys show that people decide where to live based on the availability of attractive and affordable housing, good schools, safe streets, and amenities like parks and museums.[39] Not everyone will decide to live in cities, but enough people will select urban living when those essential needs are addressed.

Sounds like a communitarian approach.

In some ways, yes. It is communitarian in its mobilization of common resources and collective effort. But it also leaves room for the more individualist strain in American life. Rebuilding housing, schools, and other local assets enables families, entrepreneurs, and others to better pursue their own hopes and dreams. The community-based revival of the neighborhood creates new opportunities for individuals. It is the best of both worlds.

The Question of Autonomy

Just because cities may possess the formal authority to act, does this mean that they will in fact use that authority?

No. Even though public officials enjoy all kinds of formal powers, they do not necessarily have the autonomy they might like to have to act as they see fit. No public official can act without engaging others. Public officials are constrained not only by local laws, agencies, and legislative processes but also by the demands and interests of a wide range of constituencies in the city. Consider taxes. While it is true that a mayor can push for higher taxes to pay for affordable housing or better schools, in reality that mayor is restrained by business and property interests that resist higher taxes. Business interests tell the mayor that higher taxes threaten their viability. That puts the mayor in a bind, where some kind of compromise policy is the only viable approach.

Or consider the mayor's control over the bureaucracy. Formally, the mayor can direct departments to do his bidding on a variety of issues. But in reality, the bureaucracy often resists the mayor. The resistance is sometimes subtle—the bureaucrat tells the mayor yes but acts as if the answer is no—but it makes a difference. Bureaucrats can come up with all kinds of excuses for not doing the mayor's bidding. At the end of the day, the mayor knows that he has to work with the bureaucracy on its own terms.

Finally, consider the city's limited autonomy. A mayor or city manager might develop a creative and efficient strategy for dealing with traffic congestion, always a major concern of people in the neighborhoods. But a neighboring community can upset those traffic policies with new highway projects, rerouting of truck traffic, or approval of a major office park or housing development that generates new traffic flows. Or what if a nearby city decides to place a new industrial plant on the two cities' shared border? Or what if that nearby city wants to build a prison or a waste treatment plant on the border? What is a mayor to do? The answer is never simple. The mayor can negotiate, prod, plead, and threaten the adjacent cities and towns—but never be assured of any result without giving something up in exchange.

Politicians are acutely aware that a decision that provides benefits to one set of interests also takes away from others—and that policy losers can punish them.

On what issues do city leaders have more autonomy?

In his influential work *City Limits,* Paul E. Peterson points out the governments can adopt three kinds of policies: distributive, in which they provide basic services to all residents; redistributive, in which they shift resources from haves to have-nots; and developmental, in which they encourage new economic activity. But city officials must be especially attentive to the needs and desires of businesses, since they provide jobs and taxes—and many businesses can and will move to another location if local tax and regulatory burdens become too great.

Peterson concedes that this threat of capital mobility exists at all levels of government, but he believes that it is especially problematic at the local level, where firms can cross jurisdictional lines more easily than they cross national boundaries. It is much simpler for a business based in Detroit employing five hundred workers to pick up and move to a suburb than it is for the company to move to Indonesia. The upshot is that local officials experience intense pressure to favor developmental and distributive policies over redistributive policies. Overall, Peterson is sanguine about this state of affairs. Peterson contends that all cities have a "unitary" interest in promoting economic activity through developmental policy. Economic growth, Peterson says, benefits the whole community by generating more jobs and tax revenues and, therefore, a higher standard of living. By increasing economic activity in the city, developmental policies enhance the well-being of all groups in the city. Peterson states: "In the policy arena the city as a whole has an interest that needs to be promoted and enhanced. Policies of benefit to the city contribute to the prosperity of all residents. Downtown business benefits, but so do laborers desiring higher wages, homeowners hoping house values will rise, the unemployed seeking new jobs, and politicians aiming for reelection." With a bigger pie, more people can get bigger slices.[40]

Local officials, even those who care about the poor, feel pressure to eschew most redistributive policies and pursue developmental policies.

American cities simply lack sufficient resources and authority to combat poverty and all of the chronic ills flowing from poverty. Peterson concludes that redistributive policies can be attempted only at higher levels of government in the federal system, preferably at the national level. Redistributive policies at the local level are suicidal.

That sounds grim for people who care about issues like poverty.

There are two responses to Peterson's argument about the limited nature of urban policy-making. First, one might contend that developmental and distributive policies can serve some of the same goals as redistributive policies. There are all kinds of things cities can do to create a better environment for all people—affluent, middle- and working-class, and poor—to pursue their lives. Even if people's income levels are unequal, they might still enjoy access to the kinds of city services that give them opportunity. If the public realm is strong and vibrant, people can enjoy significant opportunities that are not afforded by money. If a city has safe streets, good schools, libraries, parks and playgrounds, and efficient public transit—the kinds of services that fall under the category of distributive policies—even the poorest citizens have a chance to build the kinds of skills and networks they need to climb the social ladder. To be sure, such accommodations must be matched by economic opportunity. But the point is that cities can do much to enhance the position of the least well-off people by providing basic services and a strong economy. A good place to live offers its own opportunities.

Second, while urban policy-makers are constrained by the threat of capital mobility, some scholars assert that Peterson has overstated the case. To start, mayors and other public officials may convince the business community and higher-income residents to support redistributive policies targeted to lower-income residents even though such policies may result in an unfavorable reallocation of services or a higher tax bill in the short term. In the long term, investments in human, social, and physical capital of poorer citizens and neighborhoods may redound to the benefit of the entire city. Declining poverty and crime rates brought about by a redistribution of resources and services may improve the overall quality of urban life and thus stimulate new forms of business investment within a city.

Even if city government officials are unable to persuade business leaders and affluent residents that redistributive policies are in their enlightened self-interest, the city's policy choices are not as limited as Peterson claims. While politicians are certainly influenced by the risk of capital mobility, they are also guided by a powerful political imperative—the need to get elected and re-elected. Politicians understand that if they turn their backs on redistributive policies, the likely beneficiaries of those policies will eventually hold them accountable at the polls. Hence city policy-makers need to balance economic pressures presented by mobile capital with the political demands of the voters, which means that redistributive policies cannot be entirely dismissed.[41]

The Political Power of Business

But typically business interests and low-income citizens do not have the same political leverage at city hall. Don't business interests tend to wield much more clout over urban policy-making?

The obstacles to good policy-making often seem overwhelming. The title of Douglas Yates's seminal study of city politics and policy—*The Ungovernable City*—underscores the belief that it is almost impossible to provide effective leadership in a complex, divided urban setting.[42] But if a mayor or city manager is focused and strategic, he or she can identify issues and constituents that enable the construction of a coherent approach to governance.

In his classic work *Regime Politics*, Clarence Stone observes that city officials discover soon after their election that a public mandate does not give them enough authority to govern their cities. The formal power inherent in their government offices must be supplemented by the informal power that can be provided by groups with the financial, legal, technical, and media resources to convert campaign rhetoric into actual policies and programs. In most U.S. cities, the interest group best situated to help public officials get things done is the business community. The downtown business community is especially well positioned to organize its own members and provide the resources and coordination needed to take on major projects. City officials learn that establishing an informal alliance with downtown business groups may be critical to accomplishing their goals. Naturally, the business community's agenda may conflict with the priorities of government officials and the public at large. But working with the business community could give local officials the leverage they need to pursue a broader agenda.[43]

Scholars have long argued that business interests exercise undue influence over policy-making.[44] But Stone's analysis of the formation of informal alliances, or regimes, between city officials and the downtown business community offers an especially lucid argument to explain the privileged position of business in urban affairs: "In a world of diffuse authority, a concentration of resources is attractive. What is at issue is not so much domination and subordination as a capacity to act and accomplish goals."[45] By supplying "a capacity to act," business elites come to play a crucial role in setting the policy agenda and influencing who gets what, when, where, and how. To illustrate, with respect to the vital issue of urban development, even though distressed residential neighborhoods cry out for attention, it is the downtown business district that attracts a disproportionate share of public resources. Business power over city hall generally ensures that downtown interests will win out over neighborhood interests. And that pattern holds true not just in Atlanta, where Stone studied the dynamics of regime politics, but in numerous other U.S. cities such as Dallas, Baltimore, and Philadelphia.[46]

What happens when mayoral candidates who promise to pay more to the neighborhoods get elected? Are they able to resist business power?

They may try. When Maynard Jackson became Atlanta's first black mayor in 1973, he vowed to redirect the flow of resources away from the downtown business district and toward the neighborhoods. In response, the downtown business community tried to discipline Jackson by withholding resources and then publicly questioned his ability and integrity. The mayor steadfastly resisted the mounting pressure for over a year before finding himself gravitating back into the orbit of the downtown business community. Before long, Atlanta's business-led regime was operating once again, though this time with perhaps a few more nods to Jackson's supporters in the neighborhoods.[47]

Other rebellious mayors have not been so fortunate. Perhaps the most telling case of populism's defeat by business interests is Dennis Kucinich. The populist defender of neighborhood interests in Cleveland, Kucinich eventually became the target of a recall campaign organized by downtown elites. The mayor's populist crusade was shattered when the downtown business community successfully backed a candidate more attuned to its agenda.[48]

Do business interests always dominate urban politics and policy-making?

No. Even though downtown business elites possess an impressive stockpile of resources to use to reward friends and punish enemies, they are not necessarily the most powerful group within a city's governing coalition. If public officials mobilize other groups with sufficient resources to enable them to govern effectively, they will do so. In the 1980s, Chicago's Mayor Harold Washington and Boston's Mayor Raymond Flynn mobilized community-based organizations that provided significant support for a neighborhood-oriented agenda featuring numerous redistributive policies. Maintaining a governing coalition that is responsive to neighborhood interests, however, is a tall order requiring substantial political skill and effort. Relatively few mayors of U.S. cities have been able to pull it off.[49]

Bureaucracy

Is business the only powerful group that imposes limits on urban policy-makers?

Sprawling bureaucracies also pose a formidable barrier to efficient and effective policy-making. On a day-to-day basis, bureaucrats have little incentive to innovate. Taking bold stands can get them into trouble with other agencies, constituency groups, and elected officials. As a result, bureaucracies operate as stable but uncreative systems, punctuated by occasional periods of crisis. Even when more creative bureaucrats take on major projects, they often get bogged down in political and jurisdictional tangles. Bureaucrats settle into routines of action that are designed to minimize conflict. As James Q. Wilson has argued, "situational imperatives" often shape decisions more than policy logic. Agencies deal with the demands of the moment rather than broad values. Workers are socialized to adopt a persona, follow routines, and keep things under control.[50]

An even more fundamental problem is the tendency of bureaucrats to protect and expand their turf. Once a government program has been established, the bureaucrats who administer that program invariably fight to preserve and enlarge the program. By their very nature, bureaucracies contribute to the ever-increasing size and cost of government. Bureaucrats are not always hell-bent on growth. Many agencies shy away from control over new policy responsibility because they do not have the resources or they do not want to get caught in political cross fires. But over time, agency heads are more prone to take on new programs than they are to shed them.

Why don't executive policy-makers take control over bureaucratic expansion?
Easier said than done. Too often, executives have inadequate power over their underlings. If a mayor battles cops for drug testing, teachers for more time in the classroom, or firefighters for changes in work rules, those city employees may resist in all kinds of ways. They can do the bureaucratic form of going limp, doing only what is precisely asked and no more. Or they can overzealously carry out their duties—cops writing tickets for minor violations commonly understood to be acceptable—to undermine people's sense of security. Or they can flat-out ignore requests and orders from the top. Moreover, the power of bureaucrats over administrative executives and policy-makers has expanded with the rise of public-employee unions in recent decades. Before the 1960s, strikes by teachers, police officers, firefighters, and public defenders never happened. Since then, however, these employees have struck on a regular basis, which casts a shadow over every public official's efforts to control budgets and manage service delivery.

Who are "street-level bureaucrats"? Why are they so important for urban policy?
Michael Lipsky coined the term street-level bureaucrat to describe the public officials who directly deliver services. They maintain a face-to-face relationship with many of their "clients," or recipients of services. Street-level bureaucrats regularly operate in the "line of fire" and must respond to demands from most clients. Teachers and students, cops and criminal suspects, caseworkers and welfare mothers are examples of street-level

bureaucrats and their clients. Many street-level bureaucrats develop a kind of complex empathy and respect for their clients unknown to policymakers at the top levels of the bureaucracy. Street-level bureaucrats' actions usually take place out of view of high-level officials. That gives them extraordinary latitude. They have freedom to improvise, to do the best they can given the circumstances.[51]

It sounds like street-level bureaucrats could provide the kind of feedback and improvisation that would make implementation efficient.

Because street-level bureaucrats operate so far from the top, the system is often deprived of knowledge from the bottom. Information does not always flow up. Or if it does, it gets distorted along the way—like the message in the children's game Whisper Down the Lane. Low-level bureaucrats often speak a different language from their superiors; they focus on the unglamorous nuts and bolts of service delivery, rather than large-scale policy goals. Bureaucrats also learn to mold their reports to avoid difficulties from the top. Sometimes that means self-censorship of certain kinds of difficult messages.

How can policy-makers ensure that street-level bureaucrats have enough authority to confront the problems they face but not so much that they violate larger public goals?

One answer to this dilemma has come from the relatively recent movement to "reinvent government." David Osborne and Ted Gaebler advocate replacing the bureaucratic model of public administration with an entrepreneurial model. [52] Osborne and Gaebler acknowledge that public and private entities are different kinds of operations with different goals and feedback mechanisms, but they hasten to add that public administrators can learn a great deal from the innovative management practices of corporations. For instance, instead of relying so heavily upon the preference for strict rules and regulations to guide government workers, managers should set broad goals, sell those goals to their subordinates, and then let the subordinates do their best to carry out the agency's goals. If lower levels of the bureaucracy get rewards for positive results, they will not fall back on process. A good example is public education. The "effective schools" literature shows that when superintendents seek to control principals, and when principals in turn seek to control teachers, the result is a silent and bitter struggle for authority and discretion. But when superintendents set standards and tell principals and teachers to do what they need to achieve those standards, schools work better. They work even better when the superintendent's standards are devised as part of a team project with principals and teachers.

Osborne and Gaebler also call for a breakup of the government's monopoly over the delivery of services. Competition between government agencies and private providers would drive down the cost and improve the quality of service delivery. In this scenario, the role of government is to set goals, arrange for an appropriate entity to provide services, and monitor the performance of those providers. This model gives public managers more time and resources to establish policy goals and consider alternative means of attaining them. "Steering, not rowing" becomes the hallmark of reinvented government.[53] One of the preeminent practitioners of this competitive model was Stephen Goldsmith, the mayor of Indianapolis who forced numerous city government agencies to compete with private services.[54]

Conservative critics of the bureaucracy believe that the reinventing government movement is a step in the right direction, but incomplete. In their view, reforming or "reinventing" government treats only the symptoms and not the disease. If the goal is to minimize the negative impacts of the bureaucracy, then the proper approach is to go directly to the source of the problem and reduce the size of government.[55]

What about other advances in public administration? Does the revolution of management techniques in the private sector offer any new tools for city government?

It might. Corporations have long coordinated their far-flung operations with computer database systems; in recent years, corporations have used the Internet to make their everyday operations more "transparent" to customers and to automate services.

Baltimore's adoption of a program called CitiStat shows the potential for better service delivery. Every day, Baltimore's departments gather data about city workers, housing, playgrounds, streets, railroad crossings, potholes, graffiti, utilities, snowplows and other vehicles, emergency fire calls, leaf collections, and parking permits. Departments enter data into a simple computer program and every two weeks produce a ten- to fifteen-page report for the mayor's staff. The staff briefs the mayor on important trends, trouble spots, and continuing challenges. The mayor and his staff meet with department heads to hash out the data. Department officials take turns at a podium in the front of the CitiStat room—the "hot seat"—as graphs, charts, and maps flash on two huge screens. The mayor and his staff pepper the department heads with questions. The questioning is direct and rough, but is remarkable also for its tone of formality and respect.

Gathering, sorting, and displaying data for CitiStat analyses might seem a monumental task. But the $20,000 software offers a simple format for compiling information. All departments have at least a handful of computer-savvy young staffers who can do the data work. CitiStat cost Baltimore $285,000 for its first year of operation—including four full-time staffers, computer equipment and software, and new furniture for the CitiStat room. Not counting improved service delivery, officials estimate savings of $13.2 million—$6 million in overtime, $5 million in reduced costs and increased revenues, and $1.2 million in reduced absenteeism.[56]

In short, tools exist for governments that want to use them—and they can produce major improvements in service delivery as well as substantial monetary savings. What is needed are committed mayors and city managers who want to immerse themselves in the details of administration so that they can understand the big picture more clearly.

Civic Culture and Urban Policy

The structural and political constraints on urban policy-makers seem staggering. How is it even possible to contemplate the kind of public policy that will rebuild the nation's cities?

Anyone who hopes to do something about the "urban crisis" needs to acknowledge political, social, and economic constraints. But it is also important to avoid resignation and paralysis. Cities always offer room for productive maneuvering. Todd Swanstrom has spoken of "semisovereign cities" to express the idea that while urban policy-makers are limited by a host of factors—constitutional and legal restrictions, capital mobility, the power of business interests, and the inertia of bureaucracies, to name just a few—they still have opportunities to enact public policies and promote a mode of politics that seeks to remedy urban inequalities.[57]

Swanstrom's view has much support on the streets of the cities of America. In San Francisco, community-based activists who were dissatisfied with the adverse impacts and unfulfilled promises of rapid downtown development during the 1970s and 1980s waged a tireless campaign to challenge the tight grip of the downtown growth coalition and shift city priorities back to the neighborhoods. Using citizens initiatives, litigation, and grassroots planning studies to counter official planning studies, San Francisco activists were eventually able to transform the politics of downtown development to ensure that future downtown growth would be more controlled and more equitable for all city residents.[58] Activists in Boston and Seattle produced similar changes in development policy and politics— changes that created not only new policies but also a new generation of political leadership.[59] Pierre Clavel has documented the positive impact of community-based activists in broadening popular engagement in politics and engendering progressive policies in a wide range of cities including Chicago, Hartford, and Burlington, Vermont.[60]

But in those examples, community-based activists sparked local political reform. Here, the argument seems to be that public policy is the key to political change.

Both people-driven change and policy-driven change make a difference. Politics is really a collective process that involves everyone from the housing activist in the neighborhood to the mayor and local bureaucracy—and everyone in between. We know that policy-makers and others face severe constraints that limit their choices. But within those constraints, people have opportunities to make their own politics. Even modest urban revitalization policies at the outset can begin to inspire civic engagement, which can foster the development of a new political culture that respects community, participation in public life, and a more active role for government in promoting opportunity. That civic spirit will in turn generate increasing citizen support for even more substantial urban revitalization policies. It is in that virtuous cycle—as opposed to the vicious cycle of decline, disengagement, and distrust—that the hope of the cities resides.

2
Poverty and
the Divided Metropolis

What is poverty?

Poverty is want, a lack of adequate provisions for the basic necessities for living established by the society. Lacking one or more of the basic necessities—food, clothing, shelter, medical care, transportation—prevents a person from participating alongside other members of society in getting and keeping a job, raising a family, obtaining an education, and developing the resources and know-how to cope with everyday social challenges.

Scholars, policy-makers, and ordinary people differ about just how many basic provisions people need. On one end of the ideological spectrum, conservatives tend to favor an *absolute* standard, which states what income a person or household needs to pay for basic food and shelter. At the other end of the spectrum, liberals favor a *relative* definition of poverty, where people lack the resources they need to participate on a fair footing with others in the community. Bare physical survival is not enough to be considered nonpoor under this definition; one should also have access to the full range of public and private goods needed to develop oneself to the fullest.[1]

Why is poverty so pivotal to all other urban issues?

Poverty is often understood as an issue of special concern, a matter of importance primarily to those who struggle to survive day to day. But the effects of poverty ripple out beyond impoverished households and touch the lives of virtually all urban residents. When poverty rises, many other issues are affected. The city's crime rate goes up. The decay and abandonment of housing in poor neighborhoods spreads to adjacent areas. The strains on the public school system intensify. The city's fiscal condition suffers as tax revenues fall while the demand for public services jumps. Looming budget deficits force city officials either to raise taxes or to slash expenditures for programs, both of which prompt residents to relocate to other jurisdictions. The resulting erosion in the tax base further aggravates fiscal pressures, sparking additional tax hikes or budget cuts and a new wave of residents and businesses fleeing the increasingly beleaguered city.

Long-term economic insecurity also undermines the civic capacity of poor people. Communities that suffer disinvestment and depopulation experience a weakening in the bonds of civil society as social networks and neighborhood organizations atrophy. With declining civic engagement comes a drop in political participation and a reduction in the community's ability to influence local government policy-making. Class and racial segregation follow, as more affluent people distance themselves from poor communities. Citizens left behind in poor communities feel more and more disconnnected from the formal institutions of government, and their sense of political disempowerment deepens.[2]

What are the policy implications when impoverished neighborhoods become politically marginalized?

Sometimes intentionally and sometimes not, policy-makers discriminate against poor neighborhoods and their residents. Poor neighborhoods often get fewer basic services (from street cleaning to parks maintenance) and less investment in public facilities and amenities. For years, frustrated by the intensity of inner-city problems, city planners adopted a strategy of isolation and "benign neglect" to deal with the problems of the poor. While federal agencies encouraged local housing authorities and lenders to discriminate against the poor and minorities, local agencies kept the poor isolated through the siting of public housing, manufacturing plants, transit and highway systems, and various noxious facilities such as railyards and incinerators. These locational decisions were sometimes subtle, sometimes blunt, but always designed to separate the affluent and middle classes from the perceived dangers of less fortunate people. But inevitably, the problems of poor communities seeped out to the rest of the city. It is impossible to contain all of the negative aspects of life in poverty—and, in fact, concentration of those negative aspects can exacerbate them.

Poverty exists all over the United States. Is it more problematic in cities?

Poverty pervades all regions of the United States and affects all racial and ethnic groups. However, in recent decades poverty has become increasingly concentrated in urban neighborhoods, especially those in older, industrial cities. The political scientist Paul Jargowsky found that the number of poor people living in high-poverty neighborhoods almost doubled between 1970 and 1990, from 1.9 million to 3.7 million.[3] The problem fell disproportionately upon blacks and Latinos; 34 percent of poor blacks and 22 percent of poor Latinos lived in high-poverty neighborhoods in 1990, compared to only 6 percent of poor whites. Many U.S. cities witnessed a dramatic increase in concentrations of poverty among blacks and Latinos. In Detroit, for instance, only 11.3 percent of blacks lived in high-poverty neighborhoods in 1970; by 1990, that figure had ballooned to 53.9 percent. Increases in the concentration of poverty among blacks during the same period was substantial in many other cities as well (e.g., 27 percent in New York City, 22 percent in Pittsburgh, and 21 percent in Chicago). For Latinos, the increases were similarly grim (e.g., 48 percent in Philadelphia and 34 percent in Detroit).[4]

The growing concentration of poverty in American cities undermines the prospects of individuals living in impoverished neighborhoods. To start, the physical isolation makes it far more challenging for residents to find and hold good jobs. Obtaining access to employment opportunities on the other side of the city or in an outlying suburb may be difficult or impossible because of the unavailability of public transportation or the high cost of commuting by automobile. Information about job openings may be extremely limited because of the lack of social networks linking inner-city neighborhoods with more prosperous parts of the metropolitan area.[5]

Restricted access to good job opportunities is not necessarily a new problem for inner-city residents. But what is relatively new, according to the sociologist William Julius Wilson, is the outmigration of many middle-class residents, who are no longer trapped in inner-city neighborhoods by pervasive racial discrimination. As nonpoor blacks and Latinos move to more affluent areas, they leave behind the poorest of the poor, who find it increasingly difficult to sustain community organizations and institutions. As schools, churches, and clubs decline, the social organization of inner-city neighborhoods breaks down, which in turn leads to a disintegration of public order. Drug and alcohol abuse, crime, and other forms of dysfunctional behavior become commonplace, all of which further impede the life chances of neighborhood residents. Young people are particularly vulnerable to the temptations of the deviant culture of joblessness and chronic poverty.[6]

In sum, the concentration and isolation of poor people in central cities have worsened during the past few decades, with grave consequences not just for the immediate victims of poverty but for all citizens in metropolitan areas. Poverty is arguably the most serious urban dilemma today, because from it flow so many other social, economic, and political problems.

The challenge, therefore, is to understand first the nature of poverty in U.S. cities and its causes, and then how public policy might be employed to alleviate the plight of the urban poor.

Measuring Poverty

How is poverty measured?

The U.S. government measures poverty according to a simple formula devised by a Social Security Administration statistician named Mollie Orshansky in 1963. Estimating that food expenses accounted for roughly one third of the total family budget, Orshansky calculated the "poverty line" at three times the money required to pay for an emergency diet. The poverty line is adjusted according to the size of the family and the national inflation rate. Ever since, the federal government has used that definition of poverty in its formulas and calculations for antipoverty programs, education grants, housing allowances, and the like.[7] In 2000, the poverty line for a family of two adults and two children was $17,062.[8]

Experts criticize the government's official poverty line for a variety of reasons. Some say that poverty statistics are inflated because they do not take into account a number of "in-kind" benefits that many poor people receive. Two of the biggest programs directed at poor people—Medicaid and food stamps—provide real, material assistance to poor people, but their value is not calculated in determining whether a person or family counts as poor. Other kinds of assistance offered to many poor people, such as reductions in rents, hot lunches in public schools, free counseling or legal services, and allowances for clothing and furniture, are also excluded from calculations of income levels because they are in-kind goods or services.[9]

But other experts claim that the poverty rated is understated because of the poverty statistics' meager baseline of necessary goods and services. The definition of poverty, remember, begins with the emergency diet. Any healthy person can survive for a short period on an inadequate diet. Eating a lot of rice, potatoes, bread, and cereal can keep a person going for a short period. But in the long term, a deficient diet produces severe consequences for a person's energy, stress levels, and overall health.[10]

A more fundamental criticism of the Orshansky standard is that it ignores changes in the spending patterns of Americans. Although food comprised one third of the typical family budget in 1960, it comprises just one sixth of the typical family budget today. In 1995, a panel assembled by the National Academy of Sciences (NAS) proposed new criteria for measuring poverty that recognized the increased burden of clothing, shelter, and utility costs on household incomes, as well as broad regional variations in such costs. The Census Bureau later determined that if the NAS criteria had been in effect in 1997, the number of Americans living in poverty would have jumped from 35.6 million to 41.2 million, or from 13.3 percent of the nation's population to 15.4 percent.[11] However, neither the NAS criteria nor any other have yet replaced the simple measurement of poverty used by the U.S. government since the 1960s.

Why hasn't the definition of poverty been changed?

The government has resisted adjustments in the poverty formula for two reasons: money and statistics. If the definition were adjusted, the government would need to provide up to twice as much money to welfare participants in cash grants and other benefits. At a time when the welfare state is under attack for its high costs, such increases would seem impossible to sell to a skeptical public. Government officials also cling to the Orshansky definition for statistical purposes. Tracking people's well-being over time requires standard measures. However imperfect it may be, Orshansky's standard has been in use for three decades to track the well-being of poor and near-poor people.

The Orshansky definition might survive for another, more cynical or manipulative reason: it understates the degree of poverty in American society. Michael Harrington, the noted social activist and writer, put this argument most bluntly: "The bureaucracy simply did not want to establish a figure that could put 25 or 30 percent of the people—fifty or sixty million Americans—under the poverty lines."[12] A higher standard for poverty would make the country look like it had a crisis of poverty rather than a persistent but marginal problem.

Another criticism of the poverty line is that it does not place the poor person's well-being in relation to other groups in society. Today's poor fare a lot worse in comparison with the nonpoor. The standard way of measuring society's "norm" is the median of family income—the figure right in the middle of the total distribution of family incomes. The official poverty line was 54 percent of median family income in 1960, 40 percent in 1970, and 38 percent in 1979. In other words, as time has passed, poor people have gotten less and less in comparison with their fellow citizens. But that fact is not noted in most statistical reports on poverty.

In many other countries, benefits lift people at the bottom of the income scale closer to the middling level of well-being. A generous collection of benefits—both those targeted to people in need and those extended to all citizens—reduces the overall adult poverty rate by 82.9 percent (to an overall poverty rate of 3.1 percent) in Sweden, by 73.2 percent (to 5.9 percent) in the Netherlands, by 68.9 (to 8.5 percent) in France, by 59.6 percent (to 11 percent) in Great Britain, by 58.3 percent (to 7 percent) in Germany, by 43.2 percent (to 12.3 percent) in Australia, and by 25.6 percent (to 15.4 percent) in the United States.[13] Other Western nations clearly do more to supplement the income of the people at the bottom half of the population, producing much lower overall levels of poverty.

Regardless of what level of inequality exists in a country and what the government does to address poverty, many people say that poverty is more of a state of mind—that in a nation as open and prosperous as the United States, there is plenty of opportunity for those who seize it.

Critics of the welfare state often point out that poor people have access to more material benefits than ordinary people did in previous generations. Politicians who grew up in the 1940s and 1950s are fond of noting that their family may have been poor by today's standards, but did not consider themselves to be poor. People simply "did without" in the old days. People with few resources cooperated with and helped each other. It did not matter that no one on the block owned a television or radio or telephone. It did not matter that children wore hand-me-down clothing. It did not matter that children could not own their own books or games or could not afford membership in special clubs and leagues. Despite their limited resources, such people still found ways to survive and sometimes to climb the socioeconomic ladder. The implication of such a perspective is that today's poor, who have access to greater material benefits, simply need to be smarter and more diligent in taking advantage of those benefits.

Is it fair to compare the mobility prospects of the poor of today with the poor who lived several decades ago?

Not really. It is true that individuals and families in previous decades had fewer personal possessions but still managed to survive and even climb the social and economic ladders of their communities. But at the same time, even in poor neighborhoods, residents had access to a reservoir of "social capital" that we lack today. Public and social life was in many ways more vibrant in the years before suburbanization. Churches, schools, and clubs bound communities together. By contrast, community institutions in today's poor urban neighborhoods have experienced massive strain. The exodus of jobs and residents during the years after World War II caused factories, schools, churches, hospitals, and neighborhood stores to shut down. Social networks and support systems collapsed. Meanwhile, the disintegration of the nuclear family, drug and alcohol abuse, violence, and other social pathologies became increasingly common in poor communities. Prospects for upward mobility for people with limited resources trying to survive within such an environment became more and more bleak.

In addition, the "necessities" of life change over time, and these changes should be incorporated into definitions of poverty. Machines that are integral to modern life—automobiles, telephones, computers—were not necessary previously. Consider the telephone. Most families did not have a telephone during the Great Depression, but not having a telephone would create a major hardship today. People need telephones not so much because they decide the phone has useful functions, but because employers, schools, and others *expect* them to have access to a telephone.

The same case could be made for adding other goods and services that were once considered optional to the list of necessities. A telephone answering machine might be a necessity today. New clothing might also be a necessity at a time when service-sector jobs, requiring public interaction, comprise a growing part of the entry-level labor market. Automobiles are necessities in communities without extensive public transit systems. Daycare services may be essential for families with children, particularly families with only one adult.

Dimensions of Poverty in the United States

Has poverty decreased or increased in modern times?

From the end of World War II until the early 1970s, poverty declined considerably. In the late 1950s, close to 40 million Americans, or 22 percent of the population, fell below the poverty line. From 1959 to 1969, the poverty rate was cut almost in half to 12.1 percent. The poverty rate then increased to 15.2 percent by 1983 after years of stagflation (a stagnant economy accompanied by inflation), deindustrialization, and the Reagan-era recession of 1981 to 1983 before dropping again to 11.3 percent in 2000.[14]

How does the experience of poverty differ from place to place? Does urban poverty differ from rural or suburban poverty?

Urban and rural areas have experienced a reversal in recent decades. In 1959, 56 percent of all poor people lived in rural areas and small towns, while 27 percent lived in cities and 17 percent lived in suburbs. By 1985, 43 percent of the poor were concentrated in inner cities and another 28 percent lived in suburbs. Poverty became more and more concentrated in the nation's biggest and oldest metropolitan areas and in isolated areas within cities. Inner-city neighborhoods held a disproportionate number of the nation's overall poor. The poverty rate in metropolitan areas was 12 percent overall but 37 percent in "isolated poverty areas" (i.e., areas in which at least 20 percent of the residents are poor), which are usually found in the inner city. Poverty in central cities increased from 15 percent in 1967 to 21.5 percent in 1993 before falling to 16.4 percent in 1999; poverty in metropolitan areas ranged from 9.5 percent to 14.6 percent in that same period.[15]

Who are the working poor?

They are the people cleaning offices, carting garbage, entering data in computer processing centers, and caring for the sick in hospitals. Some 28 percent of all workers in household services—home child care, house-cleaning, laundering—earn poverty wages. Service workers in fields other than private household and protective services—waiters and waitresses, food service workers, janitors, and nurses—have a 16 percent poverty rate. Workers in the retail trades had a poverty rate of 12 percent.[16]

Overall, the Bureau of Labor Statistics (BLS) estimates that in 1999 6.8 million people were poor despite working. The problem for the working poor can be summed up in a simple phrase: too few hours at too low wages. The working poor spend more than half of the year—twenty-seven weeks—in the labor force but it is not enough to rise above the official poverty level. A report of the BLS summarized the dilemma: "Working full time substantially lowers a person's probability of being poor. Among persons in the labor force for 27 weeks or more, 3.9 percent of those usually employed full time were in poverty, compared with 10.5 percent for part-time workers." Still, full-time work does not guarantee an escape from poverty; some 64 percent of the working poor worked full-time.[17] Only 26 percent of the working poor work full-time all year, compared with 67 percent of the total labor force.

Besides holding low-wage jobs and moving in and out of the job market, the working poor share a number of other characteristics. The working poor are less educated; only 67 percent hold high school degrees, compared with 88 percent of all workers. As many as one third of all working poor face serious health problems that impede their ability to get to work regularly; almost half of this group stays in poverty for five or more years. Health problems are exacerbated by a lack of health care; only 18 percent get health insurance from their employer, compared with 55 percent of the total workforce. Working poor also live in broken families; about 48 percent of working poor families live in households headed by a single female. Minorities and newcomers make up disproportionate shares of the working poor population. Among noncitizens, 15 percent work but live in poverty; 14 percent of all working Hispanics live in poverty, and 12 percent of working blacks live in poverty.[18]

How can someone work full-time and still remain poor?

The wages of entry-level workers have fallen steadily in the last generation, especially in low-skill jobs. From 1947 to 1973, the real hourly wages of working people increased by 75 percent; from 1973 to 1998, however, real wages fell 9 percent. Changes in the nation's employment structure have reduced the number of low-skill jobs that pay well. As relatively high-paying manufacturing jobs migrated overseas, many displaced factory workers have had to settle for low-skill, low-paying positions in the expanding service sector—a trend that has been particularly severe in American cities.

The decline of labor unions has also contributed to falling wages on the lower rungs of the labor market. The number of organized workers has diminished from a high of more than 35 percent in the years after World War II to a low of around 11 percent in 2000. Restrictions on organizing have prevented many workers in high-growth sectors from forming new unions, undercutting workers' ability to bargain for better wages. Controlling for race, education, and other differences, unionized workers make 28 percent more than nonunionized workers in similar professions.[19]

Aren't minimum wage laws supposed to prevent full-time workers from falling into poverty?

The Fair Labor Standards Act of 1938 created the minimum wage in order to ensure "a minimum standard of living necessary for health, efficiency, and general well-being." Even though the minimum wage has been increased several times in the past couple of decades, such increases have not been enough to keep up with the cost of living. Controlling for inflation, the minimum wage in 1998 was worth 32 percent less than it was in 1968.[20] Of the eleven million Americans who earn a minimum wage, almost half are full-time workers, and many others are forced to take second jobs to make ends meet.[21]

The problem of working people in poverty, of course, reaches far beyond the adults involved. One report states:

> Children in working-poor families defy stereotype. They live in every state. Half live with two parents. . . . Most are white. Children in working-poor families face some special difficulties as a result of their parents' commitment to work. They are less likely to have health insurance than poor children whose parents don't work because they often don't receive Medicaid, yet many of their parents have jobs that don't offer health insurance. In 1996, 26 percent of children in working-poor families lacked health insurance, compared with 18 percent of poor children in families with nonworking parents."[22]

For many, working is a curse.

How about the nonworking poor? Who are they?

The nonworking poor experience deprivation because they simply cannot find a job, whether or not they have marketable skills. Some live far from job centers, cannot arrange transportation, or cannot afford to take the time from family responsibilities. Others cannot afford to lose the benefits such as Medicaid that are available to them when they live on welfare.

The African-American population has been most dramatically affected by long periods of unemployment. In the past generation, black participation in the labor force has changed substantially. In the 1950s and early 1960s, black males aged sixteen to twenty-four had a higher labor force participation rate—those either holding a job or attending school—than their white peers. In 1964, 9 percent of blacks in this cohort—almost twice as high a percentage as their white peers—did not participate in the labor force. By 1992, that figure was 20 percent and by 1997 it was 23 percent.[23]

Some poor people simply lack the skills necessary for the modern workforce. They are low-skill workers in a workforce demanding technical know-how. In his landmark study on the underclass, the journalist Ken Auletta followed the progress of twenty-six students in a worker skills training program sponsored by the Manpower Demonstration Research Corporation. Auletta found that even simple matters of style and etiquette torpedoed many would-be workers' efforts to find steady employment. This group is often so lacking in basic skills such as dressing for work or cooperating with coworkers that no employer is willing to carry them on the payroll for long. Their office skills, such as answering the telephone or composing a letter, are often worse. Many would-be workers exhibit a hostility to the rules and norms of the workplace. Even though they were given substantial incentives to attend classes that offered a way into the labor market, many students simply got bored and dropped out.[24]

You said "underclass" a moment ago. What does that mean?

The term "underclass," popularized by Ken Auletta and used by scholars such as Christopher Jencks and William Julius Wilson, describes the most desperate of all poor people. This group, which comprises 3 percent or so of the population, has a complex profile. It includes people who have never been able to get or hold a job, people who cannot function because of illiteracy or drug or alcohol addictions, and people who have engaged in crime as a regular part of life. It includes people with families—mainly female-headed households—as well as people who live alone on the streets or in single-room occupancy hotels. The underclass "liv[e] a life in which the elemental building blocks of a life—productive work, family, community—exist in fragmented and corrupted forms."[25] One leading antipoverty policy-maker describes the underclass as the unreachable class:

> There is a segment of the nation's poor, small and sometimes invisible, that does not seem to be touched by . . . any traditional sort of outreach. For all our best efforts, this sector of the population is just

about where we found them 20 years ago. To some extent, the very programs that gave many poor families the means to move out of the ghettos left behind the disorganized families and restless, unskilled individuals of this chronic underclass. Their isolation and frustration has only exacerbated the frustration and hopelessness of their life and made their condition the most dangerous and intractable problem facing the cities in which they live.[26]

In short, the underclass comprises the people who have none of the internal or external resources to use to improve their position in society.

The low skill levels and social isolation of the underclass are so extreme that even the full-employment economy of the 1990s can barely touch it. The primary challenge of the underclass is cultural. The conservative Charles Murray points out that characteristics often associated with race are really much broader. Although blacks make up a disproportionate share of the total underclass population, the raw number of poor white people is larger and they also pose important challenges. Murray writes:

> The street ethics of the underclass subculture are not "black." They are the ethics of male adolescents who haven't been taught any better. For that matter, the problem of the underclass itself is, ultimately, a problem of adolescents who haven't been taught any better. There are a lot more white adolescents than black ones, leading to the second unanswered question: How fast will the white underclass grow?[27]

Causes of Poverty

What are the many dimensions of poverty?

Like most social problems, poverty has many dimensions. We can understand poverty by adopting a levels analysis—that is, by looking at how specific dynamics affect poverty at the levels of the individual, family and community, society, economy, and government.

At the level of the individual, we can identify a number of characteristics that account for poverty: lack of education, lack of access to jobs, abuse of alcohol and drugs, medical problems and disabilities, and depression and other psychological problems. Many policy-makers believe that if the government and nonprofit organizations could address each of these problems in turn, we could do much to reduce or even eradicate poverty.

Other experts, however, look to the level of the family to explain the dynamics of poverty. The family, after all, does more to shape the individual's character and capacity than anything else. Statistics show that families headed by married couples with at least one adult working help to inculcate the values of hard work and the caring that are essential for an individual's success in life. Grimly, many families not only lack such intact and functional qualities, but are ripped by neglect, abuse, and violence. Such households undermine children's development and sense of efficacy, the feeling that they can care for themselves and make a positive difference in the world.

How can you argue with that logic—that individuals and families are susceptible to poverty if they lack the basic tools to survive in society?

As compelling as is the analysis at the individual and family levels, other theorists argue that larger social forces are more responsible for poverty precisely because they shape the opportunities for individuals and families.

So-called "structuralist" theorists believe that the structures of society create unequal opportunities for people to pursue their life plans. Structuralists point to two factors in particular. First, the structuralists argue that a market system inevitably creates a poverty class—in fact, that the existence of poor people is critical for the smooth functioning of capitalism because it allows corporate and other business entities to hold down labor costs by playing the "have-nots" off against the "have-littles." Second, the structuralists argue that a major part of capitalism is uneven development, that strong growth in one area necessarily entails sluggish stagnation in another.

Where's the government in all this?

A final level of analysis is the political system. *The government* itself has contributed to poverty by adopting a number of policies that directly and indirectly undermined some people's ability to obtain jobs, education, housing, and other necessities of life. Direct policies include welfare policies, which often created disincentives for poor people to work, attend school, or adopt the kinds of behaviors necessary for success in the job market. Indirect policies include the U.S. government's many programs that have subsidized and otherwise encouraged businesses and middle-class families to move from the cities to the suburbs. Through the creation of more opportunities in suburbs, the cities lost their capacity to employ their more vulnerable residents and the capacity of local governments to provide even basic services was undermined.

This all sounds very mechanical. Shouldn't we be concerned about about social attitudes as well as social structures?

Well, yes. Discrimination, for example. Racial discrimination and segregation have played an important role in shaping who gets access to opportunity in the United States. All newcomers to the United States have endured discrimination by employers, landlords, government agencies, and social organizations. From the time of "Irish Need Not Apply" signs in the United States to the era of racial profiling on highways, minorities and newcomers have struggled to become part of the mainstream.

The question is: How powerful and enduring is discrimination in affecting people's opportunities to climb out of poverty? Some scholars, such as Thomas Sowell, claim that overcoming discrimination usually takes two generations before a minority can become part of the mainstream—and that even when minorities suffer discrimination, they still enjoy significant opportunities to succeed economically and socially. Discrimination is unfair, but it is also part of a process of assimilating groups into mainstream values and institutions. Sowell acknowledges that blacks have taken longer than other groups to enter the mainstream. The continuing plight of blacks, Sowell says, is the result of a unique history. Blacks did not really enter the mainstream of American life until the post–World War II era:

> many of those living in the northern ghettoes today are first- or second-generation migrants from the South—at the same stage that other blacks were 50 or 100 years ago. The race as a whole has moved from a position of utter destitution—in money, knowledge, and rights—to a place alongside other groups emerging in the great struggles of life."[28]

Other scholars say Sowell understates the role of race, arguing that discrimination has posed a much more persistent barrier to opportunity to blacks and lies at the very root of poverty in America today. "A century and a quarter after slavery, white America continues to ask of its black citizens an extra patience and perseverance that whites have never required of themselves," Andrew Hacker writes in a broad study of the role of race in family makeup, schools, housing, and employment.[29] Despite numerous laws and programs aimed at achieving basic equality of opportunity, Hacker says, white Americans continue to discriminate in ways both blunt and subtle. Discrimination is a vast web that holds blacks back, isolating the poorest of the poor in dangerous and isolated ghetto communities.

The Level of the Individual

Start with the individual. What kinds of tools or capacities must an individual have to avoid poverty? And what kinds of problems prevent the individual from realizing his or her abilities?

It's very simple. To escape poverty, you need a decent income. That usually comes from a job. Well-paying jobs these days often require a basic education. To get a decent education and a job, a person needs access to an adequate school, as well as the discipline to avoid abusing alcohol and other drugs. And one needs to stay healthy, not only physically but psychologically as well.

Poor people in America often experience difficulty with one of more of these basic challenges. Even when they experience some success—holding a job, for example—they are always vulnerable. Their low level of skills, for example, makes them vulnerable to layoffs when the economy goes bad. Or their tendency toward psychological or other health problems incapacitates them.

Let's talk about jobs.

Politicians often say that the best antipoverty program is a well-paying job, and it's hard to argue against this. To understand the importance of jobs for escaping poverty, it's important to know not just whether someone is working or not, but how much and for what wages. Most poor people in America work, but their work experience is intermittent. People in poverty often hold jobs on and off for brief periods. They leave their jobs because of layoffs, family emergencies, difficulties getting to work, and a wide range of behavioral problems. Even when they work for months at a time, they work fewer hours a week than people who have escaped poverty. In order to climb out of poverty, the pattern of on-again-off-again employment has to be replaced by long hours over months and years.

Poor people face a number of barriers to work. One of the most important is known as the "spatial mismatch"—the difficulty that many people living in isolated, poor neighborhoods have in getting to where the jobs are located. Because many entry-level jobs are located outside inner-city neighborhoods, people living in those places have to find transportation. Many do not own cars, and public transportation systems are oriented toward traditional downtowns. Many poor people also experience difficulty juggling work and home responsibilities. High rates of single-parent households make working forty-hour jobs a major challenge.[30] Education is another important factor. Inner-city schools do not offer quality education to most students—test scores in urban schools are dramatically lower than those in most suburban locations—so many urban residents have little to offer employers. A survey of 693 Chicago-area firms found that almost half of the employers perceive serious deficiencies in the skills of students sent to them from job-training programs.[31]

In a detailed study of the social and economic life of greater Boston, Barry Bluestone and Mary Stevenson find that work tenure is the most important factor explaining the different fortunes of whites, blacks, and Hispanics with a high school education. The labor force participation rates for the three groups are remarkably similar for those with more than twelve years of education (89.4, 90.3, and 92.3 percent, respectively) and a high school degree or less (82.7, 86.2, and 87.2 percent respectively). But the number of working hours varies considerably. Whites with more than twelve years of education work an average of 48.2 hours a week, compared with 41.3 hours for blacks and 39.3 hours for Hispanics. Whites with a high school degree or less work 50.5 hours a week, compared with 34.9 hours a week for blacks and 43 hours a week for Hispanics.[32] Whites tended to "moonlight" more than blacks and also spend more time on their main jobs because of a wide range of factors such as discrimination, transportation access to jobs, and availability of capital to operate their own small businesses.

The problem of too few hours exists nationally for all groups of poor workers. Studies of "leavers"—the welfare recipients who left public-assistance programs for the world of work in the aftermath of the 1996 welfare reform legislation—found that 70 percent had worked at some time in the previous year. But only 60 percent of all leavers were working at a given time, and only about 40 percent found steady employment throughout the year. Even when state governments forced welfare recipients off the rolls to encourage work, the prospects for work were limited. People cut off from benefits by the state had miserable employment and income records; one three-city study found that 89 percent of those leavers were living in poverty after leaving welfare.[33]

The number of hours on the job is important for two reasons. First, the more hours you work, the more money you make. Second, the more years you work, the greater your earning power will be over the course of your career. Steady work helps workers accumulate skills and professional networks critical to climbing a career ladder and making more money over time. Bluestone and Stevenson find that a native-born black with one year of work experience makes 17 percent less than a similar white, testament to persisting discrimination in the modern economy. But six years of work experience reduces the gap to 6 percent, and 10 years of work eliminates it altogether.[34]

How important is education to getting and keeping a job—and gaining economic self-sufficiency?

A lot. Quite simply: You learn more, you earn more.

Education is the single greatest variable explaining earnings, according to a nationwide study of test scores and labor participation. Ronald Ferguson found that twenty-three-year-old whites earned 16 percent more than blacks in the period between 1986 and 1988; but when those earnings were controlled for scores on the Armed Services Qualification Test for reading and math, the wage gap fell to 5 percent. Ferguson's conclusion was simple: "Averaged across all regions and schooling levels, the residual difference in earnings between young black and white males would have virtually disappeared by the middle of the decade if blacks and whites had equal test scores."[35]

Education in this context needs to be understood broadly—as not just formal schooling but also the kinds of skills and knowledge that young people pick up in their families, among peer groups, and in recreational activities. As James Coleman argued in his classic study of education in 1966, formal education is not enough to change the life chances of poor people. Young people spend their formative time outside the classroom, and their success in the classroom depends on how much their other experiences and relationships encourage learning.[36] But the basic truth of Ferguson's study remains: to have earning power in today's economy, workers need a higher level of skills than they did in previous generations.

How do drugs and other destructive behaviors affect a person's ability to escape poverty?

Anything that impairs a person's ability to function—whether it's mental illness, a medical condition, or a physical handicap—also impairs his ability to hold a job and escape poverty. The National Institute on Drug Abuse has found a strong connection between child abuse, drugs, and poverty. In some surveys, two thirds of people in drug treatment programs report that they were abused as children. Some 30 to 59 percent of women in drug treatment programs—three times the share of men—experience posttraumatic stress syndrome that is often related to abuse. The connections between abuse, drugs, and poverty are complex and difficult, but researchers consider any severe impairment of physical and mental health to be critical to a person's ability to be self-sufficient.[37]

Inability to work because of physical or psychological disability plays a large role in poverty. People with disabilities work less, experience difficulty finding work when they seek it, and stay on welfare twice as long as those without disabilities. People with learning disabilities also drop out of job training programs because those programs do not fit their learning styles and abilities.[38]

The poor suffer mental illness at a much greater rate than the general population but have fewer opportunities to address the problem. According to one study, 42 percent of the heads of households receiving welfare suffer from clinical depression; that figure is about three times the national average. Depression is so widespread, said one researcher who has analyzed poor people's mental illness, that it "is like checking for emphysema among coal miners." According to one study, children of depressed mothers are eight times as likely as other children to become juvenile delinquents. Depression leads to a wide range of destructive behaviors that can further incapacitate a vulnerable person. One Johns Hopkins University researcher estimated that the incidence of AIDS—a disease that is increasingly suffered by poor people—could be reduced by half if proper treatment were made available: "Many people get HIV when they can't muster the energy to care anymore," the researcher said. "These are people who are utterly demoralized by life and don't see any point in it."[39]

The Level of the Family and Community

Don't many of the problems attributed to individuals have their roots in the family? How has the breakdown of the family contributed to poverty?

For years, many analysts have pointed to the increase in single-parent households as the critical variable in explaining poverty. The statistics are clear: More than half (52 percent) of all households in poverty in 1993 were headed by single women, compared to 36 percent in 1970. Some 75 percent of all black family households in poverty were headed by women, a significant increase from 54 percent in 1970. Poverty is more extreme in single-parent households. Some 17 percent of female-headed families had incomes at less than half of the poverty level, compared to 2 percent of married-couple families.[40]

Two-parent households are important for a number of reasons. Two-parent homes offer more capacity to manage the economic affairs of the family. With one instead of two adults in the home, there is one fewer person to earn wages, care for children, tend to household chores, and seek new housing and other opportunities. Two-parent households offer healthier role models for children. Men and women show commitment to making the household function; sexual relationships are understood in a matrix of love and commitment to others. In too many single-parent households, sex is seen as divorced from responsibility and families are seen as conveniences rather than as commitments. In households without adult males present, young males are often enticed by role models provided by street life—including gang leaders.

What about the problem of teen pregnancy?

Teenage pregnancy remains an important problem for inner-city families because having babies at young ages interrupts young women's education and reduces their long-term prospects for work and marriage. While 94 percent of teens believe that pregnancy would not prevent them from going to school, in reality only 70 percent complete their high school education. Most teens also believe they would marry the mother or father of the child, but fully 81 percent of women who give birth as teens do not get married to the father.[41] Teenage pregnancy is problematic not only for the mother but also for the child. Teenage mothers often possess inadequate parenting skills; they struggle to care for the child and to exert appropriate discipline. One study concludes:

> Teenage single mothers monitor their children less than older married mothers do. They are more inclined to have an inconsistent, explosively angry approach to disciplining their children. In such homes family members, including children, generally use aggressive, coercive methods to make sure their needs are met by others in the family. The parent's inability to monitor a child's behavior compounds the hostility between parent and child. . . .[42]

The rate of teenage pregnancy reached a peak in 1991 but had fallen by 21 percent by 1997. In 1997, 872,000 young women aged fifteen to nineteen—9.4 percent of the total—got pregnant; 55 percent of them gave birth, 24 percent had abortions, and the rest miscarried. Black and Hispanic young women were twice as likely as whites to get pregnant.[43]

Many people blame the problems of inner-city individuals and families on the "culture of poverty" in inner-city neighborhoods. What does that mean?

Oscar Lewis coined the term "culture of poverty" to describe a syndrome common among communities with limited economic and social opportunity. Lewis maintained that the culture of poverty was a rational response to the conditions of life under poverty. People with little opportunity for economic or social advancement, Lewis said, have less reason to sacrifice and more reason to seek instant gratification. Sex, alcohol, drugs, and fighting offer brief moments of reprieve from the hopelessness of poverty. Such a short-term orientation is destructive in the long run but provides the only real excitement for people in desperate situations. Over time, what begins as a simple response to helplessness takes on a life of its own. The attitudes and habits harden and undermine not only the prospects of the poor but also the order and well-being of the larger community.[44]

What are the characteristics of the culture of poverty?

Idleness. Fatalism and apathy. Alcoholism. Short attention spans, also known as "present orientation." Low levels of education. Inability to plan. Unstable families. Sexual promiscuity. A tendency toward violence. Impulsiveness. Unkempt appearance. Inability to control children. Absence of shame. Tribalism.

Surely not everyone agrees with this depiction of inner-city life and communities.

Liberals resist such sweeping characterizations of poor people. Scholars have found that poor people have more "middle-class" attitudes than the middle class itself. They desire the house in the suburbs, the two-parent family, the nine-to-five job, and the regular life of the community. It is, in fact, the intensity of the desire for this way of life that creates such great frustration that some poor people lash out at the system that does not seem to offer any real hope to obtain it.[45]

Increasingly in recent years, even some liberals have acknowledged that a separate "culture" develops in neighborhoods that are shut off from the life of the economy and community. William Julius Wilson has written about the social consequences of poor blacks isolated in neighborhoods, away from jobs, role models, and social institutions that could provide means of ascent. Wilson cites the work of Deborah Prothrow-Stith, who writes that young people in inner-city communities are more likely than others to see violence as a way of life: "They are likely to witness violent acts and to have role models who do not adequately control their own violent impulses or restrain their own anger." Wilson quotes an unmarried father who has made the transition from joblessness and drug abuse to employment and responsibility:

> The guys in my neighborhood, I used to be with them a few years ago when I was drugging. But, once I quit I found if someone was my friend so-called, all we had in common was drugs and once I quit drugs we had nothing to talk about because things that I was trying to do such as being at work on time and not being able to stay out until 2 o'clock on a weeknight 'cause I had to get up in the morning in order for me to be punctual at the job, that wasn't their concern because they didn't have no job and a job was the furthest from their mind.[46]

When the culture of the jobless ghetto does not provide room for work, family, and responsibility, people who seek those values struggle.

A number of other authors have written about the "oppositional culture" that develops in city slums and prevents blacks from participating in the life of the larger community. Kenneth Clark writes in *Dark Ghetto*:

> Because the larger society has clearly rejected [the black ghetto dweller], he rejects . . . the values, the aspirations, and techniques of that society. His conscious or unconscious argument is that he cannot hope to win meaningful self-esteem through the avenues ordinarily available to the more privileged individuals [which] have been blocked for him through inadequate education, through job discrimination, and through a system of social and political power which is not responsive to his needs."[47]

An example of this defense mechanism is the rise of black English, a dialect of the language that supporters embrace as a key element of racial identity. Since standard English is the language of business, education, and politics and government, the use of black English marginalizes blacks.

Oppositional culture is the undercurrent of Spike Lee's film *Do the Right Thing*. The block in Bedford-Stuyvesant depicted in the film is a rich culture filled with clever and creative characters. But underlying the coexistence of many different racial and ethnic groups is a tension that constantly threatens to burst out and wreak havoc on the block. When the film's hero, a black named Mookie, is seen talking with the Italian-American son of the pizzeria owner, Mookie's friend confronts him. "Hey Mook: stay black." Later, after a fight at the pizzeria leads to a struggle in which the police kill one of the neighborhood's combative blacks, Mookie's moment of truth comes. He works for the pizzeria owner—likes him, in fact—but takes sides in the fight. He hurls a trash can through the window of the pizzeria, inciting a riot. The imperative to reject the dominant culture for all that it has done to repress blacks dominates the ethos of the inner-city neighborhood.

But this sense of isolation is not self-imposed, is it?

No, it isn't. Its roots lie in centuries of economic and social isolation that date back to slavery. Families were broken up, parents and siblings were separated from each other, and most blacks were prevented from getting any kind of formal education under slavery. In the Reconstruction years of the last half of the nineteenth century, blacks were kept in an informal system of slavery on sharecropping farms. With the rise of new farming machinery and the growth of industrial activity in cities, blacks moved to cities in the South and North alike. When they reached the cities, they found new opportunities but also discrimination. Schools were bad, housing was substandard, public services were lesser than those of their white counterparts, and opportunities in government were nil.

In a comprehensive study of the underclass throughout American history, Jacqueline Jones found a persistent "racial division of labor" in American cities in the nineteenth and twentieth centuries. In government agencies and private mills and manufacturers alike, blacks persistently found themselves at the end of the job queue. Even in wartime, when the nation faced a deep labor shortage and recruited workers from the ranks of nonworkers, the resistance to blacks continued. When the Bell Aircraft Company in 1942 reported that it would need 40,000 new workers, it hastened to add that "approximately 75 percent may be women," giving short shrift to the area's 13,000 blacks available for work. Blacks at the time had an unemployment rate nine times as great as whites (43 percent versus 5 percent).[48] Previous newcomers to American cities—immigrants from Ireland, Italy, Germany, Russia, Poland—also faced discrimination when they first arrived in town. But these newcomers quickly found an employment niche in city government agencies as those agencies grew along with the ranks of newcomers. Irish, for example, joined police departments; Jews gained access to school departments. But by the time blacks asserted themselves in the city, such niches were no longer open.[49]

Discrimination in employment was matched by discrimination in housing and education as well. As noted in later chapters, government agencies, real-estate interests, and other city residents restricted the places where blacks and other minorities could live. And since school opportunities were tied to place, blacks usually were assigned to the worst schools in the city.

The Level of Society

Is race a useful way to understand poverty in the city?

Gunner Myrdal called race a unique "American dilemma."[50] Slavery, the Civil War, Reconstruction, and Jim Crow burnished the national psyche with race. Blacks came to the United States as property in chains, knowing that the system was designed specifically to exploit and exclude them. Other groups in this nation of immigrants came of their own will and knew they could make a place for themselves and their children within a generation or two.

Every newcomer to the United States has experienced some form of discrimination. Germans, Irish, Italians, Greeks, Chinese, and Vietnamese confronted epithets, exclusion, and even violence as they settled into American life. But most groups eventually begin to get "white" status. Established whites become willing to accept them as neighbors, coworkers, and even mates. They begin to identify themselves as white on census forms. But blacks have faced a more stubborn resistance. As Andrew Hacker notes, the United States "has chosen to reject the idea of a graduated spectrum, and has instead fashioned a rigid bifurcation."One is either white or not. The consequences are devastating for blacks. "Black Americans come from the least-known continent, the most exotic, the one remotest from the American experience. Among the burdens blacks bear is the stigma of 'the savage,' the proximity to lesser primates. . . . No other racial or national origin is seen as having so pervasive a personality or character."[51]

Statistics attest to the importance of race in American life. Blacks comprise 12 percent of the U.S. population but 55 percent of those who live in poverty for a long time and 60 percent of those who get welfare benefits for a long time. Almost seven eighths of the residents in extremely high-poverty neighborhoods are members of minority groups. Minorities in cities are much more likely to live in such communities as whites. In 1990, 14 percent of the black population and 9.4 percent of the Hispanic population residing in cities lived in extremely poor neighborhoods, compared to

Table 2.1 Persons below the Poverty Rate (percentage)

Race	1980	1990	1999
All races	13	13.5	11.8
White	10.2	10.7	9.8
Black	32.5	31.9	23.6
Asian/Pacific Islander	—	12.2	10.7
Hispanic origin	25.7	28.1	22.8

Source: http://www.cdc.gov/nchs/products/pubs/pubd/hus/tables/2001/01hus002.pdf. Centers for Disease Control, "Persons and Families Below Poverty Level."

just 1 percent of the white population.[52] Even when blacks gain the wherewithal to escape their racially segregated communities and move to white communities, whites leave those communities.[53]

Even when blacks succeed, they face barriers to full participation in every walk of American life. With all other factors "held constant," blacks still face pervasive discrimination in getting a job, securing an apartment, obtaining a home mortgage, gaining acceptance in a neighborhood, getting home owner and other forms of insurance, winning admission to schools and universities, and gaining access to a wide variety of public accommodations from retail outlets to restaurants to taxi service.[54]

How important is segregation to the perpetuation of poverty?

Segregation intensifies the experience of poverty in minority communities. Isolation from job, health care, education, and other opportunities not only hurts the individuals involved but also undermines the development of community. In their book *American Apartheid*, Douglas Massey and Nancy Denton consider a hypothetical American city with 128,000 residents and divided into sixteen neighborhoods.[55] The city's 96,000 whites (three quarters of the population) experience a 10 percent poverty rate, while the city's 32,000 blacks (one quarter of the population) experience a 20 percent poverty rate. All of these figures are roughly representative of the American urban experience.

If the city experienced no segregation, both blacks and whites would live in neighborhoods with 12.5 percent poverty rates. If four of the city's 16 neighborhoods were exclusively white, the poverty rate in the white areas would be 10 percent and the poverty rate in the other areas would be 13.3 percent. If half of the city's 16 sections were exclusively white, the mixed neighborhoods would experience a 15 percent poverty rate.

When racial segregation is reinforced by class segregation—as it almost always is—the results are even more devastating. When both black and white poor are confined to half of the city's neighborhoods, the intensity of that poverty dramatically increases. Poor blacks living in cities with low racial segregation and class segregation experience a neighborhood poverty rate of 28.3 percent. High racial segregation plus class segregation produces black neighborhoods with 35 percent poverty rates. A city completely segregated by race and class produces 40 percent poverty rates in the black neighborhoods. The situation would be more extreme if the exclusively white sections of the segregated city had 5 percent poverty rates, with a greater percentage of whites living in poverty in mixed neighborhoods, as is usually the case. In a city of half-white neighborhoods and half-mixed neighborhoods, the mixed neighborhoods would have a 20 percent poverty rate. Increase the black poverty rate from 20 to 30 percent, and the rates of poverty for the three black neighborhoods are 35, 45, and 60 percent.

That kind of concentration of poverty in black neighborhoods produces devastating effects on social structures and mores. Intensely poor neighborhoods are much more vulnerable to downturns in the economy. As noted above, a "culture of poverty" often results when the poorest of the poor are isolated from mainstream society.

In addition, poor minority neighborhoods are more likely to face a "self-perpetuating spiral of neighborhood decline." According to a study by the U.S. Department of Housing and Urban Development, once 3 to 6 percent of a neighborhood's buildings are abandoned, "investment psychology becomes so depressed that reversal of the abandonment process is impossible without major external intervention." That "tipping point" is likely to be reached with rates of neighborhood poverty near 50 percent.[56]

How can we measure levels of segregation? What do those measures show?

Blacks did not always live apart from whites, but cities and suburbs have become intensely and intricately segregated in the twentieth century.

Using an "isolation index," Massey and Denton have tracked the degree of neighborhood integration throughout the twentieth century. The index measures the makeup of neighborhoods where blacks live; a score of 100 percent indicates that all blacks live in completely black areas; a value under 50 percent indicates that a black is more likely to have whites than blacks as neighbors. In three quarters of all American cities in 1890, the index was 10 percent—meaning that the typical black lived in a 90 percent white neighborhood. By 1930, the index for Northern industrial cities had increased to 31.7 percent. By 1970, the index for the thirty metropolitan areas with the largest black populations was 69.3 percent, and in 1980 it was 63.5 percent.[57]

Much of the isolation is owed to suburbanization, which has produced white and black flight from the cities. The isolation index for blacks was

72.9 percent in cities and 39.7 percent in suburbs. Massey and Denton conclude: "Ironically, within a large, diverse, and highly mobile post-industrial society such as the United States, blacks living in the heart of the ghetto are among the most isolated people on earth."[58]

But surely many blacks have experienced great progress as a result of the Civil Rights Movement. How can that progress of the growing black middle class be squared with the extreme isolation?

The Civil Rights Movement created unprecedented opportunities for blacks in the Uunited States. For the first time in American history, blacks were guaranteed the rights to use basic public accommodations and to vote as a result of the Civil Rights Act of 1964 and the Voting Rights Act of 1965. They had the right to obtain shelter without discrimination as a result of the Housing Act of 1968. As a result of the Nixon Administration's so-called Philadelphia Plan, the forerunner of affirmative action, blacks had greater access to corporate and government jobs. Blacks earned college degrees in record numbers. At least some suburbs, usually right on the city's outskirts, opened to blacks for the first time. To be sure, most communities still practiced some subtle—and some not-so-subtle—forms of racial discrimination. But opportunities for upward mobility opened up for many blacks.[59]

One result was the rise of the black middle class. Incomes rose. Blacks dramatically increased their numbers in the professions as well as in middle-class jobs that provide a steady if unspectacular living, such as police officers, electricians, bank tellers, and medical workers. Black women did especially well. (Employers seemed to prefer women to men among blacks because they are considered more accommodating.)

Between 1970 and 1990, the income distribution of blacks shifted from a classic pyramid with gradually smaller segments in the higher salary brackets. The new distribution had a bigger base, with more poor people, and a more even distribution of the upper income brackets. That is significant, as Andrew Hacker notes, because it signals "a separation of better-off blacks from those at the lowest level." Overall, black incomes remained steady, but the distribution changed to isolate poor blacks.[60]

Middle-class blacks left the inner city for better economic opportunities, better schools, and the open spaces of the suburbs. This exodus took away some of the major supports of the neighborhood social structure in the city. Churches, political organizations, schools, and business groups all suffered from the loss of leadership and resources. Perhaps even more harmful was the loss of the moral authority of the departed middle class. Some of the most devastated areas became devoid of mainstream ideas and practices.

William Julius Wilson's book *The Truly Disadvantaged* traces the development of the underclass in America's cities. Wilson collected data from seventy-seven subdivisions of Chicago in 1970 and 1980. In 1970, only eight of these communities had poverty rates of 30 percent or more and only one had a poverty rate of 40 percent or more. Six of these communities moved from a high to an extreme poverty rate in a decade. One major reason for this more intense poverty is that 151,000 nonpoor blacks left these communities during that fateful decade. Nationally, the number of blacks living in the suburbs increased from 3.38 million in 1960 to 8.2 million in 1985. By 1989, 27 percent of all blacks lived in suburbs. These blacks had comprised the stable working class in the neighborhoods. After 1980, they were gone.[61]

How does segregation of groups affect economic mobility? Are the effects always negative?

The isolation of racial and ethnic groups has contradictory effects. On the one hand, segregation isolates minorities from a wide range of opportunities. On the other hand, segregation engenders economic and social diversity within racial or ethnic communities. In black urban communities before the Civil Rights Movement, people of all classes lived side by side. The preacher lived next door to the garbage man, the beautician next to the accountant, the teacher next to the maid. The proximity of diverse groups created a dynamic situation where people went their own ways but came to support each other in numerous ways. Black communities from Atlanta to the Los Angeles community of Watts, from Birmingham to American Beach, Florida, developed complex systems of mutuality that sustained generations of blacks from Reconstruction to the Civil Rights Movement. The most important consequence of segregation was the role model effect. Educated, upper-class families demonstrated a better way of life for the striving factory worker or janitor. The children of diverse families went to school and church together.

Ironically, when civil rights laws of the 1960s and 1970s forced whites to open up to black patronage, black businesses and communities suffered. In a study of the demise of the community of American Beach, Florida, Russ Rymer writes:

> Integration became the greatest opening of a domestic market in American history, but the windfall went in only one direction, with predictable, if unforeseen, results: the whole economic skeleton of the black community, so painfully erected in the face of exclusion and injustice, collapsed as that exclusion was rescinded. In this way, integration wiped out or humbled an important echelon of the

black community—the non-clergy leadership class that had fought so hard for civil rights and was needed to show the way to pragmatic prosperity. Today's black professionals haven't replaced the old black entrepreneurs, because the money they bring home is earned almost exclusively from white-run companies. In the past, black wealth was generated out of the black community. Money entered at the bottom of the community and worked its way up, binding the classes together in mutual dependence and a linked destiny. White business sundered that connection by inserting itself between the black professional and black consumer classes.[62]

Black neighborhoods lost their professional elites, their savings, and their consumer dollars to the larger, white-dominated system.

The Level of the Economy

Is poverty inevitable under capitalism?

Some analysts on the left argue that a class of poor and near-poor people are essential for the day-to-day operations of a market system. The logic goes like this: because firms must compete with each other for market share, they constantly search for ways to hold down costs. One way to dampen labor costs is to hold one part of the laboring class outside the mainstream—a group that Marxians call the "industrial reserve army." This reserve army consists of the unemployed, underemployed, and outsiders who could be brought into the laboring class at will when production requirements demanded—and shucked off just as easily. The existence of this group of marginal laborers gives firms great flexibility to respond to market signals. When there is a high demand for goods, companies hire itinerant workers such as women, minorities, and old people; when demand is low, those workers are returned to the sidelines of the economy. With the globalization of the economy, the pool of potential workers gets even bigger; firms locate redundant manufacturing plants around the world and keep the plants running as fully as market demand allows. During the economic boom of the 1990s, virtually every group of itinerant workers was brought into the workforce; with the onset of the recession, those workers were let loose. The reserve army serves another function as well: it keeps the wages of current workers down. Workers know that if they agitate for higher wages, they could easily be replaced by someone from the reserve army. The simple law of supply and demand holds that the more workers are available to take a job, the lower the wage will be for the workers actually on the job.[63]

Why don't workers organize and fight collectively for higher wages and better working conditions?

They do, but the reserve army also undermines collective action among workers. Workers are divided among themselves because they have different interests given their different positions in the economy. When workers attempt to form a labor union, management can hire "replacement workers" from the ranks of the reserve army. This creates conflicts between employed and unemployed workers, when both groups in fact have common interests. It also creates splits among workers. Some push for inclusive unions, some prefer exclusive unions, while still others consider organizing a waste of time or even a threat to their jobs because of company retaliation. Splits often develop along racial or ethnic lines.

How did changes in the economy affect poverty toward the end of the twentieth century?

A process known as deindustrialization changed the whole landscape of employment in America, with especially serious implications for cities and low-skill workers. In the years after World War II, U.S. firms moved some operations first to the Sunbelt and then overseas in search of lower wages; at the same time, industry after industry mechanized their operations to improve efficiency. As a result, the fraction of manufacturing jobs to all jobs in the Northeast fell from 37.9 percent to 27.9 percent, in the Midwest from 40.1 percent to 29.4 percent, and in the West from 29.5 percent to 26.6 percent.[64] In the 1970s, the unemployment rate in the U.S. increased from around 5 percent to double digits. Many of those who managed to hold on to their jobs saw their real earnings decline during the 1970s and 1980s.[65]

Deindustrialization could be seen in cities all across the United States. In Pittsburgh, Pennsylvania, and Gary, Indiana, steelworkers were laid off. In Detroit, automakers faced a stiff challenge from Japanese and German automakers, killing off one major company and almost leading to another's demise. Associated industries—machine tools, glass, engine parts, chemicals—suffered as well. Clothing manufacturers, who had already migrated from New England to the South, now moved overseas.[66] In industry after industry, the only way American producers could stay competitive was to cut workers, adopt new technologies, and establish new, "flexible," "post-Fordist" manufacturing systems.[67] The result was a lost generation of blue-collar workers who were confused and often bitter about the broken "social contract" of upward mobility that seemed to have been abrogated. Although the service industries absorbed many of the workers from the ranks of manufacturing, service wages were as low as half of those of manufacturing jobs.

But hasn't the decline in the industrial economy been offset by a rise in the postindustrial economy? Hasn't this had the effect of keeping the poverty rate down?

A postindustrial economy based on information, technology, and corporate services has certainly expanded in the United States since World War II, generating employment and income growth that has at least partially compensated for the decrease in manufacturing. However, many living in urban areas have continued to suffer for two reasons.

Many older cities in the Northeast and Midwest have not benefited from a significant increase in postindustrial activity. When major manufacturing firms such as RCA and Campbell Soups left Camden, New Jersey, for example, they were not replaced by an influx of corporate headquarters, banks, law firms, and advertising agencies; residents there were faced with an ever-shrinking base of jobs, and the unemployment rate shot upward. What happened in Camden also occurred in larger industrial cities such as Detroit and Buffalo as well as numerous smaller and medium-sized Rustbelt cities such as Lawrence, Massachusetts; Pawtucket, Rhode Island; Bridgeport, Connecticut; Patterson, New Jersey; Allentown, Pennsylvania; Utica, New York; Toledo, Ohio; Gary, Indiana; and Flint, Michigan.

Even in cities that did enjoy growth in their postindustrial sectors, that growth did not necessarily translate into good job opportunities for local residents. Many residents lacked the requisite educational background to qualify for the more skilled, higher-paying positions in the service sector. They had to settle for jobs as secretaries, custodians, security guards, hotel bellhops, waiters, dishwashers, and retail sales clerks, jobs that paid considerably less than what had been offered at the manufacturing plants before they had been shut down. In sum, the postindustrial economy led to an increasingly bifurcated employment structure characterized by highly skilled, well-paying jobs at one end of the spectrum and low-skilled, poorly paying jobs at the other end, a situation that did little to alleviate urban poverty.

Inequality in employment opportunities was further aggravated by the development policies of city governments. Believing that the nation's industrial economy was evolving into a service-based economy, most local officials backed an approach to urban redevelopment that favored downtown business districts—the presumed site of the emerging postindustrial economy—at the expense of industrial neighborhoods, whose demise was more or less taken for granted. Consequently, downtown districts flourished with the construction of high-rise office buildings, luxury hotels, convention centers, and sports stadiums, while surrounding neighborhoods and their residents were largely neglected.

The Level of Government

In what other ways has government contributed of urban poverty? Have welfare policies themselves exacerbated the problem?

Liberals and conservatives would say yes, but they have very different reasons. Conservatives contend that welfare gives poor people an incentive to avoid the world of work and achievement, that a welfare check is a kind of narcotic that prevents people from developing their abilities and providing for themselves. Liberals contend that government assistance to the poor is inadequate to help the poor achieve self-sufficiency. Some even question whether the nation's antipoverty policies are really intended to lift people out of poverty. Two of the most eloquent voices of the left, Frances Fox Piven and Richard A. Cloward, argue that American poverty policy is more concerned with quieting the voices of the poor than developing any effective remedies for their plight.[68]

How much money does the government spend to confront the poverty problem? Who gets that money, and in what form? How does spending for poor people compare with spending for better-off classes?

The federal budget for 2000, totaling $1.74 trillion, devoted roughly $226 billion to major programs involving poverty. That spending did not go completely to the assistance of the poor. The biggest program, Medicaid, cost $115 billion. In a way, that program aids the doctors, hospitals, and pharmaceutical companies more than recipients. Some $86 billion in additional spending went more directly to the recipients of Supplemental Security Income (SSI) ($29 billion), food stamps ($19 billion), earned-income tax credits ($26 billion), and Temporary Aid to Needy Families ($21 billion). Even then, some of the recipients of SSI come from more affluent backgrounds. Of course, other programs that do not primarily assist the poor, such as Social Security ($405 billion) and unemployment compensation ($26 billion), do include some poor or near-poor people among their recipients.

What is the conservative critique of welfare dependency?

The argument that welfare benefits discourage people from getting work—and encourage people to live off the dole—has been around as long as governments have devised programs to care for people. Alexis de Tocqueville's essay on pauperism might be the most eloquent statement of the dangers of dependency on the generosity of others.[69] Throughout American history, those sentiments have been echoed by prominent political figures and scholars. Franklin D. Roosevelt, for example, warned against the indolence that might result from a social welfare state. Ronald Reagan regaled conservative audiences from the 1960s through the 1980s with tales of "welfare queens" who expertly worked the system so that they would not have to get a job.

Charles Murray's book *Losing Ground*, published in 1985, is the classic argument that welfare causes poor people to abandon responsibility and become dependent on the state. Murray's claim is simple: welfare gives women and children so much support that they do not get jobs—and more important, do not marry and form families. The family structure is critical to the culture of work because it provides support and also a day-to-day imperative to take responsibility for one's own well-being. Government benefits have become so generous compared with the rewards and responsibilities of the work world, according to this argument, that men and women decide to take the dole rather than work to build a family and a future.

Murray argues that with the liberalization of AFDC, the federal government's largest cash assistance program prior to 1996, more and more people enrolled in the program. It is true that welfare rules were loosened throughout the 1960s and 1970s. For example, in 1962, states were permitted for the first time to give benefits to families with an unemployed husband, and the Supreme Court struck down the "man in the house" rule in 1968 and then invalidated residency restrictions on benefits in 1969. Such rule changes coincided with dramatic increases in the welfare rolls. According to Murray and other conservative critics, the liberalization of welfare also contributed to long-term dependency and demoralization of the poor.

To support his argument, Murray considers a hypothetical couple in Pennsylvania named Harold and Phyllis. He compares the decisions that Harold and Phyllis would make in 1960 and 1970, before and after the expansion and liberalization of the welfare state in America. Faced with a high-school pregnancy, will the couple get married and attempt to form a family? In 1960, the answer is yes. Phyllis can get a modest sum as a single mother on welfare, but not enough to make ends meet. Harold cannot be a freeloader because Phyllis has nothing to offer him. Only by combining forces can they take care of the baby and begin to achieve economic sufficiency. In 1970, though, the incentives toward marriage have been subverted by welfare. Phyllis can get a decent welfare check, and Harold can live with her and work occasionally to bring in some extra income. But since Harold's job is not his basic source of support, he can afford to be casual about it. He can get jobs on and off, collecting unemployment compensation in the off times as well as getting some money off the books in the black market. And since the couple is not married, the relationship can dissolve at any time. Rather than committing to the forces that build real assets—family and work—welfare discourages both.[70]

How does the differential in wage levels and welfare benefits discourage work and independence?

The poor are perfectly rational when they take welfare benefits and eschew work, Murray argues: "I begin with the proposition that all, poor and non-poor alike, use the same general calculus in arriving at decisions; only the exigencies are different."[71] The difference between poor people and middle-class or affluent people, Murray says, is that poor people simply have fewer choices—and welfare distorts the long-term prospects for employment and prosperity.

The rational-choice model explains some important tendencies of the poor. In an economy that does not offer a "living wage" or significant benefits for low-skill or entry-level work, taking advantage of public assistance might seem a rational decision—even if the long-term consequences are negative. Consider the case of a single mother of two children who receives AFDC, Medicaid, food stamps, and other benefits and who has the opportunity to get a minimum-wage job across town. For much of the modern history of welfare in the United States, that woman would lose most of her benefits if she took the job. She not only would be materially less well off but would also lose control of her own time and her family time. Paul E. Peterson summarizes the matter well:

> It was no longer necessary to work in order to survive; indeed, full-time employment in a fulltime, entry-level position at times yielded less after-tax, take-home pay than the income one could receive in benefits from a multiplicity of government programs. And marriage could be economically painful. The old shibboleth that two could live more cheaply than one no longer held. Instead, a single woman with children could receive more from the government than from the earnings of her potential husband. It was better— and more fun—for both if they lived apart; she could share her welfare check with him, and he could earn through episodic or parttime employment enough to sustain an adventurous street life.[72]

One study of welfare incentives found that a 1 percent increase in benefits produced a 3 percent increase in the number of beneficiaries, a four fifths of 1 percent increase in the poverty population, a 2.1 percent increase in single-mother births, a one half of a 1 percent increase in adults not employed, a 1.2 percent increase in abortions, and a 1.1 percent increase in violent crime. These figures are problematic because of the complexity of the people and places of poverty. But they suggest that the consequences of welfare policy ripple throughout society. As the author of the study noted:

> [S]tate governments may be best advised to focus welfare on the innocent—widows, the genetically or accidentally disabled, and children—and to set firm time limits on the welfare eligibility of

others. Education and a strong economic climate appear to be the most effective policy-responsive condition to reduce the remaining pathologies. A blind compassion may be admirable but a knowledgeable compassion is twice blest.[73]

As long as poor communities enjoy good educational opportunities and a range of job and housing opportunities, such an approach might make sense.

No matter what kinds of incentives there are to work, can someone really get by on public assistance?

Usually not. In fact, most welfare recipients supplement public assistance with black-market income because those benefits simply do not provide enough to survive. In a landmark study, Kathryn Edin interviewed dozens of welfare beneficiaries to determine how they survived week to week. Because of the basic need to maintain the family, the recipients engaged in a number of strategies to bring in extra cash. Both short-term and long-term welfare families seem to engage in these strategies. AFDC and food stamps covered about 58 percent of these families' expenses. Of the other 42 percent of income, about half came from family and friends, and just under half came from income from the underground economy. Many worked at under-the-table jobs, some took salaried jobs under an assumed name, and some sold drugs or engaged in prostitution. While these latter activities put the recipient in some danger, most of the jobs underscored at least a degree of networking and structure in inner-city areas.[74]

Especially in this precarious underground economy, getting supplemental income was never a sure bet. Most welfare mothers regularly cut back on the everyday necessities of life. Recipients allowed apartment defects to go months without repairs and cut back on spending for food, clothing, and other basic supplies. A quarter of the interviewees lived without telephones, which put them at a great disadvantage in getting jobs or arranging for child care. One step the Edin interviewees refused to take was moving into more dangerous neighborhoods. Even if they could have saved $150 a month, whites, Asians, and Mexicans were especially reluctant to expose their children to the dangers and temptations of the worst parts of town.

When people resort to activities outside the bounds of legality—especially dangerous and degrading activity like prostitution and drug sales—they lose faith in the larger political and social system. Christopher Jencks and Kathryn Edin conclude: "We have, in short, created a system whose rules have no moral legitimacy in recipients' eyes. . . . It is a feeling bred by a system whose rules are incompatible to everyday American morality, not by the peculiar characteristics of welfare recipients."[75] The need to survive, more than any inherent moral flaws, spurs illegality.

The Evolution of the Welfare State

How has welfare policy developed throughout American history?

The welfare state in America began in cities and towns, extended to states, and finally developed at the level of the national government—all in response to social crises of development and dislocation.

Benefits for particular classes—also known as entitlements—actually began in the Revolutionary era. Veterans were given pensions and other rewards for their service in the war against Great Britain. The pensions spurred a number of debates about who was more or less "entitled" to receive help from the government. The distinction between the "deserving" and "undeserving" poor began during this early period.[76]

Public assistance for poor people began in the towns and cities. Local governments from colonial times onward fostered cohesive communities with a strong sense of civic order and virtue. Patrician elites with strong links to political, business, and religious institutions ran the towns. They promoted the idea that the fortunate many needed to care for the unfortunate few. Caring for the unfortunate was equally a matter of public order, community cohesion, and concern for the destitute. Cities and towns established poorhouses that provided food and emergency shelter to the destitute. Political party organizations also offered the poor an occasional job or gift of turkey at Christmastime. Churches and private associations provided assistance as well. Of course, not all towns practiced such a compassionate politics. Some towns forcibly drove the poor, drunks, and other misfits from their borders.

As the Industrial Revolution gathered momentum during the nineteenth century, the demand for wage labor intensified. Waves of immigrants poured into America's cities to run the nation's factories. But while economic activity increased, so did social problems. Densely populated settlements left more and more vulnerable people in congested and unsafe housing amidst rampant disease, crime, and poverty.

City structures—formal and informal, public and private—grew out of the growing challenges of urbanism. Political party machines offered a wide range of material rewards—jobs, food, fuel—in exchange for votes. Churches, philanthropies, hospitals, settlement houses, and orphanages tended to the needs of the poor. Special commissions addressed problems concerning roads, water and sewerage systems, and parks as they arose. Reform movements emerged to institutionalize some of these informal arrangements. The motivations behind these efforts ranged from Chrisian good-heartedness to populist zeal, from a concern for economic efficiency to a desire to discipline "abnormal" people.

As economies expanded, local responses were not always adequate to addressing social problems. State governments developed programs to control the effects of social problems. Innovative governors such as Theodore Roosevelt, Al Smith, and Franklin Roosevelt in New York and Robert LaFollette in Wisconsin developed relief programs to respond to severe economic dislocations or exposure to poverty. Public works projects, housing programs, labor reform, school and recreation programs, unemployment insurance, and banking reform were some of the policies pioneered at the state level.

When did the federal government start to get involved?

The turning point was the Great Crash of October 1929, which ushered in a worldwide depression that lasted for more than a decade. When the stock market crashed, the rest of the economy collapsed. Hundreds of banks folded. More than 90,000 businesses failed. Some 13 million workers lost their jobs, with the unemployment rate reaching a high of 25 percent. For the workers with jobs, hourly wages fell by 50 percent. The international trade system collapsed, undermining the potential for exports to revive the economy. Abroad, desperate times caused once-proud nations to take the desperate measures of installing brutal dictators. Bitterness and fear were the ugly twins of the American psyche.[77]

The federal government moved slowly into social policy. President Herbert Hoover adopted a number of temporizing measures but seemed oblivious to the real desperation in the land. President Franklin D. Roosevelt took bold action from the start. His New Deal was the high-water mark of social policy. Roosevelt established jobs programs under the Civilian Conservation Corps, the National Recovery Administration, the Works Progress Administration, and the Public Works Administration. Rural development took place under the auspices of the Tennessee Valley Authority and the Rural Electrification Act. Organized labor got its "bill of rights," which allowed workers to organize, under the Wagner Act. Prospective home owners obtained loan assistance and foreclosure protection from the Federal Housing Act.

The Social Security Act of 1935 was the cornerstone of federal welfare policy for decades to come. One central component of the landmark legislation was the establishment of a system of unemployment insurance, a program that garnered widespread public support at a time when much of the nation's workforce remained idle. The other core component of the Social Security Act instituted an old-age pension; workers paid a small payroll tax on their wages, and the money was banked to provide for them in old age. This proved to be one of the most successful social welfare programs in American history. Almost by itself, Social Security has dramatically reduced poverty among the elderly, once the most vulnerable class of all. According to one study, Social Security reduced the number of elderly who would have been poor from 15.3 million to 3.8 million. In most states and around the nation, the number of poor old people would have quadrupled without the program. Three out of five people rescued from elder poverty were women. Even those who remain poor are better off because of Social Security. The total gap between the elderly poor and the poverty line was $10 billion in 1997; it would have been $70 billion without Social Security.[78]

The New Deal was based on a philosophy of public interest and access. The underlying assumption was that while all were entitled to basic opportunity, each individual should help himself. With few exceptions, people entered into a kind of social contract with the government: in return for work or other commitments, they got benefits. The jobs programs, in particular, built schools, bridges, tunnels, parks, rail stations, and other facilities that would be used by the community as a whole. Social Security, which offered the most specific benefits, was designed as an insurance program. AFDC, which was part of social security, offered mothers minimal benefits in exchange for raising their children until they could find a husband to support them.

The New Deal program had two important characteristics. First, it was experimental. Roosevelt was pragmatic and was willing to try—and abandon—any approach. FDR was famous for asking many different aides to devise programs to address a common problem and trying more than one approach. Second, Roosevelt offered a helping hand, not a comprehensive strategy. If people were hurting, Roosevelt thought they should be helped as quickly as possible. These two characteristics have become ingrained into American policy, to the consternation of many who would rather see comprehensive policy for poverty, housing, health care, and other social needs.

What happened to welfare policy after Roosevelt?

Social policy stagnated in the 1950s under presidents Harry S. Truman and Dwight D. Eisenhower. Truman proposed dramatic new extensions of the New Deal—including a federal health care program and broader civil rights protections—but was stymied by the nation's weariness with government activism and the preoccupation with the Cold War. Truman also had to fight the Republicans, who controlled Congress for two years, and conservatives in his own Democratic Party. Still, Truman persuaded Congress to pass legislation for Social Security expansion, a minimum wage, and public housing. The GI bill of rights, which provided veterans with special benefits for education and housing, was probably the greatest domestic legacy of the Truman years. The Taft-Hartley Act, which greatly weakened organized labor, was passed despite Truman's veto. Eisenhower's focus was on maintaining an even economic keel. His biggest domestic policy achievement was probably the creation of an interstate highway system, which helped to open areas outside the cities to suburban development.

John F. Kennedy ran for president in 1960 with a rousing call to "get this country moving again." Kennedy began planning new antipoverty programs in 1963 when his eyes were opened to the vast poverty in the United States by his reading (Michael Harrington's *The Other America*)[79] and personal observation (campaigning in poor communities in West Virginia). But Kennedy achieved little in his abbreviated term. Concerned that he might lose the support of segregationist Democrats from the South, Kennedy supported the Civil Rights Movement only reluctantly. Kennedy's push for a greater federal role in education and health care fizzled in Congress.

How did Lyndon B. Johnson's Great Society change American politics and policy?

Lyndon B. Johnson (LBJ), who became president upon Kennedy's assassination in 1963, used the shock of that tragedy to rally the public around a program that rivaled the New Deal. The jewels of Johnson's Great Society were the passage of the landmark Civil Rights Act of 1964, the Voting Rights Act of 1965, and the Open Housing Act of 1968. Each of these laws gave minorities and poor people tools to gain access to the basic rights of citizenship.[80]

The welfare state grew along several different lines. Liberalization of income-maintenance programs such as Social Security, AFDC, and disability pensions expanded basic means of support to individuals. New housing programs produced tens of thousands of new units of housing. Even though they were not heralded in grand speeches, the most important policy changes probably involved welfare. In the landmark 1968 case *King v. Smith*, the Supreme Court found unconstitutional the so-called "man in the house" rule, which had denied welfare benefits to children whose mother was living with a man out of wedlock; the decision added some 500,000 poor children onto the welfare rolls.[81] Other administrative changes to AFDC, covering everything from paperwork to home visits by social workers, made welfare easier to obtain. The number of AFDC recipients increased from 3 million in 1960 to 10.8 million in 1976. In the program's peak year of 1994, 14 million people received benefits.

The programs with the most material impact on poor people were straightforward grants of "entitlement" benefits. Food stamps provided vouchers for poor people to purchase nutritional necessities. Medicare provided health care to the mostly middle-class recipients of Social Security; Medicaid provided care to the poor recipients of AFDC. Housing programs operated on two tracks: subsidized construction of public housing and subsidies to help the poor pay rent.

A number of programs focused on the particular struggles of children. The Elementary and Secondary Education Act created a number of "compensatory education" programs designed to focus on disadvantaged children. The Women, Infants, and Children (WIC) Program offered support for prenatal and early infant care. Head Start offered prekindergarten education to poor children. Hot breakfast and lunch programs provided basic nutrition.

Community development programs included Model Cities, which targeted a wide range of programs to distressed neighborhoods; the Community Action Program, which provided funds for local organizing; the Legal Services Corporation, which gave the poor access to lawyers to initiate class action litigation; and Volunteers in Service to America (VISTA), which recruited young people to offer schooling and other services in poor areas. Training programs included the Job Corps.

Scholars have concluded that welfare and other public assistance programs played an important role in reducing poverty in the 1960s and 1970s. In 1965, cash transfers brought out of poverty 27 percent of the people who would have been in poverty; by 1978, the figure was 44 percent; in 1989, 40 percent; in 1995, 47 percent.[82]

When Richard Nixon ran for president in 1968, he sharply criticized the Great Society and the welfare policies of the Kennedy and Johnson years. Did that produce a major cutback in social welfare programs?

Not quite. Nixon did cut many of Johnson's antipoverty programs, such as Model Cities and Community Action. But a funny thing happened on the way to the dismantling of the welfare state: the welfare state expanded instead.

Nixon's "great experiment" was a failed effort to replace the welfare system with a guaranteed income for all citizens.[83] This ambitious plan would have eliminated the whole complex apparatus of welfare and instead offered cash grants to people whose income fell below the poverty line. This proposal passed in the House of Representatives but was defeated by a strange Senate coalition of right and left that found the benefits respectively too generous and too stingy.

Despite this failure, the Nixon years did much to bolster the nation's social welfare system. First, in 1972, Congress indexed Social Security benefits to the inflation rate through the application of cost of living adjustments. This corrected the problem of erosion in the real value of

Table 2.2 The Legacy of the Great Society

Program	Impact
Civil Rights	Laws banning discrimination in accommodations, employment, voting, and housing
Expanded welfare	More liberal eligibility opened Aid to Families with Dependent Children and other programs to a broader share of the population.
Housing vouchers and construction programs	Section 8 of the Federal Housing Act provided billions to increase supply of low-income housing and enhance buying power of poor.
Food stamps program	Vouchers for food gave poor families additional spending power.
Job training	Job Corps and other programs provided federal money for training.
Medicare	Medical coverage provided for recipients of Social Security.
Medicaid	Medical coverage provided for welfare recipients.
Compensatory education	Assistance to public schools serving low-income families provided special programs for underprivileged children.
Model Cities and other community-based programs	Inner-city revitalization efforts aimed at shoring up urban areas.

benefits during periods of high inflation. By 1998, the average benefit for all retired workers was $765 per month.

Second, in 1974, the federal SSI replaced an array of state programs for the blind and disabled. This program set uniform benefit levels for disabled people across the nation and built in adjustments for changes in the cost of living. The states supplement monthly payments to beneficiaries according to the cost of living in the states. SSI is financed through the federal government's general revenues, not the Federal Insurance Contributions Act (FICA) tax. Children qualify for SSI when they meet the requirements of disability or low income. Individuals and couples are eligible when their incomes fall below the monthly SSI benefit levels of $532 for individuals and $789 for couples. Although some critics have criticized SSI—like all benefit programs, it is subject to fraudulent claims by able-bodied people—it has provided a national approach to assisting people struggling with physical and mental infirmities. The program grew from 4.8 million to 6.5 million beneficiaries from 1990 to 1995; since then the SSI rolls have stabilized at around 6.5 million people.

President Nixon also created the Comprehensive Employment and Training Administration (CETA), which pumped billions into jobs programs over its five years of operations. CETA replaced a hodgepodge of federal job training programs with a national program that provided money to the states to develop programs that fitted their needs. The states established coherent strategies for using the program to tackle their most severe unemployment problems, usually in partnership with counties and cities. The Emergency Employment Act of 1971 provided $1 billion for some 170,000 public service jobs under CETA. Funds were targeted to communities with high rates of unemployment, although political jockeying in the states often diverted money to less-needy communities.

Finally, Nixon introduced affirmative action to American policy with the so-called Philadelphia Plan. Under the plan, the Labor Department established goals and timetables for construction projects to hire minority workers; firms that failed to go along risked losing their contracts. By linking public funds with projects undertaken by private companies, the Nixon administration hoped to bring about a real integration of blacks into the economic system—in Nixon's terms, to give minorities "a piece of the action." Since then, of course, affirmative action has become a flash point of controversy. Liberals support affirmative action in all fields, from education to government contracting, with the claim that extra efforts are necessary to redress centuries of racial discrimination. Conservatives usually oppose affirmative action, arguing that such policies discriminate against nonminorities and promote the insidious belief that minorities are incapable of competing on an equal footing with whites.

Welfare: From Discontent to Reform

What was the source of the backlash against welfare?

Starting with Barry Goldwater's insurgent presidential campaign of 1964, a growing part of the American population began to question whether welfare and other social programs worked. As Thomas and Mary Edsall have argued, three potent forces combined to unleash a "chain reaction" of anger against liberalism: race, rights, and taxes.[84] Many Americans began to question whether the Civil Rights Movement had gone "off track" and was giving blacks unfair advantages over working-class whites in the competition for educational opportunities, jobs, and social status. The race issue became a central part of tensions over urban crime, public schools, public housing, and neighborhood change. Many middle-class Americans resisted the explosion of legal rights and protections for poor people, minorities, gays, women, and others. Meanwhile, increases in taxes of all kinds undermined Americans' willingness to fund social programs.

Candidates such as Goldwater, Alabama Governor George C. Wallace, Richard M. Nixon, and Ronald Reagan played into middle-class resentments against liberal approaches to social policy. Welfare became a central part of this critique of liberalism. Rather than rewarding the people who worked hard and raised their children according to long-accepted rules, these politicians argued, welfare gave all kinds of rewards to people who did not work and allowed their children to run wild. The list of government programs for the poor—not only welfare, but also public housing, rent supplements, food stamps, medical care, even free furniture—rankled working-class voters who struggled from paycheck to paycheck.

How did this issue unfold in academic and policy circles?

In the 1970s, a growing movement of conservative scholars began to argue that welfare was not only too expensive and wasteful but actually harmed the interests of poor people. George Gilder's *Wealth and Poverty*, a favorite of Ronald Reagan, did not blame poor people for their participation in welfare, as many conservatives had for years, but blamed the system for undermining poor people's ability to develop economic independence.[85] Charles Murray's *Losing Ground* argued that poor people were behaving rationally when they chose welfare over work; when welfare was eliminated, Murray argued, not only would more poor people work and develop a stake in the economic system, but they would also form families and claim a better place in community and social life.[86]

Liberals rejected the antiwelfare manifestos of Gilder and Murray, but some of them began to acknowledge that the system contained some perverse incentives. Senator Daniel Patrick Moynihan of New York, an aide to presidents from Kennedy to Ford, expressed dismay that welfare prevented the formation of families with mother, father, and children. He regularly reminded colleagues that poverty was highly correlated with family breakdown. Moynihan also stressed the importance of work for family life; men and women, he argued, were less likely to marry when neither had a job. Welfare gave women with children an independent source of income.[87]

Didn't federal policy-makers recognize the problem?

The U.S. Congress has acted intermittently to reduce the incentives for welfare over work. In 1967, Congress passed a provision, known as the "thirty and a third" rule, which was designed to encourage welfare recipients to work. The first $30 of wages and one third of the rest of the wages could be shielded from cutbacks in welfare benefits.[88] However, the Reagan administration eliminated the thirty-and-a-third rule in 1981. After a welfare recipient received benefits for four months, her benefits would be cut $1 for every $1 she earned. Reagan repealed the thirty-and-a-third for two reasons. First, he wanted to reduce overall spending on social welfare and to concentrate remaining resources on the neediest group—the unemployed poor. Second, he wanted to replace the carrots of work incentives with the sticks of work requirements. [89]

The repeal of the thirty-and-a-third rule set the stage for another two decades of welfare reform as policy-makers struggled to find the best way to encourage welfare recipients to get jobs. Ultimately, a hybrid approach—limited eligibility for benefits, combined with more generous job training, child care, and other services—would emerge from the Clinton years in the 1990s.

One of the most powerful charges of the critics is that the welfare system encouraged young women to have babies. Did it?

The tragedy of "babies having babies"—teenage girls and young women, without independent means of support, getting pregnant—has driven much of the modern welfare debate. Critics of the welfare state argue that the extra benefits that welfare mothers get from having more children encourage them to have more and more children, which makes them ever more dependent on public assistance. But if welfare mothers can be assumed to behave rationally, getting a few extra dollars to care for additional children is not much of an incentive. The rates of illegitimacy increased dramatically in the latter years of the 1970s, even though the welfare benefit levels fell in real terms. That might be explained by a kind of lag in the mothers' realization of the consequences of their actions. Perhaps the mother made a decision to have another baby on the mistaken assumption that the extra benefits would be substantial, only to discover later on that that assumption was faulty. But an additional set of facts undermines that argument. States with different benefit packages did not have appreciably different fertility rates.

Even if the actual dollar amounts are small, welfare might encourage unmarried women to have children because of the culture of public assistance. With idleness almost forced upon recipients, one of the few ways for girls and women to find meaning in their lives is to make a family. In his portrait of Philadelphia ghetto life, Elijah Anderson notes the importance of the "baby club" in filling the "social, moral, and family void in the young girl's life." The "hip" group on the street develops a network of belonging based on getting pregnant and raising babies. Babies not only represent something to have in common, but also a way to compete and distinguish oneself. Girls who eschew sex and pregnancy until they can form a stable family get marginalized and even mocked in the inner city. When the baby leaves infancy, the urge to care for another baby sometimes becomes overwhelming, and the young women become pregnant again.[90]

When did the welfare system start to break up?

President Reagan's impressive electoral victories in the 1980 and 1984 elections did not produce the widespread GOP realignment that conservatives had hoped for. The Democrats retained control of the House of Representatives and, after losing power in the Senate in 1980, regained a majority of seats in the Senate after the 1986 election. With Congress repeatedly blocking efforts by the White House to overhaul the welfare system, the Reagan administration eventually agreed to a compromise welfare reform bill. The Family Support Act (FSA) of 1988 obligated all states to participate in the AFDC-UP program, which provided cash assistance to two-parent families (and not just single mothers) who were impoverished because of temporary unemployment. The law also strengthened the connection between welfare and work by requiring 15 percent of single-parent recipients to be enrolled by 1993 in a new program called Job Opportunities and Basic Skills (JOBS). Finally, the FSA increased "transitional" assistance in the form of literacy, English-language, job training, and child care programs to help welfare recipients find employment.[91]

Did the Family Support Act succeed in reducing welfare dependency?

No, because exemptions from the work requirements in the law (e.g., mothers with children under the age of three did not have to participate in a JOBS program) effectively excluded 50 percent of all AFDC recipients, and only 15 percent of the remaining caseload were required to participate by 1993. Also, the recession that hit the country in the early 1990s caused state governments to withhold increases in spending for the programs that were central to the FSA. Meanwhile, as the unemployment rate rose, so did caseloads. Each year seemed to bring a new record in the number of American families on welfare. Conservatives charged that the 1988 compromise was a failure and that nothing short of radical change would be satisfactory. Liberals also complained that the welfare system was broken, pointing to the two-decade-long slide in the real value of welfare benefits and thus the inability of existing policies and programs to lift poor people out of poverty.[92]

Welfare Reform

How did the big break come for welfare reform?

With the federal government stalemated over reform, the pressure for reform came from state governments. Governors were increasingly frustrated by their ever-expanding welfare rolls. They lobbied Congress for the freedom to deviate from federal regulations and design their own welfare programs, and they found a mechanism that would enable them to do just that.

A 1962 amendment to the Social Security Act allows the Secretary of Health and Human Services to waive specific rules and regulations in order for states to establish "experimental, pilot or demonstration project[s]" that promote the general purposes of AFDC. In 1992, the first Bush administration began to approve such waiver requests from states. The Clinton administration accelerated the trend by granting forty-three waiver requests between 1993 and 1996.

Leading the way were GOP governors like Tommy Thompson of Wisconsin and John Engler of Michigan. Most of the new state programs sought to build upon the FSA's goal of transforming welfare into a transitional stage on the way to a lifetime of self-sufficiency. Common elements of the state programs included tighter restrictions for program eligibility, more stringent work requirements, time limits on eligibility for welfare, and penalties for failure to comply. States also provided a range of supportive services to facilitate the transition from welfare to work. Some states adopted policies aimed at modifying the behavior of welfare recipients, such as family caps, parenting contracts, and school attendance and childhood immunization rules. The waiver process made the states into "laboratories of democracy" where new approaches to public assistance could be pursued with federal funds. Such experimenting by the states turned out to be quite important because it laid the foundation for sweeping changes in federal welfare policy within just a few years.[93]

By granting so many waivers, President Clinton obviously wanted to encourage policy innovation at the state level, but didn't he also promise to overhaul welfare policy at the federal level?

Yes, welfare reform was a prominent theme in his 1992 presidential campaign. Clinton repeatedly pledged that if he were elected, his administration would "end welfare as we know it" by offering welfare recipients a deal. If recipients would take greater personal responsibility for finding and holding onto a job, the government would assist them in navigating the transition from welfare to work by providing a variety of support services. Recipients of cash assistance under AFDC born after 1971 would be required to develop an employment plan identifying the skills they need to obtain a job. The federal government would then support the acquisition of such skills through education, job training and placement, and child care services. After a two-year period, recipients over the age of eighteen would have their cash assistance terminated. At that point, if adult recipients had not yet found employment, they would be assigned to a subsidized private-sector job or a community service position earning the minimum wage for fifteen to thirty-five hours per week. Refusal to participate in such work would result in expulsion from the program. The Clinton proposal also included measures to discourage teenage pregnancy and force parents to comply with child support orders.[94]

But the Clinton plan went nowhere. In the wake of the 1994 congressional elections, a resurgent GOP led by House Speaker Newt Gingrich and a freshman class of young, conservative Republicans had its own ideas about how to reform welfare. In August 1996, the Republican-controlled Congress enacted a bill that emphasized the need for welfare recipients to assume more responsibility for becoming self-sufficient, but the bill lacked the kind of transitional assistance contained in Clinton's earlier proposal. President Clinton called the measure "fundamentally flawed" but, in the midst of a presidential election campaign, decided to sign the bill into law anyway.[95]

Politicians often trumpet new laws as pathbreaking advances in public policy. Did the 1996 law really change welfare policy in a significant way?

It did. To start, the Personal Responsibility and Work Opportunity Reconciliation Act (PRWORA) repealed the nation's principal income assistance program, AFDC, as well as a host of related programs. This alone sent a powerful message, because poor families with children could no longer be assured of receiving cash assistance as long as they satisfied certain eligibility rules. After sixty-one years of the welfare system, PRWORA ended any entitlement to welfare from the federal government.

In place of AFDC, Congress established a new system of block grants to be distributed to each state under a program called Temporary Assistance for Needy Families (TANF). The total amount of the block grants was $16.5 billion, which is roughly the average sum that the states received from the federal government for AFDC and certain related programs each year between 1992 and 1994. The name of the new program underscores Congress's intent that henceforth the receipt of welfare would be a *temporary* condition to tide poor individuals over until they were able to secure steady employment.

Under the law, does the federal government instruct the state governments on how they are to spend their grant money?

For the most part, the answer is no. A key feature of the 1996 law is that it shifts primary responsibility for the formulation and implementation of welfare policy from the federal government to the state governments on the theory that state officials have a better understanding of local problems and how best to remedy them than do policy makers in Washington, D.C. It was assumed that devolving power to the states would encourage fresh approaches to encouraging self-sufficiency and reducing poverty. So, in general, PRWORA gives states considerable discretion in creating new programs and spending their TANF funds.[96]

Congress included in the law two crucial mandates involving time limits and work requirements. First, Congress imposed a sixty-month lifetime limit on the availability of federal TANF funds for any one family. The limit applies to the entire household, including children, and to all forms of assistance under the grant. Lawmakers felt that the prospect of a certain cutoff of cash assistance from the federal government would spur recipients to seek and retain employment. The law offered one loophole: states may grant extensions to up to 20 percent of their total caseloads by reason of hardship. States may also choose to provide *state* funds to assist families after the deadline. At the same time, in keeping with the spirit of devolution that animates most of PRWORA, states are also permitted to set time limits *shorter* than the sixty-month limit.

Second, the 1996 Act contains work participation requirements. In order to receive TANF funds, states must explain how they will require adult participants of federal assistance to "engage in work" within twenty-four months of obtaining TANF aid. Under the law, 25 percent of TANF families must participate in "allowable work activities" by fiscal year 1997 or face sanctions or penalties; that minimum participation rate rises to 50 percent by fiscal year 2002. Failure to comply with the work participation rules exposes not just welfare recipients to sanctions but also states, which may incur financial penalties. Consequently, states have an incentive to impose their own strict penalties on recipients who do not comply with work participation requirements. Although states have much discretion over what constitutes "allowable work activities," PRWORA exhibits a notable lack of enthusiasm for education and job training programs; participation in such programs to satisfy work requirements is limited to twelve months (except for teenagers completing high school) and to only 30 percent (later lowered to 20 percent) of all adult participants receiving TANF funds.

Did the 1996 Act change welfare policy in other ways?

PWRORA also included several other important components that have attracted less attention. First, along with the TANF block grant, it established a second block grant, the Child Care and Development Block Grant, to support state efforts to provide child care programs to parents and caretakers trying to move from welfare to work. Second, it triggered a set of changes intended to strengthen the enforcement of child support programs. Third, it restricted eligibility rules to qualify for food stamps in ways expected to reduce spending for the program by $25 billion. Fourth, it denied food stamps, nonemergency health care under Medicaid, and other benefits for a five-year period to *legal* immigrants who arrive after the law goes into effect.

How did the states use the discretion granted to them by Congress to recon-struct welfare policy?

Although Congress had anticipated that devolution would inspire in-novative policy-making, most states have adopted more or less the same general structure in fashioning welfare programs. The two federal man-dates have set the tone. Most states have adopted a sixty-month lifetime limit on receipt of TANF funds, which mirrors exactly the provision in PRWORA, though six states have imposed a shorter time limit.[97]

And there has been a widespread effort to "change the culture of wel-fare" from dependency to self-reliance. Almost all states require recipients of cash assistance to sign "self-sufficiency agreements" outlining their plan for becoming self-sufficient within a certain period of time. In most states, they are required to look actively for employment and provide documen-tation of their job search efforts. Agencies assist recipients in the job hunt, but not by placing them in job training programs. Less than 2 percent of adult welfare recipients are in formal job training programs. Instead, most states follow Congress's preference for immediate job placement on the as-sumption that the best training for the work world is on-the-job experi-ence.[98] Given the stress on "job readiness," there is a pronounced emphasis on the rapid development of "soft skills" such as résumé writing and inter-view techniques. Agencies also focus on changing the psychological and behavioral characteristics of many recipients in order to make them more attractive to potential employers. This may entail a battery of mental health tests and drug and alcohol screenings. As one analyst put it, "coun-seling now surpasses training as the route to self-sufficiency."[99] Finally, re-cipients are often subjected to various behavior-related rules connected not directly to work but to their roles within the family. They may be re-quired to attend parenting skills classes, immunize their children, read a specified number of books to their children each week, and meet with a child support enforcement officer.[100]

Failure to comply with any of the work and family requirements results in sanctions. Thirty-six states have adopted "full family sanctions" for non-compliance with work requirements, meaning that the *entire* family be-comes ineligible for cash assistance. This is a decisive break from past practice. Under AFDC, adult recipients subject to work requirements would lose their cash grants for noncompliance, but their children would still get their benefits. One study reports that rates of sanctioning range from 26 percent to 45 percent of families subject to a work requirement.[101]

Welfare reform seems awfully coercive. The whole approach seems to be premised on the desirability of forcing recipients off the welfare rolls through a combina-tion of time limits, work requirements, and sanctions for noncompliance.

True, but welfare reform provided a carrot to go along with the stick. Most states have significantly expanded programs designed to assist recipients in navigating the transition from welfare to work. One strategy involves "earned income disregard" policies. That's an awkward name for something that is rather simple. Remember that years ago, recipients who secured jobs were forced to forfeit in cash assistance whatever they earned through work on a dollar-for-dollar basis. Policy-makers eventually realized that this discouraged recipients from seeking employment and so they adopted the practice of "disregarding" a certain level of earned income when determining the amount of cash assistance that an individual was entitled to. In this way, recipients could secure jobs and earn income without worrying about losing most or all of their assistance under AFDC. Since 1996, forty states have put in place more favorable earned income disregard policies than had existed prior to PRWORA, typically by disregarding a higher percentage of earned income than had been disregarded under AFDC. [102]

A second strategy involves programs to help recipients absorb the costs associated with full-time employment, including higher expenses for clothing, transportation, health care, and child care. In particular, there has been a dramatic increase in state spending to provide child care assistance to working poor families. States have used hundreds of millions of dollars in TANF money and state money to provide child care for welfare mothers returning to work.[103]

Most state welfare programs take the same general approach. Most adult members of families who receive cash assistance under the TANF program are required to work. Such families are rewarded by being allowed to keep most or all of their cash assistance and by having access to certain support programs to lower transportation, health care, and child care costs. At the same time, these benefits are subject to compliance with a wide array of rules and regulations, and failure to comply may lead to a "full-family sanction." Finally, even families that faithfully follow all of the rules and regulations face a time limit on their benefits that ranges from eighteen to sixty months.[104]

Evaluating Welfare Reform

Has welfare reform been effective?

Reports in the media have ranged from cautiously optimistic to wildly enthusiastic. An example of the latter appeared in the *National Review* in February 2000: "The results are in: Welfare reform is one of the greatest public-policy successes of modern times."[105] Even liberals have offered flattering assessments.[106] The lack of public debate over welfare reform during the 2000 presidential election campaign indicates that Democrats have backed away from their predictions in 1996 of dire consequences for the nation and poor people in general.[107]

The most widely cited evidence to support claims of welfare reform's success has been the remarkable reduction in the number of families receiving assistance all over the United States. In early 1994, about 5 million families, about 15 percent of all American families, received cash assistance under AFDC. This was the peak of welfare caseloads in the sixty-one-year history of the AFDC program. But as a number of states began to implement new welfare policies under the waiver process established in 1992, caseloads began to fall. By August 1996, when PRWORA was enacted, caseloads had declined to 4.4 million families, and by June 2000 that number had dropped to 2.2 million.[108] That, in turn, has translated into substantial savings in state budgets for cash assistance. In Massachusetts, for example, where welfare caseloads fell from 103,000 in 1995 to 44,000 in 1999, the welfare budget decreased from $692.5 million in fiscal year 1995 to $272 million in fiscal year 2000.[109]

If progress is measured by caseload decline—and for many policymakers and policy advocates the paramount goal has always been a reduction in dependency on public assistance—then it is easy to see why welfare reform has been hailed as a stunning success. But the good news about diminishing caseloads is tempered by the unevenness of the decline. Progress has been slowest in urban areas, where the caseload dropped by 41 percent from 1994 to 1999 compared to the 52 percent decline nationwide during the same period. With each passing year, poverty and welfare recipients have increasingly been concentrated in cities where employment opportunities have remained constricted and job information networks are weak. By the end of the decade, Philadelphia contained 12 percent of Pennsylvania's population but 49 percent of the state's welfare recipients. Similarly, Baltimore was home to 13 percent of Maryland's residents but a whopping 58 percent of the state's caseload. Progress among minorities, and especially Hispanics who speak limited English, has lagged behind that of whites.[110]

To what extent is the decline in caseloads attributable to the booming economy of the 1990s as opposed to any changes in welfare policy?

The drop in the unemployment rate to a thirty-year low of 4 percent by the late 1990s—and the first significant gains in real wages for low-income workers in over two decades—provided an increasingly compelling incentive for welfare recipients to enter the labor market.[111]

But an economic boom cannot be considered the only factor in employment gains. If the expanding economy were such an important factor, then why did the United States not see a similar decline in caseloads during the economic expansion of the 1980s? During that decade the nation added 20 million new jobs, and yet the welfare rolls swelled by almost a half million families.[112] The debate over whether welfare reform or the economy deserves credit for falling caseloads has generated reams of academic studies, but a consensus seems to be emerging that new welfare programs were responsible for 15 percent to 20 percent of the decline during the early years of welfare reform, between 1994 and 1996, and 30 percent to 40 percent of the decline between 1996 and 1999.[113]

Even if scholars conclude that welfare reform is responsible for as much as 40 percent of the decline in caseloads, does that necessarily mean that new welfare programs have been effective? Doesn't much depend upon what happens to individuals after they leave the welfare rolls?

A whole cottage industry of research designed to answer that crucial question has developed during the past few years. The so-called "leaver studies" rely on surveys of former welfare recipients and administrative data to obtain information on people's employment status, income levels, basic needs regarding food, shelter, and health care, and general satisfaction.

On the positive side, about 60 percent of leavers are currently employed and over 70 percent have been employed at some point during the previous year. The employment rate of single mothers jumped dramatically after 1995, reaching an all-time high of 72 percent in 1999. The black child poverty rate also declined steadily during the latter half of the 1990s. Most leavers indicate in response to survey questions that the quality of their lives has improved since leaving the welfare rolls.[114]

On the negative side, a substantial minority of leavers—approximately 40 percent—are not employed. Among those who did find jobs, many were unable to hold them because of the multiple barriers to long-term employment that low-income women encounter, and a sizeable percentage were forced to return to welfare. A study by the Urban Institute drawing upon 40,000 households in its National Survey of America's Families examined individuals who had left the welfare rolls from 1995 to 1997 and 1998 to 1999. By 1999, 29.1 percent of the first group and 21.9 percent of the second group were back on assistance.[115]

Leavers who do work earn very low wages, generally between $6 and $8 an hour—not enough to lift families above the poverty line. Also, the benefits associated with such jobs are often meager; a study by the Massachusetts Department of Transitional Assistance reported that only 38 percent of such jobs include paid sick leave and only 45 percent offer health insurance as an option.[116]

Many former recipients lose their food stamp and Medicaid benefits because they assume they are no longer eligible when in fact they usually are. Because of the loss of such benefits and because wage levels are so low, quality of life remains precarious for many leaver households. A report issued by the U.S. Conference of Mayors in December 2001 found that requests for emergency food and shelter assistance increased by 23 and 13 percent in 2001.[117]

The work requirements imposed by the 1996 law may be contributing to higher levels of familial instability. Two studies of welfare programs in Connecticut and Iowa, for example, found that single mothers participating in each state's program were less likely to marry than the overall welfare population. Researchers speculated that as single mothers move from welfare to work, they become more self-reliant and thus more selective in choosing potential spouses. Another possibility is that the combination of work requirements and low-wage employment that sometimes requires women to take on more than one job to make ends meet leaves women with little time or energy to think about pursuing relationships and marriage.[118] The Iowa study also reported increased levels of domestic violence, which suggests that welfare reform may be exacerbating household stress.[119] Other studies have revealed that the adolescent children of parents participating in new welfare programs have experienced a decline in academic performance and a rise in smoking and drinking, which may be attributable to a diminished parental presence in the household due to stricter work requirements.[120]

All of these leaver studies suggest that welfare reform really isn't the spectacular success that some have claimed. How do supporters of welfare reform respond to these apparent weaknesses?

Many acknowledge that state governments and welfare agencies at the local level need to do a better job of informing current and former recipients of their eligibility for food stamps, Medicaid, child care assistance, and other benefits. Better access to benefits will improve the quality of life for many. Some champions of welfare reform also understand the need to reinvest the savings resulting from declining caseloads in programs to support recipients trying to make the transition from welfare to work. The former governor of Wisconsin, Tommy Thompson, who used the waiver process in the early 1990s to initiate a number of state government programs that anticipated the federal government's enactment of PRWORA in 1996, has pointed to Wisconsin's heavy investment in child care programs as an essential component of his state's approach to reforming welfare. When President George W. Bush nominated him to head the Department of Health and Human Services, Thompson argued for more support services for the working poor: "For welfare reform to be successful, you have to make an investment up front. It can't be done on the cheap. You can't expect welfare mothers to go to work unless they have child care. They've got to have health insurance, transportation and training. All cost money. The savings to taxpayers, and they are substantial, come later as caseloads decline."[121] So there is a recognition that more needs to be done.

At the same time, defenders of welfare reform do not interpret the leaver studies with alarm. For instance, while they concede that wage levels are low, they point out that when other benefits such as food stamps and child care subsidies are factored in (this assumes, of course, that recipients actually do receive such benefits), gross incomes rise above the poverty level. Furthermore, although most recipients start out earning entry-level wages, average incomes rise by about $1,200 annually; with each year of steady employment, prospects for promotions and higher wages improve. Defenders of welfare reform contend that no one ever said that any reform program would move former welfare recipients "miraculously from the poorest to the middle class. The journey almost certainly includes a stopover in the ranks of the working poor."[122] Advocates of welfare reform conclude that something close to a miracle *has* occurred. After several decades of ballooning welfare rolls, a trend that appeared to be irreversible to many observers, caseloads have declined by over 50 percent since 1994. The sharp reduction in welfare dependency alone is a major accomplishment.

One's interpretation of the outcomes of welfare reform so far seems to hinge upon which facts one chooses to focus on.

And how one views the objectives of welfare reform. If the goal is simply to reduce welfare dependency, then the results, indeed, have been impressive. If the ultimate goal is not just minimizing welfare dependency but reducing the extent and depth of poverty, then we still have a long way to go. Reform proponents like Tommy Thompson seem to hold this long-range perspective, but Thompson maintains that the country is heading in the right direction under the 1996 Act.

The skeptics point out that not all states are investing their savings from declining caseloads in new programs to help former recipients find and retain good jobs.[123] In some states, a pattern has begun to emerge: first, drive down caseloads through demanding work requirements, accelerated time limits with minimal exemptions for hardship, and an insistence upon strict compliance with all rules and regulations under the threat of harsh sanctions; and second, use the substantial savings from diminished expenditures on cash assistance to fund other programs unrelated to welfare reform or to cut taxes. Some of the states with the steepest declines in case-loads are also the most punitive in dealing with recipients. In South Carolina (with a caseload decline of 76 percent between 1993 and 2000), a single act of noncompliance such as being late for an appointment with a caseworker may result in a loss of benefits for the entire family, including children. Mississippi (with a caseload decline of 81 percent between 1993 and 2000) also imposes harsh sanctions for noncompliance. A study of eight counties in Mississippi revealed that only 35 percent of recipients had jobs after leaving or being forced off the welfare rolls. To make matters worse, the state has been criticized for neglecting to spend millions in accumulated funds for child care and other support services for the working poor.[124]

While most states have embraced the vision of welfare reform embedded in the 1996 Act, the vision of moving recipients from welfare to work has produced different outcomes in the states. Some have seen reducing welfare dependency as a first step toward a meaningful reduction in poverty. But other states have seen declining caseloads as the ultimate goal and thus made little effort to help the poor and working poor to achieve self-sufficiency. The wide variation in the prospects of welfare recipients among the fifty states was what many liberals feared when Congress decided to devolve power over welfare policy to the states in 1996.

So predicting what will happen to welfare recipients in the future continues to be a murky proposition?

Yes, and one that is further complicated by two additional factors that give many observers cause for concern. First, although considerable progress has been made in lowering caseloads, most analysts agree that those who have remained on the welfare rolls will be among the most difficult to employ. A substantial percentage of this group face major barriers to employment that include mental health problems, alcohol and drug addiction, or disabled children. As the lifetime limits for receipt of cash assistance loom for many of these people, it is unclear what will happen when they are cut off.[125] Second, perhaps the biggest wild card in the debate over welfare reform involves the question: What happens when the economy sours?[126] All agree that efforts to encourage self-sufficiency were greatly enhanced by the strongest domestic economy in decades. With the arrival of the recession and rising unemployment, what happens to the millions of former recipients who have been clinging precariously to their jobs? And what happens to the millions of recipients who never managed to secure employment when economic conditions were favorable?

The Future of Welfare Policy

What are the consensus "best practices" of welfare reform in the states?

The political scientist Lawrence Mead is effusive in his praise for Wisconsin Works (W-2) and its impact in urban areas: "There is no other state that has truly broken the back of urban welfare like Wisconsin. They haven't solved all urban problems. There's still a lot of poverty. But when you drive into Milwaukee today, you're driving into a city in which cash welfare payments have virtually disappeared. It's extraordinary. It's a revolution." And there is considerable evidence to support such an assessment. The state's welfare rolls dropped by an astonishing 84 percent between 1993 and 2000, a rate surpassed by only three other states. But Wisconsin did not rest on its laurels in reducing caseloads. Under W-2, the state chose to reinvest its huge surplus of TANF funds in programs to help recipients obtain and retain jobs. The state spent only 4 percent less on welfare programs in 2000 than it did in 1996, when caseloads were significantly higher. Much of the surplus was directed to an extensive child care program. Other funds were allocated to support job readiness training, health and nutrition classes, and a six-week Creative Workshop, which put participants to work knitting sweaters. As they worked, the participants tended to talk about their lives, including problems concerning domestic violence, troubled children, or negligent landlords, that could interfere with long-term employment. Meanwhile, caseworkers observed the conversations and then tried to help participants resolve those problems.[127] Such programs "boosted the sense of self-worth" of former welfare recipients and gave them "hope for the future," according to policy analyst Amy Sheridan, who sees W-2 as a model welfare reform program.[128]

All of that does sound impressive. Are there any downsides to W-2?

Frances Fox Piven, an activist and scholar of welfare policies since the 1960s, contends that Wisconsin's willingness to spend money on supportive services, while admirable, did not produce the desired effect. While the state has garnered praise for its efforts to develop and fund a child care program for the working poor, only 14 percent of eligible families participate. Many families eligible for food stamps are not getting them. In Milwaukee, where most of the state's former welfare recipients are concentrated, a host of indicators suggests that conditions are growing worse, not better. Child abuse, domestic violence, juvenile arrests, and infant mortality all increased during the 1990s, and the poverty rate remains stubbornly high at 17.4 percent in 1999, down from 18.5 percent in 1989.[129] While many former recipients have found jobs, Wisconsin has not succeeded in helping them to find jobs with decent pay and benefits. A study of W-2 by the state's Legislative Audit Bureau criticized the program for placing recipients in low-paying jobs with minimal prospects for advancement.[130] Perhaps most ominously, after making impressive gains against welfare dependency in the late 1990s, the number of people receiving cash assistance in Wisconsin jumped by 25 percent in 2001.[131]

If Wisconsin is not a compelling model for welfare reform, then what state is?

Minnesota, which shares many of the same demographic, economic, and political characteristics as neighboring Wisconsin, may be a more attractive model. Like Wisconsin, it ventured into welfare reform prior to the 1996 Act by establishing a pilot program for seven counties in 1994 before extending a modified version of the program statewide in 1998. But Minnesota appears to have been more effective not only in reducing caseloads but in lifting families out of poverty. The Minnesota Family Investment Program (MFIP) cost about 5 percent more per household then under the old AFDC program, partly because the state spent more money on support services and partly because of its generous earned income disregard policy. Under MFIP, when a welfare recipient found a job, the state would disregard 38 percent of her or his monthly income when determining the amount of cash assistance. That translated into an extra $250 per month in income compared to the old welfare system. In addition, to promote long-term economic stability, recipients were permitted to continue receiving cash benefits until their total income was 40 percent above the poverty line. The additional financial support seems to have had the further benefit of lowering the level of stress within families, which in turn resulted in greater marital stability, fewer incidents of domestic abuse, and more children thriving in school.[132]

A study by the nonpartisan, Manpower Demonstration Research Corporation (MDRC) of 14,000 Minnesota families receiving cash assistance from 1994 to 1998 produced some promising findings. Employment rates increased by about 35 percent for participants in the MFIP compared to participants in the AFDC program. The quality of the jobs seemed to improve over time; earnings among those who did find employment rose by 23 percent and the percentage of participants who obtained health insurance coverage increased from 61 percent to 69 percent for MFIP participants. Perhaps the most impressive findings involved family life. There was a nearly 40 percent surge in marriage rates among two-parent families, an 18 percent decline in reports of domestic abuse, and improvements in the school performance of the children of MFIP participants. An official with MDRC called the program's "positive effects on economic outcomes and on family and child well-being unprecedented." Analysts of welfare policy from both sides of the ideological spectrum have expressed strong interest in the Minnesota experience as a model program.[133]

Given the positive reviews, why wouldn't other states jump at the chance to emulate the Minnesota program?

Money. With its more long-term orientation and its stronger emphasis on reducing poverty, the Minnesota program costs more than most other welfare programs. Many Americans believe that the government already spends too much on welfare recipients and thus prefer the more short-term approach of rushing to cut caseloads regardless of the long-term societal costs. Even Minnesota has succumbed to some extent to these cost-containment pressures. When Minnesota extended its pilot program to cover the entire state in 1998, it followed the federal government's lead in imposing a five-year lifetime limit for cash assistance, although no time limits had existed under the original reform program. Critics of that move question whether it makes sense to offer generous support for recipients while they are working, perhaps in low-wage jobs, and otherwise playing by the rules, before suddenly cutting off the cash assistance that may keep many families above the poverty line. The new Minnesota program also cut back somewhat its supportive services for recipients of cash assistance (e.g., the ratio of job counselors to recipients increased from 50 to 1 to 80 or 90 to 1) and welfare benefits are now stopped when a household's earnings are 20 percent, rather than 40 percent, above the poverty line. Finally, no one claims that the MFIP is a panacea; wage levels remain low for many participants in the program, and many wind up returning to the welfare rolls after encountering some kind of setback.[134]

What might be done to improve welfare policy in the future?

Public confidence in the nation's welfare system increased following the enactment of PRWORA because of the emphasis on personal responsibility. But at the same time, welfare reform underscores, to reduce welfare dependency *and* poverty over the long run, the emphasis on personal responsibility must be coupled with a broader sense of public obligation. If Congress is really serious about moving people from welfare to work, it must improve support services for people with minimal skills, limited English proficiency, drug and alcohol addiction, mental health problems, domestic violence, and poor access to child care. Additional support for "difficult-to-serve" populations becomes even more pressing when the economy slumps. As one study put it: "What may have been called 'tough love' in a strong economic environment with available jobs, could create extreme hardship in a more normal economic environment with fewer work opportunities for less-skilled women." During such periods, the federal government needs to supply states with sufficient resources for public sector employment and temporary increases in cash assistance expenditures.[135]

The cyclical nature of the economy points to a second policy reform. Congress might reconsider its insistence upon lifetime limits on cash assistance. The law already allows states to exempt 20 percent of their caseloads due to hardship; states might be given more leeway to expand the hardship exemption or pursue creative options. For instance, Vermont provides community service jobs to adults unable to find a job in the private sector, California cuts off assistance to parents but not their children, and Illinois has abolished time limits altogether for families in which a parent is employed for a minimum of thirty hours per week or is enrolled in school.[136]

Congress might also eliminate the current one-year federal limit on education and job training. Although welfare reform aims to expose welfare recipients to the discipline and responsibilities of work, existing rules all too often trap people in low-skill, low-wage jobs with dim prospects for advancement. Numerous studies have demonstrated that access to education and vocational training lead to higher pay and more stable jobs.[137]

Under current law states are prohibited from using federal funds to provide welfare or health care benefits to legal immigrants who arrived in the United States after 1996 and have been in the country for less than five years. Twenty-two states, recognizing the possible long-term consequences of denying prenatal care and basic medical coverage to children, have offered at least some services for legal immigrants using state money. In a time of recession, declining tax revenues, and mounting fiscal pressures on state governments, even those state-funded programs are jeopardized. Congress should restore aid to legal immigrants for welfare, health care, and food stamps.

The 1996 law imposes a lifetime ban on cash assistance for individuals who are convicted of possessing or selling drugs. Although states are given the option of not enforcing the so-called Gramm Amendment (named after former Senator Phil Gramm of Texas), twenty-two states have chosen to deny all benefits, ten have partial bans, and another ten require drug treatment in order to be eligible for benefits. One study estimates that about 92,000 women in twenty-three states are now affected by the lifetime ban, with 135,000 children at risk. The costs endured by children as a result of this punitive measure warrant either outright repeal or its modification in order to tie continued eligibility for welfare benefits to participation in a drug treatment program.[138]

Are there other ways to combat poverty apart from welfare policy?

Sure, a major cause of poverty has been decreasing real wages over the past two or three decades, so increases in the minimum wage rate would help to alleviate poverty. This is particularly true among low-wage workers, who tend not to belong to unions and thus lack bargaining power with employers.[139]

Another increasingly popular antipoverty policy among liberals and conservatives concerns efforts to raise after-tax earnings through the earned income tax credit (EITC).[140] Adopted in 1975, this benefit has been expanded several times since. The tax credit is targeted to working poor families and because it is refundable, even low-income households with little or no tax liability are entitled to a refund check. A working parent with two children earning $9,720 in 2000 would receive a tax credit of $3,888. The amount of the credit begins to decline slowly when that family's income reaches $12,690 and is phased out altogether at $31,152. The IRS paid out $31 billion in fiscal year 1999 to about 19.2 million households, a big increase from the $6.6 billion distributed in 1989. This is a sizeable public investment, more than twice what the federal government appropriates for the entire TANF and food stamps programs.[141]

But, of course, any serious drive to combat poverty in urban America must go beyond welfare reform and income support strategies. There must also be a sustained effort to generate economic activity and promote full employment, especially jobs with good wages and benefits and prospects for advancement—just the kinds of jobs that have diminished in supply in most U.S. cities during the past few decades.

3
Economic Development
and the Construction
of Opportunity

What is economic development?

Narrowly understood, economic development is the process of stimulating business investment to expand employment and tax revenues. More broadly construed, it is a strategy for improving the economic and social assets of the community to not only promote economic activity but also foster the conditions where discovery and innovation occur and more people are brought into productive activities.[1] The former mayor of Philadelphia, Edward Rendell, used to claim that he spent 70 percent of his time at City Hall trying to promote economic development.[2] It is easy to understand why. Most cities have suffered in recent decades as a result of industrial dispersal and other forms of capital disinvestment, and the ripple effects have been devastating: soaring unemployment and poverty, population loss, a crumbling tax base, fiscal crises, deteriorating public services, and a declining quality of life. Failure to pursue new sources of business investment energetically risks dooming a city to ever worsening levels of economic distress. On the other hand, effective economic development policies promise to generate employment, reduce poverty, raise incomes, boost tax revenues, and improve public services. In the minds of most city leaders, the key to urban revitalization is economic growth. Resurrect the urban economy and the prospects of cities will brighten.

Who can quarrel with that?

Cast in those terms, nobody. The political scientist Paul E. Peterson has even asserted that cities have a "unitary interest" in adopting "developmental policies," meaning that all cities—regardless of their demographic, socioeconomic, or political profile—have an interest in pursuing strategies that will expand economic activity within their borders.[3]

The widespread consensus in favor of economic development begins to dissolve when cities have to make hard choices about how exactly they should promote growth. Should revitalization efforts be concentrated within the downtown business district or the outlying neighborhoods? Should government programs emphasize physical or human development? Industrial or postindustrial growth? How far should cities go in offering incentives to induce business investment within their borders? Does economic growth ever work against a city's interests? What should be done to help citizens adapt to the new demands of an evolving economy?

Each of these policy decisions has political consequences for the myriad constituencies that constitute any city. Inevitably, some interests will win out, while others will lose. The challenge for city planners is to devise economic development policy that is on balance both effective at stimulating economic activity and equitable for all urban groups and communities.

The Rise and Fall of the Urban Economy

At one time, American cities were dynamic engines of economic activity. Today they no longer seem as central to the nation's economy. What happened?

The condition of American cities during the past two centuries has been closely linked to broad transformations in the national and international economy. During the nineteenth century, as the United States shifted from being an overwhelmingly agricultural nation to a predominantly industrial one, the population and prosperity of urban areas swelled. Cities were ideal locations for the mass production of goods. Proximity to navigable waters and railway networks facilitated the transportation of raw materials and manufactured products into and out of cities. Urban centers also offered a growing supply of labor. As the number of factories proliferated, millions of Americans left their farms in the countryside to seek their fortune in the big city. When even that labor pool was not enough, the United States witnessed an explosion in immigration, first from Northern Europe and then from Southern and Eastern Europe and Asia. The influx of humanity pouring into cities fueled unprecedented industrial expansion. Propelled by the twin forces of industrialization and urbanization, the nineteenth century was the golden age of cities. Notwithstanding the pockets of severe poverty that existed in urban areas, especially in immigrant ghettos like the Lower East of New York, it seemed that almost everyone wanted to live and work in America's cities.[4]

Evidence of a countertrend became apparent in the early years of the twentieth century. Part of the problem was too much success. As American industrial output approached that of European powers such as Britain and Germany, factory owners sought to enlarge their plants. But expansion in the increasingly congested neighborhoods of urban America was difficult and expensive. By contrast, ample land at low cost was available just outside the city. Changes in industrial production techniques that put a premium on sprawling one-story plants that were well suited for the suburbs also spurred industrial development. After World War II, when the federal government decided to subsidize a massive construction effort to build an interstate highway system, the exodus of factories from urban to suburban areas gained additional momentum. Yet another crippling blow to urban manufacturing was the increasingly effective efforts of Sunbelt states to lure plants away from their bases in the North and Midwest by offering tax breaks, reduced utility rates, subsidies for infrastructure development, and relatively low wages in a political setting that discouraged labor union activism. In sum, for factory owners contemplating extensive renovation of existing plants or new construction altogether, remaining in the city did not make sense. By the middle of the twentieth century, cities began to experience widespread deindustrialization.[5]

How did deindustrialization affect urban life?

The impact was enormous, especially in Northeastern and Midwestern cities where industry had been most concentrated. In Philadelphia, the textiles and apparel industries represented about 25 percent of the city's manufacturing base at the end of World War II. But with cheaper labor and land costs available elsewhere, one plant after another began to shut its doors and relocate to the suburbs or the Sunbelt. By 1986, the textiles and apparel industries had lost more than 91,000 jobs, or 74 percent of their total in 1947.[6] The sociologist William Julius Wilson reported that between 1967 and 1987, Detroit lost 108,000 factory jobs, Philadelphia 160,000, Chicago 326,000, and New York City 520,000. In percentage terms, the manufacturing sector in each city declined between 51 percent and 64 percent, a crushing blow to any city's economy.[7]

Deindustrialization exacted a wrenching toll on urban neighborhoods, as the costs of a factory shutdown rippled out from the plant itself. Businesses that had provided supplies to the factory had their contracts terminated and were often forced into bankruptcy. Retail stores saw the patronage of former employees of the factory and their families fall off; many lost their leases. With jobs and residents relocating, schools, churches, and clubs suffered steady decreases in students, congregations, and memberships. Venerable institutions of the community simply collapsed. Many displaced workers endured long-term unemployment. Although some factories remained in cities, many of these cut their payrolls by becoming more technology-intensive; increased automation thus lowered the need for workers with limited skills and education—another adverse impact of economic restructuring on urban neighborhoods.[8] Some displaced workers managed to find new jobs, but in doing so settled for a sobering drop in occupational status and pay. Household incomes plummeted, leaving families vulnerable to any unexpected misfortune. A serious illness, fire, or automobile accident could wipe out whatever was left of a family's savings. Not surprisingly, plant closings were associated with a variety of physical and mental health disorders. Laid-off workers and their spouses were victims of headaches, upset stomachs, and more serious ailments such as heart disease. Many experienced heightened levels of anxiety and aggression; the incidence of alcohol abuse and suicide jumped in cities undergoing industrial decline.[9]

Barry Bluestone and Bennett Harrison describe the sense of "anomie" that afflicted local residents:

> The damage, in many cases, has far-reaching consequences beyond the apparent emotional response of anger, frustration, or victimization. Victims lose faith in the "system," leading to a kind of dependency that precludes redevelopment of their communities. Although some struggle heroically to salvage what is left after a major shutdown, there is often the widespread attitude embodied in the statement of one victim: "We put thirty years into building this mill and this community, and it has all come to naught. I can't see that I've the energy to start all over again."[10]

Why didn't people in these communities just move away?

Many did. Many concluded that they could no longer make a living by remaining where they were and so they fled their urban neighborhoods and moved to the suburbs and other regions of the country where job opportunities were more plentiful. It is no coincidence that deindustrialization during the decades following World War II coincided with the highest rates of suburbanization in American history or that the population of Sunbelt states in the South and West swelled at the expense of Rust Belt states in the North and Midwest.[11]

But mass migration was hardly a "solution" to the problem of economic restructuring for cities. To start, not everyone had the ability to relocate to the greener pastures of suburbia. The practice of exclusionary zoning in suburban towns and villages prevented lower-income individuals from finding affordable housing. Pervasive racial discrimination severely limited the mobility of people of color. The federal government's subsidized home loan program actively discriminated against blacks looking for new homes. Racial steering by realtors, as well as outright intimidation and violence by white residents, were clear signals that nonwhites were not welcome in most suburbs.[12]

The hemorrhaging of residents and jobs during the postwar period wreaked havoc upon urban neighborhoods and cities in general. Those who were unable or unwilling to leave their longtime homes lived among an increasingly poor population, a decaying housing stock, boarded-up storefronts, and an air of pessimism about the future. The situation was particularly grim in predominantly black and Latino neighborhoods, which were routinely redlined by financial institutions and insurance companies.

What does "redlined" mean?

The term comes from the practice of banking and insurance officers drawing red lines around entire neighborhoods on city maps. Those officers believed that making loans or offering insurance policies to households and businesses in those areas would be a high-risk proposition and should be avoided. The problem with redlining was that the assessment of risk was based not on objective, economic factors such as annual incomes, debt burdens, and collateral, but upon the racial identity of a majority of neighborhood residents. Entire communities were denied access to credit and insurance coverage based solely upon their racial composition. The consequences of pervasive redlining were pernicious. With potential buyers unable to secure mortgages in redlined neighborhoods, the property values of homes and businesses fell. With home owners unable to obtain home repair loans and insurance policies, the condition of housing steadily deteriorated. Housing abandonment became more commonplace. Lack of access to credit only added to the woes of struggling retail and commercial businesses in the area. In sum, the massive disinvestment associated with the redlining of black and Latino neighborhoods represented another destructive source of economic and social decline in urban communities.[13]

The downward spiral of so many urban neighborhoods was obviously bad news for cities as a whole. The loss of residents and jobs triggered by deindustrialization and other forms of disinvestment decimated the tax base of industrial cities. Tax revenues began to fall just as unemployment and poverty increased demand for social services. Cities struggled to balance their budgets; some, like Cleveland and New York, teetered on the edge of bankruptcy.[14] Mayors searched in vain for answers to the fiscal crisis that gripped their cities. Cities faced a Catch-22. On one hand, if cities raised taxes to close a budget deficit, taxpayers threatened to flee the city, thus causing a further erosion in the tax base. On the other hand, if cities reduced expenditures by slashing appropriations for law enforcement, fire protection, sanitation, parks and recreation, and schools, the quality of life in cities would further deteriorate, setting off yet another cycle of outward migration. Industrial decentralization and suburbanization left urban America in dire straits by the 1960s. As cities sank deeper and deeper into social and economic turmoil, their future appeared bleak.[15]

Urban Renewal

Notwithstanding the difficult circumstances, there must have been some policy response to the decline in economic activity in cities. How did policy-makers react to the urban crisis?

Some city officials anticipated the deleterious impacts of deindustrialization and suburbanization on urban areas long before the crisis atmosphere of the 1960s and 1970s hit. They understood just how debilitating the widespread shutdown of factories and the loss of manufacturing jobs would be. But in thinking about economic development strategies, local policy-makers chose to concentrate their time, energy, and resources not on the decaying industrial neighborhoods but on the downtown business district instead.

Why? If industrial neighborhoods were hurt the most by societal trends, then why didn't city leaders try to generate economic growth in that part of the city?

Most civic and business leaders assumed that the nation was undergoing an economic transformation that was simply beyond their control. The shift in industrial production away from central cities to suburban and rural areas in the Northeast and Midwest and then to the South and West of the United States was the result of powerful market forces. Any effort to counteract those forces by promoting new industrial development within older urban neighborhoods was bound to fail.

City leaders saw a silver lining in the otherwise dark cloud of economic restructuring. While an industrial economy seemed to be on the decline, a postindustrial economy based on services, information, and communications was on the rise. Corporations in the vanguard of the booming postindustrial economy were increasingly locating their decision-making and administrative structures within the downtown business districts of large cities. The expansion of corporate headquarters in downtown areas, in turn, sparked the proliferation of a multitude of firms offering legal, financial, accounting, advertising, and consulting services. Rounding out the downtown-based postindustrial economy were retail stores providing basic supplies and services, hotels, restaurants, and entertainment establishments. Downtown business districts were at the hub of metropolitan-wide transportation systems assuring efficient and convenient access to jobs for everyone from the top executives of Fortune 500 companies to the clerical, administrative, and custodial workers employed by those companies. If the goal was to create good jobs, expand the tax base, and revive the urban economy, then local leaders reasoned that transforming their cities into modern corporate centers based in downtown business districts was the only rational path to take.[16]

But why was it necessary to rebuild downtown if it already possessed all of these amenities?

The immediate reason is that while the basic infrastructure for a postindustrial economy was already in place, it had been neglected during the period of the Great Depression and World War II. Only one office building was constructed in downtown San Francisco between 1929 and 1959.[17] The aging building stock and mass transit systems did not inspire confidence among potential investors. By the late 1940s, most downtown districts needed a major overhaul to attract the kind of capital investment necessary to ignite a vigorous postindustrial economy.[18]

Another reason was more mercenary. Many of the civic and business leaders who advocated a downtown-centered redevelopment strategy also happened to own property in and around the downtown core. They stood to benefit handsomely if the city could convert less valuable land uses such as low-end retail stores and low-income housing into the more valuable land uses of an emerging postindustrial economy. Public officials had an interest in large-scale redevelopment too; their public image and reelection prospects could only be enhanced each time they appeared at the ribbon-cutting ceremony for a new office tower or civic structure. City officials and downtown business leaders joined together in public-private partnerships to promote downtown redevelopment as the dominant economic growth strategy for urban America.[19]

If cities were so strapped for resources because of deindustrialization and suburbanization, how did they pay for the redevelopment of downtown business districts?

With considerable assistance from Washington, D.C. Most of the funding for urban redevelopment efforts during the three decades following World War II came from the federal government under the Housing Act of 1949. What started out as a program to deal with a serious shortage of decent, affordable housing in U.S. cities soon turned into a mechanism for facilitating the reconstruction of downtown business districts. Under the 1949 law, the federal government would subsidize up to two thirds of the net cost of acquiring and clearing property designated as "blighted" by a local redevelopment authority. The property would be "taken" under the city government's eminent domain power. After existing structures were demolished and the land cleared for redevelopment, the city would then lease or sell the land to private developers, usually at a substantially reduced price.

The huge federal subsidies combined with the willingness of city governments to use their eminent domain authority created potentially lucrative opportunities for developers. It did not take long before those developers began to exploit loopholes in the law that enabled them to build highly profitable commercial office buildings, parking garages, and civic institutions as opposed to housing, which had been the top priority of the legislation. In fact, subsequent amendments to the 1949 Housing Act made it progressively easier for developers to build nonresidential projects after 1954.

Why didn't affordable housing advocates object?

They did, but the political pressure applied by commercial developers and their allies in the corridors of Congress proved decisive. In addition, the shift in priorities was consistent with the preferences of civic and business leaders in U.S. cities who had become convinced that revitalizing their downtown business districts was the key to reviving local economies. Redevelopment efforts sparked by the Housing Act of 1949 came to be known as "urban renewal," and early success stories in Pittsburgh, Philadelphia, and New Haven motivated dozens of other cities to embrace the strategy.

So was urban renewal an effective approach to economic development?

In many cases, downtown business districts were spruced up thanks to the construction of gleaming high-rise towers of glass and steel surrounded by public plazas and civic centers. The public investment also spurred substantial private investment; one study found that every one dollar of federal money leveraged four to six dollars in private funds.[20] Total assessed valuation of land within the redevelopment zones soared, thus generating significant increases in property tax revenue for revenue-starved cities.[21]

At the same time, there was a significant downside to urban renewal. The demolition of "blighted," but otherwise stable, neighborhoods uprooted numerous longtime residents and business owners, many of whom happened to be African American. Victims of urban renewal's land clearance began to call the process "Negro removal."[22] Neighborhoods that once exhibited a strong sense of community were decimated and their residents scattered to new public housing projects in isolated and impoverished sections of the city. Urban renewal did rejuvenate downtown business districts and thus contributed to the expansion of a postindustrial economy, but it also exacerbated poverty in residential neighborhoods surrounding the downtown core.

Communities victimized by urban renewal began to fight City Hall in the early 1950s, but their protests were dismissed by city leaders as little more than irritating interference with the forces of progress. It was not until the late 1960s, when the Civil Rights Movement and other social movements gave large numbers of disgruntled neighborhood residents a mechanism to mobilize more effectively against downtown elites, that the more noxious aspects of urban renewal were curtailed. Forced evictions through eminent domain decreased noticeably and the program was essentially terminated in 1974 through consolidation into the Community Development Block Grant.[23]

Inducing Business Investment

What took the place of urban renewal?

City leaders remained committed to downtown revitalization as their primary economic development strategy. In their view, the logic for pursuing a downtown-centered growth policy was as compelling as ever. Most maintained that with new advances in transportation and telecommunications, manufacturing plants had less and less reason to remain in urban neighborhoods. Indeed, by the 1970s, such plants were fleeing not only urban neighborhoods but the entire country, as economic restructuring became a global phenomenon. For most urban leaders, cities were fast becoming obsolete as sites of industrial production.[24] At the same time, local officials believed that future economic growth would be driven by a service- and information-based economy whose locus would be the downtown business district.

But it was neighborhoods outside the downtown business district that were suffering the most because of deindustrialization, right? Why wouldn't city officials divert more resources to those areas that were most in need?

Some urbanists would contend that basic morality would call for such a policy orientation. Public officials, however, worried that using the tax dollars of middle- and upper-middle-class residents and businesses to finance economic development programs in poverty-stricken sections of the city would provoke a taxpayer rebellion, and even more flight from the city.

Few were willing to risk a further erosion of the tax base when so many cities were already on the brink of fiscal collapse. Others feared that generous antipoverty programs might transform the city into a "welfare magnet" and drain city coffers of scarce resources.[25]

At the same time, downtown development promised to spawn lots of new jobs in an expanding sector of the economy and produce ample tax revenue that could be used to fund neighborhood services. Public officials felt that they really had no choice. Their thinking conformed to the conclusion reached by the political scientist Paul E. Peterson, who contended that cities have an overriding interest in avoiding redistributive policies that benefit poorer neighborhoods while pursuing development policies aimed at the downtown business district.[26] The "logic of growth politics" seemed so compelling that a broad consensus developed in support of this approach to promoting economic growth in American cities.[27]

It's still hard to believe that there was such widespread agreement over the spatial dimensions of urban development policy. Wouldn't liberal city officials with strong ties to community groups have favored a more neighborhood-centered approach to strengthening the urban economy?

Again, fears of capital flight in response to redistributive and regulatory policies gave even liberal politicians reason to pause. Beyond that, many neighborhood-oriented officials ultimately decided to support aggressive downtown development for another reason. As political scientist Clarence Stone argues in his book *Regime Politics*, elected officials realized that to govern their cities effectively, they need to reach out to groups in the private sector that have the resources to make things happen. The formal authority of elected officials is not enough to govern. The private-sector group that commands the most resources—financial, technical, legal, communications—is the downtown business community. Elected officials know that forming an alliance with business leaders will enable them to pursue at least some items on their agenda, which is certainly preferable to taking a principled stand on behalf of neighborhood interests but getting nothing accomplished. Regardless of their ideological orientation, elected officials gravitate into the orbit of the downtown business community and establish cooperative alliances on the assumption that it is "better to go along to get along." Stone called these alliances "governing regimes."[28] Other scholars dubbed them "growth coalitions" or "growth machines."[29] Whatever their label, these coalitions of public and private elites proved to be powerful advocates of downtown development.[30]

So how did the downtown growth coalition go about implementing its downtown development agenda?

The overarching goal for economic development planners remained the same: attract and retain capital investment by persuading businesses to locate downtown. The task became more challenging, however, with the phasing out of urban renewal. Not only did cities feel compelled to retreat from their extensive use of eminent domain because of mounting political opposition, but the subsidies that supported special land deals for developers were also diminishing. City officials needed to rely on other incentives to lure corporations and other firms to their growing downtown cores. The key was to foster a "good business climate." This meant convincing business leaders that the city government was committed to creating an environment conducive to corporate growth, productivity, and profits—an environment that would be superior to that of other American cities.

What did that entail?

Doing whatever could be done to reduce costs for businesses. The most important element was tax policy. Two factors determined whether a city's tax policy contributed to a good business climate in the eyes of corporate executives. First, potential investors considered the various types of taxes imposed on individuals and businesses (e.g., property, sales, and income) and the rates associated with each tax. In their view, the general tax burden typically reflected the extent to which a city pursued costly redistributive and regulatory policies. A city that was willing to hold the line on spending would minimize its relative tax burden, providing a favorable climate for capital investment. Second, city officials would also provide tax incentives in the form of credits, abatements, and exemptions to businesses contemplating expansion or relocation within the city. For instance, a city might offer a large corporation based in another municipality a 50 percent reduction in its property taxes for ten years if it agreed to relocate to its downtown district. The city might also supply below-market loans, job training programs, sales of city-owned land at discounted prices, site preparation, and the provision of infrastructure.

Dangling lots of incentives to businesses as a way to lure them to a city seems problematic. Isn't this corporate welfare?

Some critics of locational incentives would agree. They would charge that such incentives serve more as a windfall for businesses than an inducement to invest, thus enriching the private sector at the expense of the public sector.[31] On the other hand, economic development planners justify the use of locational incentives by emphasizing the greater good that will accrue to the city from the addition of new jobs and tax revenue.

What new tax revenue? Don't cities forego tax revenue when they offer abatements to entice businesses to relocate in the first place?

While a tax abatement results in a partial loss of future tax revenue for a designated period of time, if that inducement causes a major corporation such as IBM to base its headquarters in a city, that move will spark a whole series of secondary and tertiary investments by business-support firms in law, accounting, finance, and public relations, as well as hotels and restaurants, all of which will be contributing new tax revenue. [32]

Do businesses extract more from city government than they really need in terms of tax breaks and other incentives?

The underlying political context in which the negotiations take place works against the city government's interests. With fifty state governments and thousands of municipalities in the hunt for capital investment, the ferocious competition for businesses gives firms a decided advantage in dealing with city officials regarding the availability and extent of financial inducements. Cities that already enjoy vigorous economic growth may be in a position to reject excessive demands, but other cities desperate for new investment may not have that luxury. Some of them wind up offering incentive packages that prove to be unduly costly.[33] It is not just businesses from *outside* the city that are well positioned to secure extravagant concessions in exchange for a promise to relocate; some businesses already based in the city win tax breaks and other benefits simply by threatening to leave for another jurisdiction.

Just how crucial are financial incentives in influencing the locational choices of a business?

This is a hotly debated issue among scholars and policy analysts, with far-reaching implications. If such incentives are *not* that crucial in the decision-making process of corporate executives, then cities might be squandering a lot of resources for no good reason. After surveying the academic literature on the issue, the political scientist Peter Eisinger concluded that "the weight of evidence indicates that taxes and incentives are not very important in decisively influencing particular location choices. . . ."[34] What is most important to such choices are costs related to factors of production—land, labor, capital, and energy—over which local governments tend to have little control. Some studies indicate that climate and quality-of-life issues have more of a bearing on where CEOs decide to base their businesses than do financial incentives. Taxes represent such a small percentage of a business's overall costs that they are a relatively minor consideration with respect to relocation decisions.[35] This does not mean that locational incentives are completely irrelevant, however. Eisinger notes that in smaller geographical areas, financial inducements become more important. Competing cities and towns in the same region share the same general characteristics regarding factors of production, and so a sizeable tax abatement might be just enough to sway a relocation decision.[36] Tax policy can be decisive in the cannibalistic jockeying for firms in a metropolitan area.

But if financial incentives may influence locational decisions at only the metropolitan or regional level, why are they used so much as an economic development tool?

While tax breaks "are never regarded as *primary* determinants" in relocation decisions, Eisinger notes, "they are often associated with higher rates of employment and income growth, suggesting that such policies are conducive to more expansive investment behavior by resident firms."[37] In other words, tax breaks and similar inducements may convince corporate leaders already based in the jurisdiction that local government is committed to nurturing a favorable business environment and that such efforts warrant additional investment within the city.

As for why financial inducements are so prevalent in the case of cities trying to lure businesses to relocate, the most plausible explanation lies in politics. Elected officials face intense pressure to do something to generate economic growth. Sitting back and allowing their counterparts in other cities to lure businesses, especially away from their cities, would be politically intolerable. The media attention and political payoff that come with an announcement that a major new employer has agreed to relocate in the city is irresistible, especially when the cost of such a move to local taxpayers can be postponed or obscured in the details of a complex budget.[38]

So what is the bottom line? Has the use of financial incentives aimed at inducing capital investment in the downtown business districts of U.S. cities paid off?

Scholars remain skeptical of any clear causal link between city governments offering business incentives and capital investment in downtown centers. It is difficult to determine whether that investment would have occurred anyway without any incentives. What is certain, however, is that the downtown business districts of many large cities in the United States did experience a prolonged surge in commercial office construction during the 1960s and 1970s before really accelerating in the 1980s. Total office space in New York City soared by 30 percent during the 1980s.[39] More commercial office space was added to the central cities of the thirty-three largest metropolitan areas between 1980 and 1984 than during the three previous decades combined.[40]

The boom in commercial office building clearly energized economic activity in the downtown core and pleased economic development policymakers seeking to create jobs and expand the tax base. Employment opportunities in high-rise office buildings swelled with the expansion of the downtown-based, postindustrial economy. Sizeable infusions of revenue from property, sales, payroll, and other forms of taxation associated with the revitalization of downtown helped to ease the fiscal crisis that had threatened so many cities. In particular, downtown development had the intended effect of improving the class of user in the central business district, thereby elevating property values and contributing to an additional surge in property tax revenue. The image of urban America, so battered after years of disinvestment, rising poverty and crime, and racial tension, began to turn around. Mayors were able to point with pride to their cities' rapidly changing skyline as dramatic proof that an urban renaissance was under way. The downtown building boom was restoring hope for the future vitality of cities.[41]

Is there a downside to downtown development as a strategy for promoting urban economic growth?

Not all U.S. cities benefited. Large cities that already had vibrant service- and information-based economies well-connected to the emerging global economy enjoyed the most impressive growth rates during the 1980s and 1990s.[42] But smaller and medium-sized cities in the Rust Belt that had been dependent upon industrial production continued to spiral downhill, while many other cities with a more balanced distribution of industrial and postindustrial activity struggled to adjust to evolving economic structures. Downtown redevelopment efforts in such places were more of a mixed bag.

Even where downtown development was vigorous, growth produced its own costs. The building boom produced new tax revenue, but it also required new expenditures for public services. Environmentalists complained about mounting traffic congestion on downtown streets, area bridges, tunnels, and highways, as well as worsening air pollution. Preservationists lamented the demolition of historic buildings and landmarks to make way for boxlike towers of steel and glass. Still others argued that the increasing property values caused by downtown development displaced small retail establishments and residents in and around the downtown core. Gentrification became a highly visible problem in downtown and near-downtown neighborhoods at this time.[43]

The most sweeping critique of the downtown-centered redevelopment policy was that it had exacerbated inequality among urbanites. The emphasis on promoting postindustrial economic activity contributed to a market of have-lots and have-littles—an upper tier of highly-skilled, well-paid, professional and managerial workers, and a lower tier of workers employed as secretaries, custodians, security guards, hotel maids and bellhops, waiters and dishwashers, and retail sales clerks. With middle-class jobs diminishing and prospects for upward mobility constrained, the gulf between rich and poor widened as the service-based economy expanded. What made this development even more troubling was that many citizens and policy-makers did not see mounting inequality within the postindustrial economy as being unfair and thus worthy of redress; unlike inequities caused by racial and sexual discrimination, sharp divisions within the employment sphere seemed to reflect the nation's meritocracy at work.[44]

Inequality became more stark on a spatial level as well. While the downtown business core prospered with the influx of capital investment, many neighborhoods elsewhere in the city remained neglected. Contrary to the promises of the advocates of downtown development, the wealth being generated by downtown's postindustrial economy was not flowing into the neighborhoods; it was barely even trickling. Downtown tax revenue was not helping neighborhoods to rebuild crumbling streets, schools, and parks. And residents in the poorer neighborhoods were not finding desperately needed jobs in the gleaming high-rise office towers.[45]

Did public opposition to downtown development arise in response to these problems? Was there a change in policy direction?

Urban development became a controversial issue in a number of U.S. cities during the 1980s. Dissatisfaction with the negative effects and unfulfilled promises of downtown growth prompted neighborhood activists to mobilize and seek changes in public policy. In some cases, neighborhood-based protest eventually did yield policy changes. In San Francisco, for instance, a powerful growth-control movement managed to utilize a citizens' initiative process, a litigation campaign, lobbying, and various grassroots tactics to secure a strict annual cap on commercial office construction in the downtown business district, as a way to control the adverse consequences of rapid growth, and a host of so-called "linkage" policies, designed to link downtown development to community development.[46] Community groups in Boston and Seattle succeeded in bringing about similar policy changes in their cities.[47]

In most U.S. cities, however, grassroots efforts to alter economic development policy fell short. Community groups lacked the resources to battle the well-endowed and sophisticated downtown growth coalitions. They also had difficulty maintaining a unified front; progrowth advocates proved adept at exploiting differences over race, class, and national origin to keep nascent protest movements divided and weak. With the downtown growth coalitions firmly in control, the revitalization of downtown business districts, mainly through commercial office development, remained the dominant economic growth strategy through the 1980s.[48] But that came to an abrupt end at the beginning of the 1990s.

Why? What happened?

By the late 1980s, the downtown building boom had produced a sizeable glut in commercial office space. Downtown office vacancy rates, which had been 1 percent to 3 percent in many large cities at the beginning of the decade, skyrocketed to 25 percent and 30 percent by the end of the decade. Developers who had built office towers on speculation could no longer find corporate tenants for their buildings and were thus unable to pay back their loans. Many filed for bankruptcy. Credit tightened up, and the commercial office market dried up by the early 1990s. Suddenly city officials had to look for another engine to drive their urban revitalization plans besides commercial office construction.

Enticing Visitors to the City

While the downtowns of major cities became forests of skyscrapers, they also became zones of entertainment. Why?

Economic development through the arts, entertainment, sports, and tourism seemed to make sense. Many cities already boasted a variety of amenities that made them popular visitor destinations; with additional investment, existing amenities could be further improved and others added. City officials were beginning to wonder just how long they would be able to milk the office development cow. By the 1980s, more and more businesses were choosing to base their operations in the suburbs, where office rents were cheaper and employees would be closer to their suburban homes. "Edge cities" began to pop up along the beltway arteries that surround many central cities to accommodate new office parks and shopping malls.[49] And when the overall commercial office market collapsed in the early 1990s, the trend toward visitor-oriented economic development shifted into a higher gear.

Economic development through tourism is not a new idea, right? Weren't city planners urging the development of convention centers in the 1960s?

City planners have long been enamored with the economic potential of thousands of conventioneers pouring into a city for a three- or four-day stay and spending a couple of hundred dollars a day on lodging, food, shopping, and entertainment. That scenario motivated cities to finance the construction of convention centers capable of accommodating large trade associations. As local officials became interested in further developing a tourism industry, conventions offered an added bonus: they gave cities an opportunity to showcase their attractions to visitors on business in the hope that those visitors would later return with their families on vacation and spend even more money. A new round of convention center construction commenced in the 1970s, as cities expanded existing centers or built new ones. Over a hundred convention centers were constructed in the United States between 1970 and 1985.[50]

Didn't that lead to the same problem as commercial office development—a glut of convention centers?

With so many rushing to build or expand their convention centers, supply soon outstripped demand. This, in turn, put pressure on cities to compete for business in an overly saturated market. Convention bureaus found themselves compelled to offer increasingly favorable deals to convention sponsors just to keep their halls occupied. As a result, lower-than-expected revenues were often insufficient to cover operating costs and payments on construction bonds. Convention centers in popular destination cities, such as New York, Chicago, Orlando, and Las Vegas, managed to thrive, but most convention centers turned out to be financial losers. But the disappointing outcome of the first wave of convention centers did not discourage city planners from maintaining the course. Indeed, another round of convention center construction began in the 1990s, leading to an even faster rate of growth in exhibition space.[51]

Why did that happen?

Despite the saturated market, city planners believed that building or expanding convention centers was still worthwhile. Even though the centers themselves typically lost money, they still represented an investment in future tourism development on the assumption that conventioneers would return to the city later on, with, it was hoped, family and friends. Development planners believed that they could compete successfully for convention business if their governments were willing to do what was necessary to make their cities even more desirable destinations for the sponsors of conventions.

What did that require?

Enhancing cultural opportunities within the city, for one. Some cities already had a substantial arts-based infrastructure in place. New York, with Broadway, Lincoln Center, and its myriad art museums, is an obvious example. Others sought to build upon their less extensive offerings in the hope of transforming their cities into vibrant cultural centers. In the 1990s, Philadelphia decided to create an "Avenue of the Arts" along Broad Street, one of the city's principal thoroughfares. Local planners raised funds from public and private sources to construct alongside its preexisting art museums, symphony halls, and theaters a new performing arts center, theaters, jazz clubs, and a high school for the performing arts in an effort to establish a critical mass of cultural activity that would attract visitors from nearby suburbs as well as foreign countries.[52] Even smaller cities with little reputation as cultural centers jumped on the bandwagon.

Newark, New Jersey, tried to rejuvenate its long-stagnant downtown by opening in 1997 a $180 million performing arts center on the Passaic River within close proximity to existing offices, hotels, and the railroad station. The facility, which consists of a 2,750-seat concert hall and a 500-seat theater, has enjoyed high attendance rates and won praise in surveys and media reports. One study concluded that the performing arts center had contributed to a noticeable improvement in public perceptions of Newark and had sparked a renewal of development interest in the city's downtown business district.[53]

It takes more than a performing arts center to develop a tourist industry. What else have cities done?

Economic development planners searched for ways to take advantage of existing but perhaps underappreciated amenities to make their cities more inviting destinations. Cultural institutions were improved, expanded, and sometimes marketed as parts of full-fledged arts districts. City officials who had previously overlooked the value of their oldest neighborhoods came to see them as magnets for tourists interested in urban and American history. Public and private investments spruced up the Freedom Trail and Faneuil Hall in downtown Boston. Residential neighborhoods dating back to the colonial era got makeovers in Savannah, Charleston, Alexandria, Annapolis, and Newport. Historic preservation became a popular strategy not only for safeguarding a city's cultural heritage but for stimulating job growth through the rehabilitation of housing and other structures, promoting tourism, increasing property values, and enhancing the tax base.[54]

Waterfront development also took off. For generations, cities located on bodies of water had relied on their waterfronts for industrial and transportation purposes, but with the decline of manufacturing, urban waterfronts were increasingly neglected. Baltimore was one of the first cities to recognize the economic potential of revitalizing its decaying harbor. In the 1970s and 1980s, it removed its decrepit, rat-infested piers and built a waterfront promenade surrounded by an aquarium, a science museum, a "festival marketplace" of boutiques, bars, and restaurants, a restored sailing ship from the nineteenth century, and other attractions, all of which were in close proximity to the downtown business district and gentrifying residential neighborhoods. The revitalization effort paid off. Baltimore's Inner Harbor quickly became a popular destination for suburban visitors and tourists, especially on warm summer afternoons.[55] Tax revenues from the city's nearby business district jumped from $13.8 million in 1976 to $44.3 million in 1987.[56]

Other cities rushed to follow the Baltimore model. Portland, Maine, converted its aging industrial neighborhood into a contemporary com-

mercial district offering an abundance of restaurants, shops, movie theaters, and bookstores all within easy walking distance of the harbor. The
other Portland, in Oregon, undertook an unusually ambitious waterfront
reclamation project. The city closed down a busy highway alongside the
Willamette River and replaced it with a waterfront park that would be easily accessible to employees working in the nearby downtown business district as well as to out-of-town visitors.[57] The major downside to waterfront
development has been the high cost of acquiring, clearing, and redevelop-
ing valuable real estate, an obstacle that has deterred many cities from fully
embracing the Baltimore and Portland models.[58]

How does sports fit into this economic development strategy?
In a big way. One of the initial influences on the current boom in urban
sports development involved the efforts of Mayor William Hudnut of Indianapolis in the mid-1970s to establish his city as the amateur sports capital
of the nation by building a host of athletic facilities geared toward colle-
giate and Olympic sports. The goal was to attract national and international athletic competitions to the city along with all of the tourist dollars
that they would bring to the local economy.[59] Many cities without a professional sports team have bargained aggressively to lure one or more on the
assumption that a major-league franchise would add jobs and tax revenue
along with conferring major-league status upon the city and would thus
facilitate additional capital investment.[60]

At first, many city officials were reluctant to authorize the expenditure
of significant public funds for sports; some questioned the value of the
low-wage, seasonal jobs that would be produced, while others wondered
about the economic impact of a franchise that played only a few dozen
home games each year, and only ten in the case of football. The opening of
a retro-style baseball stadium with modern amenities in Baltimore in
1992—a facility that blended in cleverly with the surrounding neighborhood and was located within walking distance of downtown and the Inner
Harbor—changed some outlooks.[61] An immediate hit with fans of the Baltimore Orioles, Camden Yards was consistently filled to capacity during its
first several seasons. More important in the eyes of city planners was the
tendency of the overflowing crowds to spill out from the stadium after the
game and visit nearby attractions at the Inner Harbor or bars and restaurants in adjacent communities. In this way, sports seemed to be generating
additional economic activity in the urban core. Other cities, such as Cleveland, Denver, San Diego, San Francisco, Washington, D.C., and Detroit,
began to build their own downtown stadiums and arenas. Smaller cities
such as Lowell, Massachusetts, and Trenton, New Jersey, followed suit by
constructing homes for minor-league franchises.[62]

This may be a positive trend for sports fans, but is this the kind of economic development strategy that will counteract the ravages of deindustrialization and suburbanization?

Most scholars don't think so. Some argue that professional sports represents a tiny fraction of a city's overall economy and thus will never be a central engine of economic growth justifying huge public subsidies.[63] Others point out that the individuals who draw the highest salaries, the owners and players, usually do not spend much of their income in surrounding communities and that the trend of contemporary stadiums offering a wide selection of food and souvenirs discourages even fans from patronizing local businesses before or after games. And for those fans who do visit nearby restaurants and shops after a game, most of them are residents of the metropolitan area who probably would have spent an equivalent sum on entertainment somewhere else in the region had they not attended a ball game.[64]

Consultants and planners who defend public investment in sports stadiums acknowledge that the construction of stadiums alone will not spark an urban renaissance. But they respond that sports venues can serve a catalytic function if they are situated within an urban environment and are integrated into a city's growth strategy. A director of the Baltimore Development Corporation reports that Camden Yards pumps $30 million per year into the local economy, but cautions that the ballpark is only one element in a $4 billion campaign to rejuvenate the downtown district dating back to 1959: "It is a fabulous add-on, and it was placed downtown so it would complement 40 or 50 other attractions that we already had in place." The economist Robert Baade confirms that for a stadium to contribute to a city's economy: "It's got to be combined with a lot of other things."[65]

Cleveland's downtown baseball stadium, Jacobs Field, seems to have sparked much commercial and residential activity in its vicinity.[66] Even a scholar who has questioned the utility of sports as an economic development tool, Mark Rosentraub, concedes that Cleveland's new baseball stadium and basketball arena, which are well connected to public transit systems and other attractions, have brought large numbers of people each year to a part of the city that had become a virtual ghost town after business hours: "The 4.6 million visitors to downtown Cleveland will likely create very little new downtown development. However, downtown Cleveland is far more lively today than it was five years ago. There is a contagious vitality and excitement that should not be discounted or ignored. Downtown Cleveland is, once again, an entertainment and recreation center for the region."[67] Rosentraub goes on to note that while the $450 million price tag of the downtown projects in Cleveland may seem prohibitive, when spread out over thirty years and among the 2.5 million residents of the entire county who will pay off the debt, the cost per person amounts to $10 per year.

Sports franchises have an obvious interest in extracting as much public funding as possible, often threatening to relocate to another city absent such support. Cities that resist those demands and force franchises to assume some of the financial burden of stadium construction are much better positioned to reap economic gains. In San Francisco, voters rejected four separate ballot initiatives during the 1990s to raise public money to finance a new baseball stadium. At that point, the franchise managed to identify new funding sources from naming rights, creative sponsorship deals, seat licenses, and concession and ticket sales. The $345 million Pac-Bell Park opened in April 2000 as the first privately financed baseball stadium in 38 years.[68] Under limited circumstances—few public subsidies, venues that will be used on a regular basis, and a location that encourages fans to remain in the city—sports development might be a worthwhile economic investment.

City planners hope that out-of-town visitors lured to the city by one attraction, say by a baseball game, will decide to remain in the city and spend more money on local businesses. What do city planners have in mind besides bars and restaurants?

The revival of downtown retail has been an important economic development goal. Ever since department stores abandoned the downtown business district for the suburban mall, starting in the late 1950s, planners have tried to figure out ways to bring shoppers back to the city. One innovation has been the festival marketplace. In the early 1970s, the developer James Rouse came up with the idea of converting three historic buildings in downtown Boston that had once served as a marketplace into a contemporary, mall-like facility featuring boutique stores, restaurants, and street entertainers. Although Quincy Market lacked adequate parking and anchor department stores, it was soon popular with office workers, suburban visitors, and tourists, who liked the festive atmosphere. Rouse built another successful festival marketplace at Baltimore's Inner Harbor in the late 1970s, and before long, planners in Seattle, San Diego, St. Louis, and many other cities were following Rouse's model.[69]

Another strategy to strengthen downtown retail has been to replicate the suburban mall, on the theory that if these institutions are so popular in the suburbs, they ought to be just as popular in cities. Some cities have thus encouraged the development of large-scale shopping malls, replete with major department stores that are often connected to luxury hotels and office buildings. Examples of such "megastructures" include Copley Place in

Boston and Gallery Place in Philadelphia. Some planners criticize these megastructures for deadening street life by putting smaller, longtime retailers out of business and discouraging interaction with the city outside the mall by featuring a fortresslike, forbidding design characterized by tall, windowless concrete walls and parking garages.[70] Shopping malls that opened in the 1990s, such as the Circle Centre Mall in Indianapolis, have sought to correct such design flaws.

So has tourism-driven economic development been a worthwhile strategy?

Economic development policies that rely on the arts, entertainment, sports, and tourism to strengthen a city's inherent advantages as a social and cultural center, and thus as a desirable place to visit and spend money, have managed to revitalize urban cores in many places. Until recently, Cleveland was rarely on any tour guide's list of must-see cities, but it has witnessed a dramatic upsurge in tourism with the construction of downtown sports venues and the Rock and Roll Hall of Fame.[71] Cities that have enjoyed particular success in this regard—Baltimore, Philadelphia, and Portland, Oregon—have combined historic neighborhoods, arts and entertainment districts, waterfronts with easy public access, and sports centers in a well-integrated, human-scale, and pedestrian-friendly environment. Such an environment is all the more attractive when it encourages groups of varying races, ethnicities, classes, and cultures to mix seamlessly in civic spaces that nurture a broader sense of community.

Others are not impressed. Dennis Judd, for example, faults many cities for trying to create what he calls a "tourist bubble," a kind of antiseptic section of the city devoid of the genuine characteristics of urban life, in order to lure visitors who might otherwise be leery of big cities.[72] Other scholars have leveled similar criticisms, ridiculing tourism-based economic development policies for seeking to reconstitute cities as urban theme parks with all of the artificiality of a Disney World.[73] Perhaps the most damning critique is that, like commercial office development, arts and entertainment-based development has helped to revivify the downtown core of cities but has done little for surrounding neighborhoods that continue to struggle. For all its success in bringing visitors to downtown Baltimore, for instance, the Inner Harbor has had little noticeable effect on poorer neighborhoods elsewhere in the city.[74] Likewise, Ed Rendell's achievements in making Center City Philadelphia a more dynamic social and cultural destination failed to slow the hemorrhaging of residents and jobs from other parts of the city. Philadelphia lost approximately 270,000 residents during the 1990s, the largest absolute drop in population of any U.S. city during that period.[75] Although Rendell was always a popular mayor, residents seem to have concluded that his economic development policies made

Philadelphia an appealing place to visit but not necessarily a satisfactory place to work and live.[76]

Neighborhood Revitalization

That does seem to be a powerful point. City officials have lavished an inordinate amount of resources on their downtown districts. What has been done to create jobs and economic growth in the outlying neighborhoods that are most in need?

For many years after World War II, virtually nothing, despite the fact that deindustrialization and suburbanization were ravaging urban neighborhoods beyond the downtown core. It was not until race riots broke out in the summer of 1964 that many Americans even noticed the mounting crisis. At that point, the federal government, under the leadership of a liberal president and Congress, declared a War on Poverty, much of which was targeted at the inner city. Antipoverty programs offered comprehensive social services and stimulated economic opportunity by creating and supporting community-based businesses. The federal government also sought to empower poor people by giving them significant control over the implementation of antipoverty programs. The combination of federal money and popular empowerment raised the hopes of many that even the most distressed urban neighborhoods would be revitalized.[77]

It was not to be. The federal government began to retreat from its vision of a Great Society within just a few years. Liberals accused the Nixon administration, and later the Reagan administration, of backing policies that effectively shifted resources away from the inner city and toward the suburbs to sway Republican voters. Conservatives maintained that the War on Poverty's expansion of social service programs was making a dire situation even worse by unintentionally undermining the motivation to work and nurturing a culture of dependency.[78]

So after launching the War on Poverty in the inner city, the federal government basically surrendered?

Not entirely. Some antipoverty programs from the 1960s survived, although in a scaled-down form. In the 1970s, the Small Business Administration and Economic Development Administration implemented a number of economic development programs, and Congress enacted the Comprehensive Employment and Training Act and established the Urban Development Action Grant program to stimulate economic growth in urban neighborhoods. But while many of these initiatives showed early promise, all had become victims of retrenchment by the late 1970s and 1980s.[79]

Republican presidents Richard Nixon and Ronald Reagan shrewdly exploited escalating antitax and antigovernment fervor within the country to win presidential elections and then steered federal policy away from urban revitalization.[80] Even the Democratic administration of Jimmy Carter seemed to give up on the future of urban neighborhoods. The McGill Commission, appointed by Carter, stressed the inexorability of market forces and the futility of trying to resist or even direct those forces to improve urban areas.

> [T]he economy of the United States, like that of many of the older industrial societies, has for years now been undergoing a critical transition from being geographically-based to being deconcentrated, decentralized, and service-based. In the process, many cities of the old industrial heartland . . . are losing their status as thriving industrial capitals. . . . The historical dominance of more central cities will diminish as certain production, residential, commercial, and cultural functions disperse to places beyond them.

The commission concluded: "To attempt to restrict or reverse the processes of change—for whatever noble intentions—is to deny the benefits that the future may hold for us as a nation."[81]

How did this change in thinking about urban neighborhoods change urban policy?

The report—and other conservative theorizing—provided a rationale for slashing the budgets of many urban revitalization programs. Some policy analysts went so far as to advocate cutting back basic public services to the poorest neighborhoods on the theory that they were so sick that they should be allowed to die. Any concerted governmental effort to save distressed urban areas, however well intentioned, would be hopeless and thus a squandering of the taxpayers' money. Such analysts advised city officials to channel their increasingly limited resources into stable neighborhoods that were nevertheless at risk of succumbing to spreading unemployment, poverty, and crime. This "triage" approach to community revitalization was patterned after the grim procedures adopted by French medics during World War I to treat injured soldiers; only soldiers whose lives could be saved with immediate action were given treatment. The upshot of the triage concept in urban policy is that most distressed, inner-city neighborhoods would be abandoned.[82]

There must have been strenuous objections to such a policy!

Taken to that extreme, sure, and no city ever officially adopted a triage approach to urban neighborhoods. On the other hand, in practice, many cities did sharply curtail the flow of resources to the most distressed neighborhoods. Residents of such neighborhoods had grown accustomed to getting short shrift in the allocation of public services. More affluent neighborhoods generally do receive preferential treatment from City Hall in terms of police protection, sanitation services, and recreation, because their residents are more likely to complain to local representatives and vote them out of office if they fail to do their jobs properly. If a fiscal crisis forces painful budget cuts, it is poorer neighborhoods that are more likely to bear most of the burden. But talk of a triage policy took this practice to a much harsher level by contemplating not just a reduction in services, but complete termination.

Even commentators who had always supported antipoverty programs began to question the value of neighborhood economic development policies. Nicholas Lemann argued in 1994 that strategies designed to promote economic growth in the inner city were doomed to fail. No matter how many incentives governments were willing to provide, Lemann said, few legitimate businesses would be willing to relocate to areas plagued with such deep-seated problems. Even if jobs could be established in such areas that benefited local residents, those residents would inevitably use their new income to move to more desirable places elsewhere in the city or the suburbs. Consequently, no economic development policy targeted to the inner city since the Great Society era has ever worked and none is ever likely to work. Lemann charged that the only reason that place-based neighborhood revitalization policies persist is because place-based politicians and place-based interest groups such as local foundations and community organizations find them attractive. Cities should return to the traditional strategy for fighting poverty of tending to people's material needs, Lemann said, by providing income support, food stamps, housing vouchers, and basic health care. Such people-based policies may do little to save decaying urban neighborhoods but they enhance the mobility of citizens to escape the dire circumstances of the worst ghettos—and seek economic opportunity on their own.[83]

Maybe it does make more sense to help the urban poor gain access to jobs elsewhere in the metropolitan area.

Quite a few scholars have made just that argument. They emphasize the reality of a spatial mismatch characterized by an abundance of low-skill service jobs in the suburbs and exurbs and a glut of underskilled residents in the inner city. The most efficient way to advance economic opportunity for the urban poor, they reason, is to find ways to eliminate or minimize that spatial mismatch.[84] The economist Anthony Downs has long advocated a residential dispersal strategy that supplies inner-city residents with housing vouchers enabling them to move to jobs in the suburbs.[85] Intrigued with Downs's policy analysis, the Clinton administration enthusiastically supported a pilot program to move 6,200 poor families from Baltimore, Boston, Chicago, Los Angeles, and New York to middle-class, suburban neighborhoods. Under the "Moving to Opportunity" program, the Department of Housing and Urban Development (HUD) offered subsidies and counseling assistance to families wishing to leave the inner city. But when white residents in suburban Baltimore vociferously objected after black and Latino families began to arrive, the Clinton administration suspended the program. HUD later resumed the program after promising to disperse the inner-city residents more widely.[86]

Are there other ways to close the spatial mismatch?

Yes, and less politically charged ways too. One approach simply stresses the need to heighten awareness of employment opportunities throughout the metropolis for inner-city residents. Expanded job listings and better use of existing computer technology would be a step in the right direction.[87]

Another alternative for moving people to jobs is to improve transportation options for inner-city residents commuting to suburban jobs. This is no easy task, since metropolitan transit systems were designed to facilitate suburban-to-city commuting. Urban residents who take a train to a suburban destination often find themselves stranded miles from their place of work. If public transit is even available, it tends to be notoriously slow and inconvenient. Some businesses seeking to tap the large supply of city workers have experimented with operating their own buses and vans, but even this option has many drawbacks. Apart from their high cost, company-sponsored transit plans tend to be short-lived, either because newly recruited employees are unable to hold their jobs or because the employees who do remain buy their own cars and drive to work.[88]

Even if policy initiatives are effective at breaking down information and transportation barriers contributing to the spatial mismatch, some scholars remain skeptical that inner-city residents will benefit. Studies have demonstrated that racial discrimination continues to be a major obstacle for African-Americans and Latinos seeking employment in metropolitan areas.[89]

What should government officials say to longtime residents of such neighborhoods who are determined to remain? There is nothing we can do for your neighborhoods? Wouldn't that be terribly coldhearted?

Perhaps for that reason, even the biggest skeptics of place-based policies have not completely abandoned development policies targeted at poor, urban neighborhoods. The Reagan administration's most visible urban policy during the 1980s—enterprise zones—fell squarely within the place-oriented realm. Originating in Margaret Thatcher's Great Britain, the concept entailed identifying an economically distressed zone within a city and then shrinking government's presence by slashing taxes and cutting regulations. The assumption was that significantly minimizing government would induce businesses to relocate to the zone and unleash an entrepreneurial spirit that would engender job growth and prosperity for local residents.[90]

Enterprise zones appealed to the Reagan administration's inherent distrust of government and confidence in the private sector, but a suspicious Democratic Congress blocked efforts to enact any kind of federal legislation. At the state and local level, however, officials desperate for any kind of initiative to deal with the ever-deteriorating situation in the inner cities went ahead with their own enterprise zone programs. By the early 1990s, thirty-seven states had adopted over three thousand enterprise zones.[91]

Did the enterprise zones work as their conservative advocates had hoped?

No. It turned out that tax breaks and regulatory relief were not enough of an incentive to lure many new businesses concerned about security issues and a decaying physical infrastructure. Businesses that did move into inner-city areas tended not to hire locally, limiting the positive impact on the community. Before long, state and local officials pursued a more pragmatic approach that included a more expansive role for government. To make the zone more desirable for private investment, governments increased spending on infrastructure, law enforcement, job training, and child care. Others began to use the tax code in more creative ways to further policy goals; for instance, businesses were offered a tax credit for every neighborhood resident employed.[92] Some states reported significant gains in private investment and job growth. Even in the more successful states, some scholars questioned just how effective enterprise zones were in truly distressed urban areas, given that some had used such broad criteria in designating zones that even large tracts of vacant rural land—highly attractive to expanding businesses—sometimes counted as enterprise zones.[93]

If enterprise zones implemented by state and local governments have not lived up to expectations, what do conservatives propose instead?

Conservatives are not ready to give up on the concept of enterprise zones. They still believe that if you get government off the backs of individuals, free enterprise will flourish. In their view, what went wrong with enterprise zones was a failure on the part of entrepreneurs to appreciate the opportunities that exist in such zones.

The business strategist Michael Porter contends that inner-city neighborhoods offer four advantages that make them attractive sites for certain kinds of business investment: strategic location, local market demand, integration with regional clusters, and human resources.

Inner-city neighborhoods are often situated close to economically valuable areas such as downtown business districts and entertainment/tourist centers. As such, businesses based there are well positioned to provide goods and services in a swift and dependable manner. The fact that real estate in the inner city is often less expensive and zoning regulations are less restrictive only enhances its strategic location. Inner-city areas also offer untapped market demand. With suburban markets increasingly saturated, residents in the inner city are crying out for more retail, banking, and personal services. Although personal incomes are lower, higher population densities more than compensate by aggregating spending power. Locating a business within the inner city also creates possibilities for integration with "clusters" of companies within a region that both compete and cooperate with one another and that have established a market niche in the national or global economy. Businesses located in the inner city should be able to supply goods and services to, for example, the automobile industry in Detroit, the film industry in Los Angeles, universities and medical services in Boston, or the computer industry in Silicon Valley. Finally, the inner city provides businesses with a pool of loyal, dedicated workers.[94]

The obvious question is: If inner cities possess all of these advantages, why haven't we seen an avalanche of business investment there already?

Porter blames the government. He contends that environmental regulations have prevented the redevelopment of potentially valuable brownfield sites. He blames minority preference programs for deterring other businesses. More broadly, he believes that massive social welfare programs have produced a culture of dependency that destroys work ethics and frightens away business owners. Accordingly, Porter argues that government should confine itself to performing such traditional functions as infrastructure maintenance and law enforcement and fostering a probusiness environment by reducing taxes and regulations. In short, government should step aside and allow the private sector to assume control over redevelopment of the inner city.[95]

Sounds familiar.

That's what many of Porter's critics say.[96] Others give Porter credit for voicing optimism about communities that many conservatives *and* liberals had all but abandoned.[97]

How do Porter and other conservatives explain the competitive disadvantages of the inner city? For example, there may be a sizeable labor supply, but if it is poorly educated and inadequately trained, how is this going to attract capital investment?

Porter's claims on behalf of inner-city workers contradict what the vast majority of business owners say in interviews and surveys. He acknowledges that there are serious problems in the inner city, such as higher security and insurance costs and limited access to capital, but he insists that the private sector has the capacity to take the initiative in remedying these problems. To counteract security concerns, Porter suggests that entrepreneurs open up businesses within a concentrated area, on the theory that there is strength in numbers and that the expanded activity will deter criminal behavior. Similarly, he advises businesses to establish a business improvement district, tax themselves, and use the proceeds to hire their own private security force.

Events in recent years have added weight to Porter's argument. Many businesses have, in fact, rediscovered the competitive advantages of the inner city. Without substantial incentives from government, businesses have begun to notice the untapped purchasing power of inner-city neighborhoods. Chain drugstores were among the first enterprises to move in, followed by supermarkets. Such businesses have adopted a "micromerchandising" strategy of tailoring their products to the demographic profile of particular areas, a departure from the mass-merchandising approach that typically guides chain-store retailing, and become more flexible in terms of building designs to fit into existing urban spaces. The investment in the inner city has already paid off. For example, a Pathmark supermarket that opened in Newark in 1990 has been one of the most profitable in the 132-store chain. A Stop and Shop supermarket in a lower-income neighborhood in Boston was the highest grossing store in a 180-store chain in the late 1990s. A Foot Locker store in Harlem is among that company's most successful.[98]

Magic Johnson has more recently attracted considerable media attention by opening a series of multiplex movie theaters in Harlem, South Central Los Angeles, and other inner-city neighborhoods that have by and large lacked movie screens for decades. Those theaters have earned high profits at a time when the industry has been floundering. Buoyed by his initial success, Johnson has since participated in new ventures to open over twenty Starbucks coffee shops, six TGI Friday's, and a string of twenty-four-hour fitness centers (to be called "Magic Clubs") in inner-city neighborhoods around the country. The former basketball star's record in starting up businesses in lower-income communities has in turn prompted further investment. After Johnson and his partners announced plans for a movie theater and Starbucks in Harlem, several large companies, including HMV, Disney, Old Navy, and Modell's Sporting Goods, followed suit.[99]

Are the conservatives right after all?

Even conservative analysts would advise caution in interpreting the recent increase in private investment in poor, urban neighborhoods, given the distorting effect of the boom in the national economy during the 1990s. Beyond that, questions remain about the proper role of the government. Porter concedes that the public sector needs to be involved, if only to nurture a favorable business climate. But what does that really mean? Even if the role for government is expanded to include a stronger presence with respect to traditional functions such as infrastructure improvement and law enforcement, there is little evidence to indicate that this would be sufficient to stimulate private investment in severely distressed neighborhoods. A lot of pieces have to come together—land assembly, infrastructure, transportation, crime control—to make inner-city areas attractive to business.

The Hunts Point Food Distribution Center in the South Bronx offers a good illustration of the potential of the inner city. Founded in the 1960s in a city neighborhood with an extremely high poverty rate, it has expanded to include 160 food companies with annual sales of $7 billion. Handling over 75 percent of all fruits and vegetables and 40 percent of all meats and poultry entering the New York metropolitan area, the Hunts Point Market is considered to be the largest wholesale food market in the world. It is also central to the economic development of the surrounding community, employing 11,000 people directly and another 9,000 in related businesses nearby—20 percent of whom are Hunts Point residents, and 40 percent of whom are Bronx residents. The "spectacular success" of the Hunts Point Market is at least partly attributable to aggressive public intervention. The New York City government initiated the project by acquiring 329 acres of vacant land and then developed the site by providing spacious, modern facilities. The city retained ownership of the land and buildings and continues to be an active partner in the market complex, striving to ensure that the enterprise continues to benefit the local community.[100]

So what is needed?

With respect to neighborhood economic development, the trial-and-error experiences of state and local governments with enterprise zones have been instructive. The most successful zones have been ones in which the government has assumed a prominent role in working with business to provide necessary job training and placement programs, child care facilities, and transportation improvements along with tax incentives and regulatory relief (e.g., with respect to the cleanup of brownfield sites). Public officials have sought to ensure that the business investment that does take place within the zones actually benefits residents. Tax credits for local hires are just one example of more direct government action to advance the goal of social and economic equity.[101]

The Clinton administration was sufficiently impressed with the evolution of enterprise zones that it pushed through Congress in 1994 a federal version based on the most successful state and local programs. The Clinton program was renamed "empowerment zones" (EZs). A total of nine EZs were established, six in urban areas and three in rural areas. Each zone would receive $100 million over a ten-year period for grants, loans, and job training programs and an additional $250 million over ten years for tax incentives for businesses that agree to locate within the zone. Such businesses would be eligible for a tax credit for 20 percent of the wages of any employee who resides within an EZ (up to the first $15,000 of wages for no more than seven years) as well as higher tax deductions for new investments. To gain designation as an EZ, cities were required to prepare strategic plans demonstrating need, a holistic approach to tackling chronic problems, the availability of additional resources from the state and local governments, and the vitality of community-based organizations. The six cities eventually chosen were Atlanta, Baltimore, Chicago, Detroit, New York, and Philadelphia-Camden.[102]

How has the federal empowerment zone law fared since its adoption in 1994?

To start, the simple fact that the federal government now has a neighborhood revitalization policy is seen by many urbanists as a step in the right direction. The empowerment zone law seems to acknowledge that conditions in many inner-city neighborhoods are so desperate that local governments lack sufficient resources to make much progress without federal support. Another virtue of the program is its stress on citizen participation and grassroots planning, a notable departure from the normal elite-driven mode of urban policy making.

On the other hand, the implementation of EZ programs in the six original cities has garnered much negative media attention. The EZ in Atlanta, for instance, has been repeatedly criticized for mismanagement and poor oversight by the city.[103] The New York City EZ has been beset by political squabbles among public officials from the governor and mayor on down as well as among community leaders within the EZ. Also, while the New York City EZ has begun to attract some high-profile retail chains, small businesses contend that they have been ignored.[104] Moreover, all of the empowerment zones have suffered from excessive hype and overblown promises at the time the program was established; the prolonged application process also had the effect of unreasonably raising popular expectations about what gaining EZ designation would mean. The painfully slow distribution of funds has further demoralized residents about the prospects for any kind of broad revitalization happening any time soon.[105] Others have questioned just how much citizen input is taking place in an environment in which funds trickle down from the federal government to the state governments to the local governments, with each level of government imposing its own conditions on how the money can be used. Reports indicate that the initial burst of grassroots participation in the planning process has waned considerably.[106]

But the news is not entirely gloomy. Baltimore's EZ has been praised for its ongoing commitment to citizen control over policy-making and implementation and for wisely designating zones that feature some nearby amenity, such as the Johns Hopkins University or the gentrifying Fells Point neighborhood, to serve as an anchor for the EZ and an additional draw for outside investment.[107] The EZ in Detroit has enjoyed unparalleled success in attracting investment from the major automobile manufacturers and other large business firms, although some commentators believe that much of that would have occurred even without the EZ designation.[108]

Perhaps the most fundamental criticism of the EZ program is that it is far too limited to have a major impact. Only a handful of poor neighborhoods in just a handful of cities won federal assistance. The Clinton administration tried to remedy the limited scope of the original EZ program in January 1999 by adding fifteen new empowerment zones to the original list. The newly designated zones included Boston, Cincinnati, El Paso, Gary/East Chicago, Minneapolis, Knoxville, Tennessee, New Haven, Connecticut, Santa Ana, California, and St. Louis/East St. Louis, among others. HUD promised each EZ annual grants between $3 million and $10 million over the next ten years as well as various tax incentives. Unlike with the first round of EZ cities, there is no guarantee that each city will actually receive any federal support. Instead, all of the second-round EZ cities will have to convince Congress to appropriate the funds every year—no small task given a political climate wary, if not hostile, to federal aid for inner-city neighborhoods.[109]

Redirecting Economic Development Policy

Economic development policy has transformed central business districts but has been less successful in neighborhoods beyond the downtown core. What new policy initiatives might result in more effective and equitable economic development for cities as a whole?

Right. The common pattern is a relatively prosperous downtown surrounded by vast stretches of struggling or destitute neighborhoods. Apart from its obvious inequities, uneven development will not succeed in generating economic growth for entire cities. Widespread poverty in the neighborhoods will always be a drain on public resources, a source of upward pressure on taxes, a reason for continuing middle-class flight from the city, and a deterrent to future investment. Only when cities take a more holistic approach to economic development will the long-term prospects of cities significantly improve.

Does this require a massive redistribution of resources away from downtown redevelopment and toward neighborhood redevelopment?

Not necessarily. Cities do need a healthy downtown core. Without it, trying to rebuild neighborhoods might be akin to bailing out a rowboat without plugging the leak in the hull. City governments need to tap into expanding information- and service-based firms downtown to create jobs and raise income levels for local residents. Local government needs to make sure that the benefits and costs of downtown development are spread more evenly throughout a city. Previous advocates of a downtown-centered redevelopment policy always insisted that this would happen naturally as a result of market forces. But it has not happened. The public sector has the capacity to make downtown development more effective and equitable.

How?

One change involves the use of financial incentives to attract mobile capital to a city. Local officials often see themselves as being engaged in a partnership with business leaders in a common endeavor to foster economic development. But the balance of power often tilts toward business interests. Because of intense competition among city governments to attract capital investment, economic development planners tend to be lavish in their provision of financial inducements to business. One remedy might be for local governments to try to cooperate with each other in an effort to avoid getting ensnared in destructive bidding wars for mobile capital. Maintaining such collusion over time, especially in the highly competitive metropolitan or regional context, is difficult to do in practice.

So cities have developed other strategies to take better advantage of their use of locational incentives. Instead of offering inducements as a matter of entitlement—that is, as long as businesses meet certain preestablished criteria, they automatically obtain certain benefits—cities have relied more on discretionary incentives. A more discriminating use of tax breaks, below-market loans, land clearance and site preparation, infrastructure support, and funds for job retraining may advance broader development goals. In exchange for the provision of publicly supplied "goodies," cities might ask that businesses reserve a certain percentage of jobs for local residents. Similarly, cities might request that businesses set minimum wage levels, provide health and retirement benefits, and offer job training programs to enhance career advancement opportunities.[110]

Local planners might also take affirmative steps to see that when relocating enterprises make commitments to a city in exchange for financial inducements those commitments are honored. In an age of increasingly footloose capital, such commitments are often not honored, and cities are left holding the bag. Examples of "subsidy failure" include businesses not creating as many jobs as promised, not ensuring a sufficient number of high-quality jobs, or even relocating to another city shortly after winning financial inducements. To minimize the risk of subsidy failure, cities might enter into performance agreements with relocating firms containing clear sanctions and penalties that would apply in the event a business reneges upon a promise. Sanctions might include recision of the contract, recalibrations (e.g., reducing the subsidy amount), or "claw-back" provisions that authorize the city to recover all or part of the subsidy if promises are not kept. Such strategies might deter exploitative behavior, or at least enable cities to recoup some of their initial investment.[111]

Isn't there a risk that if cities resort to performance agreements and claw-backs, they will undermine the goal of nurturing a "good business climate"? Won't businesses turn to other cities that don't impose such nettlesome requirements?
    At a fundamental level, this question raises additional questions about the meaning of a "good business climate." Does it mean that all that businesses need to thrive is low taxes and minimal government regulations? Or are businesses more likely to prosper in an environment marked by superior public services, such as excellent public schools that produce capable employees and responsible citizens?
    Leaving this issue aside, some city officials have become more willing to risk alienating business leaders by relying on performance agreements and claw-backs. This may reflect cities' growing concern about getting drawn into expensive bidding wars for capital investment. City planning scholar Rachel Weber reported in 2002 that about half of the jurisdictions in her survey of eight cities and six states in the Midwest had enforced at least one claw-back provision within the past five years. Indianapolis was the most aggressive city in penalizing businesses that had failed to comply with job and wage criteria for business incentives set in 1993. That city's Metropolitan Development Commission identified thirty businesses in violation of performance agreements and in 1996 alone cancelled tax abatements to five of those firms for failing to honor job creation commitments. At the same time, most cities still feel compelled to move cautiously for fear of acquiring a reputation for being antagonistic toward business. To help cities walk the fine line between trying to attract capital investment while avoiding capital exploitation, Weber recommends that cities negotiate more specific performance agreements (since business leaders appreciate clarity regarding their obligations), greater use of incentives that reward positive performance after the fact, and more emphasis on third-party monitoring

and enforcement of performance agreements by grassroots organizations as opposed to city government agencies.[112]

How might the spatial inequalities resulting from downtown development be remedied?

Linkage is one possibility. Pioneered in San Francisco and Boston during the 1980s, linkage can be thought of as the reverse of financial incentives. Instead of cities offering various public subsidies to businesses to attract them to the city, linkage policies impose exactions on large residential and commercial development in the downtown business district. One rationale for such policies is that rapid downtown growth imposes certain costs on cities such as a decline in the supply of affordable housing and increasing congestion on public transportation. Community activists who advocated linkage argued that it was only fair that developers be required to accept some responsibility for sharing the costs of rapid growth.

Linkage policies also link downtown development to community development. As downtown is developed through the construction of office buildings, funds generated by linkage are placed in accounts earmarked for affordable housing production and mass transit improvements. San Francisco and Boston have adopted an employment linkage policy to expand job opportunities for neighborhood residents. Such policies help to ensure that economic development policies targeted to the downtown corporate sector benefit the city as a whole.[113]

The urbanist Marc Levine cautions that linkage policies are not a panacea for uneven development but they do give city officials a mechanism for directing some revenues to neighborhoods. Such policies also signal an important philosophical change. Levine writes: "[T]he concept of linkage inscribes in government policy a profoundly different concept of partnership [between the public and private sectors] than has heretofore existed in U.S. cities, by specifying that profit-making opportunities for developers carry social obligations."[114]

But don't all of these policies presuppose a downtown-centered approach to urban economic development? If the goal is to expand economic opportunity in outlying neighborhoods, don't cities need policy initiatives that address neighborhood problems and opportunities directly?

Sure, and something that goes beyond enterprise/empowerment zones, which have yielded disappointing results so far because of a lack of imagination, political commitment, and funding. The political scientist David Imbroscio has developed an analytical framework for thinking about alternative approaches to neighborhood economic growth. Imbroscio has identified three broad strategies, all of which deviate from mainstream policies grounded in the physical redevelopment of downtown business districts and the public provision of financial inducements to mobile capital—an entrepreneurial-mercantilist strategy, a municipal-enterprise strategy, and a community-based strategy. All three deserve attention.[115]

Much of the inspiration for the entrepreneurial-mercantilist strategy comes from Peter Eisinger's *The Rise of the Entrepreneurial State.* Instead of relying on trying to entice existing businesses into a jurisdiction through costly inducements, "the entrepreneurial state" promotes economic expansion by discovering, creating, or developing new markets for local goods and services. City planners strive to identify new market opportunities "on behalf of private actors whose pursuit of those opportunities may serve public ends." City government cooperates with local businesses, but the public-private partnership that emerges in the entrepreneurial-mercantilist model features a much more prominent role for government than the business-dominated, public-private partnerships typical in U.S. cities. With this approach to economic development, government becomes a full-fledged partner, "a risk-taker, a path-finder to new markets, the midwife to joint public-private efforts to develop and test untried technology."[116]

What exactly does local government do to identify, create, and expand new markets for local businesses?

Entrepreneurial governments supply venture capital, both by subsidizing private capital and investing public funds, to selected firms that show promise in tapping new markets. Based on analysis of the development of emerging and future markets, entrepreneurial governments support high-technology research and product development. Finally, these governments subsidize export trade by promoting products made by local firms in new foreign markets.[117]

This kind of public intervention into the private sector seems to go well beyond what city planners normally do.

That is the point. City officials would take a much more interventionist approach to promoting economic growth in neighborhoods overlooked by the private sector. This provokes controversy. Free-market advocates question the capacity of local government officials to make public investments in high-risk enterprises and industries based upon an assessment of future market demand. They ask why local government officials would be in a better position to make such complex decisions than individuals in the private sector, who presumably have decided not to invest in new firms and activities. On the other hand, the advantages of nurturing indigenous economic renewal include an expansion of local employment opportunities, a reduction in the leakage of resources from the city, and a decline in the city's reliance upon external capital.[118]

What is the municipal-enterprise strategy?

Even more extensive government engagement in the private sector in the form of public ownership of economic enterprises. This approach to economic development may sound somewhat radical, but remember that cities have always owned a wide variety of important enterprises, such as airports, convention centers, hospitals, utilities, and sports stadiums. The municipal-enterprise strategy simply proposes extending the practice to other kinds of economic activity. One rationale for doing so would be to secure greater public control over important community assets. An example might be a sports team associated with the city for decades now being wooed by another city offering extravagant incentives. Another might be a manufacturing plant owned by a large multinational corporation with little connection to the city now considering a shutdown. Local governments might also consider municipal ownership as a vehicle for generating revenue for the city.[119]

But doesn't this run counter to the dominant impulse in city government today? Instead of extending public authority, city governments have been rushing to privatize as much of their activities as possible.

Privatization of city services and expanded municipal ownership of key economic assets and enterprises are not necessarily incompatible. It would be possible for a city to obtain ownership of a profitable entity that is important to the community and then establish a competitive bidding process among for-profit and nonprofit firms for the right to operate the enterprise. A local government would not have to manage an enterprise—it could leave that to a private-sector firm with the appropriate experience and expertise—but it would retain ownership, supervisory powers, and ultimate control over profits.[120]

How would a city obtain ownership rights to a profit-making enterprise in the first place?

For years, cities have played organizing roles in urban development projects such as a festival marketplace, performing arts center, or office and hotel complex by supplying land, infrastructure improvements, venture capital, and other valuable benefits. Under the municipal enterprise model, the local government may be entitled to an equity stake in the project, which could generate profits for the city for years to come, assuming the project is financially successful.

Imbroscio acknowledges that the municipal-enterprise strategy is the least developed of the three alternative approaches to neighborhood economic development, so evidence of its viability is sparse. But some examples do exist, and they give reason for guarded optimism. Perhaps most familiar are municipally owned utilities, many of which have been operating for decades. Studies show that public utilities perform well and deliver service at a lower cost than privately owned utilities.[121] In *Reinventing Government*, David Osborne and Ted Gaebler describe a number of cities in California that have earned profits from their ownership of a minor league baseball team, an amusement park, a cable television system, and developable real estate, as well as the eventual sale of some of these assets.[122] Other scholars have reported similarly positive outcomes associated with the municipal-enterprise strategy.[123]

The third alternative approach to economic development is the neighborhood-based strategy. How does that work?

Community-based organizations that are owned and controlled by community residents leverage the resources of long-neglected neighborhoods. Community-based organizations are typically neither public nor private entities, but nonprofit enterprises that fall within what some call the "third sector." Such organizations are often animated by a strong collectivist ethic that contrasts with the more individualistic orientation of the entrepreneurial-mercantilist strategy and conventional, market-driven approaches. Such grassroots groups emphasize the spatial dimension of economic development, focusing on a distinct geographic community. The community-based strategy also emphasizes democratic control over the redevelopment process and empowering groups that historically have been marginalized by both government and the market.[124]

How do community development corporations fit into this model?

Community development corporations (CDCs) emerged in the late 1960s in wake of the grassroots activism spawned by the Civil Rights Movement and the War on Poverty. Recall that popular empowerment was a key feature of the War on Poverty, and so the federal government delegated control over many antipoverty programs directly to community-based organizations. Before long, some of these community-based organizations had begun to focus primarily on the redevelopment of inner-city neighborhoods. They took the legal step of incorporating themselves as tax-exempt nonprofit corporations governed by people with a stake in the community's revitalization. Funded through grants from government and foundations, CDCs get most of their revenue from rental income or fees from their construction and rehabilitation work.

At first, CDCs concentrated on economic development projects such as the development of small and large businesses, shopping malls, and industrial parks, but they encountered considerable frustration. Even the largest CDC-supported firms employed fewer than one hundred people. Profit levels were low, despite the availability of government subsidies. The cost of creating jobs in the first place was steep, and then keeping neighborhood residents employed required considerable investments in preparatory and ongoing training. Convincing businesses to locate within an inner-city neighborhood always presented a challenge. By the 1980s, many CDCs shifted their priorities away from economic development and toward affordable housing production, a task that seemed better suited to their capabilities. CDCs acquired abandoned or neglected properties at minimal cost, renovated dilapidated homes—often using the labor of local residents—and improved communities house by house, block by block. By 1995, over two thousand CDCs operated in every large city. Along with home construction and renovation, CDCs offer other housing programs such as home-owner and tenant counseling and homeless shelters, as well as a range of social services. Many continue to engage in economic development.[125]

How do CDCs and other community-based organizations promote economic development today?

Community-based organizations promote indigenous economic growth by trying to transform the factors of production. The community may obtain broader control over land, for example, by setting up a community land trust, a locally managed entity that acquires and holds land for the benefit of residents. The trust retains ownership of the land but leases parcels to local individuals and groups who agree to use the land for affordable housing production or local economic development. Through the control of land use, community residents are able to play a pivotal role in stimulating economic activity within their neighborhood.

The community-based strategy also attempts to transform the role of labor by creating organizational structures that enable workers to obtain ownership rights through worker cooperatives or stock-ownership plans, in which employees share in the firm's profits. Giving local residents an ownership stake in firms keeps economic enterprises anchored within the community. On a more routine level, community-based organizations provide job readiness and training programs for people in the neighborhood and then help place them in jobs. The best community-based organizations target training to the particular needs of employers that offer good wages and prospects for career advancement. A host of community-based financial institutions provide capital, the third factor of production, to spark local development. Such institutions include community development credit unions, community loan funds, and community development banks.[126]

Are there any drawbacks to the community-based strategy?

Although many CDCs do impressive work under difficult circumstances, the reality is that most are small, underfunded, and staffed by inexperienced personnel. This alone significantly limits what they are able to accomplish. The frustrations that motivated so many earlier CDCs to switch to affordable housing production as their primary activity remain. Even today, only about 20 percent of all CDCs are willing to undertake economic development projects. The vast majority of these operate on a modest scale.

The chronic shortage of financial support limits the potential of CDCs. When federal funds for affordable housing were cut in the 1980s, CDCs became increasingly preoccupied with organizational survival. Many felt compelled to choose projects that would likely turn a profit. But this meant rejecting high-risk proposals in distressed neighborhoods, even though these were the neighborhoods most in need and most likely to be ignored by private developers. The constant pressure to generate revenue has also prompted many CDCs to rely more and more on professional grant writers and other skilled experts from outside the community. The turn toward trained professionals often comes at the expense of community control, raising questions about whose interests are being pursued by the CDC.

The precarious existence of most CDCs has motivated many of them to eschew political activism for fear of alienating City Hall and other providers of desperately needed funding. CDCs that once devoted considerable energy to mobilizing citizens at the grassroots to lobby government now minimize such advocacy in favor of projecting a more conciliatory and businesslike image. Critics assert that the apolitical, even conservative, posture of many CDCs may help them to secure additional grants in the short run, but in the long run the retreat from advocacy may undercut their mission of engendering broad policy changes to transform inner-city neighborhoods.[127]

However, even the more apolitical, businesslike CDCs are often the "only game in town" when it comes to inner-city revitalization. In some places, the level of economic distress is so great that the private sector has virtually abandoned the area. CDCs that choose to remain and invest in the community give residents reason to hope. Moreover, success stories abound. To take just one well-known example, a community-based development organization in Newark, New Jersey, built a 43,000-square-foot, $12-million shopping center that included a Pathmark supermarket in a poor neighborhood served only by expensive and understocked minimarkets. Once it opened, the supermarket attracted a high volume of customers and earned impressive profits from the outset.[128] Other CDCs have succeeded in keeping large employers in the community and helping start-up businesses, all the while exploring ways to ensure that local residents share in the fruits of economic growth.[129]

How does a community-based model of economic development square with the reality of a global economy?

Cities can pursue economic development policies that exploit opportunities at both the community and global levels simultaneously. Indeed, political scientists Susan Clarke and Gary Gaile contend in their book *The Work of Cities* that cities are most likely to enjoy economic growth by developing "global-local links." A new wave of economic development policies, in fact, aim to "integrate local economies into global markets" by increasing their investment in human capital, often at the community level, through job training programs, city-college collaborations, business incubators, and school-to-work programs. Other policies strengthen global-local links through the establishment of foreign trade zones, export promotion, international development planning, and investment in telecommunications technology such as installation of fiber optic networks.[130]

At the same time that many local economic development experts focus on policy initiatives targeting the knowledge- and corporate-services sectors, others have not given up on industrial production as a source of economic vitality in urban areas. Joel Rast argues that the decline of manufacturing in cities was not an inevitable consequence of global economic change. Rather, industrial production decreased at least in part because of the public policy choices of government officials, choices that reflected power dynamics within metropolitan areas and the nation. If public policy contributed to the decline of manufacturing, changes in policy might lead to a resurgence. Some manufacturing firms have ample reason to be based in central cities. Small and medium-sized firms that specialize in one or several phases of the production process often develop cooperative relationships with clusters of similar firms. Although production costs may be higher in urban neighborhoods, these firms enjoy competitive advantages arising "through extensive subcontracting and networking relationships."

These firms often compete with each other, to be sure, but also come to share tools and equipment, information, and employees. The emphasis on subcontracting and specialization "foster[s] economies of scope, making small-batch production economically feasible and facilitating rapid response to the quickly changing consumer demands of today's markets." Simple shifts in policies related to comprehensive planning, land use zoning, capital improvement programs, and building-code enforcement, as well as the provision of debt financing and employment training programs and the establishment of business incubators, would markedly improve the prospects for industrial activity in most U.S. cities, boosting the fortunes of neighborhoods beyond the downtown core.[131]

So when all is said and done, what have we learned from past economic development policy in U.S. cities?

Too much of economic development policy has been driven by assumptions about the inevitability of broad changes in the local, national, and global economy. For those cities that benefit from market trends, the past few decades have brought great prosperity. For others, however, government's reluctance to adopt policies that mitigate the isolating or destructive tendencies of markets has produced frustration, disappointment, and a declining quality of life in the same period. Many urbanites who believe their interests have been ignored by American public policy feel disempowered, and for good reason. Sweeping stretches of the urban landscape have in fact been neglected. The inequities produced by past economic development policies have created a tale of two cities phenomenon in urban areas throughout the country.

With that growing inequality has come a fracturing of community. The redirection in economic development policy may require a more active role for government to ensure a more equitable distribution of the costs and benefits of economic growth, a stronger effort to give all citizens a more meaningful stake in the decision-making process, and a renewed commitment to revitalizing all urban places. Public policies rooted in such communitarian principles are a crucial step toward solidifying severely fragmented communities and reviving the civic spirit of deeply alienated citizens.

But promoting economic development is only one step among many to make the city whole. Along with creating good jobs, urban policy-makers also need to think innovatively about other ways to rebuild distressed communities, such as providing decent, affordable housing and schools that give students a fair chance to pursue their goals and dreams.

4
Housing and
the Structure of Place

What is housing? What are housing's functions?

Housing is a building for human habitation, a place where people find shelter and more or less permanent residence. Housing is where families conduct their work and play. Housing is also the center of the private sphere, where people live their lives apart from the necessities of the marketplace and community life.

Housing comes in a variety of different forms, from shelters for extremely poor people to mansions for extremely wealthy people. Most people live in places between these two extremes of housing—in boarding homes, apartment buildings, condominium complexes, town houses, two- and three-family homes, and single-family homes.

People understand housing in different ways, Some people see housing in a wholly utilitarian way—a roof over one's head, shelter from a storm— while others strive to build a sense of "home." Home offers much more than shelter. It offers a place where people can realize their most distinctive qualities. A home embodies all that is personal to a person: family, friends, past achievements, and future hopes. The idea of home connects individuals and families with the larger community, nurtures important ideas about the proper way to live, and provides the proper way for groups of people to live and govern themselves.

What distinguishes housing from other commodities?

Housing is "lumpy." Housing is one of the bigger and clumsier commodities in the marketplace. It is the most expensive thing that most people ever buy, often valued at several times a person's annual salary. Buying and selling housing involves a major investment of time and money.

Compare housing to another commodity, like a shirt or a computer. To buy either of these goods requires simply going to a store and putting cash or a credit card on the counter at the checkout line. Hundreds of versions of these goods can be found in any community, most of them convenient to most people's homes or workplaces. These goods are highly portable; they can be made anywhere in the world and shipped easily to sales places anywhere in the world. Consumers can set the alternatives side by side and determine which one best suits their needs. When consumers are dissatisfied, they can easily replace them with a new version.

How does lumpiness affect consumers?

Housing's lumpiness makes it less "marketlike" than other commodities. The ideal marketplace operates like a bazaar, with a wide range of buyers and sellers hawking their wares at the same time and place. If a buyer wants food or drink or clothing, she can find the full range of options at the bazaar. Likewise, the seller benefits from marketplace feedback. Buying and selling products is a never-ending process of learning and adjustment. You buy and sell groceries, clothes, office supplies, games, tickets to events, and so on, every day. Depending on your level of satisfaction, you keep buying the same things or make quick adjustments.

But buying housing is different. When you buy or rent a house, you have access to just a few of the total options; in the best of circumstances, only about 5 or 6 percent of the total market comes on line in a given year—and most buyers and renters see only a handful of properties, rarely more than a couple of dozen. It is hard to assess the products side by side, especially when another consumer might make a bid and take away your opportunity to buy. The limited exposure to the full range of products limits the transaction's "marketness."

For most people, buying a house requires years of saving and planning. Most people have little choice about when to enter the market. The right time to buy might not coincide with personal circumstances. Family events such as getting married or having a baby often dictate housing decisions. Buyers have to take what is available when they enter the market.

How does housing's lumpiness affect the supply and costs of housing?

Because it is such a large and unwieldy product, people who invest in and develop housing are essentially making long-term bets. Developers know that their investment of time and money might not pay off for a long time—years, even decades—after the project is first envisioned. By the time a project is carried to its conclusion, the economic environment could have changed. Shifts in technology, interest rates, demand, and community regulations could determine whether the bet succeeds or fails. As a result, builders tend to invest in projects that offer the best chance of success and that offer financial guarantees and incentives. They shy away from projects that, even though viable, have less margin for error—such as housing for low-income families. Property, according to this view, is a mass commodity managed by a few people and companies. Developers play with properties as if they were playing a game of Monopoly. They acquire as much as they can, betting on what pieces will produce the most gains in the long run rather than attending to the basic needs of dwellers.

Whatever its lumpiness, wouldn't people's basic need for shelter spur the housing industry to supply enough shelter at affordable prices?

Not necessarily. The poorest of the poor lack the income—the "effective demand," in economists' terms—to spur developers to produce units for them. The average income for the bottom 20 percent of the population was $15,400 in 1997; most experts say that renters should pay no more than 30 percent of their income on housing, which would mean annual rent payments of $4,620, or $385 a month. But building and maintaining those units usually costs a lot more money. In fact there were just thirty-six units considered "affordable" for every hundred U.S. households in 1997.[1]

Free-marketeers argue that low-cost housing could be built for a profit if the government cut needless regulations. Modern zoning regulations restrict the size, configuration, and location of buildings. Small multifamily housing—two- to six-family houses that were once located on fifty-foot lots—is now proscribed in most communities. Building codes also drive up the cost of housing. Standards for building materials, minimum number of rooms, room sizes, fire sprinklers, septic systems, and parking spaces drive up per-unit costs beyond the reach even of many two-earner families. Rehabilitating old buildings is expensive because new-building standards are imposed on old structures, which are often sturdy but lack modern dimensions.

A Reagan administration commission concluded in 1982 that the government should allow the building of more small units, condominiums, and mobile homes to serve the low end of the market. The liberal social policy analyst Christopher Jencks agrees, saying that the decline of "cubicle" and single-room occupancy hotels, which once offered affordable shelter to poor people in big cities, can be attributed almost completely to local regulations. These forms of day-to-day shelter once housed poor people and provided a basic level of privacy and dignity. During the three decades of economic boom before the 1973 oil crisis, state and local governments restricted or banned construction of these rooming houses. But as incomes have stagnated and families have broken up, the need for such low-cost units has increased. Jencks writes: "Rooms without windows strike many people, including me, as particularly grim. Nonetheless, when cubicles were widely available almost everyone preferred them to congregate shelters, despite the fact that shelters were free."[2]

What factors matter most in the production and distribution of housing?

Theoretically, the most important factor is land. With a few interesting exceptions, land is an exclusive, monopoly commodity. One person's occupation of space necessarily forecloses the possibility of another person occupying that space. I cannot build a house where you have already built one. When people desire greater quantities of other goods, such as sweaters or autos or hamburgers, the means to produce them usually exists. If Americans next year express a clear desire for 3 billion hamburgers instead of the 2.5 billion consumed this year, producers will gather the materials, capital, and labor necessary to meet that demand. But it is not always so easy with land.

But builders have always found ways to "make" land. Does land necessarily have an absolutely fixed supply?

Of course, entrepreneurs have in fact created habitable land where none existed before. Many neighborhoods are located on landfill, places where water has been filled in with sand, refuse, and other materials. Much of Boston was produced by filling in the Back Bay and the Fens in the nineteenth century. Battery Park City, a neighborhood on the lower tip of Manhattan Island in New York, is another example of creating new land by filling in waterways.

The episodes of land creation in American urban history point to a central truth of real estate development: the government plays a vital role in making existing land usable. Land is only as valuable as its preparation allows. Infrastructure—streets and sidewalks, parks and business districts, schools and community centers, police and fire protection, sewers and other utilities, highways and transit—makes development possible. Often the government uses public dollars to make land use viable; at other times, the government mandates certain kinds of improvements to make the land viable. In either case, it takes public action for property to be "prepared" for housing and other kinds of development. When the government invests in these basic elements of community, housing becomes valuable. As Henry George pointed out, the value of land depends upon how how society invests in that land. The value of property is social value.[3]

Cities all over the United States have hundreds of square miles of vacant land that could be the basis of a new urban renaissance. But to take advantage of these properties—many of which are environmentally damaged or lack basic infrastructure—federal, state, and local governments need to invest in preparing them for development. In some cases, government planning and taking of the land by eminent domain might be necessary to assemble the land for useful purposes. A recent survey of seventy cities found that 15 percent of all urban land was vacant, and that even the cities with few vacant parcels had numerous abandoned buildings.[4]

How does housing affect a person or family's life chances?

Housing gets the first "claim" on most people's incomes. Housing takes the most "automatic" cut from our take-home pay. Only after we have bought housing can we buy other commodities. Unlike other goods, housing does not have any real substitutes; everyone needs a roof over his head.

Housing also plays a critical role in people's access to opportunities to pursue their goals. Where people live determines their access to education, jobs, goods and services, recreational facilities, and transportation systems. The quality and location of housing determines how much people need to spend for the other necessities of life.

Education is the service most critically tied to housing. Public schools almost always enroll students according to geographic location. Families and their children get assigned to schools that are closest to them in the district. Most public school systems offer little flexibility in school assignments. As a general rule, schools in affluent districts can spend more money per pupil—and hire better teachers, obtain up-to-date textbooks and laboratory equipment, and offer more extracurricular activities—than in less affluent districts. What is more, property taxes in affluent districts tend to be lower than in less affluent districts. According to William Fischel's "homevoter hypothesis," people choose where to live—and they determine a wide range of their political preferences—based on the bundle of opportunities and costs that are tied in with their homes. Because their homes comprise a major portion of most people's wealth, most people are bound to be alert to whatever policies and practices affect their homes.[5]

The importance of the home in determining people's "life chances" is underscored by a program to disperse poor and minority families in the Chicago area. James Rosenbaum and Leonard Rubinowitz of Northwestern University tested the impact of housing and neighborhood on the lives of a number of families living in a public-housing complex in Chicago. Families were offered a chance to live in private homes scattered across the Chicago area, and their performances on a number of indicators were compared with those left in the complex. Children who were relocated had lower dropout rates (5 percent as opposed to 20 percent) and higher college enrollment rates (54 as opposed to 21 percent). Good housing in good neighborhoods produces good results.[6] In short, where you live often determines how much you learn.

Housing, Opportunity, and the City

How does housing shape the ideology of American life—the basic philosophy about the American Dream?

The home is one of the most potent and emotional symbols in American life. The expression "American Dream" usually conjures up images of the single-family dwelling with a white picket fence. Home is potent because it represents much more than a place where people can rest and sustain themselves away from the workplace. Home represents individual dignity, security, creativity and expression, career and family achievement, long-term investment, neighborhood identity, professional and ethnic meaning, and all of the complex feelings that can be tied into the notion of family. Home is the physical center of most people's identity.

How does housing opportunity differ for people of different incomes and races?

Poor people and minorities—who live disproportionately in cities—enjoy much less opportunity to live in well-maintained and located homes. More minorities than whites (15 percent versus 5 percent) live in public or subsidized housing, which tends to be less well built, maintained, and located. Many poor and working families live in close quarters, with several people sleeping in one room. Still, according to the 2000 report of the Joint Center for Housing Studies at Harvard University, only 1.3 percent of all urban home owners and 4.5 percent of unsubsidized renters lived in "severely inadequate housing," units with severe problems in plumbing, heating, electric systems, or upkeep.[7]

Urbanites are also less likely than suburbanites to own their homes (67 percent versus 50 percent). Even though urbanites and minorities experienced a major increase in home ownership in the 1990s—from 1994 to 1999, Hispanic home ownership increased from 46.1 percent to 50.2 percent and black home ownership increased from 42.5 percent to 46.7 percent, so that minorities accounted for almost 40 percent of the growth in overall home ownership—the gap between white and minority home ownership rates has held steady at about 25 percentage points.[8]

Of course, simple inequality on measures of adequacy and equity do not necessarily doom poor, working-class, and urban households. As the conservative analyst Howard Husock has noted, what is most important is whether people have the opportunity to climb a "ladder of opportunity" over the course of their lives.[9] A poor immigrant family in Chicago or

Houston might not find sharing bedrooms so disagreeable if they have the opportunity to move up to something better. A single mother or a laid-off worker can surely live in a small apartment while gaining the skills to reenter the labor force.

The really critical question for housing is whether the system is fluid, open, and dynamic enough to provide units for homes for households of all sizes, stages of the life cycle, and kinds of communities. It is not necessarily a problem that a poor or even middle-class family cannot afford a home in an exclusive "gold coast" neighborhood; neither can that family afford a Lexus car or a night at the Ritz. But what matters is that people of all backgrounds, income levels, and tastes can grab a rung on the housing ladder and find something good enough so that they can work their way to something better.

Social theorists talk of the home as the place of "social reproduction." What does that mean?

All societies require their members to conform to certain norms and activities. Housing is the first school of those norms, the place where people develop psychically and emotionally. With an established and secure home, people take the basics of life for granted. They can sleep, eat, care for children and parents, learn, and play. With a home, people can master everyday challenges of life; from there, they have a "base" to develop their life plans.[10]

Children—the wage earners and citizens of tomorrow—get their most important training and support in the home. Values such as thrift, hard work, cooperation, and respect for others are learned in the home. The home also models the workplace's division of labor, with its assignment of different responsibilities to the father, mother, children, and relatives or boarders.

How does housing affect the labor process?

The home is the preparation ground of most of the workforce. Wage earners need the security and sustenance of the home to refresh them for the rigors of the workplace. If the wage earner's needs are taken care of in the home, he will devote more time to and focus on tasks better on the job. A corporate official in America's Gilded Age observed the importance of the home in domesticating the working class: "Get them to invest their savings in homes and own them. Then they won't leave and they won't strike. It ties them down so they have a stake in our prosperity." A housing expert of the era put it more simply: "Good homes make contented workers."[11]

According to many Marxian theorists, the home softens the antagonisms of the workplace because it shifts attention from work and toward home and community. Whatever the conditions of life in a factory or a chicken-processing plant, the worker finds refuge in the home. One observer wrote:

> The place we think of as most clearly contrasting with the workplace is the home. When we think of what isn't work, what we can call "not-work," we think of the home. Although we have to do tasks at home, we don't normally think of them as being equivalent to the tasks we do at work. In the popular imagination, home is where we imagine ourselves to have stopped working, where we relax, where we unburden ourselves from the cares of the workday. Home is our refuge from work.[12]

What do feminists mean when they say housing is a "gendered" commodity?

It means that housing shapes the contours of the relations of men, women, and family. With the separation of home and workplace during the Industrial Revolution, women were expected to attend to domestic chores such as cooking, cleaning, raising children, caring for the sick and elderly, sewing, and other chores.

Delores Hayden argues: "Men could not be persuaded to sacrifice their nights and days as tireless breadwinners, nor could women be manipulated in and out of the national labor market, unless women's place was explicitly in the home."[13] The home's system of production is an important element of labor relations. The work performed in the home—the reproduction of labor power—enables the major breadwinner to get a bigger paycheck in the paid economy. But work in the home does not get compensated or counted as part of the gross national product because it exists outside the formal marketplace.

Over time, the very design of the home has come to structure all aspects of the family's activities and identities. Laborsaving devices—washing machines, vacuum cleaners, and various kitchen appliances—were sold to women and set up in a floor plan that separated living and recreation (what men got to do when they came home from work) and housekeeping (what women did to support the others in the home). With the exception of wartime, when "Rosie the Riveter" and other women were called into the factory, women historically were excluded from most male professions—leaving them only the home on which to make their mark. In recent years, as women have entered the paid labor market in record numbers, this neat division has been challenged. But surveys still show that women perform most of the work in the home, while men are more responsible for generating outside income.[14]

All of this discussion might lead one to believe that housing is a general issue, not just an urban issue. Is there anything distinctively urban about the housing crisis?

Yes. Because modern cities have to fight for their economic survival, many developers and political leaders have focused on reviving select parts of the city. The urban renewal program of the 1950s and 1960s identified key parts of the city that were considered ripe for attracting the middle class and then remade those communities on a wholesale basis. The transformation of the tenement neighborhood in Boston's West End into a discrete community of high-rise luxury apartments called Charles River Park is the most notable example of this strategy.[15] But such projects can be found across the United States, from San Francisco to New York. Such a strategy made sense for many cities that feared they would not be able to attract any new businesses or investment without a targeted approach. But while pockets of affluence developed, many residents lost their homes, and other neighborhoods suffered from neglect and lack of investment.

The "tale of two cities" extends from the city to the whole metropolitan area. People who can remove themselves from the problems of the city—inadequate schools, crime, congestion—often move to the suburbs. That movement is exacerbated by the tendency of housing developers to move outside the city along the vast highways and beltways of the suburbs. Because of labor issues, land costs, environmental issues, zoning and other regulations, city services, and employment patterns, developers find it much easier to build in the suburbs than in the city. In Philadelphia in the 1990s, developers produced more than 8,500 new units of housing a year in the suburbs but less than 160 new units a year in the city.[16] That contrast suggests a drastic separation of urban and suburban fortunes.

Does housing design matter for the way neighborhoods and cities are developed?

Indeed it does. The size, shape, and configuration of the home determine how people will interact in the community. Urban-style housing—with dense clusters of multifamily housing located close to commercial and civic spaces—allows people to tend to everyday chores by foot or mass transit. You can walk to a store or work, and that "venturing out" allows people to have a number of accidental encounters with their neighbors. The planner and author Michael D. Sorkin equates such a pattern of living with democracy itself:

> The accidental encounter is one of the things that cities are absolutely predicated upon—that accidental encounter is one of the bulwarks of democratic culture. To the degree that these kinds of accidents are precluded, either by the sterility of the mix or by more

traditional forms of segregation, cities die as democratic institutions and are forced to become sterile service centers or entertainment zones.

Public life requires people to encounter others wherever they
go.[17]

Suburban-style housing often requires the use of a car to shop, attend
school or church, or go to work or a movie. Suburban communities tend to
offer a more predictable and orderly set of spaces and routines. The home
is seen as a refuge, and community and civic activities are located in separate zones of the community. The chance of accidental encounters is much
lower in suburbs, so people tend to plan their days more precisely. That
does not mean that civic engagement is not possible, just that it takes a different form.

How do housing and neighborhoods affect local governments?

Property taxes constitute the major form of local government revenues.
The higher the property values, in general, the more revenues the local authorities can raise for basic functions such as schools and parks. Property
taxes were once considered the ideal source of revenue for education and
local services because they provided a steady and reasonably equal stream
of money to local governments. Because property assessments did not
occur regularly, revenues did not vary in boom and bust times the way
sales-tax revenues did.

But dependence on property taxes for local government has come to
cause great distortions. In the 1970s, property values in California increased dramatically as the state's economy boomed and millions of outsiders moved to the state. The average price of a single-family house in Los
Angeles, for example, increased from $37,800 to $83,200 between 1974 and
1978. Even though the higher property values produced a windfall for sellers of homes, it created hardship for the people who kept their homes or
wanted to buy new homes. The higher taxes that went with higher property values overburdened people whose incomes did not keep pace. Working-class families, young couples, retirees, and people who had assumed
big mortgages found themselves paying higher taxes, but their incomes did
not keep up. Homeowners, who were "property rich" but lacking the basic
resources for day-to-day living, could be found all over the United States,
and produced property tax revolts in California, Massachusetts, and other
states.[18]

In recent years, some analysts have suggested reducing reliance on property taxes for local government budgets. Michigan's conservative governor,
John Engler, promoted a statewide referendum in 1994 that traded a two-

thirds cut in property taxes for a 2-cent increase in the sales tax. The successful referendum, known as Proposal A, dramatically changed the basis of public school funding and quelled a nascent property-tax revolt in the state. Since then, Minnesota Governor Jesse Ventura has also promoted the idea of reducing the burden of property taxes by increasing statewide levies. The shift away from property taxes is limited but could become a major movement in American states, as courts order equalization of school spending and property-rich communities resist higher taxes.

The Character of American Housing Policy

What overarching principles guide federal housing policy?

Privatism guides most of American housing policy. The ideal of private ownership—by families, businesses, nonprofit corporations—is the foundation of every aspect of housing policy in the United States. The corollary is that collective provision of housing should be undertaken only in rare circumstances. In the United States, government wants individuals, families, and business people to own and control housing. Historically, the federal government has given subsidies to private developers to build and operate housing complexes that provide below-market rent. State and local governments also work with nonprofit corporations to develop and rehabilitate affordable housing. Many public housing authorities are turning over publicly owned stock to private firms for management and even ownership.

The federal government tends to guide housing policy indirectly. The government exerts most of its authority invisibly through the tax code. The biggest housing program of all, tax breaks on mortgage interest, powerfully influences every aspect of the housing system and provides tens of billions of dollars to mostly middle-class and upper-class home owners. The mortgage tax write-off does not require appropriations from Congress, so it operates on automatic pilot. The program is invisible, except for the millions of Americans who benefit when they fill out their 1040 forms for the Internal Revenue Service. The leading federal housing agency, the Department of Housing and Urban Development, does not have control over this program.

What is the best way to describe the structure of housing programs in the United States?

The structure of housing policy is complex, like an old Victorian house. The basic structure of American housing policy is private ownership; but that basic structure has an elaborate system of ornamentation consisting of public subsidies and regulatory requirements. Housing policy involves a number of competing goals. Some policies aim to improve the workings of the marketplace, while others aim to restrain markets. Some policies aim to build housing for the poor, while others heavily subsidize housing development for the middle class and even the wealthy. Some programs focus on new development, while the demand for rehabilitation of existing units struggles to find a foothold in policy. Over time, housing "policy" becomes a collection of sometimes helpful, sometimes contradictory and counterproductive initiatives.

Housing, the Economy, and the City

What roles does housing play in the American economy?

Housing and its supporting industries comprise about one fifth of the overall economy in the United States. The gross national product of the United States was about $9.2 trillion in 2000. The industries that directly contributed to the production and distribution of housing accounted for almost $2 trillion of that.

Housing is a "bellwether" industry. Its health is a sign of the well-being of the rest of the economy. Economic experts and journalists regularly look for the latest statistics in housing starts and sales, construction contracts, and building permits to gauge the strength of local, regional, and national economies. New housing construction increased 75 percent from 1991 to 1999. The number of permits in the fifty biggest metropolitan areas—which represent about half the U.S. market—increased 102 percent during that period. Construction in central-city locations actually increased faster than construction in the rest of the metropolitan areas. The most urban form of housing—multifamily apartments developments—increased from 33 percent to 55 percent of the total share of the national total from 1992 to 1999. Such numbers are good news not only for cities but for a wide range of related industries in construction, materials, finance, and design.[19]

Former Housing Secretary Andrew Cuomo put the matter this way: "What's good for housing is good for the economy—a very large part of the American economy. The housing finance system is in many ways the backbone of the American economic system. Housing is also—beyond the mere shelter, and even beyond the economic potential—housing is also a way for people to be vested and rooted in their society and literally own a piece of their own community."[20] During the recession that began in 2000, the housing sector managed to stay strong while various manufacturing and service industries struggled. Aided by low interest rates and a more sophisticated financial system, housing continued to build wealth for ordinary Americans, particularly on the two coasts.

What does the term "shelter poverty" mean?

Many statistical analyses of housing affordability begin with the assumption that people should pay no more than 25 or 30 percent of their income on housing. That standard once made sense—when the everyday needs of families were simpler, when taxes and spending on cars and other expenses were not as large. But the housing expert Michael Stone points out that because of the different requirements of everyday life, that fraction might not be the appropriate threshold for housing affordability anymore. A person making a good salary like $100,000 can afford to spend a lot more than one fourth of his salary on housing. Someone making just $12,000 a year cannot afford one quarter of his wages on housing.

A better way to measure housing affordability, Stone argues, is the standard of "shelter poverty." This concept begins with the understanding that the more money is required for housing, the less is available for other necessities of life. Since shelter makes the "first claim" on a household's income, it can crowd out other necessary expenses. If rents or house payments are excessive, the family necessarily suffers from a deficiency in other areas. That is shelter poverty.

So what does an analysis of shelter poverty tell us?

At the end of the economic boom of the 1990s, more than one third of the nation's population was shelter-poor, according to Stone.[21] In a nation of 101 million households, 31 million households with 89 million people (35 percent of the population) could not afford to pay for shelter and all of the other necessities of life. The number of shelter-poor households increased by 70 percent from 1970 (when 18.7 million households were shelter-poor) to the mid-1990s (when 27.4 million households were shelter-poor). Shelter poverty trends, Stone reports, are "somewhat sensitive to business cycle fluctuations, with swings up and down as unemployment and incomes shift with the overall economy." But more important than such minor shifts—about one sixth of shelter poverty can be considered cyclical—is the long-term steadiness of shelter poverty.

Shelter poverty afflicts large households more than small households, Stone found. The number of shelter-poor households increased from 9 million to 17 million from 1970 to 1997 (86 percent). The number of shelter-poor households of one or two persons increased from 9 to 16 million (66 percent) during that period.

As always, race played a major role in the level of well-being for housing. While 77 percent of all households were headed by whites, 66 percent of all shelter-poor households were headed by whites. Some 23 percent of all households were headed by minorities, while 34 percent of all shelter-poor households were minority. Gender also plays an important role in well-being. Women headed 38 percent of all households in the United States, but they accounted for almost half (47 percent) of all shelter-poor households.

Home ownership has been promoted as the true ticket to prosperity in the United States, but Stone's numbers point to problems even with home owners. Almost one quarter of all owner-occupied households (23.3 percent) were shelter-poor in 1997. Still, home owners have enjoyed a substantial—and growing—advantage over renters in recent decades. Almost half of all renters (46.5 percent) were shelter-poor in 1997. Renters account for about two thirds of the increase in shelter poverty since 1970.

How well do housing assistance programs reach families in need?

Public-assistance programs reduce the problem of shelter poverty for some people but not everyone. Admission into housing assistance programs requires an income below 80 percent of the area's median income, which is often too stringent a standard to help many in need. Public housing and rent-supplement programs have waiting lists of several years in most big cities. Programs such as Section 8 rent supplements provide virtually all assistance to about one third of the poor population. Only one fourth of all recipients of welfare received any housing assistance at all. Rent supplements were hard to get, but once received could play a major role in getting a family on its feet. But the lack of a major housing production program at the federal level created a stubborn imbalance between supply of units and the effective demand for those units—exacerbating an already difficult affordability crisis in cities like New York, Boston, Washington, San Francisco, Los Angeles, and Chicago.

No matter how extensive rental assistance may appear, it is rarely enough to escape shelter poverty. Timing is crucial. If a family is lucky enough to qualify for assistance just before its income begins to rise, then it can escape shelter poverty. But if the income rises too much, the family loses its shelter benefits and falls back below the shelter poverty threshold.

How do the high-end markets affect urban housing markets?

Gentrification—the movement of affluent people into once-depressed neighborhoods—has become one of the most powerful dynamics of local housing markets. Gentrification occurs with gays, artists, and students in the vanguard. Because they often have more disposable income to spend on housing, affluent urbanites lift the housing values in a number of neighborhoods. When they find areas with some blight but good qualities—like a strong housing stock or convenient location—the urban gentry moves in. In New York, it's Manhattan and Brooklyn Heights; in Boston, it was once Back Bay and Beacon Hill, and now it is Roxbury and

Dorchester; in Chicago, it was once the Gold Coast, and now it is the area to the west and south of the Loop.

Once the leading districts of a city get filled, housing prices rise and drive some residents to search for new places to live. Gentrification often occurs at the expense of minorities and others, who accepted some dilapidation in exchange for low rent. As the neighborhood gets spruced up, restaurants and other businesses move in, and low-income families sometimes have no choice but to move on. The city is a collection of neighborhoods ever in flux. Research has found that poor households are actually 15 percent to 20 percent *less* likely to move in gentrifying neighborhoods when "rent stabilization" regulations are in place. In New York City's 1990s revitalization, poor households actually benefited more than other households.[22]

Because more people rent housing in the cities than in suburban and rural areas, developing a rental housing policy must be especially important for urban America.

Right. The United States reached its highest level of home ownership in cities in 1998 when for the first time over 50 percent of all urban dwellers owned their own home. The home ownership rate across the United States was a staggering 67.7 percent. In traditional cities like Boston, about one third of all people live in homes that they own.

A good urban housing policy must make rental housing available to all people at reasonable rates and also ensure that rental housing is safe and secure. But not all rental housing is the same. Most cities have a mix of large-scale apartment buildings, owned and operated by professional landlords, and small-scale multifamily structures, owned and operated by mom-and-pop operations.

So how do different kinds of landlords affect the tenant's experience?

In general, the professional landlord operates his business strictly for profit and employs a number of subcontractors to look after properties—a building manager, a building superintendent, janitorial and grounds staffs, and so on. Professional landlords are more market-savvy than mom-and-pop landlords. They have more reliable information about what market rates and a greater willingness to charge whatever the market will bear. Professional landlords are in the business to make a buck. The profit-maximizing orientation tends to increase rents. To the extent that they control large blocks of real estate, professional landlords also distort rental markets.

Amateur landlords rent just a few properties as a way to earn some side income. Most amateur landlords look after their own property and develop a personal relationship with tenants. "Desire for a high return is held partly in check by concerns for the tenants' welfare, a concern bred of face-

Table 4.1 Home Ownership in the United States

	Third Quarter 2000	Fourth Quarter 1994
Nation Overall	67.7%	64.2%
Central cities	51.9%	48.2%
Minorities	48.2%	43.7%
Black, non-Hispanic	47.3%	42.9%
Other, non-Hispanic	54.3%	51.2%
Hispanic	46.7%	42.2%
Female-headed households	53.3%	48.7%
Households with less-than-median-income for the quarter	52.2%	48.6%
Married couples under 35	61.0%	57.1%

Mortgage Bankers Association of America, Archives, available at www.mbaa.org/marketdata/arch00.html. Click 10/26: "U.S. Homeownership Rate Highest in Nation's History."

to-face contact, friendship, and long-term acquaintance. Thus the amateur landlord prefers to rent to family, friends, and long-term tenants at terms well below the market."[23] Amateur landlords desire a relationship of trust more than a relationship of profiteering. Their rental properties often hold sentimental value; some are saving the house for their children or their own retirement, or as a way to maintain a stake in the community while holding onto a tangible form of wealth.

Housing Policy

What are the best ways to understand housing policy? Granted that housing is a hodgepodge of different approaches, how can we understand how those approaches come together?

Housing policy begins with the government's efforts to establish the "rules of the game." The federal government regulates how banks and other financial institutions operate, a critical area of policy since virtually all housing development requires loans that are paid off over fifteen- to thirty-year periods. Federal, state, and local civil rights laws set minimum requirements of fairness for the sale, rent, and maintenance of homes, to protect primarily racial minorities but also religious minorities, women, gays, and others who might face discrimination. State and local governments establish how developers build housing—how buildings are designed and where they can be located.

Once the rules of the game are set, governments take two basic approaches: creating more units of housing (the supply side) and improving people's purchasing power (the demand side). Because of its consumerist and individualistic public philosophy, the United States tends to favor giving people resources to pursue their own housing goals—that is, increasing their effective demand. Mortgage tax benefits comprise the most important incentive in the entire housing sector, worth upward of $70 billion a year. The biggest federal program for poor people today is Section 8, which provides vouchers for needy people to use to rent units in the private market. Many cities have enacted rent-control laws, effectively boosting the purchasing power of tenants by holding down the monthly rents that their landlords can charge.

The federal government has invested in public housing since the New Deal, usually in collaboration with local housing authorities. All three levels of government have contributed land, grants, tax credits, and other financial tools for nonprofit organizations—usually called community development corporations (CDCs)—to build housing affordable by poor and working-class tenants. Governments at all levels also finance the construction and operation of homeless shelters.

Regulating the Housing Environment
Regulating and Supporting Financial Institutions

How did the federal government's role in housing develop?

It happened during the Great Depression under President Franklin D. Roosevelt. At the center of the nation's economic crisis was a complete breakdown of the financial system. Banks failed at record rates—some 1,400 banks closed down in 1932, and the others were considered too weak to stand without help—and Roosevelt concluded that only stabilizing the financial system would provide a foundation for future economic growth. Ordinary Americans needed a stable financial sector to provide them with the opportunity to buy homes and develop their small-business assets. Roosevelt's strategy was to stabilize the lenders so that they would be willing to make loans to big builders and ordinary people alike.

How did Roosevelt shore up the nation's financial system?

Roosevelt developed a wide range of programs to protect both home owners and banks. Ever the policy experimenter, Roosevelt developed a wide range of direct and indirect approaches to protect specific interests and encourage the development of new housing for people at all income levels. Here is an overview of his top initiatives and how they evolved over the years:

- *Supplies of New Money from the Federal Government.* The Federal Home Loan Bank (FHLB) system, enacted under President Herbert Hoover, provided short-term credit to savings and loan institutions—in essence, loans to the lenders so they could lend some more. The FHLB raised money to lend to financial institutions by selling government-backed securities in the capital markets. This program was expanded under Roosevelt in 1934 with the creation of the Federal Savings and Loan Insurance Corporation (FSLIC). The FSLIC insured savings deposits in institutions that agreed to follow the program's regulations.

- *Guarantees for Deposits.* The Housing Act of 1934 created the Federal Housing Administration to insure mortgages. Deposits of up to $30,000 were guaranteed, making people less leery about putting their hard-earned cash in someone else's vault. The phrase "Member, FDIC" at the end of bank advertisements is intended to assure people that their money is safe because the Federal Deposit Insurance Corporation will cover any losses that occur as a result of bank failures.

- *Processes to Sell Notes and Get More Money to Lend.* The creation of the Federal National Mortgage Association, later renamed Fannie Mae, bought loan notes from banks so that those institutions could turn around and make more loans. The creation of a "secondary" mortgage market created fluidity in the housing market that prevented banks from getting so burdened with long-term commitments that they could not provide money to new borrowers. After World War II, when it was authorized to buy and sell the mortgages of veterans, Fannie Mae became a major force in the housing system.

- *Programs to Make Mortgages More Attractive to Borrowers.* Soon after Roosevelt became president in 1933, Congress created the Home Owners Loan Corporation (HOLC) to buy defaulted mortgages from banks and refinance the loans for longer (and hence more affordable) terms to the mortgage-holder.

The HOLC was just an emergency measure. The big initiative was a year away.

The Federal Housing Act of 1934 provided insurance for financial institutions that made long-term, low–down-payment loans to borrowers. More than any other program, this act opened the possibility of home ownership to millions of working-class people who could now save enough for a down payment and make enough to meet monthly mortgage bills. Rather than putting down 50 percent of the purchase price and paying off the balance in five years, borrowers could put down 10 or 20 percent and pay off the loan in twenty or thirty years.

By stretching out loans, the 1934 Act also kicked in one of the great bonanzas of American tax history: the mortgage deduction on federal income taxes. Home owners can write off the interest from their loans—which accounts for most of their monthly payments in the early years of the loan—when filing their tax returns on April 15. That amounts to a subsidy of as much as one third on monthly payments for shelter. These "tax expenditures," which reduce federal revenues by upward of $80 billion a year, provide disproportionate benefits to the middle-class and wealthy.

Later, the Serviceman's Readjustment Act of 1944, commonly called the GI bill of rights, guaranteed home mortgages to veterans returning from World War II. The law gave ex-GIs the opportunity to buy a home with no money down. Anyone with a job could also get a home. With interest rates low, paying off 100 percent of the price of a home was not too onerous even for working-class families.

• *Regulations against Reckless Lending Practices.* Led by the Federal Housing Act of 1934, most of the federal programs to insure and stimulate lending activity carried strong regulations about what banks could and could not do. These regulations restricted the kinds of products and services that banks could offer, set stringent standards for granting loans, and banned loans for certain speculative ventures. Banks often welcomed these measures as protecting them from their own impulses to indulge in poor lending practices when they were flush. Regulations gave banking a much-needed reprieve from the atmosphere of crisis and uncertainty that pervaded the industry in the 1920s and 1930s. They set ground rules that assured people about the predictability of the system.

Regulating Basic Fairness

What about civil rights?

The civil rights movement came late to the housing industry. The nation's first comprehensive civil rights law for housing was not passed until right after the assassination of Martin Luther King, Jr., in 1968. Because housing is largely a private market—for a commodity that has deep emotional value for all concerned—the Congress was reluctant to tell home sellers and landlords how they ought to deal with their properties. While the civil rights movement of the 1960s sought protection from discrimination in public places, no such protections were guaranteed in the housing system.

Racial and other forms of discrimination were deeply ingrained in the American housing system at all levels. Restrictive covenants—legal clauses in property sales that forbade new owners from selling to Jews, blacks, and other minorities—were the first form of housing discrimination to be held unconstitutional by the U.S. Supreme Court's decision in *Shelley v. Kraemer* in 1948. By limiting the overall pool of homes, covenants and other forms of discrimination reduced the real supply of homes for minorities and thereby drove up costs. For years, the Federal Housing Authority (FHA) actively encouraged racial discrimination by directing developers and banks to avoid building homes in minority and poor communities. The FHA's underwriting manual of 1936 warned about the "adverse influences" that included "lower class occupancy and inharmonious racial groups." The FHA's manual was a not-so-subtle signal to home builders and financiers to avoid inner-city communities.

So when did the civil right movement really reach the field of housing?

When the civil rights movement moved north toward cities such as New York, Chicago, and Newark, it became clear that basic opportunity depended on more than access to public accommodations like bus terminals and lunch counters. Even though Northern cities did not impose the same kinds of severe restrictions on public access as did the South, the everyday opportunities of blacks and other minorities were often severely limited. Blacks were condemned to slums, forced to accept the picked-over, run-down housing that whites did not want. That is what the Fair Housing Act was intended to remedy.

What did that Act do?

The Fair Housing Act—officially, Title VIII of the Civil Rights Act of 1968—bans discrimination in the sale, rental, and financing of dwellings based on race, color, religion, sex, or national origin. The law was subsequently expanded in 1988 to cover discrimination on the basis of disability or family status. The 1988 amendments also included new enforcement mechanisms.

The problem with the Fair Housing Act was that it did not provide enough enforcement "teeth" to combat discrimination effectively. To prove discrimination, a person had to prove that the landlord intended to discriminate on the basis of race. Getting a "smoking gun" for discussions and transactions that take place outside public view can be difficult. Even when housing discrimination cases made it to court, it took so long that the harm of discrimination was hard to prove. Furthermore, legal action can be expensive for ordinary people just trying to find a place to live. As former Senator Charles Mathias, Jr., and Marion Morris note: "Because they are usually between homes, they do not have the luxury of time to pursue a court case if they feel they have been given a raw deal or no deal at all by any of the actors in the home sales or rental chain. Going to court is intimidating, time-consuming, and costly for all parties."[24] Over the years, Congress has seesawed between those who favor strengthening and those who favor weakening antidiscrimination laws.

Still, racial discrimination is less of a factor in America than ever before. A recent study of the importance of race on home ownership in the twentieth century found that whites still enjoyed more opportunities to own homes than blacks, but that that difference resulted from age, education, employment, and other factors: "The pure effect of race began to decline significantly after 1960. Controlling for other factors the racial gap was about 15.5 percentage points in 1900, compared with 14.9 percentage points in 1960. By 1980, however, the pure effect of race had fallen to 9.0 percentage points."[25]

Regulating Local Development

What is zoning?

Zoning is a system for regulating what kinds of buildings can be built and where in the community they can be built. Zoning codes are enacted by local governments with minimal guidance or interference from the federal and state levels of government.

Zoning ordinances segment the city according to function (e.g., heavy and light industry, white-collar business, residential), size of structure (e.g., single-unit dwellings, high-rise buildings), and property alignments (with requirements for minimum acreage, landscaping, access to utilities). The earliest zoning law was adopted by San Francisco in the early 1800s to keep Chinese immigrants away from native-born Americans (which created the nation's first Chinatown). The first zoning law to pass constitutional muster was New York City's land-use regulations, designed to isolate the city's garment district to protect the fashionable Fifth Avenue.

As soon as the Supreme Court upheld the constitutionality of zoning in 1917, cities across the United States adopted their own versions of New York's law. The number of cities with zoning regulations increased from five in 1916 to 981 in 1930. Cities supplemented zoning with extensive processes to coordinate planning on a broad scale. The number of cities with planning commissions increased from seventeen in 1914 to 735 in 1930.[26]

Cities often adopted zoning codes to exclude poor and working-class populations from more affluent populations. Large-lot zoning sets minimum "footprints" for building homes—for example, one, two, or more acres per unit—which forecloses the possibility of poor and working-class homes being built there. By keeping out "undesirable" populations, these affluent communities keep local taxes down and keep social programs to a minimum. A resident of Greenwich, Connecticut's four-acre lot zoning argued that large-lot zoning, which limits apartment construction, was a simple matter of economics: "It's like going into Tiffany and demanding a ring for $12.50. Tiffany doesn't have rings for $12.50. Well, Greenwich is like Tiffany."[27] Like Tiffany's, Greenwich targets its policies to the upper levels of the market.

Many of the original justifications for zoning have disappeared. Whereas manufacturing was once unavoidably dirty and unhealthy—and harmful to a residential environment—today many light manufacturing processes pose no health or other danger to nearby properties. But if anything, restrictions on housing development have only increased in recent years, as cities and regions across the United States have "downzoned" their communities to allow for lower density of population. Some observers have called the resistance to new housing the "drawbridge" phenomenon, noting that people tend to draw the line on new housing once they have become safely ensconced in the community. A growing national debate about "sprawl"—the dispersal of population over wider and wider suburban territories—underscores the resistance to new housing in existing communities.

What about building codes?

Whereas local zoning ordinances determine what kinds of buildings and activities go where in the city, state building codes determine how the structures themselves should be designed.

Building codes set minimum standards for building materials, stairways, roofs, the size and placement of windows and doors, bathrooms, kitchens, garages, roofs and floors, and plumbing and electrical systems. These codes tend to set precise requirements for builders to follow. It's like a recipe. Use the ingredients that the code book says, and you'll get your permit for construction. Fail to do so, and the local authorities will not allow you to proceed with construction or occupy the building.

Do zoning and building codes create any problems?

Urban settings experience difficulties with building codes in two ways. First of all, the building standards set by the states are not always appropriate for urban areas. Three national code organizations outline the basic rules that the states adapt (the three organizations are in the process of merging into one universal international structure at the time of this book's writing). Since most new construction occurs in the suburbs, it is not surprising that the codes orient themselves to the suburbs. The codes require more space for housing and all kinds of other buildings than is needed in cities. Even though urbanites get along quite well in old structures that would not meet modern codes, they must build new structures according to the more expansive standards of the suburban-style codes.

A second and more serious problem concerns the rehabilitation of old buildings. In most states and cities, rehabilitating an old building requires bringing it up to modern code standards—which is often impossible. Here's how it works: when a developer decides to rehabilitate an old structure, the new-building code is applied according to the overall cost of the rehab job. Work that costs 25 percent of the building's value requires bringing the altered parts of the structure up to new-building standards (if you're doing work on the kitchen sink, the whole kitchen has to be brought to modern code). Work that costs 50 percent of the building's value means the entire building must be brought completely to new code standards. The problem is that abandoned buildings in inner-city areas often have little value, so any attempt to fix them requires meeting the new code standards for a whole building. That is often impossible since it requires changing the very foundation of a building, even though doing so does not make it safer or healthier.

Led by New Jersey, a number of states and cities are changing their building codes to require less expensive and elaborate rehab jobs. By simply requiring old buildings to meet certain basic health and safety goals, New Jersey has seen a blossoming of rehab work in old cities. In its first year, the new New Jersey code contributed to a dramatic increase in rehabilitation work in cities and towns across the state. In Newark, total rehabilitation spending rose from $68.1 million in 1997 to $108.5 million in 1998, the first year of the code's implementation, an increase of 59.2 percent. In Jersey City, rehabilitation spending rose from $48.5 million to $89 million, an increase of 83.5 percent. In Trenton, rehabilitation spending rose from $21 million to $29.4 million, an increase of 40.1 percent. As a point of comparison, statewide spending on rehabilitation rose from $3.79 billion to $4.08 billion, an increase of 7.7 percent. In a state with dozens of old industrial cities, a smarter rehab code can play a central role in urban regeneration.[28]

How do regulations shape the production and distribution of housing?

Regulations can usually be understood as additional costs.[29] Regulations that require housing to have minimum acreage or standard building materials require builders to pay more for construction. Every additional requirement costs the builder in materials, manual labor, and professional advice. Land, plumbing, electrical systems, fire escapes, smoke detectors, garages— all increase the cost of doing business directly and complicate the project.

Regulations could add as much as 50 percent to the total cost of housing development. The problem is not regulation per se, but regulation that goes far beyond the need to protect the health and safety of residents. Housing styles that were once the centerpiece of urban and even suburban communities—multifamily dwellings built close together with little provision for parking—are not permitted in many cities. A 1990 HUD study found that most suburbs ban residential densities of more than ten units per acre—even though many desirable neighborhoods have densities of thirty-five units or more per acre. If zoning outlaws certain kinds of decent housing, the costs of providing housing inevitably rise.

Not all regulations produce higher costs. Standard design features can reduce architectural decisions and protect builders from liability. If a builder builds a cookie-cutter structure following government guidelines, he cannot be sued if those standards are not good enough. In that sense, regulations can be considered a kind of insurance policy.

Is there a different way to make sure that housing holds up to strict standards but that regulations do not become too costly?

One way is to make regulations more commonsensical, as New Jersey officials did with their building codes for rehabilitation of old structures. But libertarians have suggested a more radical approach. Robert W. Poole, Jr., for example, suggests following the French model, which leaves most building quality issues to a voluntary code of building standards:

> The key factor protecting the public is that French law imposes strict civil liability on builders for the quality of construction. For major structural systems (roofs, walls, foundations), the builder is liable for ten years; for secondary components like windows, he is liable for two years. The liability is "enforced" in the marketplace. To protect themselves against claims, builders purchase warranty insurance. The insurance companies, in turn, hire private inspection teams to inspect buildings under construction in France. Banks and other mortgage lenders generally will not make loans to builders who do not carry warranty insurance. [30]

Even though the French set standards for quality as stringent as the Americans, there is more room for innovation. The rules establish clear standards for health and safety—but they do not say how to reach those goals.

How about regulation of the labor market?

Many states and localities mandate that housing built with public money—including all affordable housing—pay construction workers at prevailing union wages. That increases the cost of construction. Unions also stretch out the length of jobs with work rules limiting the foreman's control of the work site, timing of phases of work, and even the size of paintbrushes (small brushes mean a longer time to cover a wall). Many state and municipal governments also place a premium on affirmative-action hiring. Especially in tight labor markets, hiring a high percentage of minorities takes extraordinary money and effort.

A survey of home building in the Philadelphia metropolitan area is instructive. During the 1990s, fewer than 160 homes were built in the city, while more than 8,500 homes were built in the suburbs. Union wage rates, which prevail in the city, drive costs up as much as 50 percent. A 2,000-square-foot home would cost $74,000 to build in the suburbs but $115,000 in the city. Nonunion firms stay away from the city because of the power of unions to intimidate job sites. "When I go to the city, the pressure to do it 100 percent union . . . it's incredible," one developer said. "You go in to pull a [building] permit at Licenses and Inspection, and the union shows up at the job site before you do to set up pickets," another said.[31]

The Demand Side: Improving People's Purchasing Power
Mortgage Tax Benefits

What is the most powerful policy shaping housing in the United States?

The deduction of mortgage interest and local property taxes from federal tax bills. That policy not only doubled the portion of Americans who owned their own homes—from one third to two thirds of all households—but also transformed the metropolitan landscape by helping millions of people move from the cities to the suburbs. It is a benefit worth upward of $80 billion a year, mostly to middle-class and affluent households who buy homes and itemize their taxes.

The idea behind the mortgage-interest and property-tax deductions is simple: by providing tax breaks for home buyers, the federal government encourages people to purchase housing. By reducing the overall tax bill for home owners, the federal government effectively reduces the real cost of buying a home. The mortgage tax deduction is especially beneficial in the early years of a home loan, when interest payments comprise the bulk of the monthly payments.

Tax experts call these benefits "tax expenditures" to suggest that they offer just as much benefit to recipients as a direct grant or in-kind service. In 1999, the mortgage interest deduction cost the federal government $53.7 billion in lost revenues and the property tax deduction cost the government $33.5 billion. Those two housing-related programs combined to cost the federal government more money than the largest social tax expenditures in the federal government, the retirement savings plans ($86.9 billion) and various health care plans ($72.6 billion).[32]

Obviously not everyone benefits from this tax break.

Tax breaks favor home owners over renters. The federal government does not offer subsidies to ordinary apartment dwellers. Some states, such as Massachusetts, offer some minimal tax breaks for renters, but these offer savings of only a few hundred dollars a year for most households.

The mortgage deduction gives the greatest advantages to the affluent. Well-to-do home owners get more in tax breaks than home owners with modest incomes. Fewer than half of all home owners take advantage of the tax breaks. Switching from a tax deduction to a tax credit could make the distribution of tax benefits fairer. Families whose taxes are too simple for them to itemize their tax returns would have a way to get benefits.

The Brookings Institution has explained the bias built into the tax break: "The incentives are most valuable to those with higher marginal tax rates, the income class that would find it easiest to buy homes in the absence of tax incentives. And the incentives for homeownership are much weaker for families in the lower tax brackets whose income levels also make homeownership more difficult."[33] For example, every $1,000 deduction is worth $396 to a taxpayer in the 39.6-percent tax bracket but just $150 to someone in the 15-percent tax bracket.

Someone with an income of $40,000 gains about $800 a year from the deduction, while someone making $100,000 gets $5,600, according to an analysis of the conservative Cato Institute. "The dirty little secret of the mortgage deduction is that it is the biggest rich man's subsidy."[34] Only 24 percent of all tax filers even claim the mortgage deduction; among families making less than $50,000, only 18 percent of filers take the write-off. (Of course, for many low-end home owners, itemizing might not make sense, since they can save as much money from a standard deduction.)

Are there other criticisms of the system by which Americans buy their homes?

Yes—that this system creates an inflationary spiral, requiring thousands of dollars more to own a home. By spreading out the payments for a home over a thirty-year period, the buyer is able to afford a more expensive home. If I had to buy a $100,000 home in fifteen years, I would have to pay $898 a month at a 7-percent interest rate; if I earned an income of $40,000, I might not be able to afford that home. But if I have thirty years to pay off the loan, I have to pay only $665 a month, which might be within my budget.

But with the longer-term loan that the mortgage-interest tax deduction encourages, the cost of the home increases in two ways. First, the longer-term loan encourages people to pay out much more in total interest payments. The fifteen-year loan would cost the borrower $61,788 in interest in addition to the $100,000 loan; the thirty-year loan would cost $139,510 in addition to the $100,000 loan. That means $78,000 in the bank's coffers instead of the buyer's.

Second, by giving the buyer more monthly purchasing power, the mortgage-interest benefit encourages sellers to set the cost of a unit of housing at a higher price. Remember the definition of inflation: too many dollars chasing too few goods. The mortgage-interest deduction puts more dollars into home buyers' hands, giving sellers a chance to increase the costs.

How do local real estate taxes affect home owners?

This is a mixed bargain. On the one hand, property owners often pay property taxes of many thousands of dollars a year. Property taxes are the primary tool for financing local government services, especially public education. Like it or not, that is how states and cities have chosen to operate. Some states limit their property taxes by raising significant revenues through sales taxes, income taxes, user fees and licenses, nuisance and "sin" taxes, and revenues from lotteries and other state-run businesses. But the property tax, at least historically, has the virtue of being a stable source of revenue and easy to collect. So it remains the core element of local finance.

Home owners can deduct their local property taxes from their federal tax bill. If I pay $1,000 in local property taxes, I can reduce my taxable income by $1,000. That could mean a tax savings of $350 or more. Granted, my tax break comes on a tax that non–property owners do not have to pay. But at the same time, as a property owner I am gaining equity and own an asset that can often be sold for extraordinary profits—especially if I own the property in an economically strong community and I keep it for a number of years. Given that the value of property comes from the value created by the larger community, it is a good deal.

So is there a chance for reform?

No, because too many people—that is, *too many people who vote*—benefit from the tax break. Attempts to put a cap on the total tax benefits have met stiff resistance in Congress. The Tax Reform Act of 1986 protected the deductions for all mortgages for first and second homes.

When millionaire publisher Steve Forbes ran for president in 1996 and 2000, he made the flat tax a centerpiece of his economic program. Forbes argued for a federal income tax so simple that it could be filled out on a postcard. One of the flat tax's political drawbacks was that it would eliminate the mortgage tax deduction. The National Association of Realtors said cutting the mortgage-interest tax break would reduce housing values by 10 percent. Flat-tax boosters say that the mortgage benefit would pale in comparison to the benefits for all taxpayers of a simple—and low—federal income tax. By providing a larger personal tax allowance—the first part of

the income that is not taxed—poor and working-class voters would benefit. But Forbes's proposal never had a chance.

Section 8 Vouchers

*Tax deductions offer an indirect but powerful way for the government to in-
fluence home ownership. Does the government provide indirect assistance to
renters as well?*

One of the most popular housing programs in Washington is the Section 8 voucher, begun by the Nixon Administration in 1974 as a creative
alternative to public housing. The program combines liberal and conservative policy strategies. The liberal strategy is to offer direct financial assistance in the billions of dollars to enable poor people keep their monthly
rents down to 30 percent of their income. The conservative strategy is to
give poor people the purchasing power they need to benefit from the marketplace. Today, Section 8 provides $13 billion in subsidies for 1.7 million
households—about one third of the total HUD budget.

Under Section 8, the government gives qualifying poor people certificates that they can take to any landlord who qualifies to rent property to
them. Anyone earning less than 80 percent of the area's median income
qualifies for assistance, but preference is given to the poorest of the poor:
three quarters of Section 8 vouchers must go to people making 30 percent
or less of the median income.[35] When a landlord agrees to rent to a Section
8 tenant, the money is deposited directly into the landlord's bank account.
The landlord receives 70 percent of the community's median rent, and the
tenant pays the rest.

Supporters of Section 8 say the program offers a clean, simple way to
target federal aid to those in the greatest need but also allows free-market
mechanisms to work. Tenants have the purchasing power to seek out the best
deal for themselves in whatever neighborhood best accommodates their employment and family needs. Bureaucracy is minimal; all that the government
needs to do is to check the backgrounds of participating landlords and tenants. Providing the poor with the purchasing power they need to find the
best possible housing is intended to scatter the poor into more affluent communities. A core value of Section 8 is to end the racial and income segregation of people. If poor people need the influences and networks of better-off
classes, Section 8 is one way to provide them this opportunity.

So does it work?

Supporters say "yes, but." Yes, it puts real purchasing power into the
hands of people who need it. Yes, it avoids the bureaucratic nightmares of
public housing. Yes, it offers the possibility of integrating neighborhoods.
But there are some serious problems with Section 8. To start, only about
one third of all poor families receive Section 8 subsidies. Whether you ben-

efit from this basic program depends on how desperately poor you are, when you get on a waiting list, and how well Congress funds the program in a given year. In some cities, many poor people were so desperate to get Section 8 certificates that they entered the homeless shelter system to jump to the top of waiting lists.

But there is another problem as well from the perspective of liberal supporters. Even though the Section 8 program originally provided funds to build new housing, it does not do so any more. The Reagan administration shifted Section 8 money from a mix of construction and vouchers to all vouchers. So even if poor renters enjoy effective demand in the form of direct subsidies to landlords, many communities lack the available units and landlords to house them. In cities such as New York, San Francisco, Boston, and even Chicago, Section 8 tenants are finding that fewer and fewer units of housing are available. In booming housing markets—in which home buyers and renters face an annual housing inflation rate of 20 percent or more a year—owners decide to sell or rent to more affluent people. Many apartment buildings, long the homes of poor renters, are sold off as condominiums. Many cities have lost their allocation of Section 8 funds because they simply did not have enough units to offer renters. Some 40 percent of vouchers in Cook County, Illinois, go unused because of an inadequate supply of Section 8 housing units.

In short, without an increase in supply, providing extra purchasing power will only serve to raise the rents of apartments even further. Many liberals have called for the federal government and state governments to resume their previous role as developers of affordable housing. Given the deterioration of much urban stock and the movement of jobs to the suburbs, only the public sector can provide the incentives necessary for a new wave of affordable-housing development.

Are conservatives and other critics of government housing programs happy with this market-oriented approach.

Some are—the Reagan and Bush administrations pushed federal housing policy toward the Section 8 voucher approach—but conservatives are increasingly skeptical of the program.

To begin, Section 8 is not really a market-based approach. Critics say the program has created a protected world where none of the players has to meet the usual rules of the marketplace. Because tenants do not have to work to earn their spending power, they are less attentive to the product that they are buying. Landlords complain that Section 8 housing is subject to damage by tenants who do not have to worry about losing a month's deposit or being held legally accountable for their actions. Perhaps even more insidious is the behavior of the landlords. They know that the government guarantees their 70 percent share of the market's median rent—they do not even need to go to the trouble of collecting monthly payments—so they make little effort to screen applicants or maintain their buildings. Even when tenants do not pay their 30 percent share of the rent, landlords still profit handsomely. They get 80 percent of the area's median rent, which is usually much higher than the median rent of neighborhoods where Section 8 housing is located.

In short, Section 8 involves an unspoken bargain between landlords and tenants. Each side agrees to ask little of each other so they can both benefit from public largesse.

One might think that vouchers allow poor people to find good shelter all over the metropolitan area. Isn't racial integration one of its major goals?

Yes, that is a goal, but Section 8 does not actually disperse tenants around the city. Because Section 8 tenants are the poorest of the poor, only landlords in struggling neighborhoods are willing to accept vouchers. Many landlords buy large numbers of dilapidated housing units in struggling poor and working class communities and then rent out exclusively to Section 8 tenants. So even though they are usually located in low-rise buildings in existing neighborhoods, Section 8 communities often take on the worst characteristics of old-style public housing. Democratic Senator Barbara Mikulski of Maryland, a former social worker, says vouchers are replacing "vertical ghettos with horizontal ones."[36]

The hope of integrated communities is mocked by these concentrations of extreme poor in once-thriving working-class communities, Section 8 critics say. The southern suburbs of Chicago now house 58 percent of all of Cook County Housing Authority's vouchers. The Philadelphia suburb of Riverdale is home to a disproportionate number of Section 8 tenants. Prince George's County, Maryland, just outside Washington, D.C., is home to most of that metropolitan area's Section 8 tenants. Poor people with high rates of unemployment and illegitimacy, with low education and high crime rates, undermine the character of the community. These communities are ripped apart by drugs, alcohol, late-night noise, vandalism, and lack of engagement in civic life.

Worse, these dysfunctions exacerbate racial and class tensions. "Voucher holders have the effect of confirming the worst stereotypes," said the director of a community group in a suburb south of Chicago. As is often the case, the most needy poor and minorities are thrown together with struggling blue-collar families. Black middle-class residents also feel resentment since their efforts to escape the worst ghettos are met with a removal of ghetto elements to their new neighborhoods. "You know what bothers me?" a South Philadelphia resident asked. "I've got two kids. You know why I don't have three? Because I can't afford it. And I see people with three or four kids and no father getting a subsidy to live in my neighborhood—which means I'm paying to help them. And complaining about it makes me a racist."[37]

Enlarging the Loan Pool for Home Buyers

Besides strengthening the foundation of the banking system, how can the federal government encourage banks to make loans for ordinary people to buy homes?

One of the great innovations of the New Deal period was the savings and loan (S&L) association. Of course, S&Ls had existed for years, but the Roosevelt administration cut a deal with S&Ls to make sure that they were financially viable and that they reinvested in their communities. Here's the deal: S&Ls could make loans only for housing and they had to follow simple, uniform formulae for assessing loan applications. In return for this limited range of action, S&Ls could offer their customers one percentage point more in savings interest than other financial institutions and they could maintain low cash reserves (4 percent of deposits). For years, S&Ls operated like the Bailey Savings and Loan depicted in the classic film *It's a Wonderful Life*. Ordinary people put their savings in the hometown S&L, which then reinvested in the community by making mortgage loans at reasonable rates. The system worked well into the 1980s, when reckless lending practices produced a $500 billion industry scandal.[38]

How does the "secondary" housing market increase the pool of money available to housing development and home buyers? And who are Fannie Mae, Ginnie Mae, and Freddie Mac?

The secondary mortgage market is essentially a system that encourages financial institutions larger than banks to buy mortgages from the banks. By buying loans from the banks, the financial institutions increase the banks' available cash reserves for making more home loans.

Here is how it works. When banks make loans, they face two dilemmas. First, they take the risk that borrowers might not be able to pay back the money. Second, every loan they make reduces their pool of funds available to make new loans. That is where government-chartered companies—known as "secondary-market" institutions—enter the picture. They buy the banks' loans, freeing the banks from worry about mortgage defaults and providing them with cash to make new loans. The secondary-market institutions, using financial tools granted them by the U.S. government, then sell the loans in a variety of securities and other investment packages to investors.

The federal government established these specialized organizations beginning in the New Deal years. The biggest secondary-market agency, nicknamed Fannie Mae, is the Federal National Mortgage Association or FNMA. Created in 1938, Fannie Mae bought about 200,000 mortgages in the years before World War II. After the war, Fannie Mae bought veterans' mortgages and became a much more significant part of the housing finance system. The U.S. government does not formally guarantee Fannie Mae's investments but would be expected to intervene on Fannie Mae's behalf in the event of a financial catastrophe.

Legislation in 1968 broke Fannie Mae into two pieces. The program that continued to be known by the name Fannie Mae became a for-profit corporation and continued to provide a secondary mortgage pool for the middle-class housing market. The new program was dubbed Ginnie Mae, which stands for Government National Mortgage Association or GNMA. Ginnie Mae created a pool of money to encourage high-risk, low-income housing ventures. Ginnie Mae supports loans made by the Federal Housing Authority and the Veterans Administration (now the Department of Veterans Affairs). Ginnie Mae's mortgage-backed securities are backed by the full faith and credit of the U.S. government. That guarantee provides a stable environment for this sector of the housing market.

Freddie Mac—the Federal Home Loan Mortgage Corporation (FHLMC)—was established in 1970 to set up a pool of conventional and insured mortgages from the system of S&L institutions. Freddie Mac was designed to entice investors back to the home lending industry after investors had drifted away in the late 1960s. Freddie Mac purchases both conventional and insured loans from banks and other financial institutions. In the 1970s, in a search for even broader markets for these loans, Freddie Mac went to international capital markets. The federal government does not guarantee Freddie Mac's activities, but experts expect that the government would protect all of its investments in the event of a financial collapse.

These quasi-public corporations offered a way to make the housing market more fluid. These corporations prevented banks and other lending institutions from getting stuck with long-term loans, which would clog their ability to invest in new opportunities. With entities willing to buy their loans, the financial institutions had more money available to make new loans. Programs such as Ginnie Mae, with indirect subsidies to low-income housing, offered enticements for banks to make loans that ordinarily might not have been very attractive otherwise.

The secondary-mortgage institutions also offer home buyers a number of programs that reduce down payments, offer home-buying training, and provide other assistance. Fannie Mae, for example, backs bank loans for first-time home buyers that require only 3 percent down payments—a significant benefit, considering that the usual down payment is 10 percent.

In 1995, the United States had $3.9 trillion in outstanding (or unpaid) residential mortgages. The Big Three secondary-market institutions—Fannie Mae, Freddie Mac, and Ginnie Mae—held almost half (46 percent) of that amount. In that year, the three institutions purchased 41 percent of the year's mortgage originations.[39] It is hard to imagine the banks operating as reliably and fairly in the United States without Fannie's, Freddie's, and Ginnie's efforts. They are the ultimate support system for mortgage lending in the United States, particularly in the single-family home market.

What besides money enables the secondary mortgage market to give banks and mortgage companies stability?

Starting in 1973, Fannie Mae and Freddie Mac have used standard forms and processes for deciding whether to buy banks' loans. That makes it easy for the banks to understand what lending criteria to use when deciding whether to make loans to home buyers. When everyone knows what they have to do, business is easier to conduct. Over the years, the secondary institutions have also gathered data that demonstrate the soundness of loans to all kinds of home buyers and housing types. That is a major service, since banks had often claimed—wrongly in many cases—that poor and working class families were too risky to offer home loans.

Fannie Mae and the others have been criticized over the years for underinvesting in and inadequately promoting the multifamily housing development that is especially important to cities. While virtually all single-family home mortgages are absorbed by the secondary market, just over 40 percent of multifamily mortgages are. In short, Fannie, Ginnie, and Freddie contribute more to middle-class suburbanites than they do to working-class urbanites. "The multifamily secondary mortgage market is in the early stages of development," two housing experts note. "It could be argued that today there is more of a rationale for government sponsorship of Fannie Mae and Freddie Mac to intervene in the multifamily mortgage market than in the single-family market. In many ways, the goals of creating standards and an information base have already been achieved in the single-family market."[40] In recent years, Fannie, Ginnie, and Freddie have developed new programs to encourage home buying in urban areas, but the legacy of past practices is heavy on the cities.

How does the secondary mortgage market affect the swings of the market?

By providing slack to the mortgage lending system, Fannie and the others help to smooth over the rough patches that are inevitable in a market economy. When the rest of the economy goes through periodic busts, the housing market is assured of the funds it needs to remain stable. In California in 1996, when the state's economy was in its worst condition since the Great Depression, home loans did not suffer the way the rest of the economy did. That year, Fannie Mae had 1.3 million loans in the state. Just 10,000 of them—less than one hundredth of 1 percent—were foreclosed. Imagine the United States having that kind of cushion during the Great Depression.[41]

Rent Control

There has been a lot of discussion of rent control as a way to make housing more affordable in expensive cities such as New York, San Francisco, and Boston. How common is rent control? How well does it work?

Rent control is an attempt to keep down the costs of rental housing by restricting what a landlord can charge to tenants. Most states and cities do not control rents on privately owned units, but New York, San Francisco, and Boston have all controlled rents in the past. In the 1980s, as much as half of California's urban rental market was covered by rent-control laws. In the middle 1980s, some two hundred cities that were home to 20 percent of the nation's population had some form of rent control.[42]

Rent control operates much as price controls operated during World War II and, indeed, was adopted in scores of cities during the war to hold down the cost of living for ordinary people so that resources could be allocated to the war effort. Government agencies established standards and procedures for raising rents, usually to protect landlords from rising energy and maintenance costs. Cities adopted different standards for rent control. While some established rigid systems of rent control, others adopted looser systems of rent "stabilization" that allowed landlords substantial increases in rent when tenants left the building or when maintenance and repair costs demanded substantial new investments. Some cities limited rent-control protections to units occupied by poor, elderly, or disabled tenants.

The signal consequence of rent control is the creation of separate submarkets. Under the price-controlled market, prices are kept artificially low to the short-term benefit of renters. The long-term consequences of controls might not be so positive if landlords do not maintain their units or invest in long-term capital improvements. In the rent-controlled submarket, "shadow" markets also develop—that is, systems of exchange and barter outside the common marketplace. Occupiers of controlled units pass on units to friends and family, even when those people might not otherwise qualify for rent control. When the costs of mortgages, taxes, utilities, and upkeep exceed revenues, the unit is withdrawn from the marketplace.[43] The market-rate submarket of the housing system is also affected by rent control. Because the overall number of market-rate units is smaller than it otherwise might be, the classic conditions for price inflation result—too many buyers seeking too few goods. This situation sometimes leads landlords to gouge renters. In a market with rent control, therefore, two sets of price distortions operate side by side: one submarket with artificially low rents, the other with artificially high rents.

In cities with strong rent control laws, vacancy rates are lower than in market-oriented housing systems. Low vacancy rates produce higher costs, since too many people are chasing too few goods—the standard definition of inflation. Rent-control cities such as New York and San Francisco typically have vacancy rates of around 1 or 2 percent, while non–rent-control cities such as Chicago and Phoenix have vacancy rates of 5 to 7 percent. Most housing experts consider a vacancy rate of 5 or 6 to be ideal, since it provides enough slack for people to move when they desire and also offers a reasonable choice of units when renters and buyers enter the market.

Ironically, rent-controlled apartments often benefit middle-class and professional renters more than poor people. The economists Edward Glaeser and Erzo F. P. Luttmer have found significant misallocation of units under rent control as people in controlled units gain access to more space than they need at lower rates than their counterparts in noncontrolled units. Glaeser and Luttmer estimate the misallocation of space to be worth $500 million or more a year in New York City alone.[44] Even when rent-controlled units are originally set aside for households of modest means, they often make their way through shadow markets into the hands of people who are better off. People who once had low incomes—such as university students—make healthy wages later on but can keep the rent-controlled unit. Kenneth Reeves, the onetime mayor of Cambridge, Massachusetts, originally obtained a controlled unit as a student but kept it for years, even though his income increased substantially over the years. Educated people like Reeves tend to have more stable professional and family lives and thicker networks of friends and family to help them obtain benefits such as rent control. Once they get such a benefit, they keep it.[45]

Rent control is often difficult to reform because of the power of tenants in local elections. Because they organize to protect their direct stake in rent control—and because rent-control opponents suffer only indirectly—public officials find it difficult to change rent control laws. In New York, 1.1 million of 1.7 million renters benefit from rent control—a powerful constituency. Brave words about reform from Mayors Rudolph Giuliani and Governor George Pataki have not substantially altered the law. It took a statewide referendum in Massachusetts in 1994 to end rent control in Boston, Cambridge, and Somerville; while residents of those three localities were voting to keep rent control, the rest of the state voted to end it.

The Supply Side: Creating More Units
Public Housing

At certain times in American history—such as at the time of Franklin Roosevelt's jobs programs—the government took a direct approach to meeting the needs of the people. Is public housing a good example of government acting directly to meet the needs of the nation's "underhoused" population?

Not really. The history of public housing in the United States is as controversial and complex as any urban policy program in modern American history. Public housing reflects the ambivalence of Americans toward class and race as well as a deep skepticism about the purpose of government at all levels. It also reveals the mighty power of the real-estate lobby at all levels of government and the changing face of the American metropolis.

Public housing has provided decent housing for millions of people. The stock of public housing is high in several large cities but overall accounts for just 1.5 percent of the total housing stock. Nationwide, 1.3 million public housing units in 11,000 projects in 3,300 cities house 4 million people. Over a thirty-year period, HUD spent $440 billion on public housing—about $14 billion a year nationwide.[46]

The starkest fact about public housing for friends and foes alike is that it was transformed from a broad-based to a narrow-based program. Originally, public housing was designed to serve as a gateway to private housing for anyone in temporary need—the working class, poor people, senior citizens, and people suffering short-term need because of a family crisis or loss of job. Over the years, however, public housing has come to serve primarily the poor and the elderly. Poor people, particularly minorities, comprise almost 75 percent of the public-housing population. The median income of public-housing families is in fact about $6,500 (the nation's median income is about $35,000). Elderly people comprise more than 25 percent of the public-housing population.

But public housing has such a negative image. How come?

Over the years, public housing complexes came to be seen as unsafe, unsanitary, broken-down places that provided little access to good education or jobs. The names of some of the most notorious housing projects—Robert Taylor Homes and Cabrini Green in Chicago, Pruitt-Igoe in St. Louis, Desire in New Orleans, Schuylkill Falls in Philadelphia, Harbor Point and Mission Main in Boston—came to symbolize the worst urban conditions in America, in the words of one critic, "colorless, bleak, high, and revolting."[47] These buildings, often located in isolated sections of the city, are ravaged by crime, disease, and poverty. Gang warfare and drugs threaten children's lives. The buildings themselves are in a constant state of disrepair; a 1998 study estimated the cost of repairing the nation's public housing structures to be $25 billion.[48] Elevators are broken and stairwells are places of drugs and rape. Plumbing and electrical systems regularly fail. Broken windows and walls go months without repairs. Drug dealers occupy playgrounds, leaving no place for children to play. Supermarkets and other retailers refuse to set up shop in these areas. Tawdry outlets for check cashing, lottery sales and offtrack betting, and liquor dot the landscape.

As influential as the high-rises have been in many cities, and as vivid as the high-rises are in the public mind, most public housing is actually located in two- and three-story buildings. More than half of all buildings have fewer than two hundred units and 75 percent are in buildings with four or fewer stories. One study found that only 7 percent of all projects, with 15 percent of all tenants, could be designated "troubled."[49]

What were the public housing planners thinking?

The high-rise public-housing complexes resulted from utopian planning, racial and class segregation, highways and other large-scale development, and real-estate speculators.

Inspired by the French planner Corbusier, many public-housing planners designed high-rise buildings surrounded by open spaces but isolated from the standard street grid. The isolation of the projects was partly a matter of design, but even more it stemmed from real-estate values and speculation. Acquiring a lot of land in choice sections of the city was out of the question because private developers wanted that property. As the projects became dominated by the elderly and poor, the NIMBY phenomenon took over—middle-class neighborhoods cried "Not in my back yard" in response to proposals to build public housing units.

What accounts for the deficiency of public housing's buildings themselves?

From the very beginning, public housing has suffered from inferior design and materials. The National Association of Real Estate Boards lobbied Congress to place severe restrictions on the number and quality of public housing units. Other major lobbies, such as the U.S. Savings and Loan League and the National Association of Home Builders, joined forces to restrict the movement for public housing. At the start of the Cold War these groups tarred public housing as a "socialist" and "subversive" movement that would lead down a "slippery slope" to collectivization. By the time the Housing Act of 1949 was passed, it included provisions to prevent "extravagance and unnecessary" amenities that could put public housing into competition with the private sector. The Act pointedly failed to include provisions for racial and income integration.

The design and construction of public-housing units turned out even worse than the low design standards mandated by the federal legislation.

Because of bureaucratic incompetence, profiteering by contractors, delays from labor strife and political feuds, and spiraling construction costs, authorities did not have the money they needed to fulfill even the basic building plans. Typical was the experience of the Methunion Manor complex in Boston. A report of the Boston Redevelopment Authority found a number of structural problems:

> Concrete foundations were "in poor shape and present a bad aesthetic appearance with poor patchwork, non-matching mortar colors, very rough surfaces from worn-out or gouged forms." Stairs and landings had a reverse pitch, so they were "puddling badly and will create hazardous conditions during cold weather." Roofs leaked and created "stains and dampness on ceilings." Light poles in the parking lot were "very wobbly and globes are not set securely." Doors warped and sprung from their tracks.[50]

Local control of public housing authorities usually doomed the projects to the most isolated and least desirable parts of town. Public-housing authorities regularly interacted with real-estate interests—indeed, developers often served on authority boards—and insisted that the projects not take up valuable property that could realize greater rents and profits with private ventures.

But at least public housing increased the overall supply of housing, didn't it?

No. The Housing Act of 1937, which allowed slum clearance as part of urban housing and revitalization efforts, required communities with public housing to provide an "equivalent elimination" of existing substandard housing units so that the overall supply of housing did not increase. The housing lobby had a simple goal here: to restrict the supply of its product through the force of law so that prices did not become depressed. The equivalent-elimination provision proved a resounding success for the real-estate industry. Overall, urban renewal and public housing produced a major loss in the number of units on the market.

What was urban renewal and how did it fit into the development of public housing?

Under the Housing Act of 1949, Congress called for: "a decent home and suitable living environment for every American family." Under Title I of the Act, local authorities were given the power to clear "blighted" land for the construction of new, safer, and more sanitary housing. Urban renewal was ostensibly intended to end the "blight" in poor inner-city neighborhoods by ripping down dilapidated buildings where the poor lived and replacing them with "decent, safe, and sanitary" housing.

Often depicted as a program to improve the lot of the poor, it was quickly used to take prime territory in the city center for businesses and developers. The Act authorized 810,000 units of new housing to replace the destroyed units. But in the first dozen years of its operation, urban renewal caused the tearing down of 126,000 units of housing and replaced them with only 28,000 units. Less than one fifth of all the families and individuals evicted from their units got replacement housing, which usually cost more than the displaced families could afford. About two thirds of the displaced residents were black. Most of them simply moved to other slums rather than gaining the better housing that had been promised them.[51]

Urban renewal destroyed 177,000 homes for families and 66,000 homes for singles; only about one quarter of those units were replaced by new housing, and many of those were beyond the financial reach of the previous tenants.[52]

Would public housing work better if it included a wider range of groups?

That's the experience of public housing in European countries and the argument of poverty experts like William Julius Wilson.[53] Only when poor people are integrated into the life of the larger community will they develop the social networks, role models, and strategies to build better lives for themselves. Federal laws have historically prevented much mixing. The Housing Act of 1949 set public-housing rents at 20 percent lower than the lowest market rents in the area. The Act also allowed local housing authorities to evict tenants with middle-class incomes to make room for poor people. The effect is to restrict housing to the poor, stigmatize the projects, and undermine support for public involvement in housing provision.

The federal HOPE 6 program—which aims to destroy bad housing and disperse public-housing tenants throughout the city—builds on this thinking. Congress passed the legislation in 1992 to encourage development of mixed-use developments, blending of different income levels, and strategies to reduce the physical isolation of public-housing developments. The initiative, which was originally restricted to the nation's forty most populous cities, is now open to all local public-housing authorities.

Only in recent years, with the HOPE 6 program's destruction of many complexes to make way for scattered-site, mixed-income housing, have housing authorities begun to create communities with a healthy mix of incomes and races. HOPE 6 housing must include residents with a range of incomes and is built in clusters of low-rise garden-style apartments. Public-housing officials have, for the most part, embraced the new approach. "If you research from the old days, we were always on the wrong side of the tracks—too dense, too tall, always harboring the poorest of the poor—and we generally had a hard time sustaining how the public housing program should be run," said an official with the New York City Housing Authority.[54] Still, not all cities embrace HOPE 6. Saint Paul, which serves 20,000 residents in its public housing complexes, has made a conscious decision to make its units available only to poor households.

Suppose public housing was run by private interests or tenants themselves. Would the incentives of private ownership improve the projects' management?
In many areas of public policy, from prisons to education, private contractors have been hired to provide services that are traditionally the domain of government. The idea is simple. Private firms—operating with profit motives, modern management techniques, insulation from political intrigue, and greater technical proficiency—can produce better public services than government agencies can. Private firms quite simply have the incentive to look for better ways to do their job.

Under Section 221(d)3 of the Housing Act of 1961, the government offered below-market interest rates and subsidies to induce private and nonprofit entrepreneurs to build and operate affordable housing. As long as the building was being financed by public money, the owners were obligated to provide units at below-market rents to qualifying renters. But over the years, as owners have paid off their mortgages, they have converted thousands of units to market-rate rents—cutting off many poor people from affordable housing. Federal and state authorities have offered new subsidies to owners to keep the units affordable, but the negotiations for affordability can be long and painstaking.

The record of private construction and management of public housing is mixed. Private firms have been major players in the construction and management of public housing. But designation of contractors can be a political process, with the best-connected rather than the best-qualified getting the job. More important, with a steady stream of public subsidies and a vulnerable set of clients, many private operators do not push themselves to provide good products. Also, many private operators have a direct stake in public housing's inferiority to private housing.

Nonprofit Housing Development

So the great innovations of American cities—public housing, rent control, tenement housing—have been abandoned in recent years. What is a city to do to provide housing at affordable rents to poor people?
The nonprofit sector has become the biggest single producer of affordable housing in the United States. Community development corporations—popularly known as CDCs—have combined the aggressiveness of private-sector developers with the public mission of the government to build and renovate 60,000 units of housing a year. By developing grassroots coalitions, strong ties with banks and local businesses, and working

relationships with state and local officials, CDCs have increased their annual output of housing units from about 20,000 annually in 1988 to around 60,000 in 1997. CDCs are still spread unevenly across the United States—the movement is centered in the nation's big cities but has a less robust presence in small cities and emerging metropolitan areas—but have developed an approach that is emulated by new communities all the time.

How do CDCs operate?

CDCs are essentially deal-makers with an orientation toward poor and working-class urban neighborhoods. CDCs acquire land, coordinate community planning processes, build housing, and maintain a portfolio of housing developments.

At times, CDC housing development efforts seem as complicated as a Donald Trump project. The deals start with land acquisition. CDCs depend on government agencies for much of their land acquisition—and in most states and localities, getting land can be a long and bureaucratic process involving complex negotiations over the design of the housing development. Other nonprofit organizations—rival CDCs, health clinics, parks and gardens advocates—sometimes compete for the right to use the property. Often, property requires expensive cleanup of hazardous wastes, which in turn requires getting in line for limited public funds. Many CDCs conduct protracted community processes, hosting many public meetings to create a vision for the neighborhood.

The biggest challenge for the CDC is raising the money for a project. CDCs put together complicated financial deals involving all levels of government, banks, private investors and donors, and their own funds. The deals often take years to complete. Even when they are complete, CDCs sometimes face angry resistance from neighbors who feel threatened by the location of affordable housing in their midst. Then there is the zoning process. Even when a lot is zoned as residential, CDCs must sometimes justify their projects to skeptical officials on planning and redevelopment boards. At each step in the process, the deal can fall apart.

How does it all come together?

A lot depends on the individuals in the CDCs. Many CDCs are known throughout the community for their strong leaders. But the work of CDCs goes beyond the visible leaders. CDCs have trained a whole generation of activists in the technical and political skills necessary to make a deal work. In many states, CDCs have formed associations to provide training as well as lobbying at City Hall or Capitol Hill. Federal Reserve Bank Governor Lawrence H. Meyer has noted the sophistication of CDCs: "There has been an explosive growth in the diversity and sophistication of community development corporations. . . . Today, there is a quite identifiable community development industry, complete with a diverse set of production companies, financial intermediaries, and other support mechanisms."[55]

This sophistication extends to national support organizations like the Local Initiative Support Corporation (LISC), the Enterprise Foundation, and the National Community Development Organization. These organizations have invested billions of dollars in housing development; LISC helped produce 100,000 housing units, and Enterprise almost as much.[56] As important as providing seed money, these intermediaries also created a counterweight to old-style patronage politics in cities. Paul Grogan, the former director of LISC, says LISC refused to deal with mayors who demanded control over funds and hiring. LISC, Grogan says, helped "to challenge the prevailing power structure without acrimony and confrontation, and then [delivered] dramatic results."[57]

How do CDCs work with government agencies?

As partners. As many state and local agencies suffered staff cutbacks in the 1980s and 1990s, they were often delighted to get any help they could dealing with neighborhood planning and housing issues. They also appreciate CDCs' ability to deal with a variety of neighborhood issues. In many ways, local government has the best of both worlds with CDCs. On the one hand, by working with CDCs, public officials can get the assistance they need to mobilize their communities. On the other hand, public officials can always back off CDC plans they do not like. CDC plans can, in essence, serve as trial balloons. Officials can keep a distance from CDC plans that produce neighborhood opposition and embrace those that rally the community.

Sometimes, CDCs find themselves at odds with local officials and their own communities. When local officials and CDCs have opposing visions of how to develop vacant parcels, a struggle often results. One example will illustrate the point. In 1999 in Boston, a CDC called Urban Edge floated the idea of developing a major retail district near a transit area called Jackson Square. Urban Edge had been organizing in the area for decades, building and rehabbing housing and retail businesses in long-neglected blocks in the neighborhoods of Roxbury and Jamaica Plain. During community meetings, residents expressed a desire to attract more retailers to the area. When the Kmart retail chain contacted Urban Edge, the CDC promoted the idea. But residents and city officials rebelled, arguing that such a "big box" store—not to mention an adjoining parking garage—did not make sense in a densely populated area close to a major rapid transit station. Urban Edge persisted, opponents coalesced behind a rival CDC, and the city's redevelopment authority convened a planning process for the whole area.

How do CDCs make deals with businesses?

The most important partner for CDCs is the local bank. The Community Reinvestment Act (CRA) of 1977 requires banks to make loans to residents and businesses in inner-city communities. The idea behind the CRA is that banks should lend to the same people who make deposits; for years, inner-city neighborhoods put their money in local banks but were unable to get loans for home buying or small businesses. Over the years, the CRA has evolved into a major engine of inner-city investment. The impact of the CRA is undeniable. Total lending to inner-city neighborhoods increased from $3 billion annually in 1977 to $43 billion just twenty years later.[57]

Since the passage of the CRA, bank presidents have established community-banking divisions to provide special attention to the needs of inner-city communities. When banks announce plans to merge—a frequent occurrence in the 1990s—CDCs and other housing activists scramble to negotiate set-asides of hundreds of millions of dollars for local investment as the banks sought government approval for their combinations. Under the CRA, banks became a major funder of creative housing-development schemes, not to mention the CDC operations themselves.

Besides an occasional conflict with other actors—inevitable in the context of big-city politics—do CDCs have any major detractors?

Some people think that their housing developments cost too much. In Boston, for example, affordable-housing construction by CDCs sometimes costs twice as much as it does by private and even other nonprofit organizations. CDC officials quote a per-square-foot construction cost of $170 to $200. That translates into $170,000 to $200,000 for an apartment with two bedrooms and one bathroom—not including the cost of the land, which is usually supplied at minimal cost by the city government. Meanwhile, comparable apartments cost around $85,000 to build. The reason, CDC supporters say, is simple. Because it requires such time and skill to put together the financing and rally the public support for housing deals, the cost is higher than it would be for a simple deal.

Housing developers call the administrative expenses "soft costs." Soft costs include the fees for attorneys, accountants, and consultants. A project's soft costs also include community organizing, political lobbying, and the full range of CDC staff costs. CDC housing deals also build maintenance expenses into their cost structure. Maintenance expenses alone can add $60,000 or more to the cost of financing—per unit—which is amortized over the thirty-year term of a loan. Many critics say these costs are too high and undermine the public commitment for housing.

Other critics are concerned about the long-term implications of CDCs taking on quasi-governmental roles in the neighborhoods. By coordinating the development of housing and the delivery of a wide range of social services, CDCs become, in essence, minigovernments. But CDCs do not have to be held accountable in elections or any other forum. If they can keep developing projects and nurture their partnerships with key government bureaucrats, they can avoid having to answer for their projects. On the other hand, they get projects done in neighborhoods where others have not dared to venture, and if they cannot get along with banks or public agencies, they will fail. Maybe that's enough accountability for any community enterprise.

Finally, the ability of CDCs to deliver housing and economic development projects is limited by their access to financial resources from the state and local governments, foundations, banks, and other sources. Putting together deals is hard work, and many CDCs simply lack a basic knowledge of state tax laws, federal grant programs, and the procedures of banks and secondary mortgage institutions.

The Missing Pieces: Rehabilitation and Preservation

Does the government encourage rehabilitation of dilapidated housing units?
Even though Title I of the Housing Act of 1934 authorizes federal outlays for rehabbing existing properties, the program has never received significant funding. In recent years, the federal government has allotted about $100 million for rehabilitation, compared with around $80 billion a year for mortgage tax breaks and $30 billion for other housing programs.

The housing lobby has never been enthusiastic about federal outlays for rehabilitation. Profits are greater and programs are easier to manage for new home building. Production of new homes also creates a bigger payoff for the industries closely related to suburban residential development—highways, shopping malls, industrial parks, and various consumer goods.

In the last generation, the historic preservation movement has brought the importance of rehabbing to the forefront of discussions of housing and urban redevelopment. A number of localities, from New Orleans to Pittsburgh, have established incentives for restoring old buildings in old neighborhoods. Operation Comeback, a New Orleans program, identified seven neighborhoods with strong housing stock in need of rehabilitation and provided training and financing for people willing to invest in the areas. The program created a vehicle for a collective response to the deterioration of housing stock. Such a collective approach assures urban pioneers that they will not be alone when they invest in improving a neighborhood. No federal program provides such a coherent approach to rehabilitation of the nation's strong but deteriorating stock of old brownstones, row houses, warehouses, and industrial buildings.

The Tragedy of Homelessness

How many people are homeless in America?

Counts of the homeless in the United States range from the Urban Institute's estimate of 600,000 on any given day to homeless advocates' claim of 3 million.[59]

Homelessness usually follows a period when people without enough resources to provide for their own shelter "double up" with friends and relatives. More than three fourths of homeless people stayed with someone else at some point, and more than one third got help paying their rent before they ended up on the streets. These facts run counter to the widespread theory that homeless people do not have any social support network. The problem is that the homeless wear out their welcome after a while, and the network begins to fray. It is clear that some kind of public commitment to addressing the homeless problem—subsidized units, as well as social services—is needed to protect families and friends from getting overwhelmed.

What explains the epidemic of homelessness during the boom years of the 1980s and 1990s?

Homelessness existed long before the 1980s. But a convergence of factors increased both the number and visibility of homeless people in America. Homelessness is simultaneously a problem of housing supply and control, arson, race, employment, intense poverty, segregation, drugs and alcoholism, AIDS, mental health, domestic violence, social welfare cutbacks, economic restructuring, decay of the traditional nuclear family, and health care access.

The most immediate cause for the rise in homelessness in American cities was the process of "gentrification" in big cities. The single-room occupancy (SRO) hotels that served as home for many low-income people closed to make room for middle-class and affluent apartment buildings, retail and office complexes, workout gyms and other recreation spaces, and other more lucrative uses. The national supply of SRO hotels declined by more than half in the last generation. Some 1.2 million SRO units have been eliminated nationwide since 1970, mostly to convert into higher-priced housing units in gentrified neighborhoods.[60] Depending on the estimate of the homeless population, those lost SROs might have provided enough space to house most of the homeless population.

At the same time, the federal government cut programs for building and supporting low-income housing. The Reagan administration cut the budget of the Department of Housing and Urban Development by two thirds, from $33 billion to $11 billion, in just a few years. State and local governments attempted to take on some of the federal programs but struggled to deal with their own budget troubles.

But most homeless people do not simply lack shelter. Studies show that 30 to 70 percent of homeless people have some kind of psychological disorder. President John F. Kennedy signed the Mental Retardation Facilities and Community Mental Centers Construction Act in 1963 to end the warehousing of the mentally ill in nightmarish asylums. The idea was to offer the mentally ill closely monitored drug treatment and more human shelter in "halfway houses" as a way to integrate them into the community. By 1981, the population of mental hospitals had declined from 505,000 to 125,000.[61] The problem is that halfway houses and group homes have not picked up the slack as Kennedy and other reformers had hoped they would. Families have cared for two thirds of the deinstitutionalized patients, but they do not get the kind of financial and professional support necessary to address the severe challenges of mental illness.

Drug and alcohol addiction produces less dramatic but more insidious effects. The rate of alcoholism among homeless people is estimated to be as high as 70 percent in men and 40 percent in women; psychiatrists in Baltimore noted disorders related to drug abuse in 22 percent of men and 17 percent of women. The invention of crack cocaine in the 1980s contributed to homelessness. Crack's quick and cheap high dramatically expanded the drug culture of the inner city.

Deadly diseases such as AIDS also contribute to homelessness by incapacitating their victims and undermining their financial independence. One study found that 17 percent of all people with AIDS were homeless. AIDS taxes a person's medical and social support structure more severely than other diseases. The homeless AIDS victims were not all gay men. Intravenous drug users and prostitutes comprised a significant share of homeless people.

Despite widespread images of homelessness that suggest extreme dereliction, many working people experience homelessness. Nationwide, 44 percent of homeless people have had some employment in the previous year, according to data of U.S. Department of Housing and Urban Development.[62] Half of the residents surveyed at homeless shelters in Virginia in 1997 had had a job in the previous year. In Atlanta, the percentage was as high as 37 percent. A Los Angeles homeless activist reported that he had met homeless people who worked as telemarketers, nursing assistants, home care and child care providers, data-entry clerks and computer repair technicians.[63]

What is the federal government's strategy to address homelessness?

Right now, the federal government and most states and cities treat homelessness as an emergency. The federal McKinney Act and many local initiatives provide congregate or barracks-style shelters with hundreds of beds that offer a place to sleep but not much more. The barracks shelters are usually open from seven o'clock at night until seven the next morning. The purpose is to prevent homeless people from freezing and suffering from exposure and sometimes to provide a shower and snack.

Conditions at the barracks can be dangerous. Violence including rape, rampant drug use, disease, and noise prevent many guests from getting a good night sleep. In some cities, police report that homeless people prefer to sleep outside on grates rather than sleep in a shelter. Barracks offer the first shelter of choice for policy-makers because they seem cheap to build and operate. Because of the need to hire security officers to maintain order, however, these shelters can be expensive in the long run. New York barracks beds cost the city some $1,500 a month in 1991.[64] These shelters do nothing to address the severe problems of their overnight residents, and they release those residents into the community during the day. In times of harsh weather, the day presents dangers almost as severe as the night.

Christopher Jencks argues that improvements in the public shelter system may actually contribute to homelessness by providing a "safety net" for vulnerable people. About 2 million single-parent families live in someone else's home. The existence of shelters makes the primary dwellers of these homes more comfortable turning away people with housing problems. Staying at a shelter also improves the chances of getting federal housing assistance.[65]

The best approach to homelessness would be to treat it as a syndrome—a collection of different maladies—and to provide a wide range of services to address the particular problems faced by individuals and families without homes. A good start would be a comprehensive network of transitional and family shelters that stay open twenty-four hours a day and offer several months of alcohol and drug treatment, job training, child care, and counseling. Family shelters are an essential part of the solution. Private units in hotels and small apartment buildings, including SROs, are also important. Unfortunately, only a small fraction of the homeless population has reliable access to the full range of shelters and services needed to solve the problem.

The Future of Housing Policy

What is the future of urban housing policy in America?

It seems there are two roads to travel: the market road and the social production road.

Under the market road, local governments will remove barriers to housing development so that private developers are encouraged to produce new or rehabilitated housing for people of all income levels. Free-marketeers say that this approach not only can work, but already has. The tenement buildings of New York, Boston, Chicago, and other major cities at the turn of the nineteenth century provided housing for even the poorest of the poor without subsidies from government. When the most unfortunate people could not get access to housing—because they were disabled or otherwise incapable of caring for themselves—settlement houses took them in.

Lest we wince at the images of unsanitary and overcrowded buildings that forced people to live in inhuman conditions, it is important to state that government has an important role to play in insuring basic standards for all housing. But the government also has to allow the construction of rooming houses, reduce the required amenities for houses and apartment buildings, and otherwise get out of the way of housing developers. If there is a demand, free-marketeers say, there will be a supply.

What is the social production approach?

It is the slow, painstaking process of putting together affordable housing deals with grassroots participation. It is the model of rebuilding the city, block by block. It requires the involvement of dozens of partners—CDCs, banks, secondary-mortgage institutions, state and city agencies, universities, churches, and anyone else with an interest in low-income housing.

Because that is the model that seems to be taking hold in America's cities, it is worth describing in some detail.

How does it work?

Ultimately, all kinds of community-based housing development follow a simple formula. Stanley Lowe, a longtime housing activist and now the executive director of the Pittsburgh Housing Authority, outlines the essential strategy for housing activists everywhere.

To begin, Lowe says, the community's goal should be housing for all that meets high standards for construction and design. Traditionally, public-housing projects have had a bland appearance and a poor quality of construction that brands them as inferior. Public housing warehouses poor people in settings that isolate them from essential social networks such as business districts, schools, parks and playgrounds, and transit. The stigma of public housing is overwhelming. That has to stop, Lowe says. His goal as housing director is simple: "From the outside you're not going to be able to distinguish public housing from private houses."[66] The goal should be housing that you can be proud of, not just housing that provides basic shelter. The question is how to achieve this.

To achieve decent housing, activists need to develop a strategy that puts pressure on both the public and the private sectors. The public sector needs to invest money in affordable housing and remove regulatory barriers to housing construction and rehabilitation. The private sector needs to be prodded to commit to low- and middle-income housing, which is less lucrative than luxury housing in the short term but important for the strength of city and regional housing markets in the long term. Banks need to provide the up-front capital to make housing development possible.

Activists often begin affordable housing campaigns with campaigns to get banks to commit to make loans to poor and working-class families. Even in the absence of redlining, banks are often reluctant to take risks in poor neighborhoods because the politics and social problems in those areas are difficult to navigate. But banks have both a financial and a moral imperative to invest in the inner city. Banks in low-income neighborhoods often hold greater deposits than local banks in middle-class neighborhoods. The reason is simple: poor and working-class people are protecting themselves against crises that they have learned to expect, while middle-class and affluent families have diverse opportunities to invest their money elsewhere. Using the Community Reinvestment Act of 1977, housing activists can pressure banks to make loans to creditworthy people in low-income areas.

When banks are reluctant to make loans to people in poor neighborhoods, the only effective response is collective action. Before becoming housing director, Lowe headed a coalition of eighteen neighborhood organizations called the Pittsburgh Community Reinvestment Group. At one point, when bankers brushed off activists' requests for loans, the coalition threatened to withdraw $25 million in deposits. The bank responded. The coalition's ace card is its ability to mobilize its constituents whenever one of its member organizations meets resistance to reasonable requests for loans.

But before the coalition exercises its muscle, it is aware that it must present a comprehensive plan that banks cannot in good conscience reject. Lowe is fond of challenging fellow activists with the question: "What's the plan?" When Lowe organized his Pittsburgh community of Manchester to develop a $40 million revitalization plan, he identified not only the community's assets but also the liabilities that were sure to scare away bankers—the open-air drug markets, petty street crime, dilapidated and abandoned buildings, uninviting parks and playgrounds, and dangerous public housing structures. "We knew that if we didn't take care of them, the bankers wouldn't touch us. So we went to the banks and we said, 'We have a plan together to change our neighborhood. We know, Mr. Banker, that you can't invest here until we deal with these problems. We tell you what, Mr. Banker. We'll take care of this. This is not your job. It's our job. But when we do, it'll be time for you to invest."[67]

Cleaning up the neighborhood and providing decent, affordable housing requires great diligence. It requires reaching out to gang members as well as wary middle-class buyers. It requires attention to the "broken windows" reality of the neighborhood—that if a broken window goes unfixed, the community cannot stem the tide of decline. Maintenance of existing assets—buildings, parks, streets and sidewalks, playground equipment, transit stops—is essential to improving attitudes and alleviating fears. Even symbolic improvements make a difference. The improvement of a façade makes the place feel better, setting up the possibility of improving the whole building later.

The results of Lowe's community-based approach have been impressive. Five years after the formation of the eighteen-group coalition, banks have committed billions to previously underfinanced communities. Housing values are on the rise, and people are returning to a neighborhood once abandoned as if its population were refugees fleeing a war zone.

This is not to say that all will be fine when communities follow Lowe's demanding strategy. Serious social problems—jobs, schools, drugs, gangs, boredom—still imperil the city. It is still important to get help from the federal, state, and local governments. But at least Lowe's approach gives people in the neighborhoods a real strategy based on the imperatives of markets and community.

Under this model, housing lies at the center of any strategy to deal with the problems of the city.

Right. Housing is never an isolated commodity. It is directly tied to other aspects of the community that are essential for basic survival. But to understand how, we need to look closely at the one government service that shapes all people's lives forever—education.

5
Education and
the Ladder of Mobility

What is education?

Education is the process by which people learn how to learn. The word "education" derives from the Latin *educere*, which means "to lead or draw out." The teacher and the student work together in such a way that the student becomes excited with the learning process and knows how to pursue the questions facing people in a larger community. The teacher plays a leading role in the process, providing frameworks for analysis, supplying necessary background information and techniques, and helping the student along at difficult points in the inquiry. Ideally, education moves beyond the hierarchical relationship and into a process of mutual discovery and learning. Education requires students to learn how to take the initiative and connect their individual concerns with the concerns of the larger community.

Education contrasts with instruction. That word derives from the Latin *instruere*, which means "to build in." Instruction aims to fill students with information that might be useful in the positions they hold over their careers and lives. Instruction rests on behaviorism, the idea that people ought to be trained to perform distinct, specialized functions in a complex division of labor. Engineers receive instruction in mathematics, physics, construction methods, and technologies particular to their profession. They are told what to do, then set out to use this information in their circumscribed career roles. Even the most collaborative activities can be reduced to sets of instructions.[1]

Education and instruction might seem, by this account, to be incompatible approaches. But in reality, the two approaches need each other. Students need a certain base of knowledge in order to think critically. Basic knowledge of language, literature, history, mathematics, and science provide a basic vocabulary that enables mutual discovery and learning that is central to the ideal of *educere*. Knowledge gaps in the early grades have been especially problematic since students do not develop that strong foundation they need for later learning.[2]

In recent years, public education seems to have become the most prominent issue in American politics. Does that mean that there is something seriously wrong with public education in this country?

Many scholars and policy analysts believe so. Studies published since the 1980s indicate that American students have not performed as well as students of previous generations or other nations. Scores on standardized tests declined steadily between the mid-1960s and 1980, and then stagnated for the next two decades. Internationally, American students lag behind students from those of virtually all U.S. economic and political competitors.[3] A study by Harold Stevenson and James Stigler found that Asian parents take their children's education more seriously than American parents—a finding reflected in the time spent on homework by Asian and American students. For example, Beijing first-graders devoted twice as much time to their homework as first-graders in Chicago, while fifth-graders in Taipei spent thirteen hours a week on homework compared to the four hours a week logged by Minneapolis fifth-graders.[4] Apart from stagnant or falling test scores, too many students continue to drop out of school. And drugs and violence have become more and more prevalent in schools.[5]

And the condition of the nation's urban public schools?

Once the great assimilator in American society and the pride of the nation's educational system, urban public schools have fallen upon hard times. The gap in achievement levels and graduation rates between urban and suburban students increased throughout much of the latter twentieth century. By 1996, 60 percent of students in city schools were unable to attain basic levels of competency in reading and mathematics on the National Assessment of Educational Progress exam. About one half of all high school students in large urban school districts fail to graduate in four years.[6]

It is easy to see why sizeable gaps in academic achievement and graduation rates persist between urban and suburban students. The physical conditions of city schools are often appalling. School buildings dating from

the nineteenth and early twentieth centuries are commonplace and maintenance of antiquated structures is sporadic at best. Basic supplies, textbooks, and equipment are typically outdated or unavailable altogether.
Classrooms are overcrowded. Drug abuse, violence, and a general lack of
discipline are daily facts of life. City schools have great difficulty recruiting
and retaining qualified teachers; one study found that only 50 percent of
the mathematics and science teachers in urban schools have been certi-
fied.[7] Researchers have determined that: "instruction in inner-city schools
is often based on cognitively low-level, unchallenging, rote material."[8]

Reformers seeking to raise academic performance in urban public schools
face overwhelming obstacles, given the surrounding social and economic environment. The Council of Great City Schools, which represents the fifty
largest public school districts in the country, reports some sobering statistics
about the extent of racial isolation and poverty within those districts. For example, about 77 percent of students in the Great City Schools in 1999 to 2000
were African-American, Hispanic, Asian-American, or other students of
color, compared with about 37.7 percent nationwide. Approximately 18.1
percent of students in Great City Schools are English-language learners,
compared with about 8.4 percent in the United States as a whole. About 61.7
percent of Great City Schools students are eligible for a federal free lunch
subsidy, compared with about 37.7 percent nationwide.[9] Even more worri-
some is the fact that the societal conditions that make learning so much more
difficult for inner-city children have been getting worse. The child poverty
rate in the fifty largest cities in the United States was 18 percent in 1970;
twenty years later, it had increased to 27 percent. In 1970, 3 percent of children in the fifty largest cities lived in distressed neighborhoods with poverty
rates exceeding 40 percent; by 1990, that figure had jumped to 17 percent.
The problem is especially severe in older, industrial cities such as Detroit,
Cleveland, and Buffalo, where the percentage of children living in distressed
areas in 1990 was 62 percent, 46 percent, and 41 percent respectively.[10]

The extraordinary special needs of public schools in inner-city neighborhoods place a tremendous strain on city school budgets. Despite increases in state and federal funds for local education in recent decades,
there continues to be a yawning gap between urban and suburban schools
regarding per-pupil expenditures. One scholar asserts that "79 percent of
large city districts studied by the Council of the Great City Schools are
funded at a lower rate than are suburban schools."[11] Even where the urban-
suburban spending differential has been erased, the far greater needs of
inner-city public schools suggest that much more funding is required to
reduce the gap in academic achievement.

The availability of adequate resources is one crucial element in assessing
school performance, but it is not the only one. Even when adequate re-

sources are made available to poorer school districts by higher levels of government, academic achievement levels will not necessarily improve if the extra money is not used well. Some urban school districts are top-heavy with administration and saddled with expensive programs that take money away from the central mission of learning, while others are wracked by mismanagement and corruption. Moreover, city school districts often impose rigid rules and guidelines that constrain teachers from developing innovative approaches to educating their students.

What does all of this mean in practical terms?

Children who attend underperforming urban schools are at a decided disadvantage in competing for positions in a postindustrial, knowledge-based economy. Absent adequate credentials, individuals are relegated to low-wage, low-skill jobs with disheartening prospects for upward mobility.[12]

Not only are schools failing to prepare workers for the demands of a postindustrial economy, they are also failing to prepare citizens to participate fully in civic life. This does not have to be so. A core function of public education is to provide students with the tools to participate in public affairs and contribute actively to the resolution of issues that affect the larger community, rather than just passively following the preferences of elites who may or may not be motivated by the best interests of the community. The sense of disempowerment that pervades so much of urban America suggests yet another failing of public schools in cities.[13]

Poorly performing urban schools damage the overall vitality of U.S. cities. Especially now that crime rates have fallen, the low status of public education has been a primary reason so many middle-class families have chosen to live in the suburbs as opposed to cities. The widespread lack of confidence in urban public schools has drained cities of residents, discouraged capital investment, depleted the tax base, and undermined the capacity of urban governments to provide other basic services needed to sustain the quality of life demanded by most middle-class Americans.

The Origins and Development of Public Education

Have public schools in cities always faced such dire circumstances?

Some historical perspective would be helpful. During the colonial era, public education as we know it today did not exist. No school was entirely supported by taxpayers, and attendance was not compulsory. Most children, especially in the Northeast, managed to obtain some schooling, but this usually lasted only for a few years, just long enough to pick up basic reading, writing, and mathematics skills. School conditions were often primitive. Children of varied ages and proficiencies crammed together in the proverbial one-room schoolhouse, "dame" schools set up in kitchens of literate women living in town, or in schools established by churches or charities. Of course, the children of privileged families had access to more formal schooling and even a handful of colleges and universities, but this represented only a small fraction of the population. For the vast majority of farmers, artisans, and laborers, education was available on an informal basis and only when the demands of work subsided.[14]

The first major period of education reform in the United States occurred during the Jacksonian era. The growing democratic spirit that infused American life prompted working- and middle-class citizens to demand broader access to education. Elites recognized that reform was inevitable but sought to direct it in ways that would serve their interests. Owners of textile mills in New England viewed education as an opportunity to prepare students for factory life by instilling an appreciation for punctuality and following directions.[15]

At the forefront of education reform of the early and mid-nineteenth century were professional educators such as Horace Mann of Massachusetts and Henry Barnard of Connecticut, who advocated the establishment of free, nonsectarian, common schools that would be open to all children within the community. Such schools would be placed under public authority and supported by tax revenues. Reformers also challenged the tradition of local control, contending that tiny districts were responsible for wide variations in facilities, resources, and academic standards. They believed that a consolidation of school districts and more centralized decision-making would enhance the prospects for innovations, including compulsory attendance, a longer school year, improved teacher training, a standardized curriculum, and a series of grades based upon age and proficiency.[16]

Is this also the period when the "common school" emerged?

Yes, the most important feature of the reform agenda was its commitment to the formation of schools open to all children regardless of class, religious, or ethnic background. All students within a community would come together within one classroom, study the same curriculum, and have the same opportunity to learn and achieve. The egalitarian impulse is evident in a report by a committee of the Detroit Common Council endorsing common schools in 1842. It anticipates the "happy influence . . . upon our social and political condition" that will result from "the adoption of a system of free schools under the control of public authorities." The report goes on to state: "Here the offspring of the rich and poor, seated side by side, will drink in knowledge from the same fountains, and will learn to appreciate each other for their intrinsic values alone. No permanent and transmissible distinction in castes can ever be obtained where such a system exists and no nobility can ever be established but such as is based on intelligence and virtue."[17]

To what extent did the reformers succeed in carrying out their agenda and to what extent did the actual experience of the common school conform to the ideal?

Reformers succeeded in significantly expanding student enrollments in free, public schools at the elementary level, promoting more regular attendance, lengthening the amount of time spent in school, boosting the allocation of public money for more resources and better facilities, and enhancing the quality of education through increased teacher training and curricular improvements.[18]

However, revisionist historians have highlighted the shortcomings of the common school movement and criticized the "myth of the golden era."[19] To start, the common school never included African-Americans to any significant degree; for white professional educators, racial exclusion was an accepted part of public school systems until well into the twentieth century. Despite the intent of reformers to provide a neutral and classless education, the curriculum was imbued with a powerful cultural bias. Reformers did not disguise their ultimate goal of using education to improve the moral character of lower- and working-class children. Writing in 1851, Henry Barnard declared: "The primary object in securing the early school attendance of children is not so much their intellectual culture as the regulations of the feelings and dispositions, the extirpation of vicious propensities, the preoccupation of the wilderness of the young heart with the seeds and germs of moral beauty."[20] Irish immigrants in cities were particularly alienated by a strong Protestant influence in the operation of the common schools. Irish children who refused to comply with compulsory attendance laws found themselves whisked off to another innovation of the era, the reform school. The revisionist critique notwithstanding, the Jacksonian era witnessed tangible improvements in the quality of education, greater availability of schooling to more and more sectors of the population, and a growing belief in the inherent worth of a common education for all citizens.

We seem to have drifted away from the ideal of the common school. What happened?

With the Industrial Revolution in full swing, the division between capital and labor deepened and the gap between the rich and poor widened. A new wave of immigration from Southern and Eastern Europe further exacerbated ethnic divisions. In such a climate, pursuing the common school ideal became more problematic. The situation was further aggravated as advances in transportation technology enabled more affluent citizens to move away from congested central cities to the periphery, thus fracturing urban residential patterns. This process undermined the common-school notion that students of diverse backgrounds ought to attend the same community school and be exposed to the same teachers and curriculum.[21]

As urban areas became more segmented by class and ethnicity, the deficiencies of public schools in poor, immigrant enclaves became increasingly glaring. Such schools were ineptly managed by administrators appointed by machine politicians because of their political loyalty. Furthermore, public schools offering a standard curriculum failed to provide their diverse student populations with sufficient educational options tailored to their particular needs and interests. Finally, while earlier reforms improved access to elementary schools, few students in the late nineteenth century graduated from high school.

So how did education policy change in response to these trends?

A new wave of reformers, the progressives, emerged with a very different vision of public education. In their view, the solution to the crisis in urban schools was nothing less than a massive overhaul of the structure and organization of the public school system. The first priority was to wrest control of public education away from the machine politicians, who seemed more concerned with using the schools as patronage mills than educating children. This required abolishing the district system, in which each neighborhood of a city essentially operated its own schools, and replacing it with an independent and central board of education responsible for all schools within a city. The board would be popularly elected, but in citywide elections, which enhanced the prospects of affluent, educated, and well-bred candidates. A suitably qualified superintendent of schools would then be appointed by the board to carry out the board's policies in an honest and efficient manner. At the school level, progressive reformers tried to promote professionalism by requiring teachers to obtain teaching certificates from accredited education programs and by establishing tenure to guard against politically motivated dismissals.

In sum, the reformers embraced a bureaucratic model of organization characterized by a strict division of labor with clearly defined roles for all school personnel, a hierarchical chain of command that would assure accountability, rules, regulations, and procedures to maximize fair dealing, and an overriding commitment to political neutrality and professionalism. Insulated from the corruption of machine politics, the new public school system would showcase integrity, efficiency, and expertise.[22]

What do the centralized school districts created by progressive reformers do? How do they operate?

School districts coordinate the full range of educational activities. Districts adopt curriculum, oversee hiring of teachers and staff, and manage special programs in the schools. Districts also provide connections to governments at the city, county, state, and federal levels, as well as to corporate, philanthropic, and other interest groups within the city.

Most school districts are run by a school board and a superintendent. In 97 percent of U.S. school districts, voters elect the board members, who in turn appoint the superintendent. In some big-city systems, mayors appoint school boards.[23] With appointed members, the committee answers directly to the mayor and can avoid the mechanizations of the Byzantine city and neighborhood political structures. The appointed committee also offers a less visible platform for grandstanding and attracts more public-spirited members.

The superintendent enjoys the power to appoint the leading policy-making officials but must work with a bureaucracy dominated by career civil servants. The major divisions or departments of the district bureaucracy are curriculum, instruction, physical plant, transportation, finance, and special projects.

Did progressive reforms live up to expectations?

Progressivism was not the politically neutral phenomenon that its advocates claimed it to be. Critics charged that the dominant impulse behind education reform was social control—getting unruly and dangerous youths off the congested and chaotic streets and into formal structures where they could be taught proper values and behavioral traits. Moral regeneration was an important motivation for many reformers. Similarly, other reformers wished to Americanize the immigrant masses by ridding them of their foreign languages, customs, and religions. And still others backed the progressive agenda because of the ever-expanding demands of the industrial economy. With the need for skilled and unskilled labor perpetually on the rise, business leaders insisted that public schools acclimate students to work in the factory. They advocated the development of different curricula for different tracks, tracks that more often than not correlated with the social class of students. Thus, as one scholar put it, "[t]he older ideology of the common school—the notion that the same curriculum should be offered to all children—increasingly came under attack." Accordingly, the "soft, child-centered pedagogy" of the common school, one that sought to stimulate student interest in learning, was replaced by an emphasis on drills and recitation, a preference for instruction rather than education.[24]

As school districts expanded and took in more students, they adopted a factory model for their operations. Textbooks took on a lowest common denominator. Classes were often crowded and teachers did all they could just to keep students in line and present the basic material. Especially in low-track classes, teachers stood at the front of the class and *delivered* instruction and gave make-work tasks to students.

Beyond the classroom, the progressive reforms did not exactly succeed in sheltering school districts from outside political forces. Superintendents often found themselves doing battle with powerful interest groups. In cities such as New York, Chicago, and Boston, superintendents seem to be fighting for their jobs on an annual basis. Boston had six full-time superintendents and three interim executives over a two-decade span from the 1970s to the 1990s. Mayors, board members, parent groups, churches, and other interest groups buffet superintendents from all directions, hoping to sway their professional judgment on a wide range of issues—certainly not the apolitical atmosphere that reformers wished to nurture.

By the same token, superintendents sometimes contribute to the politicization of school districts by using their positions as springboards to more prestigious jobs in education, business, or government. Such school chiefs tend to embrace policies that attract publicity rather than doing the tedious work to build and maintain high academic standards. Research shows that superintendents who stay in their jobs for a long time produce the most favorable results. These "place-bound" leaders are committed to the community and more likely to exhibit the necessary patience to set policy and follow up on its implications.

It sounds as though public schools in cities came to resemble the factories themselves, just another form of mass production.

Yes, but given the unprecedented rates of urbanization during this period, this was predictable. With millions of people pouring into urban areas from both the countryside and other countries, city schools were overflowing with students. New York had 544,000 students in its schools, Chicago 242,000, and Philadelphia 206,000.[25] Student-teacher ratios approached 50 to 1 in some urban classrooms. With this influx of humanity, it is not surprising that city school systems came to be run as huge bureaucracies.

But why did the bureaucratic model prove to be so enduring even after urbanization rates leveled off by the mid-twentieth century?

Education planners believed that bureaucratically organized schools could offer a wide variety of courses, programs, and teaching styles to satisfy the particular desires and needs of an increasingly diverse population. The expansion of educational options available within large schools and school systems would presumably enhance opportunities for America's youth to pursue their aspirations and attain a higher standard of living. James B. Conant's 1959 study, *The American High School Today*, provided an influential academic argument for the bureaucratic model. Conant contended that only large schools could take advantage of economies of scale to provide the requisites of a good education: a wide range of required and elective classes, individualized curriculums, ability grouping, vocational education, special programs for both slow and advanced students, at least six periods in a day, special reading programs, counseling, summer school, and homerooms.[26]

Conant's manifesto accelerated an already powerful movement to consolidate schools and school districts. In the early 1930s, there were 127,000 school districts in the United States; by 1982, that number had declined to about 15,000. Although Conant was concerned mainly about schools with fewer than a hundred students, reformers and empire builders took his words to mean that only schools with one or two thousand students could serve the needs of all students. Nearly three of every four students today attend secondary school at institutions with a thousand or more students.[27]

Progressive reforms may have broadened academic choices for students and parents, but there must have been some limitations?

Although progressive reformers trumpeted the advantages of expanded choices available to diverse groups of students in large school systems, critics asked just how free student choices really were. Take the example of "tracking." Reformers assumed that students learn best when they are grouped with others of similar abilities and that teachers teach better when working with students of comparable aptitudes. Reformers also assumed that large public school systems with a plethora of course offerings and programs would motivate students to remain in school studying material they deemed relevant to their future plans.

The problem is that once a student is placed in a lower track, the prospects for moving up are limited. Even when low-level courses offer challenging lessons, the loss of bright and motivated students undermines the learning process. Researchers have found that successful classes require a "core" of committed students to set high standards for peers. Peer tutoring—students teaching fellow students—offers the most effective way to learn. Weaker students benefit by working with better-prepared students in all subjects because they get attention from peers who can relate to them as fellow learners. Stronger students also benefit from mixed-population classrooms because, in the course of working with others, they learn how to articulate the principles they are learning.[28]

Students in lower tracks also suffer because schools track teachers as well as students. In his poignant memoir of teaching in the Alexandria,

Virginia, public schools, Patrick Welsh writes: "In principle, the kids with the most problems should be getting the best teachers. In practice, the system operates in just the opposite way."[29] Because firing teachers for incompetence is a difficult task, administrators assign them to less desirable positions. The imperative to "pass the trash" is known systemwide. In some districts, assigning poorer teachers to low-level classes is actually formal policy. Alabama requires teachers with emergency teaching licenses in mathematics to teach only courses on the lower track. Ultimately, students in the undesirable classes are the victims.

Reporting on his visits to public schools across the country, the journalist Thomas Toch was dismayed to see the poor quality of instruction in lower tracks. Basic mathematics classes, for example, do not develop higher-order thinking skills but tend to drill students on rudimentary skills they should have learned earlier in their schooling. English courses on the low track do not read or discuss major works of literature but instead assign students the juvenile equivalent of pulp fiction. A question on a freshman history test on World War II asked students to identify "what C stands for in George C. Marshall." Toch concludes: "Pedagogy is far from perfect in upper-level courses, but at least there is a modicum of dialogue and debate in many of them, some cultivation of complexity and ambiguity, some demand for independent thought, and some interest in ideas and the ability to express them well."[30] Not so with classes in the lower tracks.

Yet, notwithstanding all of these problems, there was no mass rebellion against public education in this country, right? In fact, most Americans seemed relatively content with public schools well into the twentieth century.

Many citizens were grateful just to have an opportunity to attend public school beyond the elementary level. The percentage of high school graduates in the general population increased from a miniscule 2 percent in 1870 to 16 percent in 1920 to 49 percent in 1940.[31] Economic prosperity in the years following World War II obscured some of the deficiencies of public education. Jobs were readily available and income levels and standards of living were on the rise for most sectors of the population.[32]

Another wave of reformers emerged to promote an expanding ideal of equality of educational opportunity. These reformers believed that just having the chance to attend elementary and secondary schools was no longer sufficient; rather, it was now necessary to ensure that all children had more or less the same opportunity to learn and the same opportunity to pursue the American Dream. Advocates of educational equity pursued three avenues of reform: attacking racial segregation in public schools, expanding the role of the federal government in public schools by providing compensatory assistance to disadvantaged students, and overhauling the way public schools are financed.

Promoting Equity: School Desegregation

People of color have always understood that pervasive racial discrimination has severely limited their access to quality public education. The most glaring example of racial inequality was in the South, where black children were barred by law from attending public schools reserved for white children. This practice gained constitutional sanction in *Plessy v. Ferguson* (1896) when the U.S. Supreme Court upheld a Louisiana law requiring the racial segregation of railroad cars provided that the racially separate cars were more or less the same. Applied to public education, the decision permitted racially segregated schools so long as they were essentially equal in terms of facilities and resources. But, in practice, the "separate but equal" doctrine was a farce; black schools were almost always inferior to white schools. After a lengthy and arduous litigation campaign, the National Association for the Advancement of Colored People (NAACP) convinced the Supreme Court in the landmark case of *Brown v. Board of Education* (1954) to overturn *Plessy* and declare that black children in racially segregated schools were denied equal protection of the laws under the Fourteenth Amendment. In doing so, the Court established the revolutionary principle that racially separate schools were inherently unequal. *Brown* continues to be regarded as one of the seminal cases of the twentieth century because it so clearly advanced the cause of social justice and reaffirmed the nation's commitment to genuine equality of opportunity.[33]

But racial segregation in public school systems is still a pervasive problem. What happened?

Articulating a hallowed principle is one thing; implementing it is another thing altogether. Although the Supreme Court ordered desegregation to proceed with "all deliberate speed," the absence of clear guidelines for implementation enabled Southern communities not only to drag their heels but to engage in a campaign of "massive resistance." Ten years after *Brown*, only one of every fifty black children in the South attended racially integrated public schools. Progress occurred in the mid-1960s when the Johnson administration aggressively enforced the Civil Rights Act of 1964 by filing lawsuits and denying federal funds to schools that continued to engage in discriminatory practices.[34]

With the executive branch of the federal government now committed to carrying out the *Brown* mandate, the Supreme Court in the 1960s took an aggressive posture. In *Green v. New Kent County* (1968), the Court declared for the first time that it was not enough to abolish mandatory segregation but that school districts operating a dual system had an "affirmative duty to take whatever steps might be necessary to convert to a unitary system in which racial discrimination would be eliminated root and branch."[35] Three years later, in *Swann v. Charlotte-Mecklenburg Board of Education*, the Court elaborated on the nature of that affirmative duty. It held that the allegedly neutral practice of assigning students to schools based on residential patterns was unconstitutional if it reinforced existing school segregation. Since that was precisely what was happening in the Charlotte-Mecklenberg County school system, the Court affirmed the district court's cross-county busing plan to achieve racial balance.[36] Mandatory busing soon became commonplace throughout the South.

Then, quite suddenly, school disegregation became a national, as opposed to, just a regional issue. In 1973, the Supreme Court upheld a lower federal court decision finding a school district in Denver, Colorado, responsible for racial segregation in its schools and ordering districtwide busing to attain racial balance.[37] The Denver case motivated civil rights organizations to file desegregation lawsuits in dozens of cities all over the country.

How did parents and politicians outside the South react to court-ordered desegregation plans?

It was not quite the massive resistance witnessed in the South in the 1950s and 1960s, but in some places it came very close. Stable communities like South Boston were thrown into turmoil following the implementation of mandatory busing.[38] White parents resented having to put their children on buses for lengthy trips across a city when a perfectly acceptable neighborhood school was only a few blocks away. Meanwhile, black children were usually forced to endure even longer bus trips and more hostile school environments. Many of the children involved in busing controversies suffered scarring experiences that affected them for a lifetime.[39]

Was all of the hardship worth it? Were schools actually desegregated?

As noted earlier, there were clear gains in the South by the early 1970s and some gains elsewhere in the country by the end of the 1970s. However, that progress was undermined by the decision of many white parents facing desegregation plans to pull their children out of public schools and enroll them in private schools not subject to any court order or to move out of a school district altogether.[40] The phenomenon of "white flight" from public schools was particularly problematic in larger cities.

But wasn't white flight from most cities already under way long before court-ordered desegregation began?

Yes. The two decades following World War II witnessed an unprecedented migration of white, middle-class residents from urban to suburban areas. Many simply yearned for a single-family home, large yard, garage, and serenity of a suburban lifestyle. But such a lifestyle was not an option for most people of color. Housing discrimination by realtors and land-lords, not to mention physical intimidation and violence in some places, made suburbia forbidden territory for most blacks and Latinos.[41] By the early 1970s, even before the advent of school desegregation lawsuits out-side the South, city schools were increasingly attended by minority stu-dents while suburban schools were overwhelmingly white. Court-ordered busing exacerbated the problem of white flight, but the racial imbalance between urban and suburban public schools was already pronounced.

If the ultimate goal was to promote racial desegregation in public education, then it seems that one obvious remedy would have been for a court to cast a wider net and issue a desegregation order extending beyond one school dis-trict so as to include school districts within both the central city and sur-rounding suburbs.

That is what civil rights groups advocated. But hopes for desegregating public schools in metropolitan areas with regional busing were dashed when the Supreme Court ruled in *Milliken v. Bradley* (1974) that such a metropolitan remedy would be permissible only if it could be proven that suburban municipalities or the state had intentionally engaged in discrim-inatory practices resulting in the current segregation of public schools.[42] In the years following *Milliken*, plaintiffs discovered that demonstrating such intent and effect was almost impossible. Supporters of metropolitan-wide desegregation concluded that the Supreme Court had dealt them an irre-versible setback.[43]

Was that the end of efforts to achieve racial equality in the nation's public schools?

Not quite. The South was not as adversely affected by *Milliken*. First, it was possible to demonstrate intentional discrimination through the wide-spread enactment of Jim Crow laws. Second, in many areas, interdistrict busing was not even necessary. Southern school districts were often large enough to encompass central cities and surrounding suburbs, and under *Swann*, intradistrict busing would still be required to produce racial bal-ance. Ironically, then, the South became the most desegregated region in the United States by the 1970s.[44] As time passed, many Southerners came to view racial diversity as a desirable goal. Charlotte, North Carolina, is a case in point. During the 1970s and 1980s, Charlotte came to be known as the "city that made desegregation work."[45] But the city's commitment to racial diversity was called into question in 1991 when the school board ap-pointed a superintendent from outside the community who promised to phase out a long-running, mandatory busing plan. Prointegration forces rallied, and in 1995 the voters elected several new members to the school board who pledged to maintain existing desegregation policies, thus reaffirming popular support for racially balanced schools.[46]

Since mandatory busing between urban and suburban school districts usually was not an option, advocates of racial equality turned to voluntary plans to promote racial desegregation across district boundaries. The idea was to use incentives to attract white students to enroll in urban public schools. The most popular incentive was the magnet school, which offers a specialized curriculum or teaching philosophy not typically available in regular schools. Examples include schools that feature the visual and performing arts, science and technology, back-to-basics, and accelerated learning for honors students.

To fund magnet schools and to make regular schools in cities more appealing to white students and their parents, school officials hoped to take advantage of another Supreme Court decision, *Milliken II* (1977), which approved a lower federal court decision ordering the state of Michigan to provide financial relief to offset the costs of segregation endured by minority students isolated in impoverished urban schools. While suburban districts could not be required to shoulder the burden of desegregation under *Milliken* (absent proof of intentional discrimination), the Court ruled they could be asked to contribute monetarily to programs aimed at improving urban schools. Some scholars endorsed the adoption of voluntary desegregation plans offering innovative programs and a fresh infusion of desperately needed resources from the state, contending that greater reliance on carrots as opposed to sticks would alleviate racial tension, reduce white flight, and yield more diversity in city and suburban schools over the long term.[47]

What was the outcome of such voluntary desegregation plans?

The case of Kansas City, Missouri, is instructive. There, a federal district court sought to promote voluntary, interdistrict desegregation by creating a series of world-class magnet schools funded by an unprecedented $1.5 billion hike in taxes on residents within the district and throughout the state. The court reasoned that such a massive investment would lure white students and parents back into the city public school system.

The investment led to undeniable improvements in facilities, resources, and teacher salaries, and early studies reported notable advances in the academic performance of magnet schools at the elementary school level. However, progress toward desegregation was at best uneven. Although the rate of white flight subsided and students already within the city school system changed schools quite a bit, thus expanding interracial exposure, the anticipated influx of white, suburban students was never realized.[48] Also, academic achievement in the Kansas City school system's regular schools remained inadequate. In fact, in May 2000, the school system lost its accreditation when the state board of education determined it had failed to meet any of its eleven performance standards. Commentators noted that while the school district invested heavily in state-of-the-art facilities and unique programs such as Greek studies, basic learning was neglected in many of the district's regular schools.[49]

What lessons are to be learned from the Kansas City experience and other cases involving voluntary desegregation?

Voluntary desegregation plans that rely on incentives such as magnet schools and extra money enable previously neglected schools to invest in better facilities, reduce class sizes, and acquire basic supplies. All of that, in turn, reduces the degree of racial inequality in public education. At the same time, some scholars have viewed such remedies as "temporary, supplemental add-ons that are not linked to any systemic effort to redress harms of segregation."[50] In the final analysis, the additional resources yield only modest gains in educational achievement. The value of voluntary desegregation plans becomes even more dubious when one considers how little the various incentives have worked in luring white students to enroll in urban public schools.[51]

If voluntary desegregation plans have yielded disappointing results, then should we revisit mandatory segregation plans as a viable option?

Memories of the intense opposition to court-ordered busing linger, giving public officials in all three branches of government reason to pause. On the other hand, there has been evidence of growing public support for mandatory desegregation in places where it has been in operation for long periods of time.[52] And mandatory plans have produced greater racial balance in many communities in the South, where they have been most commonly employed.

However, the prospects for court-ordered busing as a desegregation tool remain constrained by *Milliken* and by more recent Supreme Court decisions making it easier for school districts to demonstrate that they have done all they could to eradicate dual segregation.[53] Even Charlotte-Mecklenburg's success story in bringing about racial diversity is now in jeopardy. A federal district court in September 1999 found that the school system had achieved desegregation "quite some time ago" and thus ordered an end to the use of race in assigning students to schools. With students now able to attend neighborhood schools, most observers predict the resegregation of Charlotte-Mecklenburg schools.[54]

In sum, nearly fifty years after *Brown*, the battle to promote racial equality in public education has produced a great deal of conflict, frustration, and demoralization. Progress in desegregating public schools in most regions of the

United States, through either mandatory or voluntary plans, has been limited. And in the one region where the most progress has been made, the South, recent Supreme Court decisions threaten to undo that progress. The consequences are particularly bleak for cities, where public schools are increasingly segregated by race. Students of color in racially isolated schools are inevitably subjected to gross inequalities in resources and facilities.

Promoting Equity: Federal Compensatory Programs

As the civil rights movement evolved, taking on issues of social justice, how did the movement for educational opportunity move beyond school desegregation?

Long before it became apparent that school desegregation would not solve the problem of racial inequality, liberal activists and politicians in the 1960s began to advocate other strategies for enhancing equality of educational opportunity. The timing was perfect. Liberals found a powerful ally in President Lyndon Johnson, who sought to use the powers of the federal government to create a Great Society. The president teamed up with a heavily Democratic Congress to enact into law dozens of new programs to eliminate poverty and promote social justice.

Where was education policy on the president's agenda?

As a former teacher himself, Johnson fervently believed that adequate schooling was the key to a higher standard of living. The appropriate starting point, he felt, was access to good public schools, but black children in the South were still being denied such access because of continuing defiance by Southern officials of the Supreme Court's mandate in *Brown*. Johnson ordered the Justice Department to enforce the recently adopted Civil Rights Act of 1964 by cutting off federal funds to Southern school districts that had failed to move toward racial integration. In subsequent years, the Great Society era's determination to reduce discrimination in education spread to other groups, such as women, immigrants, and the handicapped. Landmark legislation included Title IX of the Educational Amendment Act of 1972, which prohibited sex discrimination in school services, the Equal Educational Opportunity Act of 1974, which required schools to redress language barriers, and the Education of All Handicapped Children Act of 1975, which mandated a free appropriate education to all handicapped children.[55]

How else did the federal government try to bring about more equity in public education?

By channeling more resources to poor school districts. Policy-makers believed that removing discriminatory barriers to public education would not alone yield real equality as long as wide disparities in the quality of education persisted among school districts. The most important of these compensatory education programs was Title I of the Elementary and Secondary Education Act of 1965 (ESEA), which targeted federal money to disadvantaged students in the hope of narrowing the school achievement gap between wealthy and poor children. The additional funds would enable schools to hire new teachers for remedial reading and writing, purchase more library books, and experiment with new pedagogical methods such as team teaching and small-group instruction. Title I funds would also afford lower-income students opportunities to visit museums and other educationally rewarding places typically available to upper-income students. Finally, compensatory programs sought to encourage the involvement of parents in their children's learning through home visits and school-based activities.[56] Education policy analysts hoped that the influx of resources provided by Title I would enable public schools in central cities to offer a level of education that more closely resembled that afforded in suburban public schools.

Is Head Start also an example of one of these federal compensatory programs?

Yes. In fact, Head Start is probably the most well known of the compensatory education programs arising from the Great Society era. Its premise is simple. Many poor children face difficult circumstances with which most middle-class children do not have to contend. Hence poor children are already at a competitive disadvantage at the very beginning of elementary school. Head Start programs attempt to remedy the situation by allowing poor children to participate in preschool programs offering a nurturing, enriching environment that helps students overcome structural disadvantages and puts them on a more or less equal footing with other children by the time they are ready to enroll in elementary school.

Have these federal compensatory programs accomplished their goal of making education more equitable?

Yes and no. Policy experts generally agree that the 700,000 children who participate in Head Start benefit during the program and soon after its completion, as evidenced by higher attendance rates and a lower probability of being placed in remedial education classes. On the other hand, the long-term gains remain uncertain. Studies have found that early improvement in test scores for poor blacks fade after three or four years. Some scholars contend that this is hardly an indictment of Head Start but an indication of the inferior quality of elementary and secondary schools attended by many African-American students.[57]

That suggests that the federal compensatory grants under the ESEA have not had their desired effect.

A comprehensive analysis of seventeen studies of Title I from 1966 to 1993 by Geoffrey Borman and Jerome D'Agostino found that after a shaky start, due to flaws in the initial formulation and implementation of the program, "Title I has evolved into a more viable and effective intervention" responsible for modest improvements in student achievement. However, the study went on to assert that the program had not attained its primary objective of closing the achievement gap between advantaged and disadvantaged students.[58]

Does this mean that the federal government's long-term drive to engender equality of educational opportunity has been a failure?

Some scholars have made this argument.[59] But others question what might have happened without federal intervention. Researchers Borman and D'Agostino, for example, contend that without the compensatory funding supplied by Title I of the ESEA, "children served over the last 30 years would have fallen farther behind academically."[60]

Moreover, even at the high point of the Great Society era, the federal government never accounted for more than 10 percent of overall spending on education, and today the federal share is down to only 6 percent. Given Washington's limited role, it is hardly surprising that federal compensatory programs have had only a modest impact on reducing educational inequality. For that reason, reformers have also pursued policy changes at the state and local government levels. The most important initiative to promote educational equity at the state and local levels of government involves the long-standing campaign to reform the way in which public education is financed in most areas of the country. Critics charge that current school finance methods result in huge disparities in per pupil expenditures among school districts and that this makes a mockery of the principle of equality of opportunity.

Promoting Equity: School Finance Reform

How are public schools funded?

Property taxes have supplied the bulk of revenue for local governments in this country.[61] Most taxpayers consider property taxes to pay for schools a bargain, especially when their own children benefit directly from free public education. Even though assessment of property has always been a matter of political manipulation, property taxes offer a simplicity that other taxes do not—a simplicity that is appealing to school bureaucracies and taxpayers alike.

So why has dependence upon property taxes become a problem?

With school districts so dependent upon revenue from local property taxes, the wealth of any given tax base determines the level of school expenditures. Communities with high property values can raise more revenues to pay for high-quality facilities, resources, textbooks, extracurricular activities, teacher salaries, and advanced technology than communities with lower property values. Poorer communities often tax themselves at twice the rate of wealthier communities, but still end up with less revenue to spend on public education. The problem is particularly glaring when comparing the low tax base of cities that have suffered extensive deindustrialization and suburbanization with the relatively high tax base of surrounding suburbs, which have benefited from the inflow of businesses and residents. In the 1960s, scholars and activists began to argue that a school finance method that yielded such variations in per pupil spending from school district to school district denied students in poorer districts an equal opportunity to learn and get ahead.

Does the inequality in funding for schools really matter?

Intuitively, one would think so. But a number of influential scholars, especially economists, have raised questions about this assumption. Eric Hanushek's analysis of 187 studies found no consistent connection between higher teacher salaries, student-teacher ratios, or teacher experience and student achievement, concluding that "there is no strong or systematic relationship between school expenditures and student performance." Michael Rutter's study of twelve urban secondary schools found that costly programs such as improvement of physical plant and reduction of student-teacher ratios do not necessarily produce better outcomes. Others have pointed out that despite a 60 percent increase in real spending per student in the United States between 1966 and 1980, test scores declined steadily. Such findings reinforce the views of conservative politicians who are skeptical of "throwing money at problems," as Ronald Reagan used to say. They contend that in a wasteful system, more funding simply means more wasted money.[62]

How do liberals respond?

Many scholars have criticized those studies finding no strong relationship between school inputs and outputs on methodological grounds, especially the failure to control adequately for other explanations for poor school performance. Richard Murname, for instance, observes that many school districts receiving higher levels of federal and state assistance, such as those in distressed urban centers, happen to serve children from seriously disadvantaged family and community backgrounds; it is only logical that test scores there would be lower than in affluent suburban school districts receiving less in compensatory aid. Moreover, a large body of research has found that school inputs such as teacher education and class size do indeed affect student learning. While it is true that money alone will not improve educational performance, it is a prerequisite.[63]

Finally, it is hard to read Jonathan Kozol's depictions of inner city public schools in his book, *Savage Inequalities*, and not come away thinking that money is essential to creating a decent and productive learning environment:

> In the evening, when I drive into the neighborhood to find the school, the air at Pyne Point (Junior High) bears the smell of burning trash. When I return the next day, I am hit with a strong smell of ether, or some kind of glue, that seems to be emitted by the paper factory.
>
> The school is a two-story building, yellow brick, its windows covered with metal grates, the flag on its flagpole motionless above a lawn that has no grass. Some 650 children, 98 percent of whom are black or Latino, are enrolled here. . . .
>
> A number of teachers . . . do not have books for half the students in their classes0 . . .
>
> The typing teacher shows me the typewriters that her students use. "These Olympia machines," she says, "should have been thrown out ten years ago. Most of them were here when I had parents of these children in my class . . . "
>
> In a class in basic methematics skills, an eighth grate student that I meet cannot add five and two. In a sixth grade classroom, brownish clumps of plaster dot the ceiling where there were once soundabsorbing tiles. An eighth grade science class is using workbooks in a laboratory without lab equipment. . . .
>
> The playing field next to the school is bleak and bare. There are no goalposts and there is an illegal dumpsite. Contractors from the suburbs drive here, sometimes late at night, the principal says, and dump their trash behind the school. A medical lab in Haddon, which is a white suburb, recently disposed a load of waste, including hypodermic needles, in the field. Children then set fire to the trash.[64]

Similarly, a year after visiting and observing the dismal physical condition of Morris High School in the Bronx, Kozol returned to find little had changed: "Water still cascades down the stairs. Plaster is still falling from the walls. Female students tell me that they shower after school to wash the plaster from their hair. Entering ninth grade children at the school, I'm told, read about four years behind grade level." When the principal of

Camden High School is asked whether money matters in accounting for school performance, she responds: "I am asked to speak sometimes in towns like Princeton. I tell them, 'If you don't believe that money makes a difference, let your children go to school in Camden, *Trade* with our children—not beginning in the high school. Start when they're little, in the first or second grade.' When I say this, people will not meet my eyes. They stare down at the floor. . . ."[65] The bottom line is that parents would rather live in school districts that generate more money for their schools and their children.

How did activists concerned about such inequities propose to fix the problem?

Activists zero in on a school finance system that relies excessively upon local property taxes. Influenced by the NAACP's campaign against segregated schools, some scholars and activists advocated using the federal courts as a vehicle for social change, in particular alleging that unequal spending from district to district was a violation of the Equal Protection Clause of the Fourteenth Amendment. But unlike the NAACP's decades-long litigation effort, the campaign in federal court to overhaul school finance soon ran into a brick wall. The U.S. Supreme Court decided in *Rodriguez v. San Antonio Independent School District* (1973) that while disparate treatment based on *race* would require a compelling justification by the state of Texas, in practice a very difficult standard to meet, differences based on varying levels of *wealth* would not trigger a heightened judicial scrutiny. The state needed only to assert a rational basis in order to account for the variations in education spending from district to district, and the Court found that basis in the state's desire to preserve local control over education policy and finance. The Supreme Court's ruling shut the door on the federal courts as an arena for pursuing school finance reform.[66]

But activists did not give up on the judicial branch of government. Instead, they turned to the state court system, where they had already scored an impressive victory. The California Supreme Court in *Serrano v. Priest* (1971) became the first court of last resort in the United States to determine that a state's school finance system was unconstitutional.

Serrano decided that the heavy reliance on local property taxes unfairly discriminated against the poor because it made access to quality education dependent upon the wealth of the school district. Finding no compelling state justification, the court held that the discriminatory classification violated the Equal Protection Clause of the U.S. Constitution and the California state constitution. Two years later, the U.S. Supreme Court's decision in *Rodriguez* had the effect of overruling the first ruling, but the second holding remained intact. Public interest lawyers rushed to file lawsuits in state courts, contending that wide disparities in per-pupil expenditures resulting from wide disparities in the value of property from district to district deprived students in poorer school districts of equal protection under the law.[67]

What was the outcome of those lawsuits?

Several state supreme courts, including those in New Jersey, Washington, and West Virginia, followed the lead of the California Supreme Court in finding school finance systems that relied heavily upon local property taxes to be in violation of their state constitutions. Other states, confronted with the prospect of a long and embarrassing litigation battle, opted to reform their school finance systems by enacting new legislation.[68]

Litigation campaigns in other states, such as Arizona, Colorado, Georgia, Idaho, Illinois, New York, Ohio, Oregon, and Pennsylvania, ended in failure, with state courts choosing to follow the lead of the U.S. Supreme Court. Some courts stressed the need for judicial restraint in a policy area better suited to legislative action. Other courts expressed the concern that an equal protection violation arising from disparities in education spending would lead to a multitude of other constitutional challenges of disparities regarding other government services such as police protection and recreation.[69]

Another serious problem with the school finance reform movement in the 1970s involved the question of a remedy. As with school desegregation, winning in court did not necessarily translate into tangible changes within school districts. When confronted with a court ruling invalidating a state's school finance system, a state legislature had three basic choices if it wanted to continue to rely on local property taxes as at least one significant source of revenue for public education. First, it could narrow the gap between wealthy and poor districts by increasing state spending on public schools in the latter. Second, it could narrow the gap by imposing limits on the capacity of wealthier districts to allocate funds for public schools. Third, it could pursue a combination of the first and second options. The problem was that each option would provoke substantial public opposition. A significant hike in school spending to benefit poor school districts would require higher taxes. Tax hikes following *Serrano* produced a tax revolt that resulted in the passage in 1978 of a citizens' initiative, Proposition 13, limiting future increases in property taxes. Proposition 13 helped to ignite taxpayer rebellions in numerous other states, and the mounting anti-tax, antigovernment sentiment strengthened Ronald Reagan's successful campaign for president in 1980.[70]

Pressure on wealthier school districts to limit their outlays for schooling was also unpopular with parents in those districts eager to enhance their children's opportunities to learn. Getting popularly elected representatives in state legislatures to comply with court orders proved a difficult task. Plaintiffs who had won in court found themselves returning to court repeatedly to push state legislatures to comply with court orders. Meanwhile, the volume of litigation began to diminish. Only a handful of lawsuits were filed during the 1980s, and only the state supreme courts of Wyoming and Arkansas declared their state school finance systems to be unconstitutional.

States that experienced successful school finance litigation took actions that reduced inequality among school districts. But whether such progress in closing the gap between rich and poor school districts was responsible for any progress in reducing educational achievement differentials remains an open question.[71] Even when litigation efforts produced greater equity in educational spending, the needs of urban schools continued to surpass those of suburban schools. Even in "successful" cases, then, rough parity did not yield equality of educational opportunity or results.

Increasingly, conservative scholars and policy-makers began to assert themselves on education policy, arguing that the liberal emphasis on promoting equality had not only failed, it had caused a decline in the academic performance of the nation's schools and students. By the 1980s, the conservatives began to take center stage with their own agenda for reforming public education.

The Conservative Critique of Liberal Reforms

How does the conservatives' critique of liberal education policy shape the debate about student achievement?

While they applauded the expanded access to higher levels of education conservatives warned of a steady decline in academic achievement. Average scores on the Scholastic Aptitude Test (SAT), a standardized exam testing verbal and mathematical ability for students contemplating college-level work, began to fall steadily in the mid-1960s until about 1980. Verbal SAT scores dropped from 478 in 1963 to the 420s by the end of the 1970s, while mathematics scores decreased from 502 in 1963 to 466 in 1980.[72] Other measures of academic achievement also indicated cause for concern. Scores associated with the National Assessment of Educational Progress (NAEP)—a testing program supervised by the U.S. Department of Education which examines the achievement of students in the fourth, eighth, and twelfth grades in subjects such as science, math, reading, geography, U.S. history, computer skills, and art—revealed ongoing problems in urban schools in particular. Although the gap between white and African-American and Latino students had narrowed since the NAEP began in the early 1970s, test score differentials remained substantial.[73] International assessments of student proficiency in science and math also suggested that American students, especially those in higher grade levels, were falling further behind students in other advanced industrial countries.[74]

A handful of scholarly studies warning of a deterioration in the quality of public education soon ballooned into a cascade of studies with ominous findings and conclusions. By far the most influential of these was a report issued in 1983 by the National Commission on Excellence in Education at the request of the U.S. Department of Education. *A Nation at Risk* utilized unusually provocative language to sound the alarm bells and stimulate support for fundamental reforms:

> . . . the educational foundations of our society are presently being eroded by a rising tide of mediocrity that threatens our future as a Nation and a people. . . . If an unfriendly foreign power had attempted to impose on America the mediocre educational performance that exists today, we might well have viewed it as an act of war. . . . We have, in effect, been committing an act of unthinking, unilateral educational disarmament.[75]

The report attracted widespread media attention. At a time when the U.S. economy was already reeling from plant closures at home, OPEC oil boycotts, and the dramatic success of Japanese and German manufacturing, Americans felt vulnerable, and it made sense to them that the educational system might have been the source of many of the nation's problems.

But what was wrong with the educational system?

Some scholars maintained that nothing was fundamentally wrong. They attributed the drop in standardized test scores to the diversification of the test-taking pool. Many new students taking the SAT for the first time spoke English as a second language or had to overcome other learning obstacles. Others, however, were not convinced. Scholars such as Charles Murray and R. J. Hernstein, for example, pointed out that the drop in SAT scores for white students mirrored the overall decline. A growing number of conservative scholars took aim at the liberal policy reforms of the Great Society era, blaming them for lowering academic standards by, among other things, tolerating a proliferation of nonacademic "frills" courses and a corresponding decline in rigorous academic courses, less homework assigned each night, grade inflation, and relaxed standards for promotion and graduation. In short, reduced expectations were responsible for falling academic achievement.[76]

Later on, other conservative scholars broadened their critique of Great Society policies, contending that the expanded presence of the state and federal governments in education added new layers of bureaucracy to school systems already overly bureaucratized thanks to the restructuring efforts of earlier progressive reformers. With each level of government imposing new and onerous demands on public schools—and on matters outside the traditional domain of education—public-sector intervention became even more oppressive, stifling the creative juices of dedicated teachers, involved parents, and eager students.[77] Amid the widespread publicity generated by *A Nation at Risk*, conservative politicians and policy advocates launched several new initiatives to revitalize American education, including a campaign to raise academic expectations through rigorous standards for students and teachers, plans to restructure the organization of schools to promote flexibility and accountability, and a bold drive to give parents greater choice in selecting the schools that their children attend.

The Excellence Movement

How did A Nation at Risk *shape the education policy debate?*

The formal name of the commission that prepared *A Nation at Risk* was the National Commission on Excellence in Education, and the movement that developed to carry out its recommendations came to be known as the Excellence Movement. A core assumption underlying the movement was that the reformers of the Great Society era had gone overboard in their zeal to expand popular access to all levels of education. That egalitarian excess came at the expense of academic rigor, and leaders of the Excellence Movement felt it was now time to reorder the nation's priorities.

What exactly did the excellence movement propose?

The key idea was to raise expectations regarding the academic performance of students and teachers. Reformers pressed for a basic curriculum with a renewed emphasis on traditional academic courses in math, science, English, history, and a foreign language. A longer school day and year was another important element of the agenda. To track student performance, reformers urged increased use of standardized testing, and to hold students accountable for their performance, reformers advocated stricter promotion and graduation requirements. As for teachers, the excellence movement called for improved teacher training, test-based competency, and use of merit pay to reward effort, innovation, and above all, positive results.[78]

If the basic idea of the excellence movement was to expect high levels of achievement from students, teachers, and schools, how could anyone oppose it?

The notion of raising expectations for all aspects of our public school systems does enjoy broad support. For too long, we expected excellence only from the most intellectually talented tier of students; such students were tracked into advanced-level courses and encouraged to pursue higher levels of education. Other students were placed into standard or vocational tracks where expectations were often minimal. Challenging all students with a more rigorous curriculum and higher standards is likely to enhance academic performance and prospects for long-term success.[79]

But too many academic demands imposes costs. In the zeal to achieve excellence, researchers have found that some teachers have piled on the homework and shortened or eliminated recess. Apart from the mental health problems that may develop when children have less time to play and unwind, scholars warn that learning suffers too. Recreation builds social skills, expands vocabularies, and makes children more alert once they return to the classroom.[80] Moreover, many educators find much value in the nontraditional courses pioneered in the 1960s, whether they are courses that broaden understanding of diverse cultures and histories or a class on science fiction literature that sparks a lifelong desire to read.

How did proponents of the excellence movement motivate students?

A combination of more demanding standards and high-stakes assessment. First, task forces of educational professionals, including teachers, college professors, and policy analysts together with business leaders and other community representatives, were assembled in virtually every state to determine what students of all ages ought to know in such core academic courses as mathematics, science, English, and social studies in order to become productive members of society. Second, the same task forces considered how schools would know whether students were satisfying the new standards. The leaders of the excellence movement supported not just the periodic and widespread administration of standardized tests but wanted the tests to have consequences. No longer would schools routinely tolerate social promotions, the practice of advancing students to the next grade regardless of their performance; high school graduates would have to earn their degrees. High-stakes standardized tests would not only enable schools to assess student progress, but also serve as an incentive for students to work hard.[81]

What is the downside, if any, to this strategy?

Critics of the standards/high stakes assessment approach pose a number of objections. To start, some question whether it is possible or desirable to identify a core body of knowledge that all students ought to possess. Linda Darling-Hammond and her colleagues asserted: "to adopt what might be called the 'bunch o' facts' approach to education—let alone to specify *which* facts must be taught—is by definition to wipe out pedagogy that aims for more ambitious learning." Others worry that a core curriculum inevitably favors majority-white, middle-class perspectives while shortchanging perspectives of many minority groups. Scholars who see education as training for democratic citizenship believe that mandating a core curriculum undermines the value of teaching students how to make choices and then take responsibility for those choices—a vital skill for active participation in civic life.[82]

Still others have criticized the heavy reliance on standardized tests. Some contend that standardized tests do a poor job on content validity (i.e., measuring what they purport to measure) and construct validity (i.e., the academic standards being measured must be relevant, age-appropriate, and fair). In addition, with so much at stake for students, teachers, and schools, a number of troubling developments have become increasingly common. Teachers are under pressure to "teach to the test" by setting aside significant amounts of class time to working on test-taking skills instead of nurturing the acquisition of knowledge and a love of learning. Cheating by students and even by teachers has become more prevalent. With so much riding on the outcome of test scores, schools may also have more of an incentive to isolate low-performing students than to educate them. Some studies have shown that high-stakes testing may inhibit learning by reinforcing fears of failure and inducing many disadvantaged students to drop out of school altogether. Leaving aside the issue of how the push toward standards and accountability affects student motivation, critics believe that students without the same opportunities to learn as students in more privileged situations are at a big disadvantage.[83] What had started out as a reform to strengthen equality of opportunity, then, may exacerbate inequality.

It seems that a great deal of pressure to improve academic performance has been placed on students. What about teachers? Have they been subjected to more stringent standards and held accountable for their performance too?

This has been harder to accomplish. Teachers' unions such as the National Education Association (NEA) have become increasingly powerful in national, state, and local politics in recent decades. They have consistently fought proposed reforms intended to evaluate the performance of teachers and reward that excellence through merit pay. Union leaders believe that merit pay would compel teachers to compete with each other, thereby undermining professionalism and collegiality. They also worry that merit pay decisions would be based on biased evaluations and would generate reams of new paperwork. Few states have adopted any kind of individual teacher reward system.[84] In the case of poor performance, the ultimate sanction is dismissal, but tenure makes removal of even the most incompetent teachers extraordinarily difficult. School administrators must amass abundant supporting evidence and wage a prolonged and expensive battle. Proposals to abolish tenure have been met with massive resistance by teachers and their potent unions.[85]

Given the difficulty of implementing teacher testing and any kind of system of rewards and sanctions for teacher performance, some policy analysts have focused on what happens before teachers even begin to stand in front of a classroom. Most states require teachers to obtain certificates in teaching methods before they can become permanent members of a school faculty. Programs at both the undergraduate and graduate levels offer instruction in cognitive development, psychology, pedagogy, classroom management, and various curricular programs. About three-quarters of the nation's two thousand four-year colleges offer separate teacher education programs.

Teacher education programs have never developed the prestige or rigor of the liberal arts, sciences, or the professions. Easy and trivial courses abound. Thomas Toch reports that colleges offer "sociological foundations" courses that require students to memorize flow charts of school bureaucracies and "curriculum design" courses that provide simple blueprints for preparing lesson plans. A study of the Southern regional Education Board, which analyzed 3,283 education graduates at seventeen major universities in the South, found that prospective teachers took substantially easier courses than other college students. Three-quarters of them took no classes in philosophy, economics, foreign languages, physics, and chemistry. Elementary school teachers did only 6 percent of their course work in mathematics and 9 percent of their course work in English—two of the most important subjects in elementary education.[86]

What needs to be done?

The obvious remedy is a more rigorous curriculum. Some education programs have shored up the content and structure of their curriculums by eliminating the raft of "Mickey Mouse" courses and requiring more challenging, academic courses. Some reformers, impatient with the slow pace of progress, have advocated doing away with teaching programs altogether by opening the teaching profession to liberal arts graduates without any formal training or certification in education. As expected, teachers unions have opposed the idea. But an anticipated dearth in the supply of teachers in the next decade caused by rising student enrollments and a bulge in teacher retirements may make this proposal a matter of necessity.[87]

A review of hundreds of studies of teaching effectiveness found that certification does not enhance effectiveness in the classroom, despite the claims of advocates of teachers colleges. "Determining who is qualified to teach is a task fraught with ambiguity and nuance, far more difficult than the mechanical process of counting a teacher's coursework suggests," concluded Kate Walsh, the author of the literature review.[88] To attract the best teachers, school districts need to separate themselves from the long practice of getting teachers exclusively from teachers colleges and certifying teachers based on their college course work.

Creative educators like James Fraser of Northeastern University have embraced the critiques of teachers colleges and worked to forge a new mission for them. Fraser acknowledges that among parents, taxpayers, and politicians, "the current system of teacher preparation is seen as part of the problem, not the solution." Fraser has proposed taking away teachers colleges' role in certifying teachers. "We should let school districts, and, ideally, in many cases, individual schools make the certification and the hiring decision," Fraser writes. "Our role as teacher educators will be to provide programs that add such clear and obvious value that school districts prefer our candidates to others. If we are doing a good job, our graduates will obviously be the best teachers."[89] By forcing teachers colleges to meet the needs of schools—rather than impose their approach on schools—the whole business of teacher preparation could be transformed.

So reformers have encountered a lot of frustration in trying to improve the performance of schools by evaluating and then either rewarding or sanctioning teachers. But there must be other ways to hold schools accountable for their performance?

Yes, rather than focus only on individual actors such as students and teachers, reformers have also targeted schools and school systems. The same logic applies. Assess how well schools and school systems are educating their students and then reward or punish accordingly. Everyone associated with the institution under scrutiny will presumably have a greater incentive to achieve better results. But while public opinion backs the idea of rewarding successful schools with more state and federal funds, Louann Bierlein reports that "little real, large-scale individual or group activity has been accomplished to date."[90]

Over a dozen states now have formal procedures enabling state governments to intervene in school districts that fail to satisfy minimal performance standards. Such state intervention can range from the issuance of orders mandating the district to adopt specific remedial measures to a full-fledged takeover of school management and finances by the state government. New Jersey has been particularly aggressive in taking over school districts wracked by corruption, inefficiency, and poverty in cities such as Jersey City, Newark, and Camden.[91]

What impact has the excellence movement ultimately had? Have all of the re-forms promoting a more rigorous curriculum, higher standards, and more accountability for students, teachers, and school districts paid off?

Mixed results. Some advocates such as Diane Ravitch have maintained that public schools have largely followed the central recommendation of *A Nation at Risk*—raise expectations of student achievement by offering a more challenging curriculum. Ravitch comments:

> The most important effect of the state-level reforms of the 1980s can be seen in the dramatic changes in high school course-taking patterns from 1982 to 1992. At the end of these ten years, students across the board—whites, blacks, Hispanics, Asians, American Indians, males, and females—were taking more academic courses. . . . Enrollments in advanced courses in foreign language, mathematics, and science went up substantially for every group of students. . . . remarkable progress was made in raising academic expectations for American students.[92]

Along with advances in course-taking patterns, Ravitch notes modest gains in test scores. With respect to the NAEP, she concludes: "The trends on the whole were encouraging. Most of the improvement in student performance occurred after 1984, very likely as a result of the state-level reforms enacted after the publication of *A Nation at Risk*."[93] Other interpretations of NAEP, known as the "nation's report card," have been less optimistic. One recent review found that elementary and middle school students have improved slightly or remained the same in science, math, reading, and writing, while senior high school students have stagnated or declined: "Looked at overall and evaluated without excuses, the NAEP assessments reveal a dreadful possibility: The longer today's American students remain in the school system, the poorer their performance in comparison with their predecessors."[94] The news is particularly grim for students in inner-city schools, where NAEP scores reveal substantial majorities of students failing to reach basic levels of achievement in reading, math, and science.[95] Even worse, after the gap in NAEP test scores between white and black students steadily narrowed during the 1980s, a 2000 report by the U.S. Department of Education documented that the gap began to widen again during the 1990s.[96]

In sum, the excellence movement succeeded in stimulating virtually every state to raise academic standards and hold students accountable. Students have taken more rigorous courses and arrested steady decline in standardized test scores of the 1960s and 1970s. But for many students in middle school and high school, and especially those in central cities, there has been little improvement in academic achievement. By the late 1980s, many frustrated reformers had begun calling for much more fundamental changes in the structure and organization of public education.

The Critique of Government Control over Schooling

It was probably inevitable that a disappointment with school achievement led to a critique of the bureaucratic structure of public education. What was the basis of that critique?

Conservatives charged that attempts to reform the existing institutional structures of public education were doomed to fail because those structures themselves were inherently flawed. A proliferation of programs, multiple administrative layers, and countless rules and regulations increasingly constricted the autonomy and professionalism of principals and teachers, inhibiting their capacity to be innovative, energetic, and enthusiastic. The bloated bureaucracy that prevailed throughout the nation's public-school systems was the key obstacle to improved educational performance.

But there was nothing new about bureaucracy in public education. Reformers at the beginning of the century deliberately instituted a bureaucratic form of organization in public schools in order to eliminate the mismanagement and inefficiency associated with decentralized school systems under the control of corrupt machine politicians.

True. The bureaucratic model, with its emphasis on specialization, a hierarchical chain of command, fair rules and procedures, and professionalization, was supposed to ensure honest and efficient administration of public-school systems. And the changes in organizational structure did bring improvements. The problem was not so much that school systems were organized according to bureaucratic principles, but that bureaucracy had become bloated and unresponsive to the central mission of schools—teaching children.

Why did that happen?

Partly it was just a matter of numbers. The postwar baby boom produced an explosion in the student population requiring a rapid expansion of facilities and teachers. In the 1960s alone, high schools nearly doubled the size of their faculties from 575,000 to about one million teachers. Meanwhile, rising enrollments were accompanied by continuing consolidation. As schools and school districts consolidated, principals and superintendents needed help in running their ever-expanding institutions. The number of administrators swelled. Nationwide, the teacher-administrator ratio declined from 31 to 1 in 1920 to 16 to 1 in 1974.[97]

Another major impetus for bureaucratization has been the increase in policy demands of the federal government and various stakeholder groups in the 1960s and 1970s. Starting with school desegregation, Washington, D.C., has imposed myriad rules, regulations, and mandates. Civil rights initiatives were subsequently extended to female students too. The War on Poverty led to the establishment of school lunch and Head Start programs. Later on, the federal government acted to protect the interests of nonnative speakers by mandating bilingual education programs. A desire to serve handicapped and other special needs students led to a multitude of new programs, all of which required administrators to supervise them, and thus added layers of bureaucracy.

Teachers' unions also have fostered bureaucratization. The NEA was founded in 1857 as a professional association to promote curriculum reform, comprehensive high schools, and standardized teacher training. The American Federation of Teachers (AFT) was established in 1897 to advocate better salaries and working conditions for teachers. Starting in the 1960s, the two unions became increasingly involved in collective bargaining. In 1965, teachers' unions struck at nine school systems; a decade later, strikes shut down 218 school systems that involved 182,300 teachers. The turmoil in the schools steadily undermined the power of principals over their schools. Collective bargaining agreements restrained every aspect of school life, such as teacher assignments and transfers, control of the classroom, evaluation, and discipline. Following the teachers' example, unions for custodians and other support staff also negotiated to take away authority over everyday school operations from principals and other school officials.[98]

Conservatives are quick to blame the federal government for the burgeoning bureaucracy in public school systems, but they too have contributed to the problem. State governments responded to the recommendations of President Reagan's National Commission on Excellence in Education by mandating sweeping changes in curriculums and standardized testing with little regard for the special needs of local school districts. In the process, they expanded the centralization of policy-making and state oversight of a whole new set of government programs. Louann Bierlein observes: "Ironically, education was perhaps more regulated and centralized during the late 1980s than ever before in our country's history."[99] President George W. Bush successfully pushed for mandatory testing of all K–12 students, which will produce yet another set of bureaucratic processes.

So the key to producing better schools is to slash the bureaucracy?

Actually, the critique is more fundamental than that. Conservative critics of public education in recent years have insisted on the need to attack the underlying causes of bureaucratization by zeroing in on the political institutions that allow public-school systems to become overly bureaucratic in the first place. The problem, they say, lies in the fact that public education is under the direct control of democratic institutions of government. They maintain that democracy inevitably spawns bureaucracy.

How so?

With public education in the public realm, interest groups use schools as a forum to confront a whole range of societal ills. The phenomenon is especially apparent in inner-city neighborhoods. As community institutions come under increasing strain, well-intentioned interest groups turn to the public schools to attack virtually every major social problem facing the country: drug and alcohol abuse, teenage pregnancy, AIDS, health care, day care, depression and other mental health disorders, adult illiteracy, and joblessness, to name just a few. Schools have responded to the avalanche of policy demands by adding countless programs and functions. When businesses complained about poor job skills, schools added computer and vocational-education programs. When community groups protested the treatment of gays, schools added "sensitivity" workshops and new curricular materials. When other groups complained about required English readings or sex education classes, districts adjusted their policies. With demand after demand, administrators reacted as best they could by creating new procedures and programs.

One result has been that schools are no longer simply just places of learning; rather, they have evolved into complex, all-purpose, social-service delivery systems. Another result is that the proliferation of programs and personnel needed to supervise them has contributed to a swelling bureaucracy. Moreover, the interest groups responsible for imposing new policy demands on the schools have a strong incentive to make sure the programs are implemented in ways they originally intended; hence, the new programs often come with precise rules and procedures that limit the discretion of school officials. In this way, democratic control over public schools exacerbates the problem of bureaucracy.[100]

If these new programs are benefiting disadvantaged students, is more bureaucracy such a bad thing?

Even if we assume that such programs are beneficial—and many conservatives would certainly challenge that assumption—the growing bureaucracy inhibits the primary mission of schools. Bureaucracy promises a system of organization that is rational, accountable, and efficient, extending from top-level policy-makers down to the "street-level bureaucrats" who coordinate and implement policy, but the reality is more complex. The system is a tangle of semiautonomous structures, each with its own logic and support structure that can make it impervious to any kind of coherent authority. "Actually, there is no one central office," Gerald Grant notes in his important study, *The World We Created at Hamilton High*. "There are scores of mini-fiefdoms each with its legislative mandates, advocates, lobbies, and chains of command, many reaching from Washington through state education agencies to the local districts."[101] Orderly organizational charts notwithstanding, most school systems lack true centralized leadership. The superintendent serves more as a manager of separate operations than a vigorous leader who provides vision for teaching and learning.

This Balkanized structure produces confusion about responsibility for the overall direction of the system. Superintendents, agency heads, principals, specialists, and teachers all have distinct notions of their responsibilities and loyalties. Some even get their paychecks from separate sources. Specialists for programs for bilingual or learning-disabled students, for example, often evaluate the abilities of students differently from principals or teachers. Some teachers have charged specialists with keeping students out of mainstream classes because of a desire to preserve high program enrollments. The specialists respond that they alone have the technical training necessary to make expert judgements. Principals stand by helplessly as groups with independent power bases fight such battles.

Bureaucracy is expensive. About one third of all school spending goes for administration and "support services," such as attendance officers, guidance counselors, psychologists, librarians, transportation, and maintenance. About three fifths of the school budget pays for teacher salaries and benefits and classroom supplies. The rest goes toward food services and other noneducational programs.[102] Between 1953 and 1985, the number of specialized staff members tripled to deal with new mandates from the federal and state governments.[103]

Bureaucracy also limits the discretion of teachers and principals. All levels of government have issued a myriad of rules and mandates governing curriculum, pedagogical styles, use of textbooks, and even what can and cannot be said in the classroom. Such constraints limit autonomy, suppress creative energy, stifle innovation, and inevitably dull enthusiasm for teaching. The universal application of a standard or rule does not always conform to particular needs or interests. Nevertheless, compliance is expected. The result too often is resentment toward those establishing the standards and rules for presuming that they alone know the best way to educate students.

But this is a democracy. If citizens are unhappy with the creeping bureaucracy throughout public education, what is stopping them from going to the polls and voting in elected representatives who will address the problem?

Organized interest groups with a stake in the status quo tend to wield disproportionate influence. Stakeholders like teacher unions pay close attention to issues that affect their interests and mobilize intense pressure through lobbying, lawsuits, or the electoral process—pressure that often overwhelms the voices of unorganized citizens. Even if citizens are able to mobilize around education issues, there is no guarantee that educational priorities will prevail in the political process. Students and parents are often losers in a system of democratic control over education.[104]

It's not that grim, is it? Don't parents who are that dissatisfied with conditions in their local public schools always have the option of leaving?

That points to the ultimate problem with democratic control over public education, according to conservative critics. That exit option is actually quite limited. In most school districts, students are assigned to public schools based on residential patterns. If parents are dissatisfied with their children's schools and would prefer they attend another public school, they must relocate to another residential area, a choice that many families simply do not have. Some parents may remove their children from the public school system altogether and enroll them in private school. But tuition costs make this an unrealistic option for many.

For conservative reformers, the lack of choice that parents have over the schooling of their children highlights the core deficiency of education in this country—the government's monopoly over public schools. As long as government-funded and -operated schools offer the only game in town, public schools will have little incentive to hold down costs or improve the quality of their product. Schools face few adverse consequences for poor performance.

School Choice: Vouchers

What is the solution?

Conservative critics contend that there is no sense in trying to reform a public monopoly. This explains why all of the well-intentioned policy initiatives springing from the excellence movement of the 1980s yielded less-than-dramatic improvements in academic achievement. Instead, what is required is an all-out assault on the government's monopoly on public education by promoting competition among schools. To stimulate competition, the government might provide families with a sum of money, a voucher, which they could then use to send their children to either public or private schools. If the local public school was deemed inadequate, parents could turn to private schools, now affordable with the government-supplied voucher. In this way, school vouchers create school choice, and school choice establishes a market for education. And within that market, public schools would have an incentive to compete with one another by offering high-quality education at a reasonable cost or risk shrinking enrollments and possible closure.

Is school choice really such a new idea?

The American Revolutionary pamphleteer Thomas Paine and utilitarian philosopher John Stuart Mill both proposed some form of school choice. In modern times, the economist Milton Friedman first proposed the use of unregulated school vouchers to spark competition within public education in the mid-1950s.[105] But at a time when popular support for public schools was widespread, Friedman's proposal was dismissed as unnecessary and extreme. By the 1980s, however, amid ominous reports of the declining academic performance of public schools and with the ascendance of a privatist ideology, the Reagan administration resurrected the idea of school choice and made it a cornerstone of its education policy agenda. Democrats in Congress and powerful interest groups within the public-education sector opposed school choice, fearing that vouchers for private schools would drain students and resources away from public schools. At the state level, California voters in 1993 rejected Proposition 174, which would have given all families with children in private schools a voucher totaling about half of the average per-pupil expenditure for students in the state's public schools. Nevertheless, school choice has appealed to a growing number of Americans, especially those living in inner-city neighborhoods whose children seemed locked into severely distressed schools with bleak prospects for improvement. School choice offers hope for a way out.[106]

Have school voucher plans been adopted anywhere?

In Milwaukee, black parents, frustrated by a failed desegregation plan and other disappointing reform initiatives, decided to support a school choice program that provided vouchers worth $2,500 to up to a thousand students, about 1 percent of the city's school population. The program was targeted to families earning incomes less than 1.75 times the poverty level, and participating schools were prohibited from charging tuition to eligible students in excess of the voucher. If demand outstripped supply, schools were obligated to use a lottery to determine admission. The Milwaukee Parental Choice Program was expanded in 1995 to include 15,000 students, and religious schools were allowed to participate in the program for the first time. By the 2001–02 academic year, about 11,000 children from low-income families were receiving vouchers worth about $5,326 per year under the program.[107]

Cleveland became the second city to implement a taxpayer-funded voucher plan; it gave vouchers of up to $2,250 per year to about 4,500 students from low-income families in 2001–02. The voucher movement reached a new level in 1999, when Florida became the first state to adopt a statewide program. That program not only affords poor students a way out of inadequate schools, it also establishes a direct incentive for underperforming public schools to improve. Under the law, all students between third and tenth grades are tested each year, and schools are graded based on those test scores. Any school receiving an "F" in two years of a four-year period would be required to submit to state intervention and offer its students vouchers worth up to $4,000 which they could use to pay for private school tuition.[108]

The voucher programs in Milwaukee, Cleveland, and Florida have all been subjected to legal challenges on the ground that they violate the First Amendment's prohibition against the state "establishing" a religion. Lower federal courts had reached conflicting decisions on the issue until the Supreme Court ruled in 2002 in a 5 to 4 vote that Cleveland's provision of public funds for religious school tuition did not breach the Constitutional principle of separation of church and state. The Court's majority reasoned that Cleveland's voucher program was "neutral in all respects towards religion" because participants could use their vouchers in whatever way they wished, thus giving them a "genuine choice" between religious and nonreligious schools. Therefore the city was not using public money to endorse, promote, or establish any religion. The dissenters questioned whether parents actually had a meaningful choice regarding where to enroll their children, noting that the voucher's value ($2,250) was too low to pay tuition at most private schools. The fact that 96 percent of the children using vouchers attended parochial schools indicated, in the view of the dissenters, a breach of the First Amendment.[109]

Does the Supreme Court's decision mean that many more cities and states will now adopt school voucher programs?

Voucher advocates believe so. They contend that questions about the constitutionality of school vouchers had deterred many citizens, interest groups, and public officials searching for an alternative to malfunctioning urban public schools from pressing for legislation establishing new voucher programs. However, opponents note that the legality of such programs remains in doubt under many *state* constitutions containing stronger language prohibiting government aid to religious schools. Others argue that vouchers will never be implemented on a widespread basis throughout the United States because most people, especially in the suburbs, are generally satisfied with public schools.[110] Voucher proponents say urban families are dissatisfied with public schools, so voucher programs will attract more and more support, especially among minorities.[111]

Doesn't the likelihood of voucher programs proliferating, at least within American cities, depend upon their effectiveness? How effective have existing voucher programs been?

Education researcher John F. Witte completed a thorough evaluation of the Milwaukee program and found that the parents whose children had participated in the program were "much more satisfied" with the private schools than with the previous public schools. Indeed, Witte reported nearly unanimous parental approval of the program. Long waiting lists demonstrate strong demand for school choice in the city's lower-income neighborhoods. Witte also found that most private schools receiving public subsidies benefited as a result of physical improvements to school structures, reduced teacher turnover, and a more secure financial status.[112]

But Witte found little evidence that voucher students showed any noticeable improvement in educational performance in reading or math.[113] Other scholarly studies have reported meaningful improvements in test scores.[114] A RAND study surveying the literature on school choice found modest gains in academic achievement for African-American (but not Latino) students after one or two years in voucher schools, but cautioned that much remains unknown. RAND researchers noted that most studies have defined academic achievement narrowly by focusing on standardized test scores while overlooking continuation in school, graduation, and college attendance as well as other innovative ways to assess what actually takes place within classrooms. They also warned that most studies have ignored the systemic effects of school choices programs on students who remain in regular public schools.[115]

The vigorous demand for the program suggests that private schools must be doing something right. That raises the question of what kinds of students choose to participate in voucher programs. Are they somehow advantaged over nonchoosers? And, if so, does that exacerbate educational inequality?

This is one of the primary concerns of the opponents of school choice. They fear that the most intelligent, capable, and privileged students will be the ones most likely to participate in voucher programs, and that their transfer to private schools will leave public schools even more bereft of intellectual talent, a demoralizing prospect for all concerned with public schools. Voucher proponents have sought to minimize the likelihood of "cream skimming" by using lottery systems to determine who will be allowed to participate. But critics observe that access to information about the existence of voucher programs and procedures for applying are often inadequate and unequally distributed. Even within poorer communities, relatively better-off parents and caregivers are more likely to take the initiative to participate in a voucher program, a fact that contributes to deepening inequalities.[116]

Even when students do have sufficient information regarding school choice programs, they will not necessarily make their decisions based primarily on educational quality, as many school choice advocates assume. While some may be guided by a commitment to educational advancement, others may prefer to remain in a public school offering racial solidarity and cultural familiarity.[117]

Some private schools may be engaging in subtle screening activities to deter student applicants who may be more difficult and expensive to teach.[118] The RAND study mentioned earlier, for example, found a clear underrepresentation of students with disabilities in voucher schools.[119] More broadly, the RAND researchers went on to conclude that "unrestricted-choice programs are likely to lead to increased stratification by race/ethnicity and socioeconomic status, especially if schools are permitted to choose students."[120]

School Choice: Charter Schools

Given that vouchers arouse such great controversy, is there another model of school choice that may attract broad support?

Despite persistent questions about the impact of school voucher programs on educational achievement and equity, they remain popular among African-Americans and Latino Americans. Some have even come to see vouchers as a civil rights issue.[121] Accordingly, additional voucher programs may yet be implemented in other cities. But their expansion beyond urban borders seems less likely. Although Florida adopted a statewide program, teachers' unions and other liberal interest groups remain fiercely opposed. Many suburban communities probably will be reluctant to back any policy initiative—whether it be school desegregation or vouchers—that would enable poor, minority students from the city to enroll in significant numbers in predominantly white, middle-class schools in the suburbs.

A more politically palatable version of school choice that has already demonstrated far broader appeal than vouchers is charter schools. As a public-private hybrid, charter schools have something to offer supporters and opponents of school choice. They resemble public schools in that they are open to all, publicly funded, and ultimately responsible to a public authority for their performance. On the other hand, charter schools are not actually operated by the government; indeed, they can be established and run by almost anyone—teachers, parents from the community, a nonprofit organization, or a for-profit business firm. Like private schools, charter schools have extensive control over curriculum, personnel, finance, and scheduling. And like private schools, parents choose schools for their children; no student is assigned to a charter school based solely on where he or she happens to live.[122]

So the availability of choice to parents and students gives charter schools an incentive to offer a quality product?

Right. But in addition, charter schools offer another feature designed to foster high-quality education—the notion of accountability. Charter schools are held accountable for their results.

That is a significant departure from public school practice. How are charter schools held accountable?

Whatever group proposes to create a charter school basically enters into a contract, or a charter, with a public authority, usually a state or local board of education. That contract defines the mission of the school, the methods for achieving the goals, and anticipated outcomes. If the school fails to achieve the promised results, its charter may be revoked. The central idea is that charter schools will be given substantial autonomy to educate their students. That, in turn, enables charter schools to offer a diverse range of curricular choices and pedagogical styles, thereby expanding the educational choices available to parents and students.

The price for being liberated from the constraints of the bureaucratized public-school system is accountability. Unlike underperforming schools in the public-school system, which go on operating without any consequences, charter schools that fail to meet their goals may be shut down. The combination of autonomy and accountability is appealing to school choice advocates, who see charter schools as expanding the options of parents and students and sparking competition with conventional public schools. Voucher opponents, who are concerned about draining public schools of essential resources, tend to be more open to charter schools because they continue to operate within the public realm. President Bill Clinton, while opposing vouchers, was a forceful advocate of charter schools, proposing sizeable increases in federal aid to subsidize start-up and operating costs.[123]

Given their appeal across the ideological spectrum, how pervasive have charter schools become?

The rise of charter schools has been rather astonishing. A scholar named Ray Budde is credited with using the term "charter schools" for the first time in a 1989 article. The former president of the AFT, Albert Shanker, then picked up on the idea and promoted it. In 1991, Minnesota adopted the first charter-school law. California followed suit in 1992, and by 1999, thirty-six states and the District of Columbia had passed legislation authorizing the establishment of charter schools. By 2001, there were over 2,400 charter schools serving nearly 580,000 students.[124]

The twin principles of autonomy and accountability are appealing. It's easy to see why charter schools have proliferated so quickly. Why aren't there even more?

Political opposition is a factor, albeit less so than with school voucher programs. Critics charge that charter schools drain resources and the best students away from district schools in the public-school system. As for the first point, public funds are transferred from a district school to a charter school whenever students leave the former for the latter. But the loss of revenue to the district is offset by a decrease in the cost of educating students. Charter-school advocate Chester Finn and his associates put it this way: "The fundamental concept of any education choice regimen is that money follows children to the schools their families select. Public dollars are meant to be spent for the education of a particular *student.* They are not entitlements for *school systems.*" As for the second point, Finn et al. acknowledge that some charter schools "cream" some of the most advantaged students while leaving many of the more disadvantaged students behind in district schools, a practice that strengthens opposition to charters by the defenders of traditional public schools.[125]

Fourteen states have so far declined to adopt charter authorization laws, while other states impose onerous requirements upon groups seeking charter approval. Other states, perhaps reacting to political pressures from established interest groups, provide less than full per-pupil funding for charter-school students and little or no funding for facilities and capital costs.[126] Brand-new charter schools with enthusiastic teachers and students but with extremely limited resources are often forced to locate in abandoned schools desperately in need of repair or in former warehouses, department stores, or converted restaurants. Obtaining loans to secure better facilities and resources is problematic because charter schools are a novel entity and a risky proposition, given their uncertain cash flow and limited collateral. The fiscal constraints are compounded by a lack of business and administrative experience on the part of many charter founders, which translates into even more headaches during the first years of operation. Absent additional fiscal and technical support from the state or private sector, simply getting a charter school up and running is an achievement.[127]

How have charter schools performed?

The competitive forces unleashed by the spread of charter schools encourage teachers and administrators to experiment with innovations in curriculum and pedagogy. A group of scholars who conducted an extensive study in Arizona, a state with by far the most charter schools, confirmed that charters "have unlocked enormous energy from entrepreneurial parents and teachers."[128] Yet those same scholars also found that the extent of innovation was somewhat less than charter-school advocates had anticipated. While charter schools effectively make certain educational approaches such as back-to-basics and Montessori schooling more widely available, they have generally not developed pathbreaking forms of learning. In short, educational options have broadened, but not in the way charter school proponents had hoped.[129]

Accountability was supposed to be a hallmark of charter schools, a crucial point of distinction from traditional public schools. But even Chester Finn and his colleagues concede:

> Promising accountability systems for charter schools are still few and far between. In some states, the necessary standards and assessments are not in place; the cognizant boards and bureaucracies do not know how—or don't much want—to monitor their charter schools; or the law is muddy as to whether anyone has authority to do anything about weak performance by charter schools.[130]

But isn't this where the market is expected to play a role? Competitive pressures arising from the creation of numerous charter schools will force all schools to perform at a higher level, or parents will choose to enroll their children elsewhere. Isn't that accountability?

Sure, school-choice proponents rely heavily upon the idea that market forces will enhance educational performance. But charter-school advocates also hoped to rely on public authorities to oversee (as opposed to operate directly) charter schools and ensure that they were satisfying the goals set for them in their charters. Administrative monitoring would complement parental monitoring in promoting the overall objective of accountability.[131] However, given pervasive lapses in administrative oversight, even the most vociferous defenders of charter schools have expressed cause for some concern.[132]

How do charter schools compare to traditional public schools on the important issue of educational achievement?

A survey of empirical studies on the academic performance of charter-school students by social scientists Gary Miron and Christopher Nelson found a "mixed picture." Research from some states revealed a positive impact, while research from other states found a negative impact; still other studies reported both positive and negative impacts. Miron and Christopher concluded that "[o]verall, the charter impact on student achievement appears to be mixed or very slightly positive." Most scholars caution that it is still too early to reach firm conclusions.[133]

What effect have charter schools had on producing greater equity in educational opportunity?

This issue has generated considerable controversy. Some point out that with their freedom to deviate from "state-mandated curricula," charter schools are able to "celebrate difference over uniformity" and enable "low-income communities of color . . . to embrace their own cultural heritage." Surveys of parents confirm broad satisfaction with the power of charter schools to offer "a more culturally relevant curriculum and hire teachers enthusiastic about teaching such a curriculum." Many charter schools, particularly in inner-city neighborhoods, are established for the purpose of serving so-called "at-risk students." The smaller schools and class size offer such students, who may have dropped out of district schools, a second chance at earning a degree. Overall, Chester Finn and his associates contend that charter schools educate a higher percentage of minority students than do district schools. The fact that charter schools, due to their smaller size, are less likely to track students may also reduce the internal segregation common in many district schools.[134]

But Amy Wells and her colleagues respond that the emancipatory potential of charter schools offering "pedagogical approaches grounded in perceptions of cultural group differences" is seriously undercut by the segregative effects of charter schools throughout the country:

> At the same time that disenfranchised communities are creating sites of resistance to the traditional state-run education system through charter schools, more powerful and privileged communities are also breaking off from the public system via charter schools. Even in low-income neighborhoods, charter schools tend to serve students who are better off in terms of having parents who are actively engaged in their education.

Other scholars have reached similar conclusions about racial segregation. For example, Frank Brown's study of North Carolina found that while roughly the same percentage of white and black students are enrolled in charter schools, most individual schools are almost entirely segregated by race, and that the state's charter schools are "far more racially segregated than regular public schools."[135]

How is this happening?

One problem is simply that most charter schools, located outside inner-city neighborhoods, limit access for lower-income, minority students.[136] Apart from the physical barriers, a lack of information also contributes to the racial and economic isolation. Many inner-city parents either do not know about charter schools at all or erroneously believe that they charge tuition. For their part, charter schools do not always disseminate information widely, preferring instead to rely on informal recruiting networks. At worst, some studies report evidence of screening by charter-school administrators to discourage students with special needs from applying to minimize school costs in a climate of tight budgets.[137]

The political ramifications of deepening racial and class segregation are disturbing. Inner-city communities grow ever more isolated and alienated from the rest of society, further diminishing the potential for any kind of collective action aimed at fundamental change. As Amy Wells and her colleagues note: "Segregation and separation of the wealthy from the non-wealthy make it difficult for members of a poor, isolated community to build coalitions based on mutual interests with people who have the political and economic means to invest in public services such as schools."[138] Abandoned both physically and politically, lower-income people of color are denied an opportunity to obtain a sound education and pursue the American Dream.

The Future of Urban Education Policy

Education reform seems to have a schizoid character. Some policy-makers seem to focus on opening doors for more and more people to enjoy opportunity. Others care more about what happens once children walk through the door into the classroom—what kinds of subjects they are taught and how they are going to be held accountable. What gives?

The latter half of the twentieth century witnessed two sweeping movements to reform public education in the United States. The first sought to promote equality of opportunity in public schools regardless of one's race, gender, national origin, or class. It began with the U.S. Supreme Court declaring in *Brown v. Board of Education* that racially segregated public schools are inherently unequal. The federal government, under pressure from civil rights organizations, then embarked upon a long and halting campaign to end racial isolation in the nation's public schools. Subsequent litigation and lobbying efforts aimed to expand educational opportunities for other groups that had experienced invidious discrimination. Like-minded reformers also tried to ameliorate huge disparities in per-pupil expenditures between school districts by restructuring the way in which public schools are financed. The driving impulse behind each of these policy initiatives was a desire to make public education more equitable.

A second reform movement emerged in the 1980s, contending not only that the first reform movement had failed to achieve its goals but that it had inadvertently contributed to a protracted decline in the educational achievement levels of American students by lowering expectations and adding new layers of bureaucracy to an already bloated school system. The new wave of reformers promised to restore excellence in the public schools by establishing rigorous standards to measure the performance of students, teachers, and schools with mechanisms for holding each accountable in the event they failed to meet those standards. In the 1990s, other reformers took aim at the underlying administrative and political structures that fostered bureaucratic excess while insulating schools from the wishes and demands of their principal clients—students and parents. For these reformers, excellence could be attained only by breaking up the government's monopoly on public education, nurturing competition among schools, and allowing the magic of the market to work its wonders. School choice, especially in the form of vouchers and charter schools, became the chief vehicle for improving the quality of public education in America.

Both reform movements seem to offer something of value. Is it possible to take the best ideas from each and come up with a synthesis that might inspire even more effective policy initiatives?

The notion of fashioning policies that aspire to promote both equity and excellence is attractive and worth the effort. Let's start with school choice. Most liberals concede that even the more conservative variant of school choice—vouchers—has virtues. To start, they acknowledge that there is something fundamentally unfair about denying lower-income children the opportunity to attend public schools other than the ones they are assigned to based upon the location of their residence. If middle-class households can move to a different and better public-school district or pay tuition for a private-school education, then basic fairness would suggest that poorer families should have some options too. So it is not surprising that voucher programs are broadly popular with parents whose children are assigned to poorly performing public schools in distressed urban neighborhoods.

And there are other reasons for their popularity. The competitive pressures unleashed by voucher programs force schools to find ways to become more efficient, innovative, and responsive to the needs and interests of students and parents.[139] One result is that urban schools have begun to offer curricula and teaching styles more closely geared to the diverse groups that populate America's cities. An education that honors and respects the history and heritage of a particular group is a potential source of cultural and political empowerment.

At the same time, conservatives acknowledge that a purely market-based system has flaws. Anticompetitive practices among education producers may undermine benefits to consumers. Parents and students may lack sufficient information to make wise choices about schools. Inadequate transportation may further limit educational options. Finally, some studies suggest that unconstrained school choice exacerbates preexisting inequalities based on race, ethnicity, and class.

So can we have a voucher program that preserves the benefits of school choice while limiting its drawbacks?

Perhaps, but such a program would require a much more assertive role for government in promoting the twin goals of excellence and equity.

But isn't that a fundamental break from the libertarian vision embraced by many voucher advocates?

Some voucher advocates would object to a more assertive role for government as a step backward, but other supporters of school choice might be open to the idea. The supporters of charter schools, for example, do not insist upon the radical downsizing or near-elimination of government espoused by many voucher proponents. Instead, they see government assuming a fundamentally different role in public education. Rather than directly running schools, government would turn over responsibility for day-to-day operations to other entities within the private sector, such as a group of teachers, a community-based organization, a college, or a for-profit business firm. The government's role would be confined to setting overall goals, monitoring school performance, reporting results, and taking remedial action if needed.

Under this scenario, the government's role would be *limited*, thus preserving the benefits created by independently run schools, but *important*, in the sense that institutions of democratic control would still be responsible for the formulation and attainment of pressing societal goals such as excellence and equity.[140]

OK, then explain what the government would do in a school voucher program.

At a minimum, government would still be responsible for regulating the health and safety of public schools, no small task given the dilapidated and dangerous conditions that abound in many city schools. Government would also establish minimum standards regarding curriculum and teacher qualifications. To ensure that parents make informed choices about schools for their children, government would need to provide honest and straightforward information about all schools through direct mailings to parents, Web sites, telephone hot lines, and community bulletin boards. That information should include quantitative data on test scores, graduation rates, teachers' credentials and experience, and enrollment demographics, as well as more qualitative assessments from parents, educators, and other experts.

To minimize the likelihood of racial and class segregation, government would have to enforce antidiscrimination laws and assume a more proactive stance in regulating schools that engage in subtle screening practices to discourage student applicants who might be more difficult or costly to educate.

Finally, government might implement a progressive voucher system in which vouchers would be inversely related to household income. If the average per-pupil expenditure on schooling in the United States is now $6,500 per year, an equitable program would provide poor families with vouchers worth $10,000 to $12,000 each. Such a voucher program not only would expand access of poor students to a much wider variety of school but would also give elite schools an incentive to attract at least some disadvantaged children possessing sizeable vouchers offering an immediate infusion of resources. This version of school choice—call it "regulated school choice"—might engender a healthy competition among schools while preserving a supervisory role for government that might yield both excellence and equity.[141]

How would regulated school choice bring about greater equity in districts with charter schools?

This is where the "regulated" part of regulated school choice enters the picture. Along with setting standards for health and safety, curriculum, and teacher qualifications, the public sector would also require that charter schools have diverse student populations. At a minimum, this would entail regulations prohibiting discrimination based upon race, ethnicity, national origin, class, gender, and disability. But charter schools could also be required to take more affirmative steps to promote the ideal of equality of educational opportunity.

To combat the problem of racial segregation in public education, for instance, charter schools could be required to ensure that their student populations mirror the racial profile of their district populations. Some states already include such a requirement in their charter schools' enabling legislation. Yet this strategy's capacity for effecting racial desegregation is constrained by extensive residential segregation that renders some jurisdictions overwhelmingly white and others overwhelmingly non-white. An alternative, proposed by Charles Willie and Michael Alves, is a school-choice plan that cuts across school district boundaries. Parents and children would be allowed to choose a public school that is located within a particular geographic area, say part of a city and part of a suburb. School districts would try to respect the expressed preferences of households as much as possible while seeking to ensure a racially balanced school population. Such a "controlled choice" plan would expand educational options for parents and children, spur competition among schools, improve academic achievement, and broaden opportunities for students of color.[142]

But doesn't this resemble the racial desegregation schemes of the 1970s that provoked so much racial conflict and political opposition?

Not quite. The desegregation plans of recent decades often relied upon mandatory busing and compulsory attendance at designated schools. The Willie and Alves proposal relies upon school choice—albeit a somewhat limited version—to build popular support by giving parents some flexibility over where to enroll their children. Even a system of controlled choice would stimulate a market in public education and thus a host of benefits arising from growing competition among public schools. Still, it is reasonable to assume that many parents and students who do not get their first choice would be disappointed and thus inclined to oppose such a system.

Anticipating such a reaction, as well as other possible problems with wedding public school choice to race-based integration strategies,[143] policy analyst Richard Kahlenberg has proposed an intriguing alternative designed to improve academic achievement and educational opportunity for less privileged students. He contends that the nation's public schools are highly segregated not just by race but by class, and that schools populated by predominantly low-income children tend to perform the most poorly. Kahlenberg's idea for enhancing educational quality and opportunity is to give every child the option to attend a public school with a majority of middle-class students. Research shows that economically integrated schools increase the academic performance and life chances of poor children by giving them access to peers with larger vocabularies and knowledge bases, higher aspirations, more positive orientations toward achievement, and a lower tendency to engage in disruptive behavior. Studies also indicate that schools with majority middle-class student populations are more likely to benefit from parental involvement and attract more qualified teachers.[144]

Low-income people might have an incentive to support class-based integration, but why would middle- and upper-income people choose to send their children to economically integrated public schools?

Kahlenberg offers several reasons. First, his plan to foster socioeconomic diversity is grounded within a framework of public-school choice, although as with the Willie-Alves proposal, this version of school choice is not absolute. Still, even controlled choice expands options for parents and students and nurtures market-based competition, with all of its consequent benefits, and thus constitutes a marked improvement over the absence of any choice (short of moving to another district or abandoning public schools altogether).

Under Kahlenberg's plan every public school would have a majority of middle-class students, so parents would have no reason to fear that their children would have to attend a struggling school with mostly lower-income students. Making such an assurance is not as difficult as it might sound because 75 percent of schools in the United States already have majority-middle-class student populations.[145] Where there are school districts consisting of a large number of schools with majority-low-income student populations, some rearranging would need to take place. New districts might be created, for example, by dividing a metropolitan region into slices so that each slice contains a section of a city with a relatively high proportion of low-income students and a section of a suburb with a relatively high proportion of middle- and upper-income students.

To allay the concerns of middle-class parents worried about an influx of low-income students into their schools, individual schools could retain ability-grouping practices to ensure that students with more advanced skills would not be held back. At the same time, ability grouping could be administered with significant protections for poor children. All students would be exposed to a rigorous academic curriculum (as opposed to the common practice in previous decades of relegating most low-income students to a vocational track), though the pace of learning would vary by skill level. Schools could work to maximize mobility among ability groupings so that students initially placed in lower levels would not remain trapped there indefinitely. Ability grouping could apply to some subjects such as reading and math, but not other subjects such as social studies, music, and art. Kahlenberg concludes that economically integrated public schools would strengthen the nation's work force and produce a more socially cohesive population.[146]

This is a provocative proposal, but middle-class, suburban parents might still be expected to balk at the prospect of sending their children to public schools in distressed urban neighborhoods.

Keep in mind that most would not have to. Majority-middle-class student populations could be constructed in suburban jurisdictions by admitting low-income students from the city and low-income neighborhoods in increasingly diverse suburbs. Some middle-class suburban students will want to attend public schools in cities, perhaps out of a desire for something new and different or perhaps because the school-choice culture has inspired urban schools to revamp their curriculums and offer exciting and unique programs of study.

Maybe. But many other suburban students and their parents will still be reluctant to choose an urban school.

Local, state, and federal governments might have to step in and take more aggressive measures to encourage suburban households to make that choice. Such measures might include significant infusions of resources to enable urban schools to spruce up their physical plants, reduce class sizes, hire better teachers, offer more extracurricular activities, and provide technologically sophisticated equipment and computers.

Even if all of that is politically feasible, isn't there one other important source of potential opposition from both suburban and urban neighborhoods? Doesn't this version of school choice, not to mention many others, undermine the idea and appeal of the neighborhood school?

Neighborhood schools often play a crucial role in fostering a strong sense of community. On the other hand, Kahlenberg points out that public-school choice can nurture new kinds of communities that may be superior to spatially based ones:

> At their best schools of choice can become communities of ideas, transcending class, race, and geography. Common values—stressing back-to-basics at one school, multiculturalism and cooperative learning at another—might bind together people from different backgrounds. In a highly mobile society, in which many neighbors do not know one another anyway, a community committed to an idea may be particularly valuable, filling a void left by the lack of traditional community in residential areas. This notion, of a community of ideas and values rather than race and ethnicity, is at the heart of the American experiment.[147]

Using public school choice to bring about socioeconomically integrated schools is consistent with Horace Mann's ideal of the common school in which children from all backgrounds, advantaged and disadvantaged, would be educated under the same roof. To the extent it is possible to approach that ideal, there is the hope of creating a new kind of community that is far more inclusive than the communities produced by racially and economically segregated neighborhoods and schools.[148]

Is it possible to blend lessons learned from previous reform initiatives seeking equity and excellence with respect to other issues in urban education? What about the problem of inequalities between urban and suburban schools arising from differences in the tax bases of each?

In the 1970s, public-interest-law organizations challenged the constitutionality of school finance systems that allowed sizeable differences in per-pupil expenditures. Although some state courts found such disparities to be unconstitutional, implementation of court orders mandating equitable reforms turned out to be politically problematic. More affluent suburban districts fiercely resisted equalization policies.

Since 1989, however, a second wave of litigation has been more effective. Recent lawsuits have shifted the emphasis away from inequities associated with spending differences among disparate school districts (i.e., inputs) and toward achievement differences among disparate districts (i.e., outputs). The overall *adequacy* of an education received by students at schools with limited resources became the new focal point of litigation. Critics of school finance systems pointed to the minimal state standards for promotion and graduation—standards that presumably established the definition of an "adequate" education—and then asked whether impoverished school districts could raise sufficient resources to provide such education. Many state supreme courts found the argument compelling. In striking down school finance systems that failed to provide an adequate education in the poorest districts, judges felt shielded from charges of judicial activism because they relied on public officials for definitions of what constituted an "adequate" education. As a result, courts have issued numerous orders requiring policy reforms and an upsurge in state spending in poor school districts. This is another example of education policy incorporating elements of both reform movements on behalf of the dual goals of excellence and equity.[149]

Maybe the most intractable problem for urban education involves racial isolation. How might a synthesis of the equity and excellence movements address that dilemma?

The Supreme Court's holding in *Brown v. Board of Education* that racially segregated schools are inherently unequal continues to garner overwhelming support from Americans as an abstract principle. In practice, however, efforts to desegregate urban public schools hit a brick wall when an increasingly conservative Supreme Court decided in 1974 that a lower federal court could not impose an interdistrict desegregation plan on a metropolitan area absent evidence of a history of intentional racial discrimination. An intriguing way around the roadblock emerged recently in state courts. Following the hallowed principle established in *Brown*, the Connecticut Supreme Court ruled in 1996 that racially isolated public schools in the Hartford metropolitan area are inherently unequal and must be desegregated whether or not metropolitan-wide segregation was the result of intentional governmental action.[150]

The Connecticut Supreme Court's ruling is clearly consistent with the goal of educational equity. But how is it related to the other reform movement?

The governor of Connecticut responded to the court's decision by assembling a twenty-one-member panel of politicians, education experts, attorneys, and civil rights activists to recommend strategies for interdistrict desegregation. Five months after receiving the panel's report, the state assembly passed legislation aimed at reducing racial isolation in Connecticut's schools while improving the quality of education throughout the state, but particularly in cities. Among the remedies endorsed by the state assembly were various programs to facilitate the movement of white students from suburban schools to urban schools and minority students in the opposite direction, including interdistrict magnet schools, charter schools, and an intradistrict and interdistrict public school choice plan. To increase the likelihood that suburban students would be attracted to city schools, the state increased its funding for education by an additional $200 million, much of which would be allocated to building new school facilities (especially near city borders) and improving existing urban schools (especially regional magnet schools) by hiring better teachers, enhancing technology, and lengthening the school day.

Some education experts question whether the Connecticut strategy of expanded school choice and financial aid to urban schools will substantially reduce racial isolation, but state officials insist this is just the beginning of a long-term commitment to comply with the Connecticut Supreme Court's order. In 1999, the trial court responsible for overseeing the case expressed its satisfaction with Connecticut's progress so far.[151]

The plaintiffs in *Sheff v. O'Neill* continue to be frustrated by the slow progress in desegregating public schools in Connecticut. One ongoing problem is money. Although the state has significantly increased funding for regional magnet schools, simply bringing per-pupil expenditures up to the equivalent level in suburban schools will not be enough to lure a significant number of suburban students to city schools. A *higher* level of per-pupil expenditure will probably be necessary, but the state legislature has hesitated to make that commitment. And the state's other key segregation strategy, a voluntary school choice plan that enables urban students to enroll in suburban public schools, has been hampered by a lack of available space in the suburban schools.[152] Still, the Connecticut initiative is promising because it combines key aspects of both reform movements in seeking to improve educational performance by expanding parental and student choice while promoting greater equality of educational opportunity.

Public Education and Democracy

It's one thing to chart a new direction for public policy based on the most promising ideas and values of previous reform movements, but it's another matter to make that new direction a reality. What are the prospects for policy initiatives combining the goals of excellence and equity actually getting implemented?

Some policy analysts believe that all that is necessary is to hire an entrepreneurial school superintendent capable of pushing through desired reforms. But widespread political opposition can derail the best of ideas and the most talented school superintendent. Implementing policies that promote equity is especially difficult because of the additional costs. Any attempt to effect far-reaching policy changes must be coupled with efforts to build up the civic capacity of a polity. That entails finding ways to convince individuals who may have become deeply alienated from the political world to become engaged in the public sphere, recognize interests they have in common with similarly situated groups, forge alliances with such groups, and assume leadership roles in taking on oppositional forces. Building civic capacity entails reinvigorating public institutions and processes as sites of democratic deliberation and decision-making.[153]

In more concrete terms, building civic capacity may occur by finding connections between seemingly disparate reform movements. Groups advocating excellence and equity often hold very different values, but to the extent that it is possible to find common ground, there is a potential for a powerful coalition for change against the forces of inertia and the status quo. This is precisely what happened in the state of Kentucky during the 1980s, when groups pressing for an improvement in educational performance collaborated with groups fighting gross disparities in educational opportunities. The united campaign energized grassroots organizations in communities throughout Kentucky and resulted in landmark legislation that raised academic standards and achievement while significantly closing the resources gap between affluent and poor school districts. Kentucky's accomplishments in educational reform remain a model for other states and cities all over the nation.[154]

6

Crime and the Levels of Order

What is crime?

Crime is a violation of a community's formal rules of behavior. It can be either an act of commission or omission. Crime involves an active disrespect for borders, an intrusion of one person or group on another person or group. It is a fundamental statement of disrespect for the community as it is constituted.

The issue of crime speaks to a society's need to maintain a safe space to raise families, conduct business, and foster community. Even actions that might not directly harm others might be designated a crime if they undermine the community's overall well-being. The use of drugs such as marijuana, for example, may be perfectly harmless if done in moderation and apart from the community. But the use of such drugs can threaten the community in numerous subtle and long-term ways, such as damaging people's ability to support themselves, undermining child rearing, and creating a lethargic citizenry and workforce. Even if no one is directly harmed by drug use, its proscription might be desirable because of the likelihood that it would slowly tear apart society's fabric.

Ultimately crime gets at the very heart of a society's definition of itself. How secure do people feel about their safety in public? How comfortable are they with the social influences that their children encounter? How willing are people to confront an unruly person on a street or a next-door neighbor? What kinds of values shape the intercourse of ordinary people? What everyday relationships shape the aspirations and fears of children? What strategies and tactics can police use to resolve a domestic dispute, subdue a criminal suspect, or calm a community riot?

Has our understanding of crime changed over time?

Yes, constantly. Emile Durkheim, the great French sociologist, argued that all cultures need to maintain some basic level of "normality" to function. Ironically, to maintain that normality, every society also needs a limited but identifiable degree of abnormality in its midst. The existence of deviance gives the police and other order-maintenance institutions an "example" to teach society how not to behave. But there is a tension built into the need for deviance. When deviance increases beyond a certain threshold level, society often redefines its definition of deviance to maintain a sense of stability and order.[1]

As Durkheim suggested, there is nothing universal or fixed about crime. Understandings of crime change with different social circumstances and ideas. Use of certain drugs, to take the previous example, has not always been prohibited. To take another example: society's understanding of police brutality has shifted as understandings about authority and individuality have changed. Even the speech considered legally permissible has evolved over the years. Comments in the workplace once considered mere horseplay now are considered to be serious matters of harassment. Domestic relations, once considered a "private" matter, raise the deepest concerns about social justice and ending the cycle of violence. Defining crime produces a constant tension in which people learn the limits of their past understandings as new situations and understandings arise.

However a society defines crime, it always has an object: persons, property, and society. Crimes against persons involve violations of another person's autonomy or freedom of movement; examples include robbery, assault, rape, and murder. Violations of agreements, both formal contracts and informal expectations, are also crimes against persons. Crimes against property include takings and destruction of another person or institution's material possessions; examples include theft and vandalism. Crimes against society include any disturbance of arrangements that involve community order; examples include evasion of basic responsibilities like tax evasion, physical assault, and various forms of disorderly conduct.

The Levels of Crime

How prevalent is crime these days?

Crime is unrelenting. According to the Federal Bureau of Investigation (FBI), a crime occurs every two seconds in the United States. One violent crime occurs every seventeen seconds, one property crime every three seconds, one murder every twenty-three minutes, one forcible rape every five minutes, one robbery every fifty-one seconds, one aggravated assault every twenty-eight seconds, and one burglary every twelve seconds.[2]

The last generation has been the age of crime in America. In every category—murder, rape, burglary, robbery, theft, arson, graffiti—the crime rates have soared since the end of the baby boom in the early 1960s. The number of violent crimes for every 100,000 population increased from 160 in 1960 to 715 in 1994. In 1994, there were 23,310 murders, 102,100 rapes, 618,820 robberies, and 1,119,950 aggravated assaults in the United States. Adam Wilinsky, an aide to the late Robert F. Kennedy, noted in 1995: "In the last decade, 200,000 of our citizens have been killed and millions wounded. If we assume, with the FBI, that 47 percent of them were killed by friends and family members, that leaves 106,000 dead at the hands of strangers. Ten years of war in Vietnam killed 58,000 Americans. Over an equal period, we have almost the exact equivalent of two Vietnam Wars right here at home."[3] Since then, the crime rate has declined in many cities, but criminologists remain wary about the potential for a new wave of crime in the United States.

For the most part, the trends coincide across kinds of crime and kinds of communities. The United States has experienced four distinct crime trends in the last forty years. In the 1960s and 1970s, crime rose slowly but steadily. Crime fell in the first half of the 1980s, but rose again from 1984 to 1991, then declined again in the 1990s. The FBI reported an increase in murder from 5.1 per 100,000 residents in 1960 to 10.2 in 1980, a slight slackening to 7.9 in 1984, and increase to 9.8 in 1991, and then a drop to 8.2 in 1995 and 5.5 in 2000. The numbers for aggravated assault were 86.1 (1960), 298.5 (1980), 290.2 (1984), 433.3 (1991), 416.3 (1995), 323.6 in 2000.

Table 6.1 U.S. Crime Index, 1960–2000

Year	Murder	Rape	Robbery	Agg. Assault	Burg./ Theft	Larceny	Motor vehicle
1960	5.1	9.6	60.1	86.1	508.6	1034.7	183.0
1966	5.6	13.2	80.8	120.3	721.0	1442.9	286.9
1970	7.9	18.7	172.1	164.8	1084.9	2079.3	456.8
1976	8.8	26.6	199.3	233.2	1448.2	2921.3	450.0
1980	10.2	36.8	251.1	298.5	1684.1	3167.0	502.2
1986	8.6	37.9	225.1	346.1	1344.6	3010.3	507.8
1990	9.4	41.2	257.0	424.1	1235.9	3194.8	657.8
1995	8.2	37.1	220.9	416.3	987.6	3044.9	560.5
2000	5.5	32.0	144.9	323.6	728.4	2475.3	414.2

Source: Sarah Glazer, "Declining Crime Rates," *Urban Issues. Selections from the CQ Researcher* (2001), p. 100. Figures for 2000 come from Federal Bureau of Investigation, *Crime in the United States, 2000* available at http://www.fbi.gov/ucr/cius_00/contents.pdf.

Serious crime remains higher in the United States than in other industrialized nations. The U.S. homicide rate of 7.4 per 100,000 residents is more than twice as high as the rate for all other industrialized nations: Finland (3.1), Switzerland (2.8), Austria and Sweden (2.2), Canada and Northern Ireland (2.1), France (2), Italy (1.8), England and Wales (1.3), Japan (1).[4] New York has led the way in reducing the incidence of crime in the United States but is still bloodier than other cities in the world of a similar size. In New York in 2000, 667 murders were recorded; London, with about the same population, recorded 127 murders.[5] The United States lies roughly in the middle of overall crime victimization, with a rate of 24 per 100,000 residents, compared with a high of 31 for England and Wales and a low of 17 for Northern Ireland; as noted earlier, violent crime is more prevalent in the United States, but on the wide range of kinds of crime, the United States places somewhere in the middle.[6]

Crime is not spread evenly across society. Almost everyone has violated some basic public law over their lives, whether it's fudging a tax return, lifting office supplies, smoking a joint, or making creative insurance claims. But the kinds of crime that frighten people—direct assaults on people's bodies or possessions—are committed by a relatively small band of criminals. An influential study by Marvin Wolfgang found that 6 percent of young males aged ten to eighteen were responsible for 52 percent of the crimes committed by their age cohort.[7] That statistic has prompted police to concentrate their efforts on what they call the "predator" class, and it has prompted politicians to build prisons to lock them up when caught and convicted. Dealing with this cohort of repeat offenders is difficult because it is part of a much larger and more complex economy of crime, extending to gun dealers, money launderers, and stolen-goods fencers and sellers. No crime is an isolated act; all crimes involve a larger system. That, ultimately, is why crime is so frightening: it seems so random yet also part of a vast web of coconspirators.

How much does crime affect the economy?

Crime itself represents a major part of the American economy. To understand how, consider crime to be a vertically integrated enterprise. At the top stand the white-collar criminals who traffic in guns, drugs, and fenced goods. This group includes bankers, businessmen, and organized crime figures. They reap great rewards from operating the large-scale systems that make illegal substances and other goods available at the street level. Below them are the regional traffickers, and below them, cadres of street operators.

Estimates of the costs of crime vary depending on the methods of calculation. One study by the National Institute of Justice found that crime victimization cost some $105 billion in losses a year, including losses in property, productivity, and medical care—about $425 for every man, woman, and child in the United States. Researchers have pegged the cost at $450 billion annually—or about $1,800 per person—when calculated to include the pain, long-term emotional trauma, disability, and risk of death.[8] But the greatest impact of all may be intangible. A community that is afraid to go out at night or receive visitors at home is a society that suffers severe damage to its political and social system.

Who are the leading figures in the economy of crime?

Crime involves a whole cast of leading characters, supporting characters, behind-the-scenes operators, and ordinary people.

The leading characters can be divided into two groups: the organizations that oversee billion-dollar criminal operations, and the street-level operators who do the dirty work that makes the system work. These groups include the Mafia, gangs, drug rings, arsonists, gunrunners—and the millions of people who, one way or another, do their bidding on the streets of cities and other communities.

Although organized crime sometimes seems to be a tightly structured system with a strong hierarchy of crime bosses, studies have found that it is a loosely structured confederacy of operations. Speaking of the Colombia drug industry, which plays a major role in illegal drug trafficking in the United States, the economist R. T. Naylor writes: "Boundaries are fluid, the characters change, and their links show the same confusion of kinship relationships, formal and informal partnerships, and arms-length commercial exchanges. Despite tactical cooperation at the political level (financing electoral campaigns or running death squads, for example), there was (is) no effort to restrict product quality to control price."[9] By "following the money," Naylor discovered the fractured—but no less pervasive and deadly—character of criminal enterprises internationally and nationally.

Street gangs play an important role in organized crime. In 1992, some nine thousand street gangs with 400,000 members operated in the United States. In 1991, over two thousand people died in gang-related activities in the United States.[10] The gang business has been so successful that many gangs have established franchises in different cities. The Bloods and the Crips, the rival gangs that started in Los Angeles, now operate in thirty-five states and fifty-eight cities in the United States.[11] Experts testifying before the U.S. Congress estimate the volume of transactions by gang enterprises to be as high as $300 billion annually.[12]

Ordinary people contribute in numerous small ways to the climate of crime. Drunk drivers, petty drug dealers and buyers, inner-city thugs, and businesses that abuse tax laws and regulations on matters ranging from environmental hazards to affirmative action contracting—all contribute to the theft of other people's money, insecurity in public spaces, and damage to public and private possessions. Some of these people are usually considered law-abiding, but at the same time they are willing to cut corners or violate social norms for their own purposes.

Ordinary people's involvement in crime usually takes the form of simply looking the other way and rationalizing the "dirty hands" of cooperating with criminals. Take the case of two interior designers who in 1998 faced criminal charges of conspiracy and laundering drug money because of millions of dollars of work they did for the notorious Colombian drug lord Jose Santacruz Londono. The designers lived the high life when doing business with Santacruz, although they knew he had amassed his wealth illegally. The designers knew they were profiting from drug money, but at the same time they reasoned that they were doing honest work. When they were implicated in the drug lord's network, the designers claimed they tried to extricate themselves from the relationship, but "he made it clear that he terminates people, they don't terminate him."[13]

From America's earliest years to the settlement of the "Wild West," crime has been part of American culture. What makes the crime issue different today?

Crime has become the third rail of American politics because of the fear of random violence and the sense that crime is beyond the control of ordinary people. Interestingly, people tend to express nuanced and calm attitudes about crime when they are given some basic facts. For example, when asked whether they favor "three strikes" laws that impose mandatory life sentences for anyone convicted of three felonies, 88 percent expressed strong or moderate support; but when given the details of specific cases, 95 percent favored making exceptions when the sentence seems greater than the crimes.[14] Political and media campaigns often increase public fears. The number of people who agreed that drugs were the nation's biggest problem increased from 15 percent to 64 percent between July and September of 1989 after the Bush administration declared the latest War on Drugs.[15] From the mid-1960s on, crime has been as potent an issue in domestic politics as the Red Scare was in international politics. Politicians from Richard Nixon and George Wallace in the 1960s to Ronald Reagan and George Bush in the 1980s and 1990s made fear of crime their signature issue.

Candidates vie to depict themselves as tougher on crime than their opponents. During the 1992 New Hampshire presidential primary campaign, Governor Bill Clinton flew home to Arkansas to oversee the execution of a retarded man. Clinton had learned the lessons of the 1988 election, when

Republican George Bush used the "Willie Horton" issue to pummel Democrat Michael Dukakis. Glenn William Horton, a convicted murderer, was arrested for raping a woman while he was free from prison on a furlough program designed to help prisoners become assimilated into the larger community. The incident defined Dukakis as soft on crime. The Horton issue tapped a national fear of random violence threatening the security of people on the streets and even in their own homes. His crime evoked the deepest fears of the randomness of crime in modern America.

Crime's potency as a political issue stems in part from the way the media—especially local television news—sensationalize violence and link it to people's everyday lives in news and entertainment programming. A 1993 report of the American Psychiatric Association found that viewing violence on television increases the fear of being a victim of violence, desensitizes people to violence, and increases people's appetites for becoming involved (directly or vicariously) in violent acts.[16] People tend to care more about the crimes that endanger them suddenly rather than the crimes that hurt them invisibly. Christopher Jencks notes:

> Every year millions of Americans defraud the Internal Revenue Service by underreporting their income or overstating their deductions. The amounts stolen in this way almost certainly exceed the amounts stolen by muggers on the streets. Yet very few Americans view tax fraud as a serious threat to themselves or to the republic. The reason seems obvious. Unlike robbery, tax evasion has no individual victims. . . . Given a choice, almost everyone would rather be robbed by computer than at gunpoint.[17]

How can we assess people's fear of crime?

Despite headline-grabbing events like the sniper attacks in the Washington, D.C., area in 2002, the fear of crime has fallen throughout the United States. In a 1997 Gallup poll, 38 percent of Americans said they feared walking alone outside at night, a significant decline from 44 percent in 1992 and 45 percent in 1983. But crime remains a potent force in American life, especially in cities. The proportion of residents reporting such fears ranged from a low of 20 percent in Madison, Wisconsin, to a high of 48 percent in Chicago and Washington, D.C. The fear index was high not only in large cities such as Los Angeles (44 percent) and New York (42 percent) but also smaller cities such as Springfield, Massachusetts (45 percent), and Tucson, Arizona (40 percent).[18] Minority communities, disproportionately located in cities, report a higher-than-average fear of crime. About two fifths of blacks and one third of Hispanics reported that they were "somewhat" or "very" worried about being murdered.[19]

Even when people consider their own neighborhoods to be safe, they view the outside world as threatening—both because they know their own neighborhood and because they see the rest of the world from the perspective of crime-oriented TV programs. Media reports tend to emphasize the randomness of crime. As one analyst notes: "Drive-by shootings are particularly distressing . . . because it may appear that the target was chosen at random and innocent bystanders may be hit. . . . When there is a sense that more murders are being committed against strangers, any person can conceive of himself as a target."[20] An old expression in the news business—"If it bleeds, it leads"—is borne out by surveys of local TV newscasts. A survey of evening news programs on a hundred stations in thirty-five states found that 30 percent of programming was devoted to crime, and a wide range of violence including crime, war, and disasters (known as the "mayhem index") accounted for 42 percent of all reporting.[21]

The Causes of Crime

What factors produce public order? What factors undermine public order?

Public order develops at both the micro- and macrolevels.

At the microlevel, a wide range of institutions is required to educate, guide, and engage people in a creative and respectful cooperation with others. Families, schools, churches, clubs, associations, and sports teams bring individuals and groups into social contexts bigger than themselves. In these settings, people develop a vision and identity of themselves that reaches beyond everyday personal concerns. The "I" must become a "we" and in the process develop a commitment to cooperation, respect for others, and basic justice.

At the macrolevel, the economic system and a variety of social policies affect the economy of crime. Crime tends to increase when the economy experiences a downturn—and sometimes, paradoxically, when economic fortunes are improving but more slowly than expectations. Social programs, such as strong provision of basic income maintenance programs, education, health care, and mental health and drug treatment, can reduce the crime rate by reducing the sense of frustration and helplessness among young people and others. A generally more humane environment reduces the incidence of alcoholism, drug abuse, domestic violence, and other key triggers of crime.

What are the major theories about the causes of crime?

Two approaches that parallel the micro and macro approaches have dominated public debate about crime since the 1950s. Liberal theories, taking the macro approach, hold that criminal behavior stems largely from disadvantaged environments and bad luck. The best cure for crime is to attack "root causes" such as poverty, malnourishment, substance addiction, and illiteracy. By attacking these larger social ills, policy-makers will undermine the conditions of chaos and desperation that give rise to crime.

Conservative theories, focusing on the microlevel of the issue, counter that poverty does not in itself cause crime. Instead, they say, crime is caused by people's rational calculations of the risks and benefits of crime. Crime exploded in the 1960s and 1970s, conservatives say, because the criminal justice system went "soft" and did not hold criminals responsible for their actions. Criminal defendants won a host of new "rights" from the courts, undermining the efforts of police and prosecutors to keep them off the streets. At the same time the public justice system broke down, families and neighborhoods lost their cohesion and society at large adopted permissive attitudes toward behavior once considered deviant.

Advocates for the two positions stubbornly attack each other's research and conclusions. But when supplemented with some other perspectives, liberal and conservative positions both contain important elements of truth that can be synthesized into a rigorous theory of crime. In reality, the two schools of thought describe different stages of the production of criminal behavior. Conservatives tend to focus responsibility for crime on the individual and the family, while liberals tend to focus on larger political, economic, and social systems. In effect, both liberals and conservatives are right. The larger systems create the conditions under which individuals and families behave. To focus on any one level of the system is to simplify the situation. All of the levels of the system in fact interact and reinforce each other. It is hard to expect individuals to possess discipline and ambition when they face a house of trauma when they come home at night. It is hard for families to provide a stable environment for children when housing is expensive or employment is unsteady. It's hard for communities to develop good schools and services when tax bases are low and critical federal and state programs are cut.

The Level of the Individual

Some people say that criminal behavior can be reduced to a simple cost-benefit analysis—that is, someone will commit a crime when the potential benefits outweigh the potential costs. Is that true?

At some basic level, yes. Crime occurs when people do not feel the responsibility to contribute to the maintenance of order in society.[22] When neighbors do not bother to look after each other's homes and kids, or when cops do not deal with problems of disorder on the street, the "good" of public order is endangered. Each of these decisions not to participate in order maintenance might seem insignificant in themselves, but they add up to a relinquishment of the very idea of order.

Academics have used the notions of "collective action" and the "free rider" problem to explore this phenomenon of social withdrawal or violation of social norms. Mancur Olson's classic work *The Logic of Collective Action* argues that efforts to create "public goods"—such as public order—founder when individuals act as free riders and do not participate in the creation of those public goods.[23] This free-rider syndrome can be found in all realms of life, from labor relations to international politics, but it has special relevance to community order and disorder. The key to making collective action and public goods possible is to provide material inducements to cooperators and to punish detractors. That is why the government is such an essential force in a complex society. Without central coercion, people would not make common cause to build roads, provide open and fair schools, provide a "safety net" to all poor people, and staff a police force to maintain order on the streets.

The decision to commit a crime is the ultimate decision to be a free rider. The criminal takes advantage of other people's willingness to cooperate by striking where that cooperation is not enforced vigilantly. When people park their car or walk down a dark street, they are taking advantage of the order that the members of the community create together. To venture into common space is to live off the trust and cooperation of others. When a person violates that common space, he takes something that is produced by that community.

Many theorists have disputed Olson's collective-action theory on the grounds that people will contribute to a common good without rewards or sanctions if they identify with the values embedded in the process of creating the good. For example, most civil rights activists did not have to be bribed or pressured to take part in demonstrations and protests because their identity was at stake in the movement. The same argument could be made with the problem of crime. People contribute to the collective good of order because they identify with the values of order.

How is this cost-benefit analysis affected by the larger social structure?

People make conscious decisions about whom they will spend time with, where they will live, and whose influence will affect their behavior. People in stable, well-tended, and socially rich communities tend to be discouraged from committing crimes; there are too many people to answer to and too little to gain compared with following the community's rules. The "thicker" the network of institutions, routines, and informal relationships in a community, the greater chance that a person will rationally decide to abide by the community's codes.

Other people—from broken communities with few positive role models and little to lose from lawbreaking—are more inclined to violate social norms. In a discussion of the effects of illicit drug businesses on the community, William Julius Wilson notes the serious consequences of a breakdown in social order: "Neighborhoods plagued by high levels of joblessness, insufficient economic opportunities, and high residential mobility are unable to control the volatile drug market and the violent crimes related to it. As informal controls weaken, the social processes that regulate behavior change."[24] The costs and benefits of committing a crime change when the community is powerless to enforce formal and informal standards of behavior.

It is not just the person's immediate environment that affects propensity to law-abiding behavior. Most people also have a sense of the more distant forces that shape the consequences of their behavior. Urban tales about criminals who get away with murder, about judges who let convicts free, about prisons that brutalize inmates and social workers and parole officers who fail to track caseloads—all of these bits of information become part of the would-be criminal's decision-making process.

But rationality is not the complete story. Many criminals act impulsively, ignoring evidence about the consequences of their action. Criminals under the influence of alcohol and drugs or suffering from the lifelong effects of physical and emotional abuse do not tally up the pros and cons of actions. They see an opportunity and pounce. People with an antisocial personality disorder do not carefully consider the consequences of their actions for themselves or others. Even if there are alternative courses of action, the impulsive criminal lurches from antisocial action to antisocial action. A lifetime of conditioning and psychosocial deficiencies creates individuals who cannot empathize with the victim, feel responsible to society, or carefully consider their actions.

Criminal behavior often seems to have a life of its own. One decision leads inexorably to the next. Unanticipated crises present themselves, and people react, sometimes badly. Subtle and not-so-subtle pressures from collaborators, cops, and victims sometimes push a person to do something he might otherwise avoid.

How does the social environment—the ideas and images that people are exposed to—shape people's propensity to commit crime?

Criminologists draw a connection between social attitudes toward crime and the level of crime itself. To sort out how much ordinary attitudes about crime matter, we need to understand the long chains of attitudes and behavior that involve home, school, media, and public spaces. George Kelling and Catherine Coles explore the issue:

> When are disorderly acts really serious? At what point does their seriousness merit intervention? Why should some persons engaged in disorderly behaviors be warned and/or arrested, and not others?

The answers to these questions require a determination based upon two measures: first, the seriousness of virtually any crime—major as well as minor—is determined not solely on the heinousness of the act itself, but also by the context in which the behavior takes place. Second, the seriousness of any crime is similarly dependent not upon the harm done to the immediate victim alone, but also upon the injury to and impact on the entire community.[25]

When a crime occurs, its impact ripples throughout the community. When people are exposed to crime, not only do they feel less safe but over time they get desensitized and inured to crime. That changes the overall context of crime. People change their behaviors to accommodate the reality of crime. They avoid going to a particular street or part of town. They avoid public transportation. They install expensive security equipment in their cars and homes. They withdraw from the public space. Over time, they accept the inevitability of crime and fear.

Eventually, a society begins to mirror, in muted form, the characteristics of the criminal elements in that society. Family and community ties weaken. People become emotionally cold and distant and lose their empathy for the real victims of society's ills. People become impulsive and willing to lash out at anyone who threatens their sense of security. People develop a fatalistic attitude that nothing they do can improve the security and vitality of their community. In such circumstances, fighting crime becomes even more difficult because the battle loses the ordinary people who must stand up to crime in everyday life.

What demographic variables account for most crime?

Gender and age. Most crimes that threaten the safety and property of ordinary people are committed by young men. In 1990, 11 percent of the total population consisted of juveniles aged ten to seventeen and accounted for 32 percent of property felonies and 16 percent of violent felonies. That was a decline from 1980, when the 14 percent of the population aged ten to seventeen committed 41 percent of the property crimes and 22 percent of the violent felonies.[26] Sliced a different way, the overall homicide rate in the United States was 9.4 per 100,000 population in 1989, but the rate for minorities was significantly higher. Black males, for example, had a rate of 51 per 100,000 compared with 8.1 for white males.[27]

The tendency of young men to commit crime troubles criminologists, who note that the juvenile population in the United States will increase from 27 million in 1990 to 33 million in 2010. Young people—those between the ages of fifteen and twenty-five—accounted for only 14 percent of the total population but 40 percent of all arrests in 2000.[28] Of course, only a small share of the total youth population engages in regular crimi-

Table 6.2 Percentage Distribution of Total U.S. Population and Persons Arrested for All Offenses

Age Group	U.S. Resident Population	Persons Arrested
Age 14 and younger	21.2%	5.5%
Age 15–19	7.2%	21.8%
Age 20–24	6.8%	18.7%
Age 25–29	6.4%	12.6%
Age 30–34	7.1%	11.4%
Age 35–39	8.0%	11.3%
Age 40–44	8.2%	8.7%
Age 45–49	7.3%	5.0%
Age 50 and above	27.9%	5.0%

Source: Kathleen Maguire and Ann L. Pastore, eds. *Sourcebook of Criminal Justice Statistics* [online], available from http://www.albany.edu/sourcebook/1995/pdf/ t44.pdf.

nal activity. A massive study of Orange County, California, found that 8 percent of first-time juvenile offenders committed three or more additional crimes after their first offense, meaning they were responsible for half of all crimes by this group. A six-year follow-up study found that the 8 percent group averaged more than twenty months of incarceration.[29]

Who Does the Crime?

The explanations for youth crime are simple. Young people tend to be physically active and unattached to jobs and family. They have energy but often lack the maturity to channel that energy constructively. Many young men out of school or work do not have the guidance and engagement in constructive activities that they need. Social theorists have begun to appreciate the powerful role of peer groups in the criminal behavior of young people. In the absence of meaningful family and community ties, gangs offer to many young people a sense of belonging.[30]

For many young men, alternatives to crime seem worthless. Broken families, especially, do not nurture or respect young men. Bad schools do not engage them. Companies do not offer decent jobs with real prospects of advancement or learning.

In the late 1980s and early 1990s, the rise in the youth crime rate alarmed criminologists, who predicted the rise of a "predator class" with the increase in the overall youth population. The thinking was that once the size of the youth population reached a "tipping point," the antisocial tendencies in that group would feed off each other, leading to a dangerous increase in crime. In fact, the overall youth share of the crime problem actually declined in the 1990s.[31] Despite the good news from the 1990s, it is probably prudent to be concerned with the increased size of the segment of the population that contributes the most to street crime.

What about the location of crime?

Sadly, crime takes place much more frequently in cities than in suburbs or rural communities. The media homicide rate in the twenty largest cities in the United States in 1992 was 27 per 100,000 population, compared to a national rate of 9.7 per 100,000. Nineteen of the top twenty cities exceeded the national norm. These twenty cities, which were home to 11.5 percent of the nation's population, accounted for 34 percent of the criminal homicides reported in the nation. What is more, crime is concentrated in certain sections of the city.[32] High-risk neighborhood rates are two and three times the rate of other neighborhoods. Two criminologists summarize their findings: "New York City's aggregate homicide rate may be 27 per 100,000, but many residents of New York City live as safely on the borders of Central Park as do the residents of Sioux City, Iowa."[33]

Does genetic makeup contribute to the propensity of people to commit crime?

The idea that criminals have a genetic disposition toward crime conjures up legacies of quack psychology a century ago and, worse, Nazi theories of determinism in the 1930s. The genetic explanation—advanced most recently by Richard Herrnstein and Charles Murray in their controversial 1994 book *The Bell Curve*—suggests that people are born with a biological predisposition to engage in violent acts. The best response to crime, according to this thinking, is to isolate criminals and others with violent and antisocial dispositions.

Some evolutionary psychologists see violence as part of the inherent makeup of humans, especially males. "Men have evolved the morphological, physiological, and psychological means to be effective users of violence," state Martin Daly and Susan Wilson, two popularizers of the argument that violence is built into human nature. Like other animals, human males must compete violently for status and control of the female. Men's tendency toward violence, Daly and Wilson say, is dampened by the modern state's monopoly on violence. "But wherever the monopoly is relaxed—whether in an entire society or in a neglected underclass—then the utility of the credible threat becomes apparent."[34] When society loses its power to impose order, the inherent unruly tendencies of people come to the fore.[35]

Christopher Jencks offers a wise caution when looking at genetic explanations for crime or any other behavior. To be sure, he says, physical constitution can play an important role in shaping behavior. But even genetic tendencies can be counteracted by environment. A child's aggressive tendencies can be lessened or exacerbated by conditions in the family, school, and community:

> A medical analogy is helpful here. Suppose you have a deaf child. The disorder may be inherited, or it may be the result of a childhood disease or accident. But the prospects of curing the disorder do not depend in any direct sense on whether it is a product of nature or nurture. Rather, they depend on what is actually wrong and how much your doctors know. Furthermore, if your disorder cannot be cured, the question of how you educate such a child does not depend, at least in any simple way, on what caused the problem. The same principle holds for behavioral problems.[36]

Probably the best approach to the issue is to understand that nature and nurture interact in complex ways, and that humane and smart public policy can make the best of whatever physical traits we have.

The most distressing aspect of the genetics argument is that it offers an excuse not to respond to the troubles of poor or other young people before those troubles reach a critical state. The emphasis on genetics is fatalistic. If the genetic disposition toward crime is coded into a person before birth—if criminal behavior is inevitable—then government programs and policies can do little to prevent violence and criminality. The best policy response, according to this logic, might be to isolate potentially dangerous people.

Some people say that a person's creative life—the person's ability to "play" in the world—is the most important element in crime. Why?
Humans are not strictly instinctual animals. People have the intellectual capacity to imagine the world as it might be, to devise scenarios for themselves and others. The ability to conceive schemes, develop strategies and tactics, and execute the schemes is essential to human growth and development. The ability to articulate your hopes and dreams is also critical.

Illiteracy may play a central role in the production of crime in America. A survey of 1,100 inmates from federal and state prisons found that seven of ten inmates finished on the bottom two levels of a five-level literacy test. Just 51 percent of inmates had a high school degree, compared with 76 percent of the general population.[37] The fifteen-year-old inmates in juvenile facilities read, on average, at a fourth-grade level. In a survey of teachers who provide instruction in prisons, 90 percent said that their inmate students could not even read "material composed of words from their own oral vocabularies."[38]

The most obvious reason for literacy's importance is that it gives a person the basic tools to operate in the economy and society. Someone who can read a machine operator's manual or operate a computer keyboard can get and keep a job. Holding a job is the key to becoming part of a law-abiding culture and to feeling good about oneself. But the impact of literacy goes far deeper. Literacy gives people a sense of power over themselves and a sense of competency in their relations with others. Without basic literacy—and without the sense of logic and order that comes with literacy—people get easily frustrated. They cannot articulate their desires, fears, and inadequacies and so they become aggravated over time. "When frustration can find no resolution in constructive or productive activity," the educator Michael S. Brunner has written, "one response, although not necessarily the only one, is aggressive, anti-social behavior."[39]

The Level of the Family

No matter how important an individual's own character and intelligence might be, that character is shaped in the family, right? How do criminologists view the role of the family in fostering or preventing crime?

Conservative and liberal theorists have long agreed that the family is an important factor affecting whether a young person will turn to crime—and perhaps even the most important factor of all. Beginning in the 1960s, liberals have sought to find ways to strengthen the family—or at least ameliorate the deficiencies of families—in social programs. Conservatives have long argued that strong "family values"—intact, two-parent households with strict discipline and care for children—would provide the most effective response to crime and other social problems.

The family is the most important place for the development of personal character and integrity. In early infancy, people learn the capacity for empathy—the ability to feel for other people and care enough about other people to treat them with kindness and respect. In childhood, a person learns how to work and play with others and develop cooperative approaches—sharing, taking turns, sharing credit. In adolescence, a person learns how to be an adult, taking responsibility for decisions and shedding the innocence of youth to understand the complexity of life. In adulthood, a person begins to take responsibility for creating and caring for life beyond the cares of selfish individual needs.

Being part of a family can be the most exciting and comforting part of life. The family can be a cradle of care and development—in the words of Christopher Lasch, a "haven in a heartless world."[40] But the family can also be where people's lives break down. In an environment lacking love and care, an environment where distrust, violence, and inconsistency prevail, young people can experience difficulty growing into whole human beings.

According to the U.S. Justice Department, "intimate partners" commit almost a million violent crimes against women annually. Some 503,485 women and 185,496 men are stalked by an intimate partner. About half of all women on welfare have suffered from domestic violence as adults—more than twice the larger population's rate of 22 percent. Many suffered sexual or physical abuse as children. Most states have adopted tough laws against domestic violence and stalking, but enforcement is spotty at best. Police often tell women who are afraid for their safety that they cannot do anything to restrain their abusers until they commit new acts of violence.[41]

How does domestic violence contribute to crime?

People who experience abuse and neglect as children are more likely to engage in criminal behavior than people from stable, nurturing homes.

Independent studies have consistently demonstrated a strong correlation between domestic violence and later criminal activity. A longitudinal study of the lives of 253 men raised in 232 families from 1939 to 1945, whose records were tracked down from 1975 to 1979, presents powerful evidence of the linkage. The study examined how boys were treated, the overall environment of their homes, and the later behaviors of the boys. Child abuse and neglect produced later criminal behavior—but an even more powerful relationship was found between parental rejection of a child and later criminal behavior.[42] A study by Albert Bandura found that parents of aggressive and destructive youths relied on ridicule, physical punishment, and deprivation in raising their children. Another study by Donald West found that the disciplinary practices of delinquents' parents included "attitudes of indifference, positive rejection or neglect, overstrict or erratically varying discipline, and harsh methods of enforcement." Dorothy Lewis and her colleagues found that nearly four fifths of all seriously violent youths had witnessed extreme violence in their home growing up. A longitudinal study by Leonard Eron and associates at the University of Illinois documents this connection. Some 23 percent of the eight-year-old boys labeled as highly aggressively were later convicted of a crime, compared with 15 percent of the boys judged to display moderate levels of aggression and 9 percent of the boys judged to display low levels of aggression.[43] Daniel Scheinfield's study of inner-city children found that achievers' parents displayed trust and encouragement for the children to develop their own direction, while the parents of low achievers were more concerned with controlling their children's behavior.

Conservatives and liberals do not disagree about these basic facts. They disagree about what causes what—about what particular factors cause families to behave dysfunctionally. Does it have to do with poverty and the deep and bitter frustration that arises out of want in an age of affluence? Does it have to do with inadequate education? Liberals emphasize these factors. Conservatives, by contrast, talk about the decline in public standards of morality—permissive teachers and parents, depraved mass media, and the crushing effects of divorce on the nuclear family.

The liberal criminologist Elliott Currie sums up the connection between poverty, domestic violence, and crime:

> The parents most at risk for serious child abuse have low incomes and are most often poorly educated; they were typically subject to greater than ordinary barrage of social stresses, including frequent unemployment and excessive geographic mobility; where there are men in the home, they are disproportionately often out of work or employed in low-level jobs; the families are often very large, with at least some of the children unplanned and unwanted; the parents are likely to be very young, frequently under twenty; they have few parenting skills and are generally unprepared for the complexities and frustrations of child-rearing; and they are unusually isolated from sources of social support—extended family, friends, community organizations, or adequate public social services.[44]

Here is the real connection between poverty and crime, especially in poor or disorganized communities, many of which happen to be in urban areas. It is not the absence of things, or even an envy of other people having things, that causes people to commit crimes. It is instead the accumulation of problems and the lack of control—the lack of "life skills"—that create the environment where people are so overwhelmed that they do not develop an understanding of society's rules or the capacity to follow those rules.

Analyses of brain composition and behavior have found great deficiencies in criminals which can be traced back to their severe abuse as children. Brain scans of neglected children show that the cortical and subcortical regions are 20 to 30 percent smaller than normal.[45] The brain's development was undermined at its most sensitive period by the blows of a parent's fist, a wall, or a household object. Abuse also damages the interaction between the right and left sides of the brain. The left side of the brain, the site of logic and language, is especially damaged in abuse victims.

Children with healthy backgrounds typically go to the aid and comfort of their peers when they sense those peers are distressed or unhappy. Children with histories of physical abuse, however, show no emotion and do not aid their peers in distress. They show no affect at all. They do not feel badly when one of their playmates feels bad or suffers. It does not matter to them if a peer is hurt or crying or afraid. It is easy to see how such a child can grow up to be a violent criminal. Not only is his or her ability to judge levels of danger undermined, but so are feelings of consequence or responsibility for acting impulsively and violently.

The Level of the Community

The question of community seems to pose the ultimate "nature or nurture" question for criminologists.

That's right. Criminologists have concluded in recent years that the character of a person's environment—what it looks like, how other people behave, what kinds of norms get enforced, what kind of disorder is allowed—produces a powerful impact on people's behavior. When people live in pleasant and safe places, all other things being equal, they behave well; when they live in dysfunctional places, they lose their humanity and become capable of bad deeds. Psychologists have conducted experiments that show that ordinary people placed in inhumane surroundings quickly become violent and uncaring.

A Stanford University researcher created a pretend prison block where he placed twenty-one well-adjusted volunteers and asked them to play the roles of guard and inmates. One prisoner was released after thirty-six hours when that person became hysterical; four more were released because of "extreme emotional depression, crying, rage, and acute anxiety." The role-playing was halted after six days because of the emotional trauma experienced by the participants exceeded allowable standards for human-subjects research. Other experiments have found that people become willing to cheat, steal, and mistreat others when the environmental context changes even slightly. In summary, a person's very character and behavior can change in unhealthy or inhumane environments.[46]

How can the analogy of the "broken window" explain the tendency of people to commit a crime?

How people respond to a broken window—or any other outward sign of disturbance, for that matter—shows how a community might respond to other threats against public order. When residents of a community act quickly to fix a broken window—or any other disturbance—that community sends a powerful signal to both insiders and outsiders. The message is that the community notices and cares about any threat to stability and order. When the window does not get fixed right away, the opposite message goes out, that residents are too busy or apathetic to notice social disturbances. By not fixing the window, the community advertises its vulnerability to future breaches of order and respect. That message spurs more crime, since malefactors have no reason to believe that their actions will be noticed or countered.

James Q. Wilson and George L. Kelling, Jr., popularized the broken window theory in an article that appeared in *The Atlantic Monthly* in 1982.[47] Wilson and Kelling recounted an experiment conducted by a Stanford psychologist named Philip Zimbardo. Zimbardo wanted to see how passersby would respond when he placed cars by the side of the highways in the Bronx, New York, and Palo Alto, California. The Bronx car was stripped and then destroyed within ten minutes—first by a family and then a succession of vandals. Nothing in the Bronx area sent a message that the community would watch over the car. The Palo Alto car stood undamaged for a week. After Zimbardo took a sledgehammer to the car—sending a powerful signal that the car was untended and unclaimed—it was destroyed by a succession of vandals within a period of a few hours. Most of the vandals were respectable-looking, middle-class whites. Commenting on the Zimbardo experiment, Wilson and Kelling write:

> Untended property becomes fair game for people out for fun and profit, and even for people who ordinarily would not dream of doing such things and who would probably consider themselves law-abiding. Because of the nature of community life in the Bronx—its anonymity, the frequency with which cars are abandoned and things are stolen or broken, the past experience of "no one caring"—vandalism begins much more quickly than it does in staid Palo Alto, where people have come to believe that private possessions are cared for and mischievous behavior is costly. But vandalism can occur anywhere once communal barriers—the sense of mutual regard and the obligations of civility—are lowered by actions that seem to signal that "no one cares."[48]

How people respond to threats make all the difference. When there are signs that people have withdrawn from public space and engagement, crime and disorder ensue. Any balanced community can stand some measure of disorder; in fact, the existence of disorder can act as a safety valve and actually increase the strength of the overall order. But once the degree of disorder reaches a "tipping" point, all of the formal and informal means of reinforcing order suffer.[49] Some criminologists have used the metaphor of "epidemic" to describe the loss of order. Just as a disease can be contained so long as it lacks a basic means of reproducing itself, the phenomenon of disorder is limited as long as it is isolated within a system of order.

What are some of the danger signs?

Sometimes something as simple as spray paint or loitering around a video store is a signal that criminal elements are "staking out" parts of the neighborhood. If a part of the neighborhood gets taken over by gangs, drug pushers, or even petty criminals, there is that much less public space where members of the community can actively engage in maintaining order.

These destructive activities often begin in places that are outside the public view. If they go unchecked, these activities spill over into more public spaces. Deals are made in the hidden recesses of abandoned buildings, alleys, and subways. Over time, criminal elements take over city blocks, putting them off-limits to law-abiding people. Graffiti, vandalism, blocked entryways, display of gang colors—not to mention the sight of intimidating thugs overseeing an area—create a zone of avoidance. If unchecked, this zone can expand into nearby communities. The public realm is ceded to the elements of disorder.

What do critics of the broken-window model say?

In a word, that the theory is simplistic. Broken-window critics say quite simply that improving the appearance of a community—conveying the message that someone cares, that antisocial behavior will not be tolerated—is never sufficient to combat crime.

In a groundbreaking work, the legal scholar Bernard E. Harcourt rejects the idea that fixing broken windows is enough to combat crime. In reality, fixing broken windows was just part of a larger effort to police the streets more aggressively—to pick out disruptive youths, find the multiple offenders among them, and put them behind bars. Fixing broken windows offers a first step in a larger process of taking control of the streets. Armed with "enhanced powers of surveillance," police can focus their manpower and other resources on the most troubling elements of society. Cops enjoy a greater license to confront loiterers, subway fare-beaters, and unruly street people and to gather useful information about street crime through these contacts. But taken alone, improving the appearance and maintenance of public spaces does not lead to dramatic decreases in crime. To take one example: after implementation of an anti–gang loitering program in Chicago, gang-related homicides actually increased over an eight-year period. Of course, a number of other factors play into gang violence besides their ability or inability to gather in public places, but that's just the point.

Harcourt's summary of the New York experience also captures his research on broken windows elsewhere:

> The quality-of-life initiative probably has contributed to some degree to the decline in crime in New York City. To whatever degree, though, the mechanism is probably not a reduction in litter, fixing broken windows, or beautifying neighborhoods—although all of these may have some minor positive neighborhood effects. The primary engine of order-maintenance policing is probably the enhanced power of surveillance offered by a policy of aggressive misdemeanor arrests.[50]

In short, fixing broken windows is just part of a much broader strategy of restoring order and a sense of civic responsibility to a neighborhood. Confronting antisocial behavior—and isolating the most egregious violators of public order—is even more important.

How do people's perceptions of the safety of public spaces affect the actual functioning of those spaces?

When people develop abnormal fears of crime, they look suspiciously on their neighbors and withdraw from public spaces. But when people are given reason to believe that public spaces are safe, they are likely to use those spaces and make them even more safe. It is a self-fulfilling prophesy.

That is one reason why the "quality of life" approach to crime-fighting, followed by New York Mayor Rudolph Giuliani, has been so effective. By working to create a more attractive public realm, Giuliani reduced the vague sense of unpleasantness that people experience on the streets, in parks, on subways, and in public buildings. Petty crimes that had been ignored by cops—loitering, subway turnstile–jumping, urinating in public, street-walking by prostitutes, disorderly behavior—were attacked by Giuliani and Police Commissioner William Bratton.

The rewards were twofold. First, the police found that people they arrested for petty crimes often had other crimes to answer for. Someone who jumps a turnstile in a subway station, *ipso facto*, is someone likely to disrespect other rules of social conduct. Second, once the city's public spaces look more inviting and safe, people repopulate public spaces—and bring even more surveillance by ordinary people on the streets. When fare evasions dropped from nearly 200,000 daily in 1990 to 45,000 daily in 1996, the effect was palpable for law-abiding users of the system. The system was safer and more orderly than it had been in years, and ordinary people were drawn back underground to use the subways. "Eyes on the street" are one of the most important deterrents to crime. Crime flourishes where people do not look, but it moves away when people keep an eye on each other and each other's things.

Eyes on the street are one thing, but what about weapons on the street? Does the growing availability of guns in society increase the rate of violent crime?

Probably. As Geoffrey Canada notes in his memoir *Fist Stick Knife Gun*, the danger of crime is related proportionately to the power of the weaponry.[51] Conflicts that in earlier eras would have led to mere street brawls today often lead to the use of firearms. With heavier firepower, the conflict affects not only direct participants but bystanders as well. In the 1980s and 1990s, American TV news was filled with reports and images of stray bullets from gang warfare killing innocent bystanders.

A few simple statistics shed some light on the role of guns in violent crime in the United States. Although conflict of most kinds is similar in the United States and Great Britain, the United States suffers a dramatically greater incidence of gun violence because of guns' simple availability. From 1980 to 1984, the total number of gun killings in England and Wales was 213, a rate of .86 per 1 million population; in the United States, there were 63,218 gun killings, a rate of 54.52 per 1 million population. Other forms of homicide are also higher in the United States than Britain. During the 1980-to-1984 period, there were 2,416 nongun killings in Britain (a rate of 9.75 per 1 million) and 41,354 nongun killings (35.67 per 1 million in the United States. Clearly, America is a more violent society, a fact that is only exacerbated by the availability of guns.[52]

The Level of Society

Regardless of a community's sense of mutual regard—whether or not the people in the community fix the proverbial broken windows and keep a lookout for each other—larger social forces affect a person's criminal tendencies. Let's talk about poverty and inequality.

In the American mind, poverty is strongly associated with street crime. The popular images of poverty in the United States mirror the popular images of crime: inner-city neighborhoods with dilapidated housing, widespread vandalism, damaged parks and other public spaces, young men hanging out on the streets, rambunctious youths carrying on even during school hours, drug dealers and prostitutes plying their trade in the open and in well-guarded crack houses.

Liberal theorists argue that limited economic opportunity and a sense of despair drive people in poor communities to commit crime. Poor education reduces employment opportunities. High unemployment leads to acute frustration and unstable home life. Unstable home life leads to an inability to cope with the challenges of raising children, which often leads to domestic violence. Violence in the home produces frightened children who know of no ways to cope with difficulties other than impulsive and violent action. And so on.

What do the numbers show?

Economists Stephen Raphael and Rudolf Winter-Ebmer found a strong correlation between unemployment and crime, arguing that the risk factors change when people are out of work, in several categories of crime. From 1992 to 1996, when the unemployment rate fell, levels of crime fell in virtually all categories. The economists calculate that a decline in the unemployment rate of 2 percentage points produced a 9 percent decline in burglary, a 14 percent decline in rape and robbery, and a 30 percent decline in assault. An increase in the unemployment rate of 1 point would have resulted in 500,000 more crimes in the United States, the authors estimate.[53]

But the poverty/crime connection goes beyond joblessness. A strong correlation exists between poverty, inequality, and crime. A two-decade study showed a clear connection between falling real wages and the crime rate. From 1979 to 1997, federal statistics revealed a 20 percent decline in real wages for people without a college education. During that same period, property crimes increased 21 percent and violent crimes increased 35 percent. The study estimated that the 20 percent fall in real wages of men without college educations accounts for a 10.8 percent increase in property crimes and a 21.6 percent increase in violent crimes. Interestingly, wages had a larger effect than unemployment on the crime rate. The link between economic deprivation and crime was especially telling in assault and robbery figures—but there was little connection between economic well-being and rape and murder.[54] "A decline in wages increases the relative payoff of criminal activity. It seems obvious that economic conditions should have an impact on crime, but few studies have systematically studied the issue," said one of the authors of the study. "The fact that murder and rape didn't have much of a connection with wages and unemployment provides good evidence that many criminals are motivated by poor economic conditions to turn to crime."[55]

Race is an important dimension of both inequality and crime in the United States. Blacks make up 30 percent of the federal prison population and 46 percent of the state system, even though their overall share of the population is only about 12 percent. Here is the key: blacks' unemployment rates are twice as high as the rest of the population and their poverty rates are three times as high. Hispanics have similarly unequal rates of unemployment and poverty—and make up 28 percent of the federal prison system and 17 percent of the state prison system, even though they comprise only 10.2 percent of the nation's population. This is not to say that there is anything inherently criminal in the racial makeup of these populations, but that they suffer the greatest poverty and therefore contribute disproportionately to the crime problem. In 1993, New York City police reported that the vast majority of all homicides occurred in the city's poorest neighborhoods. A total of 854 homicides occurred in twelve precincts in the poorest areas of Harlem, the Bronx, and Brooklyn, while only thirty-seven murders occurred in twelve affluent precincts.[56]

Education and unemployment have to be a big part of the issue. Lack of education leads to not only spotty work records and family formation but also a sense of despair.

Prisoners tend to be far less educated than the general population. According to the U.S. Department of Justice, about 40 percent of the inmates in state prisons lacked a high school education or its equivalency. Some 14.2 percent had an eighth-grade education or less, another 28.9 percent had only some high school education, 25.1 percent had a GED (an equivalent of a high school education, obtained outside of high school). Only 18.5 percent were high school graduates and 10.7 percent had some college experience. Just 2.7 percent of the inmates had earned college degrees.[57]

What is meant by the expression "relative deprivation"?

The tendency for poverty to engender crime increases when poor people are exposed to affluence. The relative deprivation theory—first developed by Alexis de Tocqueville to explain why the French Revolution occurred at a time of prosperity—helps to explain the role of poverty in producing crime. People understand their own situation with reference to others. If everyone is poor or working-class, no one is deprived relative to another. But in highly stratified communities, the sense of deprivation is aggravated by seeing others succeed. Cities with extremes of wealth or poverty experience more violent crime than cities with more evenly distributed wealth. This tendency is exacerbated by extreme or abrupt reversals of fortune. When a group gains ground economically, and then suffers a downturn when others do not, the opportunity gap is much more obvious. Crime is an expression of helplessness and frustration, of exclusion from the community, as much as anything else.

But surely economic deprivation alone is not the problem. Lots of poor people—the vast majority, in fact—are law-abiding citizens. What accounts for the poverty-crime connection?

Poverty in America is an experience of isolation. Theorists on the right, such as Edward Banfield, and on the left, such as William Julius Wilson, agree that the isolation of poor, unemployed, ill-educated people with broken families and few positive role models make a strong equation for crime. Whether you call it "culture of poverty" or "social isolation," experts agree that poverty and isolation can be a lethal combination. Here is Banfield's summary of the situation:

> Because the lower-class style of life involves an unremitting search for sex and for relief from boredom, it tends to bring the individual

into situations in which he is likely to break the law. Moreover, he has little or nothing to lose—no job, no money, no reputation—by being charged with a crime. In the lower-class world it is taken for granted that everyone "gets in trouble" and may go to jail now and then. Being known as vicious and violent may give one a certain prestige in the slum, as it does in prison. Finally, since he is unwilling or unable to keep a job or acquire a skill, the lower-class individual's opportunities for income are relatively poor. Even if the "wage rate" for "hustling" were low (in fact it is often very high) that might be the best "job" open to an unskilled youth, especially one who prefers the "life of action" to regular work.[58]

Banfield's "culture of poverty" argument posits that people's antisocial behavior goes far beyond their economic straits. People can choose to be law-abiding even when they are poor. But the inner-city creates a culture that encourages destructive behavior.

Is there any way to compare poor people who are isolated—and hence prone to antisocial behavior—with poor people who are integrated into the values and norms of the larger society?

A recent study of the Moving to Opportunity (MTO) program offers some clues. Under MTO, the U.S. Department of Housing and Urban Development offered some poor families in ghetto tracts the opportunity to move to integrated, middle-class communities. The experiment was brought to five cities: Baltimore, Boston, Chicago, Los Angeles, and New York. One set of families was given housing subsidies, counseling, and help with housing searches to move to communities with less than 10 percent poor populations. A second set was given just the subsidies so they could search for their own housing outside ghetto neighborhoods. A third set of families—the control group—was given no special assistance and forced to fend for themselves in their existing ghetto neighborhoods.

A study of the Baltimore program found striking results. More than three quarters of the participating households reported that the prospect of escaping the problems of gangs and drugs was the first or second reason for enrolling in the program. Program participants were arrested for violent crimes at about one half the rate of their peers in the control group. A decline in robbery arrests accounted for about half of the difference, even though robberies comprise only about 16 percent of total arrests for the population sample as a whole. The authors of the study conclude that the results are robust for different slices of the population, including those with no preprogram arrests and girls as well as boys.[59]

The Level of the System

Once a person commits a crime, the criminal justice system has to respond. The question is whether the cops, prosecutors, courts, and prisons form a coherent enough system to combat crime, isolate dangerous people, and rehabilitate the offenders who might play constructive roles in society.

The U.S. criminal justice system is not a coherent, unified structure. The justice system is instead a confederation of semiautonomous operations—from local police departments to federal, state, and local court systems, prosecutor's offices, prisons and jails, parole boards, and community organizations.

When a crime is committed, a whole chain of events is set into motion that involves these actors in turn. That chain of actions can lead to the successful prosecution and imprisonment of the perpetrator, but it usually does not. In fact, the criminal justice system imprisons only about one person for every hundred violent crimes that occur. About one in five reported crimes ends in an arrest, and less than 30 percent of all arrests result in imprisonment. Of those convicted of violent crimes—about 165,000 in 1992—only 10 percent go through a full trial. The other 90 percent accept a guilty verdict of a lesser crime through plea bargaining.[60]

To understand the consequences of crime, it is useful to examine the sequence of events that occurs with the commission of a crime. The system is binary. At each stage of the process—investigation, arrest, booking, initial court appearance, preliminary court hearings, bail or bail hearings, and the trial itself—charges and pieces of evidence are either pursued or dropped. Each stage in this process, which might be compared to a filter, reduces the chances that a criminal suspect will be convicted and sent to jail.

Let's look at the front line of the criminal justice system—police. How does a cop's behavior affect the life of the community—the way that lawbreakers and law-abiding citizens act on a daily basis?

Police are always part of the complex ecology of order and disorder. Police actions lead the criminal element to adjust its strategies and actions—ironically, often producing an increase in deviant behavior. When police seek to apprehend a suspect, for example, the suspect often engages in even more violent and destructive acts. Riots, high-speed chases, and an escalation of drug-related violence often occur when police confront people on the street. Police confrontation produces a string of efforts of criminals to avoid capture.

When police use their discretion and do not enforce the law—when they use informants, for example, or avoid confrontation to "keep the peace"—they often subtly encourage criminals to step up their illegal behavior. One police detective commented: "Any junk dealer that you work with as an informant is moving junk when you're working with him. It has to be. You can't waste time chasing after some churchgoing Mary. If he's selling onions, what's he gonna tell you? The only way he can know what's coming down is if he's doing business."[61] One notorious example of the corrupting influence of informants is the case of James ("Whitey") Bulger, a South Boston organized crime boss who was paid by the FBI from the 1970s to the 1990s to inform on fellow mobsters, and whose FBI liaison became entwined in the crimes of the underworld.[62] The real tragedy of the Bulger scandal was that it undermined the whole practice of insider informing, which can be critical for law-enforcement authorities to confront drug dealers, weapons traffickers, money launderers, organized crime families, and others engaged in complex operations.

Why are police brutality and corruption important problems?

Police brutality occurs whenever a cop uses force that exceeds the needs of the situation. When a cop roughs up a suspect or someone on the street, it might be considered brutality. Given the dangerous and unpredictable circumstances police often find themselves, it is inevitable that police will make mistakes. Inevitably, police will misjudge the danger of a situation and use too much of their muscle power and firepower to subdue someone that they think poses a physical danger to themselves and the community. Some would even say that verbal abuse should count as police brutality. When people's dignity is attacked by a cop's verbal abuse, the effect can be as profound as physical abuse.

The harshest critics of police brutality recognize the difficult situations that police face every day. A document from Human Rights Watch states this understanding eloquently:

> Human Rights Watch recognizes that police officers, like other people, will make mistakes when they are under pressure to make split-second decisions regarding the use of force. Even the best recruiting, training, and command oversight will not result in flawless behavior on the part of all officers. Furthermore, we recognize that policing in the United States is a dangerous job. During 1996, 116 officers died while on duty nationwide (from all causes—shootings, assaults, accidents, and natural causes). Yet, precisely because police officers can make mistakes, or allow personal bias or emotion to enter into policing—and because they are allowed, as a last resort, to use potentially lethal force to subdue individuals they apprehend—police must be subjected to intense scrutiny.[63]

There are two major reasons to maintain vigilance against police brutality. First, even occasional corruption undermines the legitimacy of the whole police force. Second, even if the public were willing to look the other way, rough street tactics actually undermine police effectiveness. Police need a network of helpers in order to track down criminal activity. Most crimes do not have direct witnesses who will talk to police, so police must piece together an endless string of clues to nab a criminal. Developing relationships with people in the neighborhood requires gaining their trust.[64]

How can we assess the levels of police brutality? How extensive is it? What breeds brutality in police departments?

Contrary to sensational news reports, incidents of police force are really quite rare. Just 1 percent of people who had encounters with police reported that the police used or even threatened the use of force. In a survey of arrests involving the police taking a suspect into custody, one in five involved some use of force. When injuries occur, it is almost always when the suspect resists arrest physically.[65] According to a 1999 study of arrests in six cities, police used force 17 percent of the time; that larger figure includes verbal encounters and chases as well as the use of restraint, physical force, and weapons. A study conducted in Miami–Dade County found that in 97 percent of all encounters involving force, the suspects physically resisted police actions.[66]

Ultimately, the problem of police brutality stems from the everyday stress and culture of the police department.[67] Cops, like other people, are social animals. They learn and take their cues from peers. Jack Maple, the legendary cop who helped turn around crime in New York in the 1990s, puts it this way: "Cops are not from another planet. Their backgrounds, their weaknesses, are the same as any other human being's. They are not descended from Planet Honest. We get them from Earth."[68]

Police corruption thrives when there is no independent oversight of police departments. The New Orleans Police Department's Chief of Operations, Ronald Serpas, notes: "If a doctor is guilty of malpractice, well, sooner or later people will go to another doctor. In our case, if the police are guilty of malpractice, where is the community supposed to go? When we've lost their trust, what do they do? Find *another* police force?"[69] To promote honest policing, departments need to establish clear rules and lines of authority, public access to information about police behavior, independent means of investigating complaints of police misconduct, and swift punishment of cops who violate citizens' rights. Nationwide, more cities have created independent review commissions to provide oversight of police behavior and hear complaints from citizens. Close to a hundred cities have established outside civilian review bodies, up from just one in 1970. Seattle, Portland, San Jose, and Los Angeles County all have independent officials who review the police.[70]

OK, back to the structure of the criminal justice system. Once someone has been arrested, the criminal process moves from the cops to the courts. What happens then?

If the police and prosecutors decide that they have enough evidence to bring a case to court, the case moves to the courts. Getting to a court trial can be difficult, because police and the courts are so overworked that obtaining the evidence needed for a trial can be time-consuming—and sometimes impossible. Prosecutors often decide not to try cases because of a lack of compelling evidence, a decision to strike a plea bargain with the accused, or a simple decision that the case is not as important as other cases in the docket. When a case makes its way to court, anything can happen. Many courts are so overloaded that they have delays that last for months or even years. Winning cases in court requires that everything go right—good evidence from the police, strong legal arguments by the lawyers, and a willingness to convict on the part of juries and judges. If the prosecutors do win a conviction, the defendant can appeal to a higher court.

Critics of the court system complain that judges let defendants off too easily. But the real winnowing of cases occurs because the criminal-justice system moves through so many stages. Of every hundred felony arrests in the United States, thirty-five are immediately diverted from the system because they involve juveniles who cannot be tried in an adult court. Of the sixty-five cases brought to the district attorney, forty-five are approved for prosecution. Ten of those are dismissed by the judge or involve a suspect who fails to appear, leaving thirty-five cases. Thirty of those thirty-five cases plead guilty—usually as part of a deal with prosecutors—and the other five go to trial. Three of the five get convicted, the other two acquitted. Of the thirty-three convicts, nineteen go to prison and fourteen get probation. Eleven are jailed for less than a year and eight for more than a year.

The real discretion during this series of decisions is exercised by the prosecutor. A prosecutor's decisions usually depend on the practical considerations of caseload management and not so much on a concern for legal niceties. There are only so many cases a prosecutor can push through the system. Prosecutors consider many factors: the seriousness of the offense, the suspect's record, the weight of the evidence, in-house rules or norms on how to treat different kinds of cases, the workload at the police department, what kinds of special tools prosecutors can use (such as the federal Racketeer Influenced and Corrupt Organizations Act or the forensics laboratory), and the political climate (such as the public fervor about drugs). One recent shift in the criminal-justice system is a greater focus on repeat offenders. Race and gender also play a role, but in ways that are often hard to figure. The public tends to get a distorted view of the process through such cases as the homicide conviction of British nanny Louise Woodward in 1997 and the murder acquittal of OJ Simpson in 1995.

Some people say that judicial activism—particularly regarding the rights of criminal defendants—has undermined the ability of the police to maintain order.

Ever since Richard Nixon's "law and order" campaign of 1968, conservative critics have claimed that the courts' protection of the rights of criminal suspects has undermined the ability of police to protect the public. Instances abound of violent criminals being set free because of technical violations of police or courtroom procedure, only to commit crimes again when they are out of custody. At issue is a basic tension between the rights of the community and the rights of the individual.

The controversy began in the 1960s, when the Supreme Court issued a number of rulings that extended basic protections to all people charged with a crime. *Gideon* v. *Wainwright* (1963) requires courts to appoint a lawyer to defendants who cannot afford their own. *Miranda* v. *Arizona* (1966) and *Escobedo* v. *Illinois* (1964) require police to inform suspects of their rights and tell them that they may refuse to answer questions and have a lawyer present for questioning. *Mapp* v. *Ohio* (1961) requires courts to exclude evidence obtained in illegal searches and seizures. *Duncan* v. *Louisiana* (1968) requires jury trials for state criminal trials involving serious charges and sentencing. *Katz* v. *United States* (1967) defines an illegal wiretap as an unreasonable search and seizure. *Malloy* v. *Hogan* (1964) extends a person's right to remain silent to state cases.

More recent cases have reduced the reach of these protections. *Arizona* v. *Fulminante* (1991), for example, says that courts may use illegally obtained evidence if it is supported by legally obtained evidence. *Coleman* v. *Thompson* (1991) restricts the right to counsel in appeals cases. *Harris* v. *New York* (1971) rules that illegally obtained statements cannot be used to implicate a person in a crime; they can be used to impeach a person's character in a trial. *New York* v. *Quarles* (1984) allows statements that violate Miranda warnings if those questions are asked with a desire to protect safety. *Nix* v. *Williams* (1984) allows the use of unlawfully obtained evidence if that evidence could have been obtained legally.

Have "liberal" court rulings in fact prevented cops and courts from getting arrests and convictions?

Contrary to the popular image, few court cases are damaged by minor violations of police or courtroom procedure. Judges do not set many criminal defendants free because of technical violations of search-and-seizure

What Is the Sequence of Events in the Criminal Justice System?

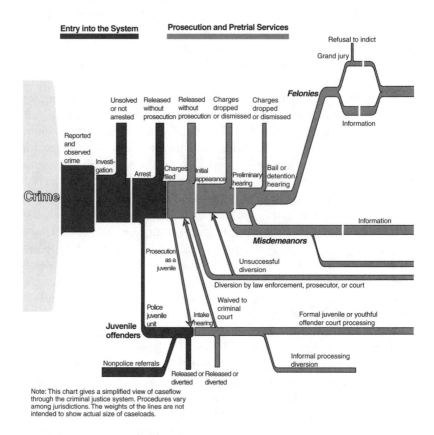

Note: This chart gives a simplified view of caseflow through the criminal justice system. Procedures vary among jurisdictions. The weights of the lines are not intended to show actual size of caseloads.

law or cops' failure to inform criminal suspects of their rights. Fewer than 1 percent of all felony arrests are dropped for technicalities, usually in drug cases when police have used questionable search methods. It is impossible to judge how many would-be suspects are not arrested in the first place because of constitutional rules for gathering evidence, but few scholars believe that the numbers are significant.[71]

The decade of the 1990s might be known as the era of imprisonment in American life. About 2 million Americans were behind bars by the turn of the century. That must have a profound impact on the crime problem in the United States.

The move toward a lock-'em-up approach to crime has changed the life of the street. Under various mandatory sentencing laws, judges have no

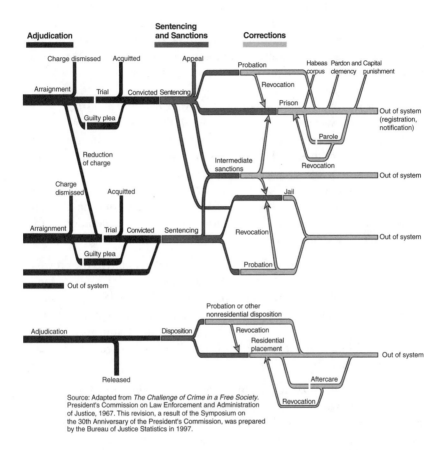

Adjudication

Sentencing and Sanctions

Corrections

Charge dismissed Acquitted Appeal

Probation Habeas corpus Pardon and clemency Capital punishment

Arraignment Trial Convicted Sentencing Revocation

Prison

Guilty plea

Out of system (registration, notification)

Parole

Reduction of charge Intermediate sanctions Revocation

Out of system

Charge dismissed Acquitted Jail

Arraignment Trial Convicted Sentencing Revocation Out of system

Guilty plea Probation

Out of system

Probation or other nonresidential disposition

Adjudication Disposition Revocation

Residential placement Out of system

Released Aftercare

Source: Adapted from *The Challenge of Crime in a Free Society.* President's Commission on Law Enforcement and Administration of Justice, 1967. This revision, a result of the Symposium on the 30th Anniversary of the President's Commission, was prepared by the Bureau of Justice Statistics in 1997.

Revocation

choice but to put offenders in jail, even for first-time petty drug offenses. Thirty states have adopted some form of mandatory sentencing laws; in Arizona, California, Illinois, Indiana, and Maine, judges have almost no discretion in sentencing. So-called "presumptive" guidelines in states such as Minnesota, Pennsylvania, and Oregon allow judges discretion only under specific conditions. Surveys show that an overwhelming proportion of federal judges oppose mandatory sentencing because it prevents them from developing "proportionate" responses to the criminal activity.

New York State offers a stark example of the new toughness. Under the notorious Rockefeller drug laws, the state now imprisons two nonviolent drug offenders for every one violent felon; twenty years ago, the state sent six violent criminals to prison for every one nonviolent drug offender.[72] The growth in the prison population has captured a wide range of people and cut them off from society, so they can do no harm to innocent people. But the paradox of the prison strategy is that some of the more dangerous elements elude capture, while the tamer elements get caught. Because drug kingpins possess knowledge of larger criminal operations, they are often able to plea-bargain their way out of prison sentences while otherwise law-abiding people do years in prison for minor drug offenses.

What is the role of prisons in the American system of criminal justice?

Prisons lie at the center of the debate about the American system of justice. The threat of going to prison serves as the major political deterrent to committing crimes. Police work is oriented toward apprehending criminals for possible prosecution—with the threat of jail—rather than community development or order maintenance. The American public, frustrated with the seeming failure of liberal strategies of rehabilitation, seems to have adopted a lock-'em-up attitude in the last generation. Alfred Blumstein typifies the modern sentiment:

> For the short term, there is little we can do but respond to the growing violence with arrest, conviction, and incarceration, at least for the period when the individual [criminal] can be expected to continue to act violently. In order to do this, we have got to make room in the prisons for those for whom prison is most appropriate for reasons of incapacitation, those who are likely to engage in violence on the outside.[73]

The public's motivations for the incarceration strategy go further than incapacitation, however. A basic search for order lies at the root of the public impulse. One study found that the primary concern of people supporting the "three strikes and you're out" sentencing strategy is a concern about "moral cohesion" in society. To allow the community to heal, the cancer of crime must be removed, according to this view.[74]

The inmate population is growing so fast—by about 8 percent annually—that prison officials estimate a need for about a thousand new beds each week.[75] The problem with this emphasis is that it ignores the organic nature of crime, the way that criminal acts grow out of the very character of the society. Ultimately, if a community is to combat crime, it needs to foster the ideals of respect and order—and the formal and informal social systems that reinforce those ideals in day-to-day life. A reliance on the criminal justice system focuses too much on responding to the failure of those ideals and systems.

How do prisons affect the level of street crime in the United States? How does the growth in the prison population affect the overall levels of crime?

The nation's prison population has increased at an unprecedented rate in recent years. From 1980 to 1990, the number of inmates in state and federal prisons jumped from 330,000 to 883,000; by the mid-1990s, the population passed the 1 million mark. By 1990, 2.5 million people were on probation and almost another half-million on parole. In 1993, forty states and the District of Columbia were under court orders to relieve overcrowding and substandard prison conditions. New sentencing guidelines have increased the average time served in prison from twenty-four months in 1984 to forty-six months in 1990.

Conservatives make a compelling argument about the cost-effectiveness of imprisoning street criminals who steal property and commit violent acts. Despite the high cost of imprisonment, former California Attorney General Dan Lundgren says jailing repeat offenders is a bargain. Keeping a prisoner costs some $30,000 to $35,000 a year, but the cost to society of crime is greater still. According to a National Institute of Justice study, the cost of crimes to victims and society ranged from $1,400 for each burglary to $2.9 million for each murder. For multiple offenders, those figures add up fast. One RAND study found that burglars commit between seventy-six and 118 burglaries a year, while lesser larcenists like pickpockets and shoplifters average 135 to 202 acts a year. Sentencing one hundred convicts to jail costs the system about $25 million but saves $400 million.[76]

The major question facing American courts today is: Who should be imprisoned, and why? Draconian mandatory sentences have put 300,000 people behind bars for myriad drug offenses—one in five federal prisoners are first-time petty offenders—while at the same time violent prisoners are often released because of prison overcrowding. Thousands of people with no history of crime have been put behind bars, sometimes for indirect involvement like unpacking crates from trucks. One federal judge, J. Lawrence Irving, resigned rather than implement the laws. "It's insanity," he said. "We are putting young people in prison for ten years on their first offense without the possibility of parole, a longer sentence than is served in many states for murder."[77] Large-scale drug dealers get lesser sentences because they can bargain with prosecutors to exchange their insider knowledge of the drug business for reduced sentences.

Ultimately, society has to decide whether prisons should even contain people who do not pose a physical threat to the community. Should prisons hold white-collar criminals like Webster Hubbell along with violent predators like John Wayne Gacy? In *Between Prison and Probation*, Norval Morris and Michael Tonry argue that when the criminal does not pose a direct threat to society, punishment should be shifted toward greater use of heavy fines, electronic controls (such as "bracelets"), community service, and supervised probation and parole.[78]

What's prison life like?

For the most part, bad and getting worse. The modern impulses behind the explosion in the prison population is expressed by one inmate at the Nottoway Correctional Center in Virginia: "The idea is to make prison a secular hell on earth—a place where the young potential felon will fear to go, where the ex-con will fear to return. But an underlying theme is that 'these people' are irredeemable 'predators' (i.e., 'animals'), who are without worth."[79] Prisons are supposed to convince would-be criminals that any rewards from a crime pale in comparison with life behind bars.

Prisons also serve as breeding grounds for criminal resentment. Some have dubbed prisons the "graduate schools for criminal behavior" because the subculture of crime there offers numerous lessons on criminal technique and survival. Convicts in prison often brag to each other about their exploits and talk about every conceivable factor they face on the street—cops, security systems, guns and other weaponry, what works and what does not.

A study by Human Rights Watch found that many jails have unhealthy and dangerous conditions. Security officials often abuse restraining devices and other disciplinary tools to control inmate populations. Both men and women prisoners are subject to sexual abuse by both fellow inmates and prison guards. Prisoners with mental illness and other handicaps are abused. In Corcoran State Prison in California, more than fifty prisoners have been shot by guards; in 1988, prison guards were indicted for putting on gladiator-style fights among prisoners and using guns to break up the violence.[80]

The harsh picture of prisons contrasts with the liberal notion of "corrections" that prevailed throughout much of the 1960s and 1970s. In response to years of barbaric conditions, where rape, violence, and disease were commonplace, federal and state courts ordered prisons to adopt standards and programs so that determined prisoners could reform themselves and make a new life for themselves. Courts ordered states to improve basic conditions, such as the size of cells and the quality of diets and health care, and reform-minded states such as New York and Massachusetts offered educational and work programs in an attempt to rehabilitate prisoners.

But since the 1980s, states have eliminated many of the programs and services that were intended to provide inmates with an incentive to improve their lives and become better citizens when they were released. With prisons doubling and sometimes tripling in population, just maintaining order poses a major challenge to prison operations. Meanwhile, a debate rages about whether educational programs in prisons ought to be required or optional, while some argue that prison should provide punishment for antisocial behavior, not new opportunities for the perpetrators. New York State eliminated state tuition assistance programs in 1995, and many prisons have cut back on work opportunities within prison walls. The percentage of inmates who are employed in prison jobs ranges from a low of 1 percent to a high of 30 percent; the median is 9 percent.[81]

Prison officials and scholars often bemoan the inmate's lack of opportunity for self-improvement. One study of male inmates in Wisconsin found that when prisoners are enrolled in high school classes, they are about 10 percent less likely to be rearrested once they leave prison. Studies also show that work opportunities reduce the disciplinary problems in prisons. Education and work are not only ways to rehabilitate the prisoner but also an important safety valve. J. Michael Quinlan, the former director of the Federal Bureau of Prisons, stated: "I've never met a prison administrator who didn't want more inmates working."[82]

Rates of recidivism are high for released prisoners. A national survey found a recidivism rate of 31.2 percent for male property offenders sentenced to felony probation. Recidivism among white, black, and Hispanic probationers was 25, 35.8, and 39.8 percent, respectively. Other researchers have identified five factors that contribute to recidivism: youth, minority status, gender, drug problems, and previous arrests.[83] Experts have begun to worry about how prison crowding and cutbacks in education and other services will affect the ex-con once he gets on the street. Assaults in prisons doubled in the 1990s, according to the Criminal Justice Institute. Jerome Miller, the president of the National Center on Institutions and Alternatives, sums up the problem this way: "As sentencing laws get tougher and punishment proposals get more vicious, there's a tendency toward a great wave of dehumanization of inmates."[84] Such a dehumanization is not only problematic from a human rights standpoint but also feeds the spiral of violence that hurts the larger community.

Policy Responses to Crime
Jobs, Education, Training, Social Services

If we really wanted to confront the street crime that concerns so many people, what kinds of social programs might we adopt?

A comprehensive approach to crime would look at root causes and develop programs to address the needs of the people most susceptible to criminal behavior—before, during, and after these people engage in any criminal activity. If low levels of education are part of the cause of criminal behavior, then local governments should develop literacy programs for those in need—high school dropouts, parolees, unemployed people, members of substance-abuse groups. Prisons should do the same, to make the time behind bars as productive as possible and prepare inmates for life outside prison.

Likewise, if low job skills are part of the problem, then state and local authorities might develop programs that teach skills among the most desperate populations and communities. One of the biggest problems for troubled populations is that career ladders have many missing rungs—that is, jobs might be available at the lowest levels, but there are no processes for helping the worker advance to higher rungs. It is not enough to assure that troubled people will get entry-level jobs during boom times. It is also necessary to create ways for workers to improve their skills, get advice from mentors, and become part of networks.

If drug addiction is a big part of the criminal world, then communities and prisons should provide treatment on demand for the full range of substance abuse problems, from alcohol to cocaine to harder drugs. Treatment is expensive in the short term but cost-effective in the long term. With more than 1.2 million prisoners addicted to some kind of drug, treatment is critical to improving their opportunities for joining mainstream society on their release. The National Center on Addiction and Substance Abuse found that the cost of drug treatment and a variety of other educational and social services was $6,500 a year. The Columbia University–based center estimates that comprehensive treatment for all addicts in prison would cost $7.8 billion and would yield benefits worth $8.26 billion if only 10 percent of the inmates were treated successfully. Furthermore, experts estimate that drug-addicted ex-cons commit a hundred property and violent crimes per year after their release, so every ten thousand successfully treated ex-convicts would result in 1 million fewer serious crimes a year.[85]

Mental health problems should also be addressed as part of a comprehensive crime-prevention strategy. As the growing numbers of homeless people on city streets attest, mental illness can exact a terrible price not only for victims but also for their families and the larger community. The best time to reach people with mental illnesses is during their youth. One study found that 63 percent of all incarcerated juveniles have had more than one diagnosis of mental illness. Another study of ninety-seven male adolescents with mental health problems after they left prison found that all but six were imprisoned again as adults; most of them had received no treatment at all for their illness.[86] As grim as it may sound, arrest and imprisonment could serve as an effective way to identify young persons with mental problems.

But that approach would take a long time to be effective.

Yes and no. Addressing root causes of crime does take a long time. It sometimes takes years—and many failed attempts—to help someone get off drugs or address mental illness. Treatment for deep-seated problems is not cheap and it requires the kind of support—from family, friends, church—that often does not exist. It also requires a commitment on the part of the person who experiences the problem.

On the other hand, doing nothing makes the problems even more intense. The costs of crime are so much more expensive than the costs of treatment, even when the treatment succeeds only a fraction of the time. The ultimate goal of self-sufficiency and responsibility can be reached only when the deep-seated problems are addressed.

The Private Security Approach

What effects do the private security industry—for-profit police forces, alarm and security systems companies, architects, and planners—have on the overall level of crime and on the community's ability to confront the economy of crime?

In the past generation, in terms of manpower, private security firms have become the most dominant part of the criminal justice system. Three times as many private security officers patrol streets and guard buildings than public cops. In all, some 1.5 million security officials under private contract patrol neighborhoods, office parks, business improvement districts, and other places. Nationwide, there are only 500,000 publicly paid and controlled police officers. In addition, security technology has enmeshed the metropolis in a separate system of surveillance and control. Developers design residential communities and commercial strips to restrict access.

Private security officers are hired by apartment complexes and stores, neighborhood associations and business improvement districts. The purpose is to create a visible presence in the streets and buildings—to send a message to criminal elements. In addition, many public agencies contract out with private security forces. Many cities now resemble checkerboards, with certain high-profile neighborhoods protected by private security, and other neighborhoods protected by public cops.

Public and private security forces tend to have different priorities. Public police focus on "index crime," the serious instances of violent acts that require apprehension, investigation, and prosecution. Cops must follow bureaucratic and legal procedures; they must be accountable to the public at large, which means that they cannot tailor their actions to specific constituencies. Private security forces, however, focus more on creating a feeling of security. Rather than relying on formal authority, they develop a pragmatic, decentralized, coalitional approach to preventing crime. Private security forces, in other words, embody the basic concepts of community policing. Their growing numbers in the two decades have educated Americans on the importance of the preventive approach based on community participation.

What is the most appropriate balance between public police forces, on the one hand, and private security forces and community groups, on the other?

As with all areas of urban policy—poverty, housing, education, public health, parks and recreation—the public realm needs to establish the foundation for the individuals and groups. The public realm exercises a unique sense of authority because of its grounding in constitutional and legal strictures, electoral accountability, and bureaucratic regulations and procedures. Because it aspires to govern the whole community, it makes a claim for the public interest that no other institution can match.

But for the public realm to be effective and to enjoy the support of citizens and institutions, public authorities need to understand that their role is to establish the foundation and then get out of the way. The local government needs to meet basic public needs—infrastructure, public education, law enforcement and public order, fire protection, care for the indigent, and some degree of public health and recreation—and then allow the private sector and local groups to take over. Real order develops when public-spirited action is taken by individuals and families, clubs and block associations, small and large businesses, church and fraternal organizations, and advocacy groups.

If police departments can provide a foundation for order—with community-based patrolling of streets, assistance to crime watches, professional attention to crime hot spots, and rigorous but sensitive enforcement of laws—then the people can "deputize" themselves to do the rest.

Policing

What different approaches to public order have been pursued by big-city police departments?

Policing, like all social and political activities, moves through cycles. Policing strategies swing back and forth between engagement and separation from the community, between emphases on technology and on "street smarts," between centralized and decentralized control, and between an aggressive, punitive approach and a community-based, developmental approach. James Q. Wilson outlines three major styles in his classic *Varieties of Police Behavior.*[87]

The original model of police behavior was the "night-watchman." The police officer's job was to walk the beat and maintain a basic order in the community. The physical presence of the cop on the street—where everyone, law-abiding citizen and scofflaw alike, could see him—directly deterred crime. The night-watchman exercised great discretion in deciding what signs of disorder to confront. Police had the power to decide whether to confront teens loitering on a corner, bars operating after hours for illicit purposes, and men making exchanges on empty lots. The night-watchman made these decisions based on his intimate knowledge of the community and his judgment about what activities were acceptable and what kinds of intervention would work. The cop ran his own show, with little interference from police headquarters. He was a free agent. The problem with this model is the opportunity for cronyism and corruption. A cop with strong personal ties to a neighborhood could lose sight of his responsibilities. Accommodation, rather than the law, dominates the night-watchman model.

The "legalistic" model stands in almost complete opposition to the night-watchman. The legalistic cop is more concerned with processing violations of the law strictly according to the book than with maintaining community order. This cop is a bureaucrat in blue. Under the direction of superiors in headquarters, the legalistic officer responds to complaints rather than serving as a larger community presence. The cop hears about a crime, interviews people who might know something about the crime, and "closes" the case one way or another. There is little contact with the community.

The legalistic cop's routines and identity reflect the ideals of Max Weber's model of bureaucracy. Cops work in clear and separate jurisdictional areas, operate in a hierarchical system in a permanent structure, record all actions in a system of written documents and files, and develop a professional commitment and identity with all of the trappings of that status (formal tests and standards, tenure and career orientation, fixed salary structure).[88]

Often, to impress superiors, the legalistic officer acts to pad his statistical record. Making arrests, issuing tickets, getting to the scene of a crime in record time—rather than preventing crimes from occurring in the first place—were all too often the preoccupation of the legalistic cop. The emphasis is on scientific measurement of performance. The courts' insistence on protecting the rights of the accused leaves little room for the informal order-maintenance of the night-watchman. One police chief remarked: "We used to be able to get a boy on juvenile delinquency charged for almost anything. We never had trouble finding some grounds for bringing the boy in. The new [state] juvenile code makes it a lot tougher to arrest him."[89] The legalistic cop sees his task narrowly; there is little of the ambiguity of the night-watchman's role.

Where the legalistic or bureaucratic style is mechanistic, the "service" model is more organic. The service model sees the police officer as a friend of the community—indeed, the community cop is a vital part of the fabric and texture of the community. The cop is expected to mediate disputes and intervene to offer assistance to home owners, schools, churches, and anyone else who asks. The service cop is a uniformed jack of all trades. He or she can settle domestic conflicts, mediate disputes between members of different ethnic groups, help neighborhood kids get jobs, help shop owners deal with graffiti and loitering, and guide substance abusers to treatment programs. The service model is at the heart of the contemporary community policing movement, which aims to prevent explosions of violence and disorder rather than simply respond to specific crimes.

The most important element of the service model is the social compact that is informally negotiated every day between the cop and diverse members of the community. Like a natural organism, the community has a delicate equilibrium. To maintain the equilibrium, police and other community leaders nurture bonds and arrangements among the members of the community. Sometimes those bonds are informal, as when people develop relationships simply because they know that they must all deal with each other on a day-to-day basis. At other times, cops, priests, or other community leaders use their prestige and authority to arrange a more formal working relationship among people. However these relationships develop, they tie people's interests together. That is something that no top-down bureaucratic organization could accomplish.

Critics say the service model could turn the purpose of policing upside down. Rather than developing strategies to prevent and control crime, police gain popularity in neighborhoods by meeting social needs that are better served by families, schools, churches, boys and girls clubs, and the like. Social services are critical in developing safe communities, but police resources need to be focused on attacking the activities that more directly challenge order.

What has been the predominant model in the post–World War II era?

The model of policing from World War II to the 1980s and 1990s was the professional police officer who plays a specific and circumscribed role in a larger bureaucratic setting.

The leading figure in police reform was August Vollmer, the police chief for Berkeley, California, from 1905 to 1932. Vollmer established the first dispatching systems, in which precincts sent police out to respond to complaints telephoned to central headquarters. Vollmer's thinking was that even if night-watchman police were unimpeachably honest and hardworking, their movements could be detected by criminal elements, who could close down a numbers operation if they saw a cop moving in on them.

Vollmer's rapid-response system had spread nationwide by the 1940s and 1950s. Cops moved from foot patrols to car patrols so that they could respond more quickly to calls for help. People facing any kind of problem—burglary, domestic violence, noisy neighbors—could call 911 to alert the police. Dispatchers at the police departments could then alert cops cruising in patrol cars to get to the scene.

To this day, newspapers and the public judge police effectiveness by how quickly they respond to 911 calls. Journalists regularly look to 911 response times to gauge how well police departments respond to community needs. A press release by the Nashville-Davidson County Police Department illustrates how police play into this approach: "Overall average police response time to calls from citizens decreased 2.07 percent during calendar year 2000 despite more than a 24 percent jump in requests for service."[90] Police and media use the 911 standard so frequently that ordinary people begin to think that the number lies at the core of their relations with police. At the turn of the twenty-first century, city police departments across the country received an estimated 268,000 calls a day; about four fifths of all calls are for police assistance, the rest for ambulances and fire departments. In New York City, 911 calls are expected to total 12.5 million by 2005.[91]

What are the limitations of this approach?

Even taking into account the changes made by Vollmer and his followers, cops cover very little ground in a typical city. Nationwide, there are 500,000 police officers—or about one per five hundred citizens. When you take into account that the cops need to be dispersed over many shifts, you can get only about one cop overseeing two to three thousand people at a time. Taking into account that many officers work in pairs or do desk work, you realize that you can only get one cop to oversee several thousand people at a time. Ultimately, then, the police need to rely on the help of the communities that they police to maintain order. Order cannot come from the presence of a badge, only from the presence of a community that polices itself.

Somehow the cop needs not only to oversee thousands within his or her precinct but also to work inside the contentious world of the criminal justice system.

One of the greatest difficulties facing cops is the jurisdictional complexity of the criminal justice system. Combating drugs provides the clearest illustration of what happens when too many agencies are charged with combating crime. Drug enforcement at the federal level falls under the jurisdiction of dozens of agencies, including the State Department, the Pentagon, the CIA, the FBI, the Coast Guard, the Immigration and Naturalization Service, and the Drug Enforcement Administration. State and local efforts are even more fragmented.

Given the limitations of the catch-'em-afterward approach, how might police do a better job of stopping crime?

Community policing has been the most important shift in urban policy in the last generation. The strategy begins with a major reversal of attitude, from an emphasis on the actions of individual lawbreakers to an emphasis on the way that all members of a community work together to maintain order. Lawrence Friedman explains the dominant culture of the post–World War II era:

> In our individualistic age the state, the legal system, and organized society in general . . . seem more and more dedicated to one fundamental goal: to permit, foster, and protect the self, the person, the individual. A basic social creed justifies this aim: each person is unique, each person is or ought to be free, each one of us has or ought to have the right to create or build up a way of life for ourselves, and do it through free, open, and untrammeled choice.[92]

Community policing begins with the notion that the individual can thrive only when all the members of a community contribute to the maintenance of order. Policy cannot do it alone but requires the assistance of residents, shopkeepers, and even visitors.

Community policing is a term that describes any conscious effort to coordinate the strategies and tactics, resources, and know-how among all levels of a community. Community policing restores the original purpose of modern police departments in the United States and Britain: maintenance of public order. Historically, police considered it their top priority to create and foster public order by combating a whole raft of minor crimes: aggressive panhandling, public drunkenness, drug dealing, gambling, urinating in public, graffiti, prostitution, loud radios, and other disturbances of the peace. By tackling these problems, police created a more pleasant environment in which ordinary people can go about their business.

But in the post–World War II generation, police moved away from public order as a major preoccupation. Partly, the shift was due to changing social mores. In the liberal social climate of the 1960s, many of these offenses came to be understood as "victimless" crimes that ought not to concern public authorities. Prostitution, for example, was a transaction restricted to the john, the prostitute, and her pimp—so why should the police or the public care? But there was an even more compelling reason for the police to overlook petty crimes that undermined the public order. Serious crimes like murder, rape, armed robbery, and burglary had skyrocketed. Serious crime was probably the dominant single issue of domestic politics from the 1960s to the 1980s, and police felt they had no choice but to launch an all-out offensive. As a result, police spent more and more time responding to serious crimes and less and less time responding to petty crimes.

As inner-city neighborhoods deteriorated, ordinary people started to demand a return to some basic standards of order and civility in public spaces. And academics such as Wesley Skogan started to notice a connection between the deterioration of public spaces and the incidence of serious crime.[93] Kelling and Coles sum up the argument:

> [D]isorder, both directly and as a precursor to crime, played an important role in neighborhood decline. By lowering community morale and giving the community a bad reputation throughout the city, disorder both in itself, and through increased crime, undermined the stability of the local housing market: fearful residents moved out, and real estate values plunged. At the same time local businesses could not attract customers, and investment in the community plummeted. All these factors contributed directly and indirectly to decline and decay.[94]

That's when police departments—oh so tentatively—started to challenge the modern bureaucratic model of crime fighting and develop models of community policing.

Community policing attempts to restore the old goal of order maintenance by engaging the members of the community in efforts to identify problem spots and respond to those problems collectively.

Under the rubric of community policing, police have worked with neighborhood associations, business groups, kids on the streets. Rather than riding around in a squad car or responding to 911 calls all day, police were assigned to neighborhood beats. On the beat, police developed working relationships with people in the neighborhoods, which improved levels of trust and cultivated important sources of information. Police could mediate conflicts and identify dangerous situations before they blew up. In short, working with neighborhood activists, cops began to knit together the complex relationships that are necessary for order in any community.

But can walking the beat provide the kind of information cops need to confront crime strategically?

No, probably not. Carefully targeting resources makes community policing a strategy. That is the logic behind New York City's CompStat, a computer-based crime-tracking program that police use to attack crime systematically throughout the city. CompStat, says New York's former Police Commissioner Howard Safir, is "like a shot of adrenaline to the heart of law enforcement."[95]

CompStat is the brainchild of a longtime New York transit cop named Jack Maple. On his own, Maple used wall-sized sheets of paper to track the location of crime at New York's hundreds of subway stations. The daily formatting of crime data helped New York reduce subway crime by 27 percent between 1990 and 1992. When Rudolph Giuliani took over as New

Table 6.3 Traditional versus Community Policing: Questions and Answers

Question	Traditional	Community Policing
Who are the police?	A government agency principally responsible for law enforcement	Police are the public and the public are the police: the police officers are those who are paid to give full-time attention to the duties of every citizen
What is the relationship between the police and other public service departments?	Priorities often conflict	The police are one department among many for improving the quality of life
What is the role of the police?	Focusing on solving crimes	A broader problem-solving approach
How is police efficiency measured?	By detection and arrest rates	By the absence of crime and disorder
What determines the effectiveness of police?	Response times	Public cooperation
What view do police take of service calls?	Deal with only if there is no real police work to do	Vital function and great opportunity
What is police professionalism?	Swift effective response to serious crime	Keeping close to the community
What kind of intelligence is most important?	Crime intelligence—study of particular crimes or series of crimes	Criminal intelligence—information about the activities of individuals or groups
What is the essential nature of police accountability?	Highly centralized; governed by rules, regulations, and policy directives; accountable to the law	Emphasis on local accountability to community needs
What is the role of police headquarters?	To provide necessary rules and policy directives	To preach organizational values
What is the role of the press liaison department?	To keep the "heat" off operational officers so they can get on with the job	To coordinate an essential channel of communication with the community
How do the police regard prosecutions?	As an important goal	As one tool among many

Source: Malcolm K. Sparrow, *Implementing Community Policing,* National Institute of Justice, November 1988, pp. 8–9.

York's mayor in 1994, Maple brought the system to the entire police department. Every day, police input data on different crimes into computer databases, which in turn are linked to maps of the city. Crime patterns and trends show up starkly on the maps that police use to target their policing strategy for the day. If one block has an abnormal number of assaults, for example, police can be deployed there to make arrests. If another block has a large number of drug sales, the police can devise strategies not only for making arrests but also to target the neighborhood drug boss. Maple explains the strategy:

> The narcotics people have to know about the murders, the detectives have to know where the crack houses are, everybody needs to know where the fences [stolen-goods merchants] are, where the chop shops are, where the quality of life problems are happening. . . . By looking at this, you can figure out where you need to be and when. You can figure out what time the pickpockets are working. You can look at stolen cars—where they are being stolen from and where they are being recovered. If only the bones [parts] are being found, you know there is a chop shop nearby.[96]

When the full range of activities is logged onto a computer-based mapping system on a daily basis, the police get an accurate portrait of the city's hot spots. Information drives strategy. Not only can police amass forces where the most street activity is occurring but they can also develop long-term strategies to attack behind-the-scenes drug dealing, stolen-goods rackets, prostitution rings, gunrunning, and sweatshops.

When police move into an area, it doesn't necessarily mean that crime is eliminated. It just moves to another neighborhood, right? Or it gets driven underground.

Sometimes, yes. But when all areas of a city are tracked and when police action in hot spots is relentless, the tactics of criminals change. In New York, when police went after illegal gun possessions, drug dealers and others stopped carrying guns on the street. In August 1995, the proportion of people arrested carrying guns was 39 percent lower than it was two years before. Overall crime in New York dropped by 12 percent, compared with a 1.1 percent drop nationally, and homicides fell by 19.8 percent, compared with a 5 percent drop nationally.[97] If criminals are forced to reduce their firepower, it is likely that they will commit fewer crimes.

Give an example of how CompStat works on specific crime problems.

The most noteworthy example is the turnaround of the New York subway system. In many ways, New York's subway system is a city within a city.

On an average workday, 3.5 million people ride the system's 230 miles of lines to go to work, meet friends, or otherwise get around the city.

In the 1970s, the subways were dangerous and intimidating places. Ridership fell and crime skyrocketed. Graffiti marred the appearance of trains. Many trains were badly vandalized. Subway riders were regularly accosted for money and subject to verbal and physical abuse. Surveys reflected the dangers and fears. Some 97 percent of riders reported that they took some form of defensive action before entering the subways, 75 percent avoided wearing expensive clothing or jewelry, 69 percent avoided "certain people," and 68 percent avoided certain positions on the platforms.[98]

Graffiti seemed an intractable problem that undermined people's sense of comfort when they used the system. Under David Gunn's direction, the Metropolitan Transit Authority (MTA) devised a strategy to make sure that new trains never rode the rails with graffiti: he simply took any train with graffiti out of circulation. Since graffiti artists desire above all else to "mark" the trains, removal of marked trains from circulation deprived them of their pride of authorship. Within five years, all of the system's trains were cleaned up. Around the same time, the MTA bought newer trains with a special property: because of a special chemical makeup of the metal, paint does not stick to the train.

The MTA also confronted an epidemic of panhandling and other forms of disorder. Despite a series of legal challenges, the MTA established clear standards of conduct for the subways and instructed transit cops to enforce them. William Bratton, who became head of the MTA's police department in 1990, ordered cops to arrest subway users who committed petty crimes such as aggressive panhandling, urinating in public, and jumping turnstiles. Ejections from the subways tripled in Bratton's first few months on the job and continued to rise afterward. Bratton set up special "booking buses" outside subway stations to arrest, process, and release suspects.

Arresting fare-beaters proved an especially useful strategy for restoring order. Police found that some of the same people who jumped turnstiles also committed other crimes. At their bookings, many were found to be possessing illegal weapons and many more had outstanding warrants for arrest on other charges. Arrest them for jumping a turnstile and keep them for more serious offenses. Arrests for beating fares had the effect of removing the perpetrators of serious crimes from society.

One problem with this deployment strategy in the eyes of many critics is that cops might become too aggressive where they expect to find crime. If it's true, community policing doesn't have a chance.

Today, most police seem to be big believers in a balanced community-based approach to crime prevention. A survey of police chiefs by the National League of Cities found the following priorities for anticrime strategies: 1) strengthening family stability, 63.6 percent; 2) jobs and economic development, 48.4 percent; 3) more police officers, 39.8 percent; 4) after-school programs, 33 percent; 5) neighborhood watch programs, 33 percent; 6) more foot patrols, 32.2 percent; 7) school-to-work programs, 31.2 percent; 8) more recreational programs, 30.4 percent; 9) early childhood education, 29.8 percent; and 10) reintroducing punishment in schools, 18.1 percent.[99] This list hardly supports the stereotype of a baton-wielding, rights-violating cop.

Of course, the old values of cops—force and aggression—still exist in all major departments. A report of Human Rights Watch found pockets of police brutality to be "persistent" in cities that it studied, including Atlanta, Boston, Chicago, Detroit, Indianapolis, Los Angeles, Minneapolis, New Orleans, New York, Philadelphia, Portland, Providence, San Francisco, and Washington. The report stated that "problem officers"—police with significant records of abuse or citizen complaints—result from inadequate recruitment, background checks, training, and monitoring. A "code of silence" among cops makes it hard to root out brutality and corruption, even when honest cops are the rule. [100]

Removal from the System

Some people say that you cannot eliminate the aggressive or antisocial tendencies of some people, so the best you can do is send then a strong signal that crime does not pay—and remove antisocial forces from the street.

The logic of deterrence is simple: if the punishment for a crime carries high costs, any rational person will choose not to commit the crime. If the costs are low, however, many people will be tempted to commit the crime. The challenge for the criminal justice system is to create a system of punishments that convinces the potential criminal not to take the risk.

The problem with this logic is that criminals do not always act rationally; many crimes are committed impulsively, without any consideration of all but the immediate consequences. Even assuming that would-be criminals behave rationally, however, we must also understand that people calculate the costs and benefits of actions in different ways.

Here is where the idea of proportionality comes in. How long a person is sentenced for a crime ought to depend on the severity of the crime. Violent criminals ought to do more time than nonviolent criminals. People who cause greater damage to people and property should sit behind bars longer than people who commit lesser offenses. This is what has troubled observers about the crackdown on drug users in recent years. Onetime marijuana users sometimes serve more time than drug lords and even murderers; the combination of mandatory sentences for drug offenses and plea bargaining for people with broad knowledge of the criminal world is responsible for that absurd state of affairs.

Would tougher sentencing affect a person's decision about whether to commit a crime?

Tough sentencing amounts to a wager by judges and juries. The bet is that would-be criminals will calculate the costs and benefits of offenses before committing them. A lack of consequences produce a willingness to violate the law; steep consequences give the criminal pause. James Q. Wilson states the logic elegantly:

> [C]rimes will be committed more frequently if, other things being equal, crime becomes more profitable than other ways of spending one's time. Accordingly, ... one major reason why crime has increased is that people have discovered they can get away with it. By the same token, a good way to reduce crime is to make its consequences to the would-be offender more costly (by making penalties swifter, more certain, or more severe), or to make alternatives to crime more attractive (by increasing the availability and pay of legitimate jobs), or both."[101]

The problem is that many crimes are committed in the heat of the moment, without careful deliberation. Domestic disputes, fights with drug suppliers, and escalation of street confrontations are not always rational. Logic alone is not a deterrent.

The most popular sentencing reform of recent years is the "three strikes and you're out" law passed by Congress and many state legislatures. The laws give mandatory life sentences to criminals convicted of felonies or violent crimes for the third time. Critics say the law is arbitrary and hence works against rationality. Someone convicted of two vicious crimes could have a better chance of release than someone who committed three less dangerous crimes, such as petty dealing in marijuana. The three-strikes law also places too much discretion—and pressure—in the hands of the prosecutor. When a criminal suspect faces his third strike, it is up to the prosecutor to decide whether to try to lock him up for good. That creates a difficult climate in which even the most hard-nosed prosecutors might have an incentive to reduce or even drop charges.

In addition, critics such as the American Civil Liberities Union and Human Rights Watch argue that it does not make sense to lock up criminals for life. First, maintaining order in jails requires at least the hope of release. Prisoners have no incentive to be on good behavior if they have no chance of release. Second, most criminal careers fizzle as the person ages. Keeping three-strikes cons in jail into old age turns prisons into expensive retirement homes.

Below is a summary of the average time that convicts spend in federal and state prisons according to offense. The figures were calculated by multiplying the length of sentence imposed by the courts by the percentage of time expected to be served.

But what happens to convicts when they leave prison, as almost all do within a few years?

That is the most difficult predicament for the lock-'em-up approach. If they are simply allowed to rot in prison, convicts enter the "real world" with little money or know-how to live a better life on the outside. In recent years, as educational and drug rehabilitation programs have been cut from prison budgets, ex-cons are ill equipped to live productive lives in their old neighborhoods. Even when the old gangs have broken up, there are still barriers to getting jobs, housing, health care, and treatment for chemical dependencies.

Is it possible to shut down criminal enterprises by going after the leaders of the major criminal syndicates?

Going after large-scale criminal entrepreneurs—the mob, banks, drug producers, black-market mercantilists—can change the dynamic of the crime economy. But in many cases the "big busts" cause criminal activity to shift to a new market or system rather than shutting down the operation.

The federal Racketeer-Influenced Corrupt Organizations (RICO) law—was designed to give federal law-enforcement agencies the authority to gather evidence from banks, telephone logs, and other private files. The federal authorities have used the law systematically to go after crime families all over the United States. One FBI official summed up the effect of

Table 6.4 Doing Time

Offense	Time Served in State and Federal Prisons
Murder/manslaughter	10 years and 6 months
Aggravated assault	3 years and 3 months
Rape	7 years and 3 months
Drugs, all offenses	2 years and 4 months
Drug trafficking	2 years and 9 months
Burglary	2 years and 3 months
Larceny	1 year and 7 months
Auto theft	2 years and 1 month

Source: Bureau of Justice Statistics, *Sourcebook of Criminal Justice Statistics 1996,* Washington, D.C.: U.S. Government Printing Office (1997), p. 476, Table 5.58.

RICO on the mob in major American cities. Philadelphia: "Almost everyone is in jail." Cleveland: "Technically, there is no real [crime] family." Detroit: "The family's still there, but I think good things may occur in the future." Kansas City and St. Louis: crime families "have almost ceased to exist."[102]

But at the same time as the traditional Mafia of the Cosa Nostra families has declined, new families have formed. Russian and Chinese mobsters have established beachheads in Brooklyn and San Francisco, where their organizational structures and operating techniques still confound federal agents. Their crimes—drug dealing, auto theft rings, tax and health care fraud, and money laundering—have dramatically changed the way of doing business on their turf. Local businesses must buy protection for as much as $100,000.

The international scale of organized crime can be overwhelming to city police departments. Clearly, city officials need the assistance of state and federal authorities, who in turn need help from foreign governments to confront the problems of drugs and other organized crime. Drug dealers operate out of Asia, South America, and the Middle East. Colombian drug traffickers dominate the global market for cocaine, while Asian countries and Colombia dominate the heroin market and Latin American countries dominate marijuana trade. The cocaine business is vertically integrated, with drug lords controlling every aspect of the industry from cultivation to processing to exports to military production. Other drug industries are more dispersed, with different drug lords dominating different parts of the world market. Efforts to interdict drugs have been successful, but that success has been at best irrelevant and at worst a major spur for traffickers to increase their production. Andean nations produced some 820 to 855 metric tons of cocaine in 1994, of which 303 metric tons were seized by authorities worldwide. Those 303 metric tons were just considered a cost of doing business—like the costs of bribes, assassinations, and shipping and handling.[103]

Reconstituting the Social Order

Virtually all anyone talks about in discussions of crime policy is achieving peace and order in the community. But is all conflict bad? Somehow people have to learn how to live with one another. Can't conflict help people to learn how to live together?

When conflict forces people to deal with each other, to learn how to settle disputes without recourse to police or other authorities, the overall result could be a decline in violence and crime.

The sociologist Richard Sennett argues that for a community to maintain order, it needs a healthy degree of conflict. Only when people engage each other—arguing over a wide range of important and petty matters—can they learn how to deal with each other and rely on each other. Sennett complains that the prosperity of modern America has enabled people to separate themselves from people and things that they dislike. By living in gated and other "purified" communities, people lose contact with the everyday diversity and discord that teach them how to solve problems at the street level. Sennett proposes increasing the density of urban communities, fostering the ethnic and social complexity of specific neighborhoods, and removing centralized bureaucracies from the management of everyday street life. "For example, police control of much civil disorder ought to be sharply curbed; the responsibility for making peace in neighborhood affairs ought to fall to the people involved."[104]

Sennett's thesis has found support in the research of Matthew A. Crenson. In his study of neighborhood politics in Baltimore, Crenson found that the neighborhoods where people experienced a great amount of day-to-day tensions were best able to maintain basic levels of public order. Hostility toward neighbors, Crenson found, was a critical factor behind the kinds of political activity that are essential for a well-ordered democracy. Tension is a critical ingredient in informal political discussions, from gossip about neighborhood characters to debate about the mayor's latest headlines. Tension is an even more important factor behind the delivery of what Crenson calls "impromptu public services"—shoveling sidewalks, delivering supplies during emergencies, policing the streets, and the like. "Residents who perceive many severe problems in their neighborhoods are more likely than others to take informal direct action to cope with these problems," Crenson says. "Possibly because they have such troubled perceptions of their neighborhoods, they are also more likely than others to believe that they live among fellow residents of inferior quality."[105]

Crenson's findings go against the grain of some communitarian approaches to politics, which suggest that people ought to come together to develop common visions in friendly and respectful settings. But it could be that the tension that drives urban politics in Crenson's reckoning might also lead to a community of mutual respect. Richard Sennett notes: "[T]he scene of conflict becomes a community in the sense that people learn how to listen and respond to one other even as they more keenly feel their differences."[106] When people are challenged to pick up the garbage, discipline youngsters, tend to parks, and look after someone in need, they are challenged to become part of something greater than themselves.

7
Re-Placing the City

The challenges facing American cities are overwhelming. Practically every do-mestic problem that we face as a nation is located—often more intensely—in cities. Is a new urban agenda possible?

We have reason to be guardedly optimistic. After several decades of steady decline, many cities stabilized during the 1990s, and some even ex-perienced resurgence. In many urban areas, poverty, unemployment, wel-fare dependency, and crime rates dropped—in some cases dramatically. Low vacancy rates and high rents in the office buildings of many down-town districts indicate that central cities continue to be desirable places to do business. Many urban neighborhoods, especially those near to the downtown core, are enjoying a revival brought about by an influx of young adults, empty nesters, and immigrants.

And yet, if some American cities have shown signs of recovery, that re-covery remains precarious. Shifts in the national economy or in other soci-etal trends could just as easily spark another downturn in the fortunes of cities. Moreover, in those cities that seem to be enjoying a renaissance, the prosperity tends to be confined to particular populations and neighbor-hoods. Entire groups of citizens and broad stretches of the urban land-scape have had little to cheer about. So the need for reform remains compelling, but the constraints on urban policy-makers also continue to be formidable.

The precariousness of urban vitality is no clearer than in the current age. The terrorist attacks on New York and Washington on September 11, 2001, serve as a chilling reminder of the fragility of complex societies. Cities lesser than New York could have been ruined by such an attack. In an increasingly global economy, communities become more and more dependent on outside forces. A company that provides jobs for people can shut down or move its operations overseas, leaving the locals vulnerable. Or low wages elsewhere could pressure the firm to depress wages. Strikes and protests could cripple ports and downtown business districts and school districts. Natural disasters, from hurricanes to floods, could overwhelm communities. Or the banking system could crash, as it did totally in 1929 and has done less completely several times since then. Or—we could continue this litany endlessly—world energy prices could explode, as they did in 1973 and 1979, creating a massive ripple effect on the global economy.

A political system's ability to solve its problems depends on the scope of the community and the scope of the problems. No small town can solve the problems posed by a catastrophic increase in oil prices or jarring "corrections" in the stock market. It is appropriate that a higher form of government, with more tools in its toolbox, should confront some of those issues.

What is the biggest job facing the people who want to save American cities?

Cities need to generate enough economic, political, and social dynamism so that enough people will live and work there to support the basic requirements of such a large and complex organism. When the people and economic activity flow out of the city, the city is in trouble. The visionary urbanist Jane Jacobs has called upon urban specialists to pay attention to the balance of trade for cities just as economists track the balance of trade for nations.[1] When we understand the economic flows in and out of an area—products, labor, capital—we develop an appreciation for creating the conditions that generate life in cities.

What does a healthy city look like? It is a place where people on all rungs of the economic ladder can afford a home. It is a place with a diverse economy, where import-replacing industries set up shop, where businesses gather together so that producers and sellers benefit not only from economies of scale but also from the specialized knowledge of the cluster. It is a place where students learn, where principals lead communities of learning and teachers teach without the distractions of petty pedagogical and community battles. It is a place with areas that people occupy in common—whether it is an old railroad station, a park or a waterfront, a school or post office, a museum or theater, a university or medical campus, a bike trail or nature preserve, and even (or especially) a government building. It is a place where police operate aggressively but within the bounds of respect for individual liberties and in cooperation with people in the neighborhoods. It is a place where people are motivated to take part in politics, where elections are fought hard, and where the winners have the opportunity to implement their programs. It is a place where data about all aspects of policy—from emergency medical response times to public works contracts to school performance—are gathered thoroughly and made "transparent" to policy-makers and citizens alike.

Notice that with all of these elements of a good city, the people within that city have the capacity to make it happen. In fact, all of the above elements are achieved in cities across the country. The challenge for urban America is to make sure that all of the elements are in place together. As programs like the Institute for Government Innovation have found, there is no shortage of "best practices" in communities of all sizes in the United States. The trick is to apply the best practices in all areas of urban life in ways that are appropriate for different city contexts.

Constraints on Urban Revitalization

How optimistic! But don't cities in fact face severe constraints?

Yes, the constraints begin with the city's own political authority. If a city wants to revise welfare rules, it needs to cooperate with the federal and state governments. If a city wants to develop a new park, it often needs to work out rights of way with state agencies. If a city wants to cluster housing around transit stations—build old-fashioned "urban villages" that house lots of people and relieve road congestion and air pollution—it needs to collaborate with the independent transit authority and often neighboring towns. If a city wants to modernize its ports or airports, design schools that fit into the urban neighborhood context, track down drug dealers in troubled sections of town, or create affordable housing, that city needs to develop strong working relationships with dozens of federal and state entities.

Even if cities possess the legal authority to pursue their agendas, the money problem remains. Cities often lack the resources they need to deliver basic services and address the extraordinary problems in their midst. Ideally, cities would be able to raise all of their funds locally to pay for police and fire protection, schools, housing, and job training. But this requires a healthy tax base with a large middle class and a vibrant local economy. City officials are always cognizant, therefore, of the need to attract and retain business investment. This is not as simple as it once was, when businesses were more dependent on the strategic location of cities—near ports, railroad crossroads, and vital resources. In the modern economy, most revenue-generating businesses are footloose. Even when they do not move across the nation or to the developing world for low wages, they do have the capacity to move to another part of the metropolitan region.

In a global economy, urban policy-makers feel constrained in terms of their policy options. Many would like to adopt aggressive policies to revitalize poor neighborhoods, but they worry that such policies would require tax hikes that would deter new investment while prompting existing businesses and middle-class residents to leave.[2]

So how can cities attract the resources they need to address the concerns that local tax revenues do not cover?

Because of their precariousness in the larger economy, some scholars have argued that cities need a steady infusion of money from the federal and state governments just to maintain basic services. In fact, cities depend on higher levels of government for resources to provide affordable housing, family assistance, homeless shelters, park acquisition, and a host of other core needs and amenities.

Paul E. Peterson, a leading scholar of urban affairs, has argued that Washington, D.C., should assume full responsibility for social welfare policies, including policies that seek to rebuild distressed urban neighborhoods, largely as a matter of default. Local governments are simply too vulnerable to the problem of capital mobility. It is much easier for a business that is disgruntled with city government to move to an adjacent community than it would be for the same business to relocate overseas because of unhappiness with the federal government's welfare policies. Peterson asserts that the problem of poverty and want is national in scope and requires a national response.[3]

Is a national urban policy the answer?

Many scholars and urban officials would say yes.[4] The obvious problem, however, is a lack of political support throughout the country for such an ambitious undertaking. At a time when the suburbs now hold a majority of the American population, winning support for federal and state funding can be a challenge.

The ultimate challenge for urban policy lies in the suburbs. Developing a national urban agenda requires convincing at least some suburbanites that their interests are connected with the fortunes of cities. Making that case is difficult. After all, many suburbanites live where they do specifically to get away from the ills of urban life, real or perceived. Suburbanites look aghast at the poor quality of schools, the inflated cost of building new housing, the crime in inner-city neighborhoods, and the degradation of brownfields sites.

In recent years, many suburbanites have come to appreciate how their fortunes are connected to the life of the cities. A nascent national movement to confront sprawl—the uncontrolled development of tract housing and office parks, connected by highways—has brought together urbanites and suburbanites. Al Gore's 2000 presidential campaign raised the sprawl issue as a concern for basic quality of life for all Americans. But developing an urban-suburban coalition needs to go beyond sprawl. Economic development, housing, the environment, and taxes are just a few issues that might serve as the basis of a new "grand coalition" of people throughout the metropolis.

Does the government's financial commitment have to be at the national level? What about state and regional government?

The states have played an increasing role in city finance and development in recent years. Prompted by state court battles over inequities in school funding, many states across the United States have significantly increased their funding for urban schools. Many states have also created major programs for job training, affordable housing, and environmental remediation. The states have also taken the lead on crime by increasing mandatory sentences for major crimes and doubling prison capacity.

But much of the financial power available for cities resides in their own regions. It is a truism that well-off suburbs live side by side with struggling cities and working-class communities. Former Albuquerque Mayor David Rusk argues forcefully that when the cities and towns in a region pool their resources, everyone is better off. Rusk begins with the finding that development will not occur in a city that has less than 70 percent of the average income of the suburbs. For some reason, that 70 percent mark is the "tipping point." To bridge that gap, cities need to become part of the larger metropolis. Regional governments such as Metro in Nashville and Unigov in Indianapolis have the capacity to gather the resources necessary to provide coherent local governmental programs for economic development, education, health care, housing, and environmental issues. As recently as 2002, voters in Louisville, Kentucky, acknowledged that the fortunes of all of the metropolitan area were tied together—approving a referendum to create a regional government that shares revenues and streamlines public agencies.

When cities can take in the robust tax revenues of the whole metropolitan area, they have the resources to assure that police get deployed, kids get educated, parks and infrastructure get maintained, and communities get developed.[5]

But wouldn't any campaign for regional government encounter political resistance too?

No doubt, and not just from suburbanites worried about rising taxes. Some urban politicians and interest groups tend to oppose regionalism for fear they might lose some of their political clout. Nevertheless, there is a compelling rationale for people from diverse jurisdictions to come together and pool their resources. Myron Orfield, who represents Minneapolis in the Minnesota state legislator, has worked to cobble together political coalitions of have-nots and have-littles in metropolitan areas across the United States. Orfield's reasoning is that many urban and suburban communities suffer from the same problems of economic disinvestment, fiscal stress, unequal school funding, environmental degradation, and underinvestment in public infrastructure. Once these communities realize their common plight, they might come together to create a metro-politan-wide coalition. Orfield argues that this coalition can produce a powerful movement for regional government.[6]

This sounds reasonable. Is regionalism the answer?

Maybe, but we have to make sure that regional government does not create as many burdens as it addresses. To be sure, communities would benefit from a fair share of funding for infrastructure and public services. But that does not mean that a centralized regional body should determine how communities develop or deliver services. Sometimes it is possible to respond to regional problems—from economic development to housing to education—without necessarily adopting regional government. By pro-viding adequate resources and policy standards—and then allowing locali-ties to make their own decisions about how to pursue those standards—metropolitan areas can pursue their larger social values while allowing the diversity and creativity of the larger community to flower. In his provoca-tive book *Emergence*, Steven Johnson explores how simple rules without command-and-control planning foster both order and creativity in sys-tems ranging from ant colonies to cities.[7] Urban policy-makers can follow this wisdom by understanding what basic tools and standards all commu-nities need and then allowing those communities to develop their own ap-proaches to development and social services.[8]

We've been focusing on the lack of resources available to cities as a constraint on urban revitalization. But isn't there more to it than this? Many people sim-ply don't have confidence that government at any level is capable of spending its resources efficiently and wisely.

Regardless of what level of government is involved—regional or local—public officials need to think creatively about reforming their government to make it more efficient, effective, and responsive. In the heyday of the spoils system, mayors placed followers in public "hack" jobs as rewards for their political support. Later, bureaucracies became havens for civil-service workers and public-sector unions, who have been loathe to develop man-agement systems that compromise job security or control over the work-place. Many urban bureaucracies are connected closely with interest groups that have a stake in their everyday functioning—from housing (large-scale developers, community development corporations) to educa-tion (parent-teacher associations, unions) to welfare (public-interest lawyers) to public safety (neighborhood watch groups, legal-aid firms).

The bureaucracy poses a major challenge. Think of what a bureaucracy is: a collection of diverse people with different technical and social skills, operating under rules that were written decades before, using information that is fragmented and incomplete, often with outmoded technologies, working at low levels of pay, with little incentive to perform with courage or distinction, for bosses who might be gone in three years, for clients that often resist what the government is trying to achieve, and in communities where complaints seem to overwhelm ideas for constructive engagement. Oh, yes, and with the stigma of a being part of a bureaucracy.

One basic reality is that mayors and managers cannot oversee everyone who is working for the government. The best that mayors can do is to appoint people who are both knowledgeable on the issues and capable of working in a political environment—and give those officials the tools they need to get on top of their departments. That is why Baltimore's experiment with CitiStat is so powerful. The mayor has given all of his department heads state-of-the-art computer databases and demanded that they update everything that happens in the department . . . every day, as a matter of course. The data are analyzed every two weeks, and the mayor and his chief of staff review each department's performance at least twice a month for at least two hours at a time. At the very least, the mayor and his team know what is going on in their city government. That basic knowledge gives them the ability to spot patterns, see who is performing well and who is not, and actually work with the staffs to do what needs to be done.

Another useful model—competition between public and private entities to deliver basic services—was pioneered by Mayor Stephen Goldsmith of Indianapolis. The idea was simple: neither the public nor the private sector has a monopoly on the best ideas for providing services such as public transportation, fleet maintenance, towing, operating jails, garbage pickup, and street repair. Whether a service should be done by public or private operators depends on which mobilizes to provide the best plan and engage its workers more effectively. Indianapolis identified some sixty-eight city services that could be opened to competition among public agencies and private firms. Rather than fighting the bureaucracy over the details of day-to-day management, the competition challenged the bureaucracy to come up with better approaches. Labor unions responded favorably to the opportunity to develop better service-delivery strategies, despite some early grumbling among rank-and-file workers. Over his eight years in office, Goldsmith cut costs, held the line on taxes, and produced better results in a wide range of services. The public-*and*-private approach spurred government managers to specify what kinds of outcomes they were seeking. Street-level workers who had never been asked to identify better ways to deliver services were actively engaged in developing strategies for meeting public needs.[9]

Another useful model comes from Minnesota, where a state board gives local governments temporary waivers from state regulations if they can develop better ways to meet public goals. The Minnesota Board of Government Innovation and Cooperation has granted waivers of regulations and joint-operation authority for health care delivery, social services, school programs, data management, environmental remediation, sewage treatment, and teacher training and evaluation. If the innovation of the locality proves successful, the board petitions the state legislature to make adjustments in state laws.[10]

Whatever level of government dominates an urban scene, it's absolutely vital that the federal government set the tone by vigorously enforcing basic civil rights.

Yes, indeed. The national community has the responsibility to assure that all of its citizens enjoy their basic rights wherever they happen to live. By the 1960s, virtually all Americans agreed with the proposition that people's civil rights—the right to public accommodations, fair housing, equal opportunity in employment—should not vary from region to region. The Supreme Court also established the principle that for any citizen to enjoy individual liberties, there must be consistent rules and procedures for all. The United States has less consensus on giving all citizens the basic means of survival. Social insurance programs such as Social Security and Medicare garner across-the-board support, and programs for poor children such as Head Start and school lunches also enjoy backing among Republicans and Democrats alike. But programs designed to help poor people have always been controversial, largely because of the nation's ideology of "rugged individualism." The Welfare Reform Act of 1996 resulted from decades of complaints about the goals, costs, and results of welfare and other antipoverty programs. Even though most poor people are children, and even though many adults on welfare have little opportunity for work, middle America resents people getting "something for nothing." To be sure, welfare—like all government programs—has produced its share of abuse and warped incentives. And to be sure, many people support the basic principles of assistance for the less fortunate. But the antiwelfare sentiment has played as large a role in American domestic politics as the Cold War played in foreign policy.

Resentment toward the poor remains one of the most stubborn and troubling aspects of the American system. As many metropolitan areas become more segregated, it is hard to imagine how middle-class and working-class Americans might develop a greater sense of empathy and common cause. The answer might lie in the kind of broad eligibility for benefits associated with programs such as Social Security and Medicare. Because so many Americans have benefited or stand to benefit from these programs, they enjoy widespread public support. If the United States—at either the national or the state level—could build a consensus for universal health care, day care, job training, and employment, maybe there would not be so much resentment over the benefits offered the poor.[11]

However you think about the proper arena for urban policy—whether programs should be directed by a strong national government or left to the discretion of states and localities—all public policy requires a vibrant public realm.

The Public Realm

What do you mean by "public realm"?

The public realm is the space and activities that people in a community share. Ideally, the public realm offers people access not only to the necessities of life but also to the resources and people they need to develop and enrich themselves. A healthy public realm aims to give people access to the tools they need to live productive lives. There is no guarantee that people will achieve their ambitions; the public realm assumes only that society should provide a basic equality of opportunity, not equality of result.

There are two ways of looking at the public realm: physical and programmatic. The physical public realm is where you go when you walk out of your front door or leave your workplace. The public realm includes the community's streets and sidewalks, parks, transportation systems, museums, and schools and other public buildings. It includes a wide range of private or quasi-private spaces, such as churches, office building plazas, fronts of buildings, private stores, stadiums, and colleges and universities. It is the place where people come together and affect the lives of each other.

The programmatic public realm is less tangible. It is the collection of systems that structure people's access to the core ingredients of opportunity. A loan program for a college education is a part of the public realm because it helps young people get access to common tools they need to develop themselves. The "safety net"—welfare, food stamps, health care, hot meals programs—is also part of the public realm because it gives people a common, basic level of subsistence. The delivery of vital services such as police and fire protection, child immunization programs, and old-age insurance are also elements of the public realm.

Both senses of the public realm are vital to democracy. They enable people in a community to "add up" to more than a collection of individuals. A good public realm gives people a place to come together to explore common problems, debate different points of view, and develop common visions while at the same time acknowledging the importance of their different qualities. Ultimately, the public realm empowers people to play a meaningful role in governing themselves.

So the public realm offers people a certain foundation on which they can build better lives for themselves.

Yes, the idea is that all citizens should enjoy a rich store of social and economic opportunities regardless of their race, class, or background. In a provocative study of liberal social policy, Mickey Kaus argues that the United States will never significantly redistribute wealth through taxes or social programs. The biased system of interest-group politics is enough to prevent in the United States anything approaching socialism similar to the welfare states of Sweden, Great Britain, France, Italy, and Germany. If anything, the American social system is becoming more unequal. Looking at the growing rates of inequality in the United States, Kaus concludes that a strategy of "social equality" is not a realistic goal. The imperatives of both politics and economics at the turn of the century foreclose the possibility of major efforts to redistribute wealth in the United States. If anything, the trend is toward greater inequality of income and wealth.

But that does not mean that a community cannot provide a meaningful equality of opportunity to all its citizens. If we offered all our citizens good schools, health care, public transportation, decent housing, access to parks and civic spaces, job opportunities, and vital communal experiences, we would be offering a basic equality of opportunity. At the same time, we need to demand some basic sacrifices of all citizens—starting with a requirement of national service with no exceptions. The particulars of Kaus's agenda are debatable, but there is no arguing that it could foster a real sense of membership in our common enterprise. Kaus quotes the British reformer R. H. Tawney: "If men are to respect each other for what they are, they must cease to respect each other for what they own."[12] When they share more basic things in common, what they own individually matters less.

So the public realm needs to teach people about a greater commitment to community?

If it is properly constituted, the public realm absolutely demands commitment and sacrifice from its people. The public realm *teaches* people about the need to contribute to the well-being of the larger community. The public realm goes far beyond a materialistic sense of entitlement toward an expectation that people must contribute to others even under the most difficult circumstances. They must do the right thing, even when the circumstances seem unfair.

A strong public realm teaches people to be part of a community in countless ways. It teaches in schools. It teaches in playgrounds, libraries, volunteer activities, churches and temples, museums, adult-education classes, choirs, election campaigns . . . the list goes on. If a community can build public spaces and foster meaningful interaction with other people, then its members will have the capacity to ask what life expects of them rather than what they expect from life.

This public education requires a strong interaction between the leaders and the led. In the past generation or so, however, this relationship has been attenuated. The rise of the modern bureaucratic state—with its attendant entitlements, legalistic rules and regulations, and interest groups—has pushed most policy issues out of the public arena and into the behind-the-scenes maneuvering of policy elites. In an insightful analysis of the "downsizing" of democracy in the United States, Matthew A. Crenson and Benjamin Ginsberg argue that political candidates no longer seek to mobilize as much of the public as they can, because most political issues get settled outside the electoral process. "Today's parties . . . occupy generally consistent and distinguishable positions on issues like abortion, social welfare, gay rights, taxation, the environment, and economic regulation," Crenson and Ginsberg write. "But as their positions have come into focus, they have pared down their popular followings to the reliable, mailing-list voters who have helped make American elections invitation-only affairs for an electoral elect."[13] Politicians do not issue "calls to arms" as they once did in America. As a result, much of the public watches passively as armies of interested advocates contest the issues of the day.

How can local government address some of these problems?

Local government provides the contact point between ordinary citizens and the larger political regime. The city is the place where people come face to face. If properly constituted, local politics forces people to justify what they are doing at all times. The simple fact of being seen and known by others can play a powerful part in shaping people's attitudes toward others. When I know that the people I deal with are going to see me again, I am likely to consider the long-term consequences of my actions.

The directness of local politics gives rise to what social scientists call "intermediary institutions." Intermediary institutions or associations connect individuals and the larger political regime. As Alexis de Tocqueville observed in *Democracy in America*, when they are isolated, individuals are powerless, but when they form an association, they become a force to be reckoned with. Tocqueville writes:

> Feelings and opinions are recruited, the heart is enlarged, and the human mind is developed, only by the reciprocal influences of men upon each other. . . . As soon as several of the inhabitants of the United States have taken up an opinion or a feeling which they wish to promote in the world, they look out for mutual assistance; and as soon as they have found each other out, they combine. From that

moment on they are no longer isolated men, but a power seen from afar.[14]

When people come into regular contact with each other and form associations, they develop a capacity to act and to engage the whole community on the great political questions of the day.

A review of the evolution of democracy in America shows that the greatest advances occurred when ordinary people with common causes *found each other* and made common cause in opposition to government, corporations, and other monolithic forms of power. It started slowly—a couple of people, face-to-face—but expanded to involve a widening circle of people. Abolitionism, suffragism, populism, progressivism, tenants, labor, civil rights, farm workers, feminism, gay rights, the environmental movement, antiwar demonstrations, the crusade against land mines— these great movements all started with face-to-face encounters of ordinary people. It is inconceivable to imagine American history without understanding the political and social movements of ordinary people.[15]

New York City suggests the power of urban community to confront a crisis. Many of the early commentaries on the city's remarkable response to the terrorist attacks of September 11, 2001, focus on the leadership of Mayor Rudolph Giuliani or the heroism of the firefighers and police. It is certainly appropriate to laud the responses of these visible people. But we should also remember the countless acts of cooperation, assistance, and sacrifice of ordinary people during the awful aftermath of the attacks. No one will mistake New Yorkers for the white-picket-fence communities celebrated on television. New Yorkers definitely have an edge, an impatience, a willingness to confront others. It was just that level of hardness, combined with a healthy ability to just get along with complete strangers on a daily basis, which gave the city the fortitude it needed most during the crisis.

Local government can act as the great connector. People can make a direct connection with local government almost everywhere. In most cities, an ordinary citizen can make contact with the mayor and council members. Most of local government interacts on a daily basis with people in the neighborhoods.

Political Change

All of this talk about a vibrant public realm as the key to urban revitalization sounds very appealing, but it also seems far removed from the political realities of twenty-first-century America.

It is true that we live in an era in which public spaces are often neglected and even abused, in which government is widely disparaged as inefficient, ineffective, and unresponsive, and where political participation is limited to casting a vote for president every four years—and half of the electorate does not even bother to do that. Apathy and alienation pervade our political culture. In the eyes of many citizens, the political system is broken. Government seems distant and out of touch. Politicians seem to be consumed by partisan bickering instead of tackling and resolving the problems that matter most to people. When government does address important issues, the process seems painfully slow and unsatisfying.

In a democracy, if the citizens are disgruntled with their government, they have the power to voice their displeasure by voting their elected representatives out of office. But the electoral system is fraught with problems. Almost regardless of the level of popular discontent, incumbents enjoy huge advantages over any challengers and are usually elected by overwhelming margins. Money seems to dictate who wins and loses. Gerrymandered districts suggest that many electoral outcomes are rigged in advance. Even the actual process of voting can turn into an exasperating ordeal thanks to faulty voting machines and confusing ballots. It is little wonder that so many citizens, feeling isolated and powerless, simply give up. Dropping out of politics becomes a rational, if not a wise, course of action.

Given this political climate, how is it possible to create the kind of public realm conducive to rebuilding the nation's cities?

While the political system is marred by a multitude of defects, it still offers opportunities to effect meaningful change if people from diverse communities come together, discover common ground, and fight together for real solutions to their problems. The obstacles are immense, but they can be overcome, and have been at times in the past. In thinking about how that might happen, it is logical to contemplate various strategies of political mobilization and how citizens might use both conventional and unconventional mechanisms to advance their common interests.

Can you give some examples of public policy strengthening the public realm?

Start with something as basic as community policing. After years of increasing crime—historic levels of murder, rape, assault, auto theft, burglary, and a variety of more petty degradations of public space—police departments around the United States changed their policing strategies. Boston, San Diego, and Seattle pioneered a strategy of community policing. Cops got out of their squad cars and worked with community groups to identify problems before they happened. From after-school programs to better coordination of parole programs, community policing put the emphasis on maintaining order rather than just responding to 911 calls. Meanwhile, New York used technology to track patterns of criminal activity and deploy officers to the city's "hot spots." New York cops also targeted petty crimes such as turnstile-hopping and pot selling, both to foster a sense of public order and to nab perpetrators who more often than not were involved in other crimes as well.

Once a community feels safe, people feel free to come outside again. Once you get people out of their homes, you can work on rebuilding the public realm even more. In Boston, Mayor Thomas M. Menino created twenty "Main Streets" districts to bring local shop owners, residents, and activists together to improve neighborhood business districts. The program represented a major expansion of a program designed by the National Trust for Historic Preservation to spruce up small towns. In New York, a program called Partnership for Parks has worked wonders in engaging ordinary residents in rehabilitating long-neglected neighborhood parks and waterfronts all over the city. In Chicago, mayor Richard Daley has used streetscape amenities—neighborhood and downtown parks, public festivals, and a lakefront museum complex—to bring people together. Across the United States, charter schools have offered new opportunities for civic-minded people to create new communities of learning, with a special focus on minority communities.

Are the institutions of city politics and government capable of bringing about genuine equality of opportunity?

Sure, but efforts to improve opportunity depend on the structure of local government. It matters whether or not the city council can assert reasonable power against the mayor. It matters whether the bureaucracy is structured and given incentives to carry out policy. It matters whether policy-makers have access to timely information and can coordinate what the different parts of the system are doing. It matters whether local government can attract the "best and brightest" to make and implement policy. It matters whether the government reflects the city's diversity. It matters whether city officials learn from the failures and successes of other cities. It matters whether city governments strike reasonable deals with public employee unions, and whether reasonable new work methods are folded into government operations. It matters whether local government takes an entrepreneurial approach to service delivery, seeking out new technologies and systems that can improve efficiency.

Leadership, of course, goes beyond elected officials and government workers. Civic organizations play an essential role in guiding debates and consolidating interests. Organizations such as the Municipal Art Society in New York and the Citizens League of Greater Cleveland created a citywide conversation on matters of concern to everyone in the city: education, factory conditions, housing, transit, sewers and other infrastructure, annexation, parks, and art and other enhancements of the public realm. Look at the early platforms of the Progressive Era's "goo-goo" (good government) organizations, and you look at a list of some of the greatest achievements of cities in America, such as safe and sanitary housing, public aid for the unemployed and destitute, care of orphans, and great public amenities like parks, libraries, and public art.[16]

For more than a century, public referenda have focused the public mind on issues that interest groups and politicians have been unwilling to confront. A public referendum can produce an open and vigorous public dialogue. Almost every state in the United States has some kind of referendum mechanism. The ballots can produce binding policy or express sentiment to lawmakers. On matters ranging from affordable housing to open-space acquisition, from civil rights to education reform, from public works to taxes, referenda provide a vehicle for ordinary people to tell their governments about their policy priorities.[17]

In sum, using political institutions and organizations to revitalize cities consistent with a communitarian vision of politics is complicated and difficult, but not impossible.

OK, but what are the prospects for fundamental political change in cities without visionary leaders and resourceful grassroots activists?

The political scientist Theodore Lowi contends that the causal arrows may point in the opposite direction too. He notes that public policy might also stimulate a new kind of political engagement.[18] Even in cities lacking a communitarian political ethos, political leaders may enact and implement policies that have the effect of promoting civic engagement and encouraging individuals to see beyond their own immediate self-interests to the well-being of the city as a whole. Even modest policy reforms guided by a communitarian ethos will gradually nurture political activity throughout the city that will lay the cultural and political foundation for more ambitious urban revitalization policies. Over time, changes in policy could yield a transformation in local culture, which could in turn produce better policies.

Responsibility and Commitment

Isn't it expecting too much to assume that individuals will set aside their personal interests for a broader conception of the common good?

People will always take care that their individual needs and interests are pursued, whether they are concerned about jobs or taxes or property values. That is fine. The trick is to create common life that is robust enough that people see their individual needs as inseparable from their common needs. Once that broader communitarian vision emerges, many of the divisive squabbles of city politics can recede, and we can engage in debate and compromise about how to order our lives together.

So where does that leave local policy-making in the United States?
Ultimately, any political system is only as good as the political culture.

Robert Putnam's study of local politics in Italy found that the regions that prosper under decentralization are those with a strong civic culture, regardless of the natural and other resources at their disposal. Civic-minded people mobilize and organize themselves well when confronted with common problems. They put the community before their separate, selfish interests. In his more recent work, focused on America, Putnam has established a direct connection between civic participation and income, public safety, health, and education. The stronger our "civic capital," Putnam shows, the better off we are in all realms of life in our cities and towns.[19]

Constructing the civic culture requires action on many fronts. It requires challenging people to improve their part of the world and then letting them carry out their own strategies. Neighborhoods need the tools for reviving their commercial districts and housing stock—including eminent-domain powers and powers to police violations of lots and buildings. Business districts need to be able to raise revenues to enhance streetscapes and security. Entrepreneurs need the right to provide public services now monopolized by unresponsive agencies such as transit authorities and taxi commissions. Housing projects need to be able to kick out drug dealers and reshape their buildings and grounds into mixed-use communities. School principals and teachers need to be allowed to work with parents to take charge of schools. Workers have to be allowed to organize to improve working conditions.

Democracy requires that people exercise choice and responsibility. Letting bureaucracies and politicians run the show is a form of surrender, especially when systems of accountability are allowed to atrophy. Having democracy requires *doing* democracy.

When will people rise to the challenge?
When people feel a direct stake in their community, when they feel a connection to the community's past and future, they will take action. The biggest problem facing our cities is a pervasive sense of alienation, the feeling of estrangement from government and economic forces that shape our everyday lives and choices. Mass media, urban renewal, and the automobile—to mention just three pervasive forces of our time—have also separated us from our neighbors and from our own past. We have lost our

sense of attachment to place that gives us the burning commitment to build community and better our lives.

Consider the case of Stanley Lowe, who began his career as an advocate of urban renewal and later became one of the nation's leading neighborhood preservationists. Lowe was in the midst of working on an urban renewal plan for his Pittsburgh neighborhood of Manchester when a friend showed him the Georgetown section of Washington, D.C., for the first time. Learning that Georgetown was once targeted for urban renewal but was saved by preservationists and neighbors, Lowe had his epiphany. He realized that tearing down old buildings robbed us of not only material resources but spiritual resources as well. Lowe now speaks eloquently about the need for people to be connected with their communities, their governments, and their formal and informal social institutions:

> We made some horrible mistakes. The tragedy about it is that we made so many monumental mistakes [that] people don't even know we made them, because they don't have any memories of what was here. . . . We have so little to protect. . . . What we have is irreplaceable. When you tear a building down, you must be absolutely sure. There must be no doubt. You must be unequivocal that you are doing the correct thing. Because when you tear down the building, you're tearing down the neighborhood, and they don't come back as fast as they disappear."[20]

The same can be said of every resource in the city—physical and human. We could be talking about a beautiful block of row houses, a great old park, access to the waterfront, or a well-maintained transit system. We could be talking about a generation of schoolchildren, disenfranchised factory workers, or victims of crime. It's all there for the cities to nurture and develop—or to destroy. Once it's destroyed, it's hard to get back.

Notes

Preface

1. Quoted in Stephen Goldsmith, *The Twenty-First Century City: Resurrecting Urban America* (Washington, D.C.: Regnery Publishing, Inc., 1997), p. 6.
2. Buzz Bissinger, *A Prayer for the City* (New York: Random House, 1997).
3. C.f. Paul S. Grogan and Tony Proscio, *Comeback Cities: A Blueprint for Urban Neighborhood Revival* (Boulder, Colo.: Westview Press, 2000); and Roberta Brandes Gratz, *Cities Back from the Edge: New Life for Downtown* (New York: Preservation Press, 1998).

Chapter 1

1. Lewis Mumford, *The Culture of Cities* (New York: Harcourt, Brace and Co., 1938).
2. Jane Jacobs, *The Death and Life of Great American Cities* (New York: Random House, 1961); and Jane Jacobs, *The Economy of Cities* (New York: Random House, 1969).
3. Steven Johnson, *Emergence: The Connected Lives of Ants, Brains, Cities, and Software* (New York: Scribner, 2001), p. 107.
4. Jon C. Teaford, *The Unheralded Triumph: City Government in America, 1870–1900* (Baltimore, Md.: Johns Hopkins University Press, 1984).
5. Kenneth T. Jackson, *Crabgrass Frontier: The Suburbanization of the United States* (New York: Oxford University Press, 1985).
6. *Place Matters: Metropolitics for the Twenty-First Century* (Lawrence, Kans.: University Press of Kansas, 2001), p. 24.
7. C.f. William Julius Wilson, *The Truly Disadvantaged: The Inner City, the Underclass, and Public Policy* (Chicago: University of Chicago Press, 1987).
8. Thomas Sowell, *Ethnic America: A History* (New York: Basic Books, 1981).
9. See Malcolm Gladwell, *The Tipping Point: How Little Things Can Make a Big Difference* (Boston: Little, Brown, 2000). See Gladwell's complete writings at http://www.gladwell.com.
10. Thomas Byrne Edsall and Mary D. Edsall, *Chain Reaction: The Impact of Race, Rights, and Taxes on American Politics* (New York: W.W. Norton, 1991); Demetrios Caraley, "Washington Abandons the Cities," *Political Science Quarterly* 107 (1992).
11. See Elizabeth Arens, "The Democrats' Divide," *Policy Review* 108 (2001), available at http://www.policyreview.org/AUG01/arens.html.
12. Robert Reich, "Secession of the Successful," *New Perspectives Quarterly* 13 (Spring 1996). See also Evan McKenzie, *Privatopia: Homeowner Associations and the Rise of Residential Private Government* (New Haven, Conn.: Yale University Press, 1994).
13. C.f. Paul S. Grogan and Tony Proscio, *Comeback Cities: A Blueprint for Urban Neighborhood Revival* (Boulder, Colo.: Westview Press, 2000) and Roberta Gratz, *Cities Back from the Edge* (New York: Preservation Books, 1998).

14. Stephen J. McGovern, "Mayoral Leadership and Economic Development Policy: The Case of Ed Rendell's Philadelphia," *Policy and Politics* 25 (April 1997): pp. 153–72.

15. For an overview of the issue, see www.smartergrowth.net.

16. Gerald E. Frug, *City Making: Building Communities without Building Walls* (New York: Princeton University Press, 1999).

17. Myron Orfield, *Metropolitics: A Regional Agenda for Community and Stability* (Washington, D.C.: Brookings Institution Press, 1997).

18. The individualist society and culture described here are rooted in classical liberalism, a political philosophy associated with Thomas Hobbes, John Locke, and James Madison. It is important to understand the distinction between classical liberalism, which entails a narrow role for government, and contemporary liberalism, which assumes that government has an important and far-reaching role to play in bringing about a just, orderly, and fair society.

19. President's Commission for a National Agenda for the Eighties, *Urban America in the Eighties* (Washington, D.C.: U.S. Printing Office, 1980).

20. The communitarian vision is grounded in a political philosophy developed by thinkers such as Aristotle, Jean-Jacques Rousseau, and John Dewey.

21. For a fascinating account of how immigrants from the Dominican Republic affect their native country and their new community of Boston, see Peggy Levitt, *The Transnational Villagers* (Berkeley: University of California Press, 2000).

22. Kevin P. Phillips, *The Politics of the Rich and Poor: Wealth and the American Electorate in the Reagan Aftermath* (New York: Random House, 1990); Robert Pear, "Number of People Living in Poverty Increases in U.S.," *New York Times*, September 25, 2002, p. A1.

23. Kevin P. Phillips, *The Politics of Rich and Poor*.

24. Charles Taylor, "Liberal Politics and the Public Sphere," in *The New Communitarian Thinking*, ed. Amitai Etzioni (Charlottesville: University Press of Virginia, 1995).

25. See the discussion of how decentralization in American politics spurs Americans to action without state authority, in Alexis de Tocqueville, *Democracy in America*, Richard Heffner, ed. (New York: Signet, 2001), ch. 5.

26. See Charles C. Euchner, *Extraordinary Politics: How Protest and Dissent Are Changing American Democracy* (Boulder, Colo.: Westview Press, 1996).

27. Lawrence Goodwyn, *The Populist Moment: A Short History of the Agrarian Revolt in America* (New York: Oxford University Press, 1978).

28. For an overview of MacPherson's work, see Joseph H. Carens, ed., *Democracy and Possessive Individualism: The Intellectual Legacy of C. B. MacPherson* (Albany: State University of New York Press, 1993). The seminal study of "narcissism" in American life is Christopher Lasch, *The Culture of Narcissism: American Life in an Age of Declining Expectations* (New York: Norton, 1978).

29. Robert N. Bellah, Richard Madsen, William M. Tipton, *Habits of the Heart: Individualism and Commitment in American Life* (Berkeley: University of California Press, 1985).

30. Robert D. Putnam, *Bowling Alone: The Collapse and Revival of American Community* (New York: Simon and Schuster, 2000).

31. Daniel Bell with Will Kymlicka, *Communitarianism and Its Critics* (New York: Oxford University Press, 1993).

32. Sandra E. Black, "Do Better Schools Matter? Parental Valuation of Elementary Education," *The Quarterly Journal of Economics* (May 1999).

33. C.f. Evans Clinchy, ed., *Creating New Schools: How Small Schools Are Changing American Education* (New York: Teachers College Press, 2000).

34. Ann Whiston Spirn, *The Granite Garden: Urban Nature and Human Design* (New York: Basic Books, 1984), p. 261.

35. David Scobey, "Putting the Academy in Its Place: A Story about Park Design, Civic Engagement, and the Research University," lecture, University of Miami, February 10, 2000, available at http://www.artsofcitizenship.umich.edu/about/02102000.html.

36. *Clinton v. Cedar Rapids and Missouri River Rail Road Company*, 24 Iowa 455 (1868).

37. See David Rusk, *Cities without Suburbs* (Washington, D.C.: Woodrow Wilson Center Press, 1983), and Orfield, *Metropolitics*.

38. Paul S. Grogan and Tony Proscio, *Comeback Cities: A Blueprint for Urban America* (Boulder, Colo.: Westview Press, 2000).

39. See, for example, *Money* magazine's annual September survey of the factors that affect ordinary people's decision to locate in a particular city or town.

40. Paul Peterson, *City Limits* (Chicago: University of Chicago Press, 1981), pp. 17, 21.

41. Paul Kantor, *The Dependent City Revisited: The Political Economy of Urban Development and Social Policy* (Boulder, Colo.: Westview Press, 1995).

42. Douglas Yates, *The Ungovernable City: The Politics of Urban Problems and Policy Making* (Cambridge, Mass.: MIT Press, 1984).

43. Clarence N. Stone, *Regime Politics: Governing Atlanta, 1946–1988* (Lawrence, Kans.: University Press of Kansas, 1989).

44. C.f. Floyd Hunter, *Community Power Structure: A Study of Decision Makers* (Chapel Hill: University of North Carolina Press, 1953).

45. Stone, p. 229.

46. Stephen L. Elkin, "State and Market in City Politics: Or, The 'Real" Dallas,' in *The Politics of Urban Development*, eds. Clarence N. Stone and Heywood T. Sanders (Lawrence, Kans.: University Press of Kansas, 1987); Robert P. Stoker, "Baltimore: The Self-Evaluating City?" in *The Politics of Urban Development*; Scott Cummings, ed., *Business Elites and Urban Development: Case Studies and Critical Perspectives* (Albany, NY: State University of New York Press, 1988).

47. Stone, see Chapter 5: "Challenge and Response," in Stone and Sanders.

48. Todd Swanstrom, *The Crisis of Growth of Politics: Cleveland, Kucinich and the Challenge of Urban Populism* (Philadelphia: Temple University Press, 1985).

49. Pierre Clavel and Wim Wiewel, eds., *Harold Washington and the Neighborhoods: Progressive City Government in Chicago, 1983–1987* (New Brunswick, N.J.: Rutgers University Press, 1991); Peter Dreier, "Urban Politics and Progressive Housing Policy: Ray Flynn and Boston's Neighborhood Agenda," in *Revitalizing Urban Neighborhoods*, eds. W. Dennis Keating, Norman Krumholz, and Philip Star (Lawrence, Kans.: University Press of Kansas, 1996).

50. James Q. Wilson, *Bureaucracy: What Government Agencies Do and Why They Do It* (New York: Basic Books, 1989).

51. Michael Lipsky, "Toward a Theory of Street-Level Bureaucracy," in Willis D. Hawley and Michael Lipsky, eds., *Theoretical Perspectives on Urban Politics* (Englewood Cliffs, N.J.: Prentice Hall, 1974).

52. David Osborne and Ted Gaebler, *Reinventing Government* (Reading, Mass.: Addison-Wesley, 1992).

53. Ibid.

54. Stephen Goldsmith, *The Twenty-First Century City: Resurrecting Urban America* (New York: Regnery Publishing Co., 1997).

55. William D. Eggers and John O'Leary, *Revolution at the Roots: Making Our Government Smaller, Better, and Closer to Home* (New York: Free Press, 1995).

56. This section is drawn from Charles C. Euchner, "Cities Using New Technology to Manage the Unmanageable," *Boston Herald*, July 7, 2001. See also Christopher Swope, "Restless for Results," *Governing* (April 2001).

57. Todd Swanstrom, "Semisovereign Cities: The Politics of Urban Development," *Polity* (Fall, 1988).

58. Stephen J. McGovern, *The Politics of Downtown Development: Dynamic Political Cultures in San Francisco and Washington, D.C.* (Lexington, Ky.: University Press of Kentucky, 1998).

59. Peter Dreier and Bruce Ehrlich, "Downtown Development and Urban Reform: The Politics of Boston's Linkage Policy," *Urban Affairs Quarterly* 26 (March 1991): 354–75; Roger W. Caves, "Seattle, Washington: Capping Downtown Growth," in *Land Use Planning: The Ballot Box Revolution* (Newbury Park, Calif.: Sage Publications, 1992).

60. Pierre Clavel, *The Progressive City: Planning and Participation, 1969–1984* (New Brunswick, N.J.: Rutgers University Press, 1986); Clavel and Wiewel, eds., *Harold Washington and the Neighborhoods*.

Chapter 2

1. Sara S. McLanahan and Marcia J. Carlson, "Poverty and Gender in Affluent Nations," in *International Encyclopedia of the Social and Behavioral Sciences* (Oxford: Elsevier Science Limited, 2002).

2. Thad Williamson, David Imbroscio, and Gar Alperovitz, *Making a Place for Community: Local Democracy in a Global Era* (New York: Routledge, 2002).

3. In Jargowsky's research, census tracts are proxies for neighborhoods, and high-poverty neighborhoods are defined as census tracts with poverty rates of 40 percent or higher. Paul A. Jargowsky, *Poverty and Place: Ghettos, Barrios, and the American City* (New York: Russell Sage Foundation, 1997).

4. Paul A. Jargowsky, "Sprawl, Concentration of Poverty, and Urban Inequality," in *Urban Sprawl: Causes, Consequences and Policy Responses*, ed. Gregory D. Squires (Washington, D.C.: Urban Institute Press, 2002), p. 43.

5. Ibid., p. 63.

6. William Julius Wilson, James M. Quane, and Bruce H. Rankin, "The New Urban Poverty: Consequences of the Economic and Social Decline of Inner-City Neighborhoods," in *Locked in the Poorhouse: Cities, Race, and Poverty in the United States*, eds. Fred R. Harris and Lynn A. Curtis (Lanham, Md.: Rowman & Littlefield, 1998). It is important to note that many inner-city residents are not impoverished. Moreover, Wilson stresses that even a majority of the poor in the inner city subscribe to mainstream values and aspirations. They develop coping mechanisms that enable them to get by in spite of overwhelming obstacles. Still, their situation is always precarious and their prospects for advancement are bleak. See also Katherine S. Newman, *No Shame in My Game: The Working Poor in the Inner City* (New York: Alfred A. Knopf and Russell Sage Foundation, 1999).

7. Alice O'Connor, *Poverty Knowledge: Social Science, Social Policy, and the Poor in Twentieth Century U.S. History* (Princeton, N.J.: Princeton University Press, 2001).

8. For the U.S. Census Bureau's definitions of the poverty line and the latest statistical overviews, see http://www.census.gov/hhes/www/poverty.html.

9. C.f. Robert Rector, "Not So Poor," *National Review* 51; 20 (October 25, 1999): 28.

10. Deborah A. Stone, "Making the Poor Count," *The American Prospect* 17 (Spring 1994); Patricia Ruggles, *Drawing the Line: Alternative Policy Measures and Their Implications for Public Policy* (Lanham, Md.: Urban Institute Press, 1990).

11. In calculating the new poverty line, the NAS panel included a number of noncash benefits such as food stamps and housing subsidies but excluded Medicaid and Medicare health benefits while at the same time deducting certain expenditures from gross income such as income taxes, social security payroll taxes, child care costs, job-related transportation costs, and out-of-pocket medical and health insurance costs. Spencer Rich, "Poverty by the Numbers," *National Journal* (March 10, 2001): 694.

12. Michael Harrington, *The New American Poverty* (New York: Penguin Books, 1984), p. 71.

13. The poverty rate used for this comparison is the international standard of below 50 percent of the nation's median income. See Timothy M. Smeeding and Katherine Ross, "Social Protection for the Poor in the Developed World: The Evidence from LIS," prepared for the Conference on Social Protection and Poverty, February 4, 1999, available at http://www.iadb.org/sds/doc/864.eng.rtf.

14. Jorg Sancho Pernas, "Poverty and Statistics in the U.S.: Problems of Statistical Assessment," http://tiss.zdv.uni-tuebingen.de/webroot/sp/spsba01_W98_1/usa4.htm. See also *Historic Poverty Tables*, U.S. Census Bureau (Table 7), June 4, 2001.

15. *Historic Poverty Tables* (Table 8), U.S. Census Bureau, June 4, 2001.

16. Marlene Kim, "Problems Facing the Working Poor," paper presented at Economic Policy Institute symposium on June 15, 1999, available at http://www.lights.com/epi/virlib/studies/2000/balancinga/chapter4.pdf.

17. U.S. Bureau of the Census, Bureau of Labor Statistics, "A Profile of the Working Poor, 1999," Report 947, available at http://www.bls.gov/cpswp99.htm.

18. Kim, "Problems Facing the Working Poor."

19. Economic Policy Institute, Washington, D.C., State of Working America, 2000–01, available at http://www.epinet.org/books/swa2000/swa2000intro.html.

20. Edward N. Wolff, "The Rich Get Richer: And Why the Poor Don't," *The American Prospect*, February 12, 2001, available at http://www.prospect.org/print/V12/3/wolff-e.html. The minimum wage was first set at 25 cents in 1938; it was raised twenty times over the next sixty years, reaching $5.15 in 1997. In 1998 dollars, the minimum wage began in 1938 at $3.52 an hour, reached $5.07 an hour in 1950, $6.27 an hour in 1961, and a high of $7.49 an

hour in 1968. The modern low of $4.40 occurred in 1989 and by 1997 it was $5.23 an hour. "Value of The Federal Minimum Wage, 1938–1997," U.S. Department of Labor, available at http://www.dol.gov/dol/esa/public/minwage/chart2.htm.

21. Rick Wartzman, "As Officials Lose Faith in the Minimum Wage, Pat Williams Lived It," *Wall Street Journal*, July 19, 2001.

22. William O'Hare and Joseph Schwartz, "One Step Forward, Two Steps Back," *American Demographics* (September 1997).

23. Charles Murray, "The Underclass Revisited," American Enterprise Institute Papers and Studies, available at http://www.aei.org/ps/psmurray. htm.

24. Ken Auletta, *The Underclass* (New York: Random House, 1982). William Julius Wilson explores the controversy over the "underclass" concept in "Studying Inner-City Social Dislocations: The Challenge of Public Agenda Research," *American Sociological Review* 56 (February 1991), pp. 1–14.

25. *Murray, "The Underclass Revisited."* The use of the term "underclass" has fueled controversy. But the term is still useful to suggest the persistence of poverty for a particularly isolated and unskilled group of people. See, for example, *The Underclass" Debate: Views from History*, ed. Michael B. Katz (Princeton: Princeton University Press, 1993).

26. *Mitchell Sviridoff, former vice president of the Ford Foundation, quoted in Auletta, p. 30.*

27. *Charles Murray, "And Now for the Bad News,"* Wall Street Journal, February 2, 1999.

28. Thomas Sowell, *Ethnic America: A History* (New York: Basic Books, 1981), p. 224.

29. Andrew Hacker, *Two Nations: Black and White, Separate, Hostile, Unequal* (New York: Charles Scribner's Sons, 1992).

30. For a discussion of these and other issues, see Margaret Pugh, "Barriers to Work: The Spatial Divide Between Jobs and Welfare Recipients in Metropolitan Areas," The Brookings Institution, September 1998.

31. Lena Lundgren and Iris Cohen, "The New Skills Mismatch? An Examination of Urban Employers' Perceptions about Public Job Training Participants as Prospective Employees," *Journal of Social Services Research* 25 (1999): 109–124.

32. Barry Bluestone and Mary Stevenson, *The Boston Renaissance: Race, Space, and Economic Change in an American Metropolis* (New York: Russell Sage Foundation, 1999), pp. 219–224.

33. See Jared Bernstein and Mark Greenberg, "Reforming Welfare Reform," *American Prospect*, January 1–15, 2001; see http://www.prospect.org/print-friendly/print/V12/1/bernstein-j.html.

34. Bluestone and Stevenson, p. 235.

35. Quoted in Barry Bluestone and Mary Stevenson, p. 205.

36. James S. Coleman, *Equality of Education Opportunity* (Washington, D.C.: U.S. Government Printing Office, 1966).

37. Neil Swan, "Exploring the Role of Child Abuse in Later Drug Abuse," *NIDA News* 13, available at http://www.nida.nih.gov/NIDA_Notes/NNVol13N2/exploring.html.

38. For a review of the literature on work and disabilities, see the U.S. Department of Health and Human Services site at http://aspe.hhs.gov/hsp/isp/ancillary/disability.htm.

39. Andrew Solomon, "A Cure for Poverty," *New York Times Magazine*, May 6, 2001, pp. 116–117.

40. Linda L. Swanson, "Household Structure and Resources in Female-Headed Family Households," paper presented at the annual meeting of the Population Association of America, San Francisco, April 1995, available at http://www.cpc.unc.edu/pubs/paa_papers/1995/wanson.html.

41. The Henry J. Kaiser Family Foundation, *The 1996 Kaiser Family Foundation Survey on Teens and Sex: What They Say Teens Today Need to Know, and Who They Listen To* (Menlo Park, Calif.: The Henry J. Kaiser Family Foundation, 1996), Chart 6.

42. Patrick Fagan, "The Real Root Causes of Violent Crime: The Breakdown of Marriage, Family, and Community," The Heritage Foundation, Backgrounder No. 1026, March 17, 1995, available at http://www.heritage.org/Research/crime/BG1026.cfm.

43. "National and State-Specific Pregnancy Rates Among Adolescents—United States, 1995–1997," *Morbidity and Mortality Weekly Report*, July 14, 2000 / 49(27);605–611, available at http://www.cdc.gov/mmwr/preview/mmwrhtml/mm4927a1.htm.

44. Oscar Lewis, *La Vida* (New York: Random House, 1965).

45. The classic argument is in William Ryan, *Blaming the Victim* (New York: Pantheon, 1971).

46. Wilson, p. 74.

47. Kenneth B. Clark, *Dark Ghetto: Dilemmas of Social Power*, 2nd ed. (Middletown, Conn.: Wesleyan University Press, 1989), p. 13.
48. Jacqueline Jones, *The Dispossessed: America's Underclasses from the Civil War to the Present* (New York: Basic Books, 1992), pp. 226–7.
49. Stanley Lieberson, *A Piece of the Pie: Blacks and White Immigrants Since 1880* (Berkeley: University of California Press, 1981).
50. Gunnar Myrdal, *An American Dilemma: The Negro Problem and Modern Democracy* (New York: Harper Brothers, 1944).
51. Hacker, *Two Nations*, pp. 13, 15.
52. Paul A. Jargowsky, *Poverty and Place*, pp. 68–70 .
53. Lincoln Quillian, "Migration Patterns and the Growth of High-Poverty Neighborhoods, 1970–1990," Institute for Research on Poverty, Discussion Paper no. 1172–98, September 1998, available at http://www.ssc.wisc.edu/irp/pubs/dp117298.pdf.
54. For a sophisticated analysis of the effects of race and other factors in poverty, see Joseph V. Stefko, "The Effect of Racial and Poverty Concentrations on Urban Employment: A Geographic Assessment," State University of New York at Buffalo, paper presented at the American Political Science Association meeting in Atlanta, Georgia, September 2–5, 1999.
55. The following discussion is based on Douglas S. Massey and Nancy A. Denton, *American Apartheid: Segregation and the Underclass* (Cambridge, Mass.: Harvard University Press, 1993), ch. 5.
56. Ibid., p. 93.
57. Ibid., ch. 3.
58. Ibid., p. 77.
59. Stephan Thernstrom and Abigail Thernstrom, *America in Black and White: One Nation, Indivisible* (New York: Simon & Schuster, 1997).
60. Hacker, p. 103.
61. William Julius Wilson, *The Truly Disadvantaged: The Inner City, the Underclass, and Public Policy* (Chicago: University of Chicago Press, 1987), pp. 46–62.
62. Russ Rymer, "Integration's Casualties," *New York Times Magazine*, November 1, 1998, p. 48.
63. See Robert Pollin, "Globalization, Inequality, and Financial Instability: Confronting the Marx, Keynes, and Polanyi Problems in Advanced Capitalist Economies," Political Economy Research Institute, University of Massachusetts at Amherst, 2000, available at http://www.umass.edu/peri/pdfs/WP8.pdf.
64. Gail M. Johnston, "The Transformation of American Families: Employment, Dislocation, and the Growth of Female-Headed Households," Carolina Population Center, available at http://www.cpo.unc.edu/pubs/paa_papers/1995/johnston.html.
65. From 1973 to 1993, the average median earnings for males working full-time fell by 11 percent even though the Gross Domestic Product of the United States rose by 29 percent. In the 1980s, the incomes for the lowest quintile of twenty-two- to fifty-eight-year-old men fell by 34 percent, and the incomes for women in the same age bracket fell 4 percent. Charles M. Benny, Jr., "Great Expectations," Minnesota Center for Corporate Responsibility, paper, April 1996.
66. See Barry Bluestone and Bennett Harrison, *The Deindustrialization of America: Plant Closings, Community Abandonment, and the Dismantling of Basic Industry* (New York: Basic Books, 1982). Also see Paul Kantor with Stephen David, *The Dependent City: The Changing Political Economy of Urban America* (Glenview, Ill.: Scott Foresman, 1988), ch. 9; and William W. Goldsmith and Edward J. Blakely, *Separate Societies: Poverty and Inequality in U.S. Cities* (Philadelphia: Temple University Press, 1992).
67. For a discussion of post-Fordism, see David Harvey, *The Condition of Postmodernity: An Inquiry into the Origins of Cultural Change* (New York: Blackwell, 1988).
68. Frances Fox Piven and Richard A. Cloward, *Regulating the Poor: The Function of Public Welfare* (New York: Vintage Books, 1983).
69. Alexis de Tocqueville, "Memoir on Pauperism," *The Public Interest* 70 (Winter 1983), pp. 102–120.
70. Charles Murray, *Losing Ground: American Social Policy, 1950–1980* (New York: Basic Books, 1984), ch. 12.
71. Murray, p. 155.

72. Paul E. Peterson, "The Urban Underclass and the Poverty Paradox," in Christopher Jencks and Paul E. Peterson, eds., *The Urban Underclass* (Washington, D.C.: Brookings Institution, 1991), p. 14.
73. William A. Niskanen, "Welfare and the Culture of Poverty," *Cato Journal*, Spring/Summer 1996 16:1.
74. Kathryn Edin and Christopher Jencks, "Welfare," in Jencks, *Rethinking Social Policy*, p. 208 (Cambridge, Mass.: Harvard University, 1992). See also Kathryn Edin and Laura Lein, *Making Ends Meet: How Single Mothers Survive Welfare and Low-Wage Work* (New York: Russell Sage Foundation, 1997).
75. Edin and Jencks, p. 205.
76. Laura S. Jensen, *The Origins of Social Welfare in the American Nation* (Cambridge: Cambridge University Press, 2003).
77. For a summary of the impact of the Great Depression on the American economy and society, see Charles Kindleberger, *The World in Depression* (London: Allen Lane, 1970).
78. Kathryn H. Porter, Kathy Larin, Wendell Primus, "Social Security and Poverty among the Elderly: A National And State Perspective," Center on Budget and Policy Priorities, April 1999, http://www.cbpp.org/4-8-99socsec.pdf.
79. Michael Harrington, *The Other America* (New York: Macmillan, 1962).
80. For a good overview of the Great Society initiatives and their precursors, see James L. Sundquist, *Politics and Policy: The Eisenhower, Kennedy, and Johnson Years* (Washington, D.C.: Brookings Institution, 1968). For studies of the Great Society programs, see Marshall Kaplan and Peggy Cuciti, eds., *The Great Society and Its Legacy: Twenty Years of U.S. Social Policy* (Durham, N.C.: Duke University Press, 1986); and John E. Schwarz, *America's Hidden Success: A Reassessment of Twenty Years of Public Policy* (New York: W.W. Norton, 1983).
81. *King v. Smith*, 393 U.S. 309 (1968).
82. Robert D. Plotnick, Eugene Smolensky, Eirik Evenhouse, and Siobhan Reilly, "The Twentieth Century Record of Inequality and Poverty in the United States," July 1998, available at http://ideas.repec.org/p/wop/wispod/1166-78.htm.
83. Vincent J. Burke and Vee Burke, *Nixon's Good Deed: Welfare Reform* (New York: Columbia University Press, 1974). See also Tom Wicker, *One of Us: Richard Nixon and the American Dream* (New York: Random House, 1991); Richard P. Nathan, *The Plot That Failed: Nixon and the Administrative Presidency* (New York: Wiley, 1975).
84. Thomas Byrne Edsall and Mary D. Edsall, *Chain Reaction: The Impact of Race, Riots, and Taxes on American Politics* (New York: W.W. Norton, 1991).
85. George Gilder, *Wealth and Poverty* (New York: Basic Books, 1981).
86. Charles Murray, *Losing Ground*.
87. For a guided tour of Daniel Patrick Moynihan's twists and turns through the welfare debate from his work in the Johnson Administration's Labor Department through his service in the Senate during the Clinton administration, see Jacob Heilbrunn, "The Moynihan Enigma," *American Prospect*, July 1–August 1, 1997.
88. For example, without this rule, if a woman moves from a $300-a-month welfare package to a thirty-hour-a-week job that pays the minimum wage of $510 a month, she would lose all $300 in benefits and make a net gain of $210 a month. With the rule, she could keep the first $30 in wages and one third of the remaining $480 in wages, or $160, would be shielded. In other words, the woman would be allowed to keep $190 in welfare benefits along with the $510 in wages, for a total income of $700 per month. So under the "thirty and a third rule," the differential in monthly income between welfare ($300) and work ($700) would increase to $400, thus significantly strengthening the incentive to move from welfare to work.
89. Sheldon Danziger, "Welfare Reform from Nixon to Clinton: What Role for Social Science," December 1999, paper delivered at conference on Social Sciences and Policy Making at the Institute for Social Research, University of Michigan, p. 13.
90. Elijah Anderson, *Streetwise: Race, Class, and Change in an Urban Community* (Chicago: University of Chicago Press, 1990), pp. 123–124.
91. Charles Noble, *Welfare as We Knew It: A Political History of the American Welfare State* (New York: Oxford University Press, 1997).

92. James T. Patterson, *America's Struggle against Poverty in the Twentieth Century*, rev. ed (Cambridge, Mass.: Harvard University Press, 2000).

93. For a good overview of the waiver process, see Joel F. Handler, *The Poverty of Welfare Reform* (New Haven, Conn.: Yale University Press, 1995).

94. Elizabeth Shogren, "Clinton Unveils Welfare Reform," *Los Angeles Times*, June 15, 1994, p. A1.

95. The *New York Times* commented that President Clinton's decision to sign the bill represented "a remarkable retreat from the vision of welfare that he had outlined in 1992." Peter T. Kilborn and Sam How Verhovek, "Clinton's Welfare Shift Ends Tortuous Journey," *New York Times*, August 2, 1996, p. A1.

96. PWRORA does impose a "maintenance of effort" obligation on the states, so that a state's block grant may be reduced if it fails to spend at least 80 percent of what it had been spending on welfare programs in 1994. But states have considerable discretion in determining how to spend their TANF funds since they now have the power to decide who is and who is not eligible for assistance.

97. Many states exempt families from the lifetime limit during periods when enforcing work requirements would result in undue hardship (e.g., caring for children under the age of two or coping with a personal or family crisis).

98. "Welfare Reform: Four Years Later," *Spectrum: The Journal of State Government* 73 (Fall 2000).

99. Sanford F. Schram, "In the Clinic: The Medicalization of Welfare," in *After Welfare: The Culture of Postindustrial Social Policy*, ed. Sanford F. Schram (New York: New York University Press, 2000), p. 75.

100. Janet L. Finn and Lyne Underwood, "The State, the Clock, and the Struggle: An Inquiry into the Discipline for Welfare Reform in Montana," *Social Text* 18 (Spring 2000); Marcia K. Meyers, "How Welfare Offices Undermine Welfare Reform," *American Prospect*, June 19–July 3, 2000.

101. Sarah Brauner and Pamela Loprest, *Where Are They Now? What States' Studies of People Who Left Welfare Tell Us* (Washington, D.C.: The Urban Institute, 1999).

102. LaDonna A. Pavetti, "Creating a New Welfare Reality: Early Implementation of the Temporary Assistance for Needy Families Program," *Journal of Social Issues* 56 (Winter 2000).

103. Ibid.

104. Ibid.

105. Stephen Moore, "A Success to Trumpet, and Protect," *National Review* 52; 3 (February 21, 2000): 37.

106. Liberal commentator Michael Kelly declared: "The reform of the welfare system is a great triumph of social policy—so great, indeed, as to restore some legitimacy to the whole concept of large-scale social policy." "Assessing Welfare Reform," *Washington Post*, August 4, 1999, p. A21.

107. Amy Goldstein, "Forgotten Issues: Welfare Reform's Progress Is Stalled," *Washington Post*, June 1, 2000, p. A1.

108. Isabel Sawhill, "From Welfare to Work," *Brookings Review* 19 (Summer 2001): 4. Taking a more long-term perspective, 147,000 families received cash assistance under AFDC in 1936, the first full year of the program. Caseloads increased gradually until the 1960s, when there was a 230 percent surge due mostly to programmatic changes during the Great Society era that enabled more poor people to obtain easier access to benefits. Another surge in caseloads occurred between 1989 and 1994, partly because of an economic recession and partly because of a rapid increase in cases in which only children received benefits, including American-born children of parents who were undocumented immigrants and children of parents addicted to crack cocaine under the care of relatives. Douglas J. Besharov and Peter Germanis, "Welfare Reform—Four Years Later," *Public Interest* 140 (Summer 2000): 18–9.

109. Tina Cassidy, "Majority Off Welfare Employed, State Says," *Boston Globe*, December 6, 2000, p. A1.

110. Sawhill, p. 6.

111. Jared Bernstein and Mark Greenberg, "Reforming Welfare Reform," *American Prospect* 12 (January 1, 2001). See also a study by the Manpower Demonstration Research Corporation of Connecticut's welfare program which found that 81 percent of families randomly assigned in 1996 to a control group that would continue receiving cash assistance under pre-

1996 rules left welfare by 2000, a rate only slightly lower than that of Connecticut families who were subjected to the new rules including work requirements and time limits. This suggests that the booming economy was a major factor in enabling welfare recipients to find jobs regardless of PRWORA. Nina Bernstein, "In Control Group, Most Welfare Recipients Left the Rolls Even without Reform," *New York Times*, February 20, 2002, p. B5.

112. Ron Haskins, "Giving Is NOT Enough," *Brookings Review* 19 (Summer 2001).

113. Besharov and Germanis, pp. 25–6.

114. Jared Bernstein and Mark Greenberg, "Reforming Welfare Reform," *The American Prospect*, January 1, 2002, available at http://www.prospect.org/print/v12/1/Bernstein-j.html.

115. Pamela Loprest, "How Are Families That Left Welfare Doing? A Comparison of Early and Recent Welfare Leavers," *New Federalism: National Survey of America's Families* (Washington, D.C.: The Urban Institute, 2001).

116. Ralph Ranalli, "Welfare Reform's Success at Issue," *Boston Globe*, February 21, 2001, p. B1.

117. U.S. Conference of Mayors, "A Status Report on Hunger and Homelessness in America's Cities," December 2002, available at http://www.usmayors.org/uscm/hungersurvey/2002/onlinereport/HungerAndHomelessReport2002.pdf.

118. Nina Bernstein, "Strict Limits on Welfare Discourage Marriage, Studies Say," *New York Times*, June 3, 2002, p. A1.

119. Cheryl Wetzstein, "Iowa Welfare Study Finds Job Success, Family Life Failures," *Washington Times*, June 12, 2002, p. A7.

120. Carla Rivera, "Study Examines Effect of Welfare Programs on Teens," *Los Angeles Times*, March 1, 2002, p. A42; Laura Sessions Stepp, "Welfare Reform's Unexpected Difficulties," *Washington Post*, July 31, 2001, p. A3. See also Ellen K. Scott, Kathryn Edin, Andrew S. London, and Joan Maya Mazelis, "My Children Come First: Welfare-Reliant Women's Post-TANF Views of Work-Family Trade-Offs and Marriage," in *For Better and Worse: Welfare Reform and the Well-Being of Children and Families*, eds. Greg J. Duncan and P. Lindsay Chase-Lansdale (New York: Russell Sage Foundation, 2001).

121. Robert Pear, "Gains Reported for Children of Welfare-to-Work Families," *New York Times*, January 23, 2001, p. A12.

122. Amy Sheridan, "The Lessons of W-2," *Public Interest* (Summer 2000): 41.

123. Tami J. Friedman, "How States Are Spending Their Welfare Money—Or Not," *Dollars & Sense* (March 2002).

124. Karen Houppert, "You're Not Entitled!: Welfare Reform Is Leading to Government Lawlessness," *The Nation* 269 (October 25, 1999); see also Joshua Green, "Tough Sanctions, Tough Luck," *American Prospect*, June 19, 2000. Nationwide, a recent study found an 89 percent poverty rate among sanctioned leavers. Jared Bernstein and Mark Greenberg, "Reforming Welfare Reform," *The American Prospect*, January 1, 2001, available at http://www.prospect.org/print/v12/1/bernstein-j.html.

125. Mark Sappenfield, "Now, the Tough Part of Welfare Reform," *Christian Science Monitor*, May 8, 2001, p. 2.

126. Jonathan Peterson, "As Economy Slows, Gains of Welfare Reform Tested," *Los Angeles Times*, April 22, 2001, p. A1.

127. Stephanie Simon, "Thompson's Welfare Reforms Cut Rolls But Also Safety Net," *Los Angeles Times*, January 12, 2001, p. A1.

128. Sheridan, p. 41.

129. Frances Fox Piven, "Thompson's Easy Ride," *The Nation* 272 (February 26, 2001). See also Phil Wilayto, "The Folly of Looking to Wisconsin as a Model for Welfare Reform," *Minneapolis Star Tribune*, June 4, 2000, p. 23A; Steve Schultze and Tom Held, "Welfare Rolls Plunge in State, But Figures Show Fewer Gains against Poverty, Especially in Milwaukee," *Milwaukee Journal-Sentinel*, June 5, 2002, p. A1.

130. Jennie Tunkieicz, "Are the Poor Better Off under W-2?" *Milwaukee Journal-Sentinel*, April 15, 2001, p. 1Z.

131. Robert E. Pierce, "Welfare Reform's Big Test," *Washington Post*, December 27, 2001, p. A1.

132. Virginia Knox, Cynthia Miller, and Lisa A. Gennetian, "Reforming Welfare and Rewarding Work: A Summary of the Final Report on the Minnesota Family Investment Program," Manpower Demonstration and Research Corporation, September 2000. See also Lisa A. Gennetian and Cynthia Miller, "Children and Welfare Reform: A View from an Experimental Welfare Program in Minnesota," *Child Development* 73 (March-April 2002): 601–621.

133. Marlene Cimons, "Welfare Plan Gives Families Surer Footing, Study Says," *Los Angeles Times*, June 1, 2000, p. A1; Robert Pear, "Changes in Welfare Bring Improvements for Families," *New York Times*, June 1, 2000, p. A16.
134. Jean Hopfensperger, "Families Fare Well under State Welfare Overhaul," *Minneapolis Star Tribune*, June 1, 2000, p. 1A; Jean Hopfensperger, Welfare Rolls Shrinking More Than Ever," *Minneapolis Star Tribune*, January 18, 2001, p. 5B.
135. Rebecca M. Blank and Lucie Schmidt, "Work, Wages, and Welfare," in *The New World of Welfare*, eds. Rebecca M. Blank and Ron Haskins (Washington, D.C.: Brookings Institution Press, 2001).
136. Jean Hopfensperger, "Clock Is Ticking for Some on Welfare," *Minneapolis Star Tribune*, April 23, 2001, p. 1A.
137. Jeanne Kohl-Welles, "Work-First Shouldn't Erect Roadblocks to College Degree," *Seattle Times*, March 10, 1999, p. B5; Carla Rivera, "'Work-First' Approach Earns Critical Report Card," *Los Angeles Times*, April 24, 1999, p. B1.
138. "Report Analyzes Impact of Lifetime Ban on Women," *Alcoholism and Drug Abuse Weekly* 14:12 (March 25, 2002): 3.
139. David Card and Alan B. Krueger, *Myth and Measurement: The New Economics of the Minimum Wage* (Princeton, N.J.: Princeton University Press, 1995).
140. Liberals support the EITC because it has been such an effective weapon in fighting poverty. The Center of Budget and Policy Priorities estimated that the EITC was responsible for lifting almost 5 million people above the poverty line in 1998. Conservatives support the EITC because it requires recipients to work and because it does not contribute much to an expansion of the government's bureaucracy to administer the program. Jared Bernstein, "Two Cheers for the 2000 EITC," *American Prospect*, June 19–July 3, p. 64.
141. Albert B. Crenshaw, "IRS Is Writing More Checks to Working Poor," *Washington Post*, April 16, 2001, p. A6.

Chapter 3

1. Peter K. Eisinger, *The Rise of the Entrepreneurial State: State and Local Economic Development Policy in the United States* (Madison, Wis.: University of Wisconsin Press, 1988), pp. 3–4.
2. Dave Davies and Paul Maryniak, "High Profile and Growing," *Philadelphia Daily News*, June 3, 1993, p. 4.
3. Paul E. Peterson, *City Limits* (Chicago: University of Chicago Press, 1981).
4. Allan R. Pred, *The Spatial Dynamics of U.S. Urban-Industrial Growth, 1800–1914: Interpretive and Theoretical Essays* (Cambridge, Mass.: MIT Press, 1966); see also Erik H. Monkkonen, *America Becomes Urban: The Development of U.S. Cities and Towns, 1780–1980* (Berkeley: University of California Press, 1988).
5. Barry Bluestone and Bennett Harrison, *The Deindustrialization of America: Plant Closings, Community Abandonment, and the Dismantling of Basic Industry* (New York: Basic Books, 1982); John F. Kain, "The Distribution and Movement of Jobs and Industry," in *The Metropolitan Enigma*, ed. James Q. Wilson (Cambridge, Mass. Harvard University Press, 1968); Leon Moss and Harold F. Williamson, "The Location of Economic Activity in Cities," *American Economic Review* 57 (1967): 211–222.
6. Carolyn Adams et al., *Philadelphia: Neighborhoods, Division, and Conflict in a Postindustrial City* (Philadelphia: Temple University Press, 1991), p. 31.
7. William Julius Wilson, *When Work Disappears: The World of the New Urban Poor* (New York: Random House, 1996), pp. 29–30.
8. Richard D. Bingham and Zhonghai Zhang, *The Economies of Central-City Neighborhoods* (Boulder, Colo.: Westview Press, 2001), p. 3.
9. Bluestone and Harrison, p. 51–66.
10. Ibid., p. 79.
11. Kenneth T. Jackson, *Crabgrass Frontier: The Suburbanization of the United States* (New York: Oxford University Press, 1985); Jon C. Teaford, *City and Suburb: The Political Fragmentation of Metropolitan America* (Baltimore, Md.: Johns Hopkins University Press, 1979); Carl Abbott, *The New Urban America: Growth and Politics in Sunbelt Cities* (Chapel Hill, N.C.: University of North Carolina Press, 1981).

12. Michael N. Danielson, *The Politics of Exclusion* (New York: Columbia University Press, 1976); Dennis R. Judd and Todd Swanstrom, *City Politics: Private Power and Public Policy* (New York: HarperCollins College Publishers, 1994), pp. 200–207; W. Dennis Keating, *The Suburban Racial Dilemma: Housing and Neighborhoods* (Philadelphia: Temple University Press, 1994).

13. Gregory D. Squires, *Capital and Communities in Black and White; The Intersections of Race, Class, and Uneven Development* (Albany: State University of New York Press, 1994).

14. C.f. Martin Shefter, *Fiscal Crisis/Political Crisis: The Collapse and Revival of New York City* (New York: Basic Books, 1985).

15. The gloomy mood was captured in the title of a widely read book at the time: Douglas Yates, *The Ungovernable City: The Politics of Urban Problems and Policy Making* (Cambridge, Mass.: MIT Press, 1977).

16. Thierry J. Noyelle and Thomas M. Stanback, *The Economic Transformation of American Cities* (Totowa, N.J.: Rowman and Allanheld, 1983).

17. Chester Hartman, *Yerba Buena: Land Grab and Community Resistance in San Francisco* (San Francisco: Glide Publications, 1974).

18. Jon C. Teaford, *The Rough Road to Renaissance: Urban Revitalization in America, 1940–1985* (Baltimore, Md.: Johns Hopkins University Press, 1990).

19. John R. Logan and Harvey Molotch, *Urban Fortunes: The Political Economy of Place* (Berkeley: University of California Press, 1987); John H. Mollenkopf, *The Contested City* (Princeton, N.J.: Princeton University Press, 1983); Jeanne R. Lowe, *Cities in a Race with Time: Progress and Poverty in America's Renewing Cities* (New York: Random House, 1967).

20. Robert Groberg, "Urban Renewal Realistically Reappraised," in *Urban Renewal: The Record and the Controversy*, ed. James Q. Wilson (Cambridge, Mass.: MIT Press, 1966), p. 521, cited in Eisinger, p. 96.

21. Richard M. Flanagan, "The Housing Act of 1954: The Sea Change in National Urban Policy," *Urban Affairs Review* 33 (November 1997): 265–286.

22. Martin Anderson, *The Federal Bulldozer: A Critical Analysis of Urban Renewal, 1949–1962* (Cambridge, Mass.: MIT Press, 1964).

23. Hartman, *Yerba Buena.*

24. David Harvey, *The Urbanization of Capital* (Baltimore, Md.: Johns Hopkins University Press, 1986); Robert A. Beauregard, ed., *Economic Restructuring and Political Response* (London: Sage, 1989); Richard Peet, "Industrial Restructuring and the Crisis of International Capitalism," in *International Capitalism and Industrial Restructuring*, Richard Peet, ed. (Boston: Allen and Unwin, 1987).

25. Paul E. Peterson and Mark C. Rom, *Welfare Magnets: A New Case for a National Standard* (Washington, D.C.: Brookings Institution Press, 1990); see also Paul Kantor, "The Dependent City: The Changing Political Economy of Urban Economic Development in the United States," *Urban Affairs Quarterly* 22 (1987): 493–520.

26. Peterson, *City Limits.*

27. The phrase comes from Todd Swanstrom, *The Crisis of Growth Politics* (Philadelphia, Pa.: Temple University Press, 1985).

28. Clarence N. Stone, *Regime Politics: Governing Atlanta, 1946–1988* (Lawrence, Kans.: University Press of Kansas, 1989).

29. Harvey Molotch, "The City as Growth Machine," *American Journal of Sociology* 82 (September 1976): 309–332.

30. Gregory D. Squires, ed., *Unequal Partnerships: The Political Economy of Urban Redevelopment in Postwar America* (New Brunswick, N.J.: Rutgers University Press, 1989); Scott Cummings, ed., *Business Elites and Urban Development: Case Studies and Critical Perspectives* (Albany: State University of New York Press, 1988).

31. Timothy Barnekov and Daniel Rich, "Privatism and the Limits of Local Economic Development Policy," *Urban Affairs Quarterly* 25 (1989): 212–238.

32. Michael A. Pagano and Ann O'M. Bowman, *Cityscapes and Capital: The Politics of Urban Development* (Baltimore, Md.: Johns Hopkins University Press, 1995); Daniel Mandelker, *Reviving Cities with Tax Abatement* (New Brunswick, N.J.: Rutgers Center for Policy Research, 1980).

33. Desmond S. King, "Economic Activity and the Challenge to Local Government" in *Challenges to Local Government*, eds. Desmond S. King and Jon Pierre (London: Sage, 1990);

Irene S. Rubin and Herbert J. Rubin, "Economic Incentives: The Poor (Cities) Pay More," *Urban Affairs Quarterly* 23; 1 (September 1987): 37–62.

34. Eisinger, p. 202.
35. C.f. Roger W. Schmener, *Making Business Location Decisions* (Englewood Cliffs, N.J.: Prentice Hall, 1982).
36. Eisinger, p. 202.
37. Ibid., pp. 215, 202.
38. Todd Swanstrom, "Semisovereign Cities: The Politics of Urban Development," *Polity* (Fall) 1988.
39. Susan S. Fainstein, *The City Builders: Property, Politics and Planning in London and New York* (Oxford: Blackwell, 1994).
40. Michael Rich, "UDAG, Economic Development and the Death and Life of American Cities," *Economic Development Quarterly* 6 (1992): 150–172.
41. Donald B. Rosenthal, ed., *Urban Revitalization* (Beverly Hills, Calif.: Sage, 1980); see also ch. 7, "Messiah Mayors and the Gospel of Urban Hype," in Jon C. Teaford, *The Rough Road to Renaissance: Urban Revitalization in America, 1940–1985* (Baltimore, Md.: Johns Hopkins University Press, 1990).
42. Saskia Sassen, *Cities in a World Economy*, 2nd ed. (Thousand Oaks, Calif.: Pine Forge Press, 2000).
43. C.f. David R. Goldfield, "Private Neighborhood Redevelopments and Displacement: The Case of Washington, D.C.," *Urban Affairs Quarterly* 15 (June 1980): 453–468.
44. Barry Bluestone, "The Inequality Express," *American Prospect* 20 (Winter 1995): 81–93; Thomas M. Stanback and Thierry J. Noyelle, *Cities in Transition: Changing Job Structures in Atlanta, Denver, Buffalo, Phoenix, Columbus, Nashville, Charlotte* (Totowa, N.J.: Allanheld, Osmun & Co., 1982).
45. C.f. Marc V. Levine, "Downtown Redevelopment as an Urban Growth Strategy: A Critical Appraisal of the Baltimore Renaissance," *Journal of Urban Affairs* 9; 2 (1987): 103–123; Susan S. Fainstein, Ian Gordon, and Michael Harloe, eds., *Divided Cities: New York and London in the Contemporary World* (Cambridge, U.K.: Blackwell, 1992).
46. Stephen J. McGovern, *The Politics of Downtown Development: Dynamic Political Cultures in San Francisco and Washington, D.C.* (Lexington, Ky.: University of Kentucky Press, 1998).
47. Peter Dreier and Bruce Ehrlich, "Downtown Development and Urban Reform: The Politics of Boston's Linkage Policy," *Urban Affairs Quarterly* 26 (March 1991): 354–375; Roger W. Caves, "Seattle, Washington: Capping Downtown Growth" in *Land Use Planning: The Ballot Box Revolution* (Newbury Park, Calif.: Sage Publications, 1992).
48. McGovern, *The Politics of Downtown Development*.
49. Joel Garreau, *Edge Cities* (New York: Doubleday, 1991).
50. Dennis R. Judd, "Constructing the Tourist Bubble," in *The Tourist City*, eds. Dennis R. Judd and Susan S. Fainstein (New Haven, Conn.; Yale University Press, 1999).
51. Ibid., see also Lawrence Tabak, "Wild about Convention Centers," *Atlantic Monthly*, April 1994, pp. 28–34.
52. Stephen J. McGovern, "Mayoral Leadership and Economic Development Policy: The Case of Ed Rendell's Philadelphia," *Policy and Politics* 25 (April, 1997): 153–172.
53. Elizabeth Strom, "Let's Put on a Show! Performing Arts and Urban Revitalization in Newark, New Jersey," *Journal of Urban Affairs* 21; 4 (1999): 423–35; Andrew Jacobs, "A Newly Cool Newark Says, "C'mon Over!" *New York Times*, November 24, 2000, p. E1.
54. Joni Leithe, "Profiting from the Past: The Economic Impact of Historic Preservation in Georgia," *Government Finance Review* 16 (April 2000); Alexander J. Reichl, "Historic Preservation and Progrowth Politics in U.S. Cities," *Urban Affairs Review* 32 (March 1997): 513–535.
55. For example, approximately 18 million people visited the Inner Harbor's festival marketplace during its first year in operation. Judd and Swanstrom, p. 348.
56. Ibid., p. 349.
57. Philip Langdon, "How Portland Does It," *Atlantic Monthly*, November 1992, p. 136; see also Ann Breen and Dick Rigby, *Urban Waterfronts: Cities Reclaim Their Edge* (New York: McGraw-Hill, 1993).
58. David L. A. Gordon, "Financing Urban Waterfront Redevelopment," *Journal of the American Planning Association* 63 (Spring 1997): 244–265.

59. William H. Hudnut, *The Hudnut Years in Indianapolis, 1976–1991* (Bloomington, Ind.: Indiana University Press, 1995).

60. Charles C. Euchner, *Playing the Field: Why Sports Teams Move and Cities Fight to Keep Them* (Baltimore, Md.: Johns Hopkins University Press, 1993); Robert A. Baade and Richard F. Dye, "Sports Stadiums and Area Development: A Critical Review," *Economic Development Quarterly* 2; 3 (1988): 265–275.

61. The model for the ballpark at Camden Yards was a minor league stadium in Buffalo featuring a revivalist architecture that local planners hoped would help resuscitate a declining downtown district. The same architectural firm went on to design the baseball stadium in Baltimore and more than a dozen others elsewhere in the United States.

62. Arthur T. Johnson, *Minor League Baseball and Local Economic Development* (Chicago: University of Illinois Press, 1993).

63. Roger G. Noll and Andrew Zimbalist, eds., *Sports, Jobs, and Taxes: The Economic Impact of Sports Teams and Stadiums* (Washington, D.C.: Brookings Institution Press, 1997); Mark S. Rosentraub et al., "Sport and Downtown Development Strategy: If You Build It, Will Jobs Come?" *Journal of Urban Affairs* 16 (1994): 221–239.

64. Robert A. Baade, "Professional Sports as a Catalyst for Metropolitan Economic Development," *Journal of Urban Affairs* 18; 1 (1996): 1–17.

65. Steve Rock, "New Stadium No Cure-All, Experts Say," *Kansas City Star*, July 1, 2001, p. A1.

66. Thomas V. Chema, "When Professional Sports Justify the Subsidy: A Reply to Robert A. Baade," *Journal of Urban Affairs* 18; 1 (1996): 18–22.

67. Mark S. Rosentraub, "Does the Emperor Have New Clothes? A Reply to Robert A. Baade," *Journal of Urban Affairs* 18; 1 (1996): 23–31.

68. Peter Waldman, "If You Build It Without Public Cash, They'll Still Come," *Wall Street Journal*, March 3, 2000, p. A1.

69. Bernard Frieden and Lynne B. Sagalyn, *Downtown, Inc.: How America Rebuilds Cities* (Cambridge, Mass.: MIT Press, 1989).

70. Ibid., p. 189; but see Witold Rybczynski, "The New Downtowns," *Atlantic Monthly* 271 (May 1993).

71. Chema, "When Professional Sports Justify the Subsidy."

72. Judd, "Constructing the Tourist Bubble."

73. Michael Sorkin, ed., *Variations on a Theme Park* (New York: Hill & Wang, 1992).

74. Richard Hula, "The Two Baltimores," in *Leadership and Urban Regeneration: Cities in North America and Europe*, eds. Dennis R. Judd and Michael Parkinson (Newbury Park, Calif.: Sage Publications, 1990); Levine, "Downtown Redevelopment as an Urban Growth Strategy."

75. Population Estimates Program, Population Division, U.S. Census Bureau, March 9, 2000; available at http://www.census.gov/population/estimates/county/co-99–4/99C4_42.txt.

76. McGovern, "Mayoral Leadership and Economic Development Policy."

77. C.f. "Symposium: Antipoverty Programs," *Law and Contemporary Problems* 31; 1 (Winter 1966).

78. Michael B. Katz, *In the Shadow of the Poorhouse: A Social History of Welfare in America* (New York: Basic Books, 1986); Charles Murray, *Losing Ground: American Social Policy, 1950–1980* (New York: Basic Books, 1984).

79. Rich, "UDAG, Economic Development and the Death and Life of American Cities."

80. Thomas Byrne Edsall with Mary D. Edsall, *Chain Reaction: The Impact of Race, Rights, and Taxes on American Politics* (New York: W.W. Norton & Co., 1991).

81. President's Commission for a National Agenda for the Eighties, *A National Agenda for the Eighties*, (Washington, DC: Government Printing Office, 1980), pp. 67, 66. Quoted in Dennis R. Judd and Todd Swanstrom, *City Politics: Private Power and Public Policy* (New York: HarperCollins, 1994), pp. 293–4.

82. C.f. Roger Starr, "Making New York Smaller," in *Revitalizing the Northeast*, eds. George Sternlieb and James W. Hughes (New Brunswick, N.J.: Rutgers University Press, 1978).

83. Nicholas Lemann, "The Myth of Community Development," *New York Times Magazine*, January 9, 1994.

84. John D. Kasarda, "Urban Change and Minority Opportunities," in Paul E. Peterson, ed., *The New Urban Reality* (Washington, D.C.: Brookings Institution, 1985); John F. Kain, "Housing Segregation, Negro Employment, and Metropolitan Decentralization," *Quarterly Journal of Economics* 82; 2 (1968): 175–197. For a critique of spatial mismatch theory, see David T.

Ellwood, "The Spatial Mismatch Hypothesis: Are There Teenage Jobs Missing in the Ghetto?" in *The Black Youth Employment Crisis*, eds. Richard B. Freeman and Harry J. Holzer (Chicago: University of Chicago Press, 1986).

85. Anthony Downs, *New Visions for Metropolitan America* (Washington, D.C.: Brookings Institution Press, 1994).

86. Ann Mariano, "Hill Panel Halts Plan to Move Poor Families," *Washington Post*, September 3, 1994, p. E1. Other programs aimed at dispersing inner-city residents throughout a metropolitan region have shown promising results with respect to employment opportunity. Moreover, the children of moving households have been more likely to remain in school and secure better jobs after graduating. But political obstacles have frustrated efforts to expand such dispersal programs. C.f. Peter Dreier and David Moberg, "Moving from the 'Hood': The Mixed Success of Integrating Suburbia," *American Prospect* 24 (Winter 1996).

87. M. Hughes and T. Madden, "Residential Segregation and the Economic Status of Black Workers: New Evidence for an Old Debate," *Journal of Urban Economics* 29 (1991): 28–49.

88. John F. Kain, "The Spatial Mismatch Hypothesis: Three Decades Later," *Housing Policy Debate* 3; 2 (1992): 371–460; Rochelle L. Stanfield, "The Reverse Commute," *National Journal*, November 23, 1996: 2546–9.

89. C.f. Chris Tilly, et al., "Space as Signal: How Employers Perceive Neighborhoods in Four Metropolitan Labor Markets," in *Urban Inequality: Evidence from Four Cities*, eds. Alice O'-Connor, Chris Tilly, and Lawrence D. Bobo (New York: Russell Sage Foundation, 2001); Susan C. Turner, "Barriers to a Better Break: Employer Discrimination and Spatial Mismatch in Metropolitan Detroit," *Journal of Urban Affairs* 19; 2 (1997): 123–141.

90. Stuart M. Butler, *Enterprise Zones: Greenlining the Inner City* (New York: Universe Books, 1981).

91. Karen Mossberger, "State-Federal Diffusion and Policy Learning: From Enterprise Zones to Empowerment Zones," *Publius* 29 (Summer 1999).

92. William Fulton and Morris Newman, "The Strange Career of Enterprise Zones," *Governing*, March 1994, pp. 32–36; Robert Greenbaum, "An Evaluation of State Enterprise Zone Policies," *Policy Studies Review* 17; 2/3 (Summer/Autumn 2000).

93. Roy Green, ed. *Enterprise Zones: New Directions in Economic Development* (Newbury Park, Calif.: Sage Publications, 1991).

94. Michael Porter, "The Competitive Advantages of the Inner City," *Harvard Business Review* 73 (May-June, 1995): 55–71.

95. Ibid., pp. 67–9.

96. David S. Sawicki and Mitch Moody, "Déjà-vu All Over Again: Porter's Model of Inner-City Redevelopment" in *The Inner City: Urban Poverty and Economic Development in the Next Century*, eds. Thomas D. Boston and Catherine L. Ross (New Brunswick, N.J.: Transaction Publishers, 1997).

97. Edward J. Blakely and Leslie Small, "Michael Porter: New Gilder of Ghettos," in *The Inner City*. Some observe that Porter's stature within the corporate world also gave his arguments added credibility among business leaders, all of which works to the advantage of inner-city neighborhoods.

98. Michael Hickens, "Hot Time in the City," *Management Review*, March 1999, p. 23; Michael A. Fletcher, "More Retailers Are Sold on Cities," *Washington Post*, March 5, 1999, p. E1; and Gregg Gatlin, "Markets Moving Back to Inner City," *Boston Herald*, June 13, 1999, p. 33.

99. Larry Platt, "Magic Johnson Builds an Empire," *New York Times Magazine*, December 10, 2000, p. 119. The wave of investment by chain stores is not without skeptics. Some point out that excessive dependence on large chain retailers siphons resources out of the community. C.f. Christopher Gunn and Hazel Dayton Gunn, *Reclaiming Capital: Democratic Initiatives and Community Development* (Ithaca, N.Y.: Cornell University Press, 1991). Others respond that investment by chains is only the first step in stimulating smaller-scale, community-based businesses. Moreover, aside from giving local residents more product choices at lower prices, the retail chains offer significant employment benefits. For example, Magic Johnson's various enterprises are estimated to employ three thousand inner-city residents throughout the United States. Ibid.

100. Susan S. Fainstein and Mia Gray, "Economic Development Strategies for the Inner City: The Need for Government Intervention," *Review of Black Political Economy* 24 (Fall/Winter 1995). In highlighting the city's crucial role in developing the Hunts Point Market, Fainstein's and Gray's only criticism is that even more government activism would have

been useful: "The chief deficiency of the city's role has been its passivity with regard to fostering ancillary development around the market and its grudging commitment to further investment."

101. Richard C. Elling and Ann Workman Sheldon, "Determinants of Enterprise Zone Success: A Four State Perspective," in *Enterprise Zones: New Directions in Economic Development*, ed. Roy E. Green (Newbury Park, Calif. Sage Publications, 1991).

102. The empowerment zone law also established ninety-five urban and rural enterprise communities that would be eligible for much smaller levels of federal funding—only $3 million for each enterprise community and no federal tax incentives. Soon after HUD announced which cities had been designated as empowerment zone cities, it responded to criticism of the selection process by asking Congress to create two supplemental zones for Los Angeles and Cleveland; those zones would receive a slightly reduced amount in federal grants and fewer tax incentives. Ronald Brownstein and John Schwada, "Clinton Seeks Larger Aid Program to Include L.A.," *Los Angeles Times*, December 21, 1994, p. A1; Evelyn Theiss and Miriam Hill, "Owning the Neighborhood," *Cleveland Plain Dealer*, January 1, 1995, p. 1A.

103. Ernie Suggs, "State Finds Atlanta Empowerment Zone Lagging," *Atlanta Journal and Constitution*, August 29, 2000, p. 1A.

104. Amy Waldman, "Thin Support and Red Tape Mire New York City Development Zone," *New York Times*, May 24, 1999, p. 1A; Abby Ellin, "A Harlem Power Zone Weakens Some," *New York Times*, January 4, 2000, p. B4.

105. Eric Siegel, "Renewal Efforts Move at Slow Pace," *Baltimore Sun*, January 10, 2000, p. 1A.

106. Alison Grant, "Enterprise Zone Effort Falling Short at Midpoint," *Cleveland Plain Dealer*, September 26, 1999, p. 1A. See also Marilyn Gittel et al., "Expanding Civic Opportunity: Urban Empowerment Zones," *Urban Affairs Review* 33 (March 1998): 530–558.

107. Siegel, p. 1A.

108. Jennifer Dixon, "Detroit Developers Discover Opportunity in Places Once Known for Blight," *Detroit Free Press*, January 17, 2000.

109. Bruce Alpert, "Regional Linkages Empowered Winners," *New Orleans Times-Picayune*, January 14, 1999, p. B1.

110. John P. Blair and Rishi Kumar, "Is Local Economic Development a Zero-Sum Game?" in *Dilemmas of Urban Economic Development: Issues in Theory and Practice*, eds. Richard D. Bingham and Robert Mier (Thousand Oaks, Calif.: Sage Publications, 1997).

111. Daniel Monroe Stillman, "Local Governments as Risk Takers and Risk Reducers: An Examination of Business Subsidies and Subsidy Controls," *Economic Development Quarterly* 16; 2 (May 2002): 115–126; Alan H. Peters, "Clawbacks and the Administration of Economic Development Policy in the Midwest," *Economic Development Quarterly* 7 (1993).

112. Rachel Weber, "Do Better Contracts Make Better Economic Development?" *Journal of the American Planning Association* 68 (Winter 2002): 43–56.

113. McGovern, *The Politics of Downtown Development*.

114. Levine, p. 30.

115. Much of the following section on alternative approaches to neighborhood economic development is derived from David L. Imbroscio, *Reconstructing City Politics: Alternative Economic Development and Urban Regimes* (Thousand Oaks, Calif.: Sage Publications, 1997).

116. Eisinger, p. 9.

117. Ibid., see chapters 10–12.

118. Imbroscio, pp. 51–9.

119. Imbroscio, pp. 141–4.

120. David Osborne and Ted Gaebler, *Reinventing Government* (Reading, Mass.: Addison-Wesley, 1992).

121. Imbroscio, p. 152.

122. Imbroscio, pp. 152–3.

123. Pierre Clavel, *The Progressive City: Planning and Participation, 1969–1984* (New Brunswick, N.J.: Rutgers University Press, 1986); Gunn and Gunn, *Reclaiming Capital*.

124. Imbroscio, pp. 97–100.

125. Sara E. Stoutland, "Community Development Corporations: Mission, Strategy, and Accomplishments," in *Urban Problems and Community Development*, eds. Ronald F. Ferguson and William T. Dickens (Washington, D.C.: Brookings Institution Press, 1999); Herbert J. Rubin, *Renewing Hope within Neighborhoods of Despair: The Community-Based Development Model* (Albany, N.Y.: State University of New York Press, 2000).

126. Imbroscio, pp. 100–4. See also William T. Dickens, "Rebuilding Urban Labor Markets: What Community Development Can Accomplish," in Ferguson and Dickens, *Urban Problems and Community Development.*

127. Margaret Weir, "Power, Money, and Politics in Community Development," in *Urban Problems and Community Development.* See also Benjamin Marquez, "Mexican-American Community Development Corporations and the Limits of Directed Capitalism," *Economic Development Quarterly* 7 (1993): 287–295.

128. Rubin, p. 15.

129. W. Dennis Keating, Norman Krumholz, and Philip Star, eds., *Revitalizing Urban Neighborhoods* (Lawrence, Kans.: University Press of Kansas, 1996).

130. Susan E. Clarke and Gary L. Gaile, *The Work of Cities* (Minneapolis: University of Minnesota Press, 1998).

131. Joel Rast, *Remaking Chicago: The Political Origins of Urban Industrial Change* (DeKalb, Ill.: Northern Illinois University Press, 1999), pp. 15–17.

Chapter 4

1. Department of Housing and Urban Development, *The Widening Gap: New Findings on Housing Affordability in America,* 1999, available at http://www.housingall.com/STEPUP/AffabilityGap.htm.

2. Christopher Jencks, "Housing the Homeless," *New York Review of Books,* May 12, 1994, p. 44.

3. Henry George, *Progress and Poverty* (New York: Appleton and Co., 1879).

4. Michael A. Pagano and Ann O'M. Bowman, "Vacant Land in Cities: An Urban Resource," Brookings Institution report, January 2001, available at http://www.brook.edu/dybdoc root/es/urban/pagano/paganofinal.pdf.

5. William A. Fischel, *The Homevoter Hypothesis: How Home Values Influence Local Government Taxation, School Finance, and Land Use* (Cambridge, Mass.: Harvard University Press, 2001).

6. James Rosenbaum and Leonard Rubinowitz, *Crossing the Class and Color Lines: From Public Housing to White Suburbia* (Chicago: University of Chicago Press, 2000).

7. Joint Center for Housing Studies at Harvard University, *The State of the Nation's Housing 2000* (2000), p. 36.

8. Joint Center for Housing Studies, pp. 16, 17, 34.

9. Howard Husock, *Repairing the Ladder: Toward a New Housing Policy Paradigm,* Reason Foundation Policy Study, No. 207, July 1996.

10. As Fred Block points out in *Postindustrial Possibilities: A Critique of Economic Discourse* (Berkeley: University of California Press, 1990), the whole concept of the "market" is problematic. Classical economic theory posits that buyers and sellers constantly respond to market signals. But Block argues that the behavior of economic actors is "embedded" in a variety of social relations. Long-term relationships between buyers and sellers, for example, cannot be constantly disturbed by fluctuations in price, or else the whole market will be thrown into chaos. Markets depend, then, on non-market-like behavior.

11. Delores Hayden, *Redesigning the American Dream, The Future of Housing, Work, and American Life* (New York: W.W. Norton, 1984), p. 33.

12. Charles Bertsch, "Secrets of the X-Files," *Bad Subjects* 28 (October 1996).

13. Hayden, *Redesigning the American Dream.* p. 149.

14. A University of Michigan study found that women do twenty-seven hours of housework a week and men do sixteen hours a week. See Thomas Juster, Hiromi Ono, and Frank Stafford, "Time Use: Diary and Direct Reports," paper presented at the annual meetings of the Sloan Centers for Work and Family, San Francisco, March, 2000.

15. See Herbert Gans, *The Urban Villagers: Group and Class in the Life of Italian-Americans* (New York: Free Press, 1990).

16. Nathan Gorenstein, "Building Union Pay Far Higher in City than Suburbs," *Philadelphia Inquirer,* August 12, 2001.

17. Michael D. Sorkin, "Cities and Suburbs: A Harvard Magazine Roundtable," *Harvard,* January-February 2000, available at http://www.harvard-magazine.com/issues/jf00/citysuburb. html.

18. Robert Kuttner, *Revolt of the Haves: Tax Revolts and Hard Times* (New York: Simon and Schuster, 1980).
19. See National Multi Housing Council, "Apartment Construction in Cities and Suburbs: Multifamily Picks Up Market Share," available at http://www.nmhc.org/Content/Serve Content.cfm?ContentItemID=553.
20. "Transcript: Housing Secretary Cuomo Remarks in Shanghai," available at http://usinfo. state.gov/regional/ea/uschina/cuomo2.htm.
21. The following discussion of shelter poverty comes from Michael Stone, "Housing Affordability: One-Third of a Nation Shelter-Poor," in Rachel Bratt, Chester Hartman, and Michael Stone, eds., *Housing: Foundation for a New Social Agenda* (Temple University Press, forthcoming).
22. Lance Freeman and Frank Braconi, "Gentrification and Diaplacement," *The Urban Prospect*, Citizens Housing and Planning Council, January/February 2002, available at http://www.chpcny.org/pubs/UP2002–1.pdf.
23. John I. Gilderbloom and Richard P. Appelbaum, *Rethinking Rental Housing* (Philadelphia, Pa.: Temple University Press, 1988), p. 93.
24. Charles Mathias, Jr., and Marion Morris, "Fair Housing Legislation: Not an Easy Hoe to Row," *Cityscape* 4 (1999): 27.
25. William J. Collins and Robert A. Margo, "Race and Home-Ownership, 1900–1990, available at http://www.eh.net/Clio/Conferences/ASSA/Jan_00/margo.shtml.
26. Kantor, p. 107.
27. Dennis Judd and Todd Swanstrom, *City Politics: Private Power and Public Policy* (New York: HarperCollins, 1994), p. 227.
28. See Charles C. Euchner, "Rebuilding the City, One Building at a Time," February 7, 2000, http://www.curp.neu.edu, Digest section.
29. Charles C. Euchner, with Elizabeth G. Frieze, "Getting Home: Overcoming Barriers to Housing in Greater Boston," Rappaport Institute for Greater Boston and Pioneer Institute for Public Policy, January 2003, available at http://www.ksg.harvard.edu/rappaport/downloads/ gettinghome.pdf.
30. Robert W. Poole, Jr., *Cutting Back City Hall* (New York: Universe Books, 1981), p. 144
31. Nathan Gorenstein, "Building-Union Pay Far Higher in City Than in Suburbs."
32. Eric J. Toder, "The Changing Composition of Tax Incentives: 1980–99," Urban Institute report, March 1999, available at http://www.urban.org/tax/austin/austin_toder.html.
33. Quoted in Cushing Dolbeare, "How the Income Tax System Subsidizes Housing for the Affluent," in Bratt et al., *Critical Perspectives on Housing*, p. 265.
34. "Mortgage Deduction Blocks Tax Reform," *Orange County Times-Herald Record*, March 30, 1998.
35. See "Housing Choice Voucher Program Fact Sheet (Section 8) on the site of the U.S. Department of Housing and Urban Development (http://www.hud.gov/about/Section8.cfm).
36. Howard Husock, "Let's End Housing Vouchers," *City Journal*, Autumn 2000, available at http://www.city-journal.org/html/10_4_lets_end_housing.html.
37. Ibid.
38. The system broke down in the 1970s when high rates of inflation and the development of other investment opportunities undermined the attractiveness of simple savings accounts as investments. S&Ls were squeezed by volatile interest rates, which reached a high of 21.5 percent in 1981. S&Ls had to offer customers high savings rates and at the same time they had to carry a generation of low-interest loans. The S&Ls suffered a period of deep decline: "[D]epositers withdrew nearly $110 billion from savings accounts in 1974 and the same amount in 1975, nearly matching new money coming in, so that thrifts had virtually no money to lend for mortgages." In 1972, S&Ls in the U.S. had a total net worth of $16.7 billion. Eight years later, they had a negative net worth of $175 billion. Alexander Garvin, *The American City: What Works, What Doesn't.* (New York: McGraw Hill, 1996), p. 157. The industry sought relief. In 1980 and 1982, Congress passed legislation that guaranteed federal deposits up to $100,000, allowed an even lower level of reserves (3 percent), and, most important, allowed S&Ls to make loans for a wide range of investments. Ownership of S&Ls, once dominated by local business people, fell under the sway of larger institutions without local ties. With little federal oversight, these entrepreneurs engaged in reckless activity that would cost the nation hundreds of billions of dollars. Rogue S&L operators such as Charles

Keating and James McDougall made loans to their friends and to sham corporations for sham projects. Even when they were not outright dishonest, they were often reckless. Caught up in the go-go economy of the 1980s, S&Ls invested in ski chalets and suburban condos that could not be sustained by the marketplace. When S&Ls could no longer pay their depositors or their bills, they crashed. The federal government was forced to pick up the pieces. By the time all the losses are settled, experts expect the S&L crisis to cost the U.S. government upwards of $500 billion. That makes it the biggest financial scandal in the nation's history.

39. Jean Cummings and Denise DiPasquale, *A Primer on the Secondary Mortgage Market,* (Boston: City Research Corporation, 1997), p. 10.

40. Ibid., p. 10.

41. "American Dream May Have Nightmarish Effects," *American Banker.com,* June 24, 1999.

42. William Tucker, "How Rent Control Drives Out Affordable Housing," *Policy Analysis* 274 (May 21, 1997).

43. Denton Marks, "The Effects of Partial-Coverage Rent Control on the Price and Quantity of Rental Housing," *Journal of Urban Economics* 16 (1984): pp. 360–369.

44. Edward Glaeser and Erzo F.P. Luttner, "The Misallocation of Housing Under Rent Control," National Bureau of Economic Research, Working Paper No. 6220, October 1997.

45. Rolfe Goetze, *Rent Control: Affordable Housing for the Privileged, Not the Poor. A Study of the Impact of Rent Control in Cambridge* (Cambridge, Mass.: GeoData Analysis, 1994).

46. Center for Community Change, "The Public Housing Initiative," available at http://www. communitychange.org/ph.htm.

47. Judd and Swanstrom, *City Politics,* p. 148.

48. Abt Associates, "Capital Needs of The Public Housing Stock in 1998: Formula Capital Study," January 2000, available at http://www.abtassoc.com/reports/20008744720691.pdf

49. Rachel G. Bratt, "Public Housing: The Controversy and Contribution," in Rachel G. Bratt, Chester Hartman, and Ann Myerson, eds., *Critical Perspectives on Housing* (Philadelphia, Penn.: Temple University Press, 1986), p. 344.

50. Quoted in J. Anthony Lukas, *Common Ground: A Turbulent Decade in the Lives of Three American Families* (New York: Random House, 1986), p. 189.

51. Judd and Swanstrom, *City Politics,* p. 147.

52. Judd and Swanstrom, *City Politics,* p. 146.

53. William Julius Wilson, *The Truly Disadvantaged: The Inner City, the Underclass, and Public Policy* (Chicago: University of Chicago Press, 1987), pp. 143–44.

54. Ron Scherer, "Public Housing Moves toward Rich, Poor Together," *The Christian Science Monitor,* February 8, 1999.

55. Paul S. Grogan and Tony Proscio, *Comeback Cities: A Blueprint for Urban Neighborhood Revival* (Boulder, Colo.: Westview Press, 1999), p. 70.

56. Grogan and Prosci, p. 88.

57. Grogan and Prosci, p. 90.

58. Grogan and Prosci, p. 120.

59. William Tucker, *The Excluded Americans: Homelessness and Housing Policies* (Washington, D.C.: Regnery Gateway, 1989).

60. The discussion in the following four paragraphs relies on Christopher Jencks, "Housing the Homeless," *New York Review of Books,* May 12, 1994.

61. See Richard D. Lyons, "How Release of Mental Patients Began," *New York Times,* October 30, 1984.

62. "44 Percent of Homeless Have Jobs, Officials Find," *Dallas Morning News,* December 21, 1999.

63. Mary Otto, "The Working Homeless Is a Growing Reality," *Miami Herald,* December 26, 1999.

64. Thomas Morgan, "Fear and Dependency Jostle in Shelters," *New York Times,* November 4, 1991.

65. Jencks, "Housing the Homeless," p. 44.

66. Richard Moe and Carter Wilkie, *Changing Places: Rebuilding Community in the Age of Sprawl* (New York: Henry Holt, 1997), p. 129.

67. Ibid., p. 133.

Chapter 5

1. Bruce Wilshire, *The Moral Collapse of the University: Professionalism, Purity, and Alienation* (Albany, N.Y.: SUNY Press, 1990), ch. 2.

2. E. D. Hirsch, "Neglecting the Early Grades," in Paul E. Peterson, ed., *Our Schools and Our Future . . . Are We Still At Risk?* (Stanford, Calif.: Hoover Institution Press, 2000). see E. D. Hirsch, *Cultural Literacy* (Boston: Houghton Mifflin, 1987). Since the success of this book, Hirsch has written and edited a number of works that attempt to identify the elements of a strong cultural literacy for Americans at different stages of learning.

3. Diana Jean Schemo, "Worldwide Survey Finds U.S. Students Are Not Keeping Up," *New York Times*, December 6, 2000, p. A1. Tests of 180,000 students in the eighth grade in thirty-eight nations in 1999 revealed that American students performed at a lower level than students in Singapore, Taiwan, Russia, Canada, Hungary, the Netherlands, and Australia; they performed better than students in Iran, Jordan, Chile, Indonesia, Macedonia, and South Africa.

4. Harold W. Stevenson and James W. Stigler, *The Learning Gap: Why Our Schools Are Failing and What We Can Learn from Japanese and Chinese Education* (New York: Summit Books, 1992), p. 55.

5. It should be noted that not all education policy analysts view the condition of public schools in such dire terms. C.f. Richard Rothstein, *The Way We Were? Debunking the Myth of America's Declining Schools* (New York: Century Foundation, 1998); David C. Berliner and Bruce J. Biddle, *The Manufactured Crisis: Myths, Fraud, and the Attack on America's Public Schools* (Reading, Mass.: Addison-Wesley Publishing, 1995); Gerald W. Bracey, "Why Can't They Be Like We Were?" *Phi Delta Kappan* 73 (October 1991); Iris C. Rotberg, "I Never Promised You First Place," *Phi Delta Kappan* 72 (December 1990).

6. *The State of the Cities: 1999*, U.S. Department of Housing and Urban Development (Washington, D.C.: Government Printing Office, 1999), p. 18; see also Jean Anyon, *Ghetto Schooling: A Political Economy of Urban Educational Reform* (New York: Teachers College Press, 1997).

7. Linda Darling-Hammond and Eileen Sclan, "Who Teaches and Why: Dilemmas of Building a Profession for Twenty-First Century Schools," in *Handbook of Research on Teacher Education*, 2nd ed., eds. John Sikula, Thomas Buttery, and Edith Guyton (New York: Macmillan, 1996), cited in Jean Anyon, *Ghetto Schooling*, p. 7.

8. Anyon, *Ghetto Schooling*, p. 7.

9. Council of the Great City Schools, "Beating the Odds II: A City-by-City Analysis of Student Performance and Achievement Gaps on State Assessments" (June 2002), available at http://www.cgcs.org/reports/beat_the_oddsII.html.

10. John Portz, Lana Stein, and Robin R. Jones, *City Schools and City Politics: Institutions and Leadership in Pittsburgh, Boston, and St. Louis* (Lawrence, Kans.: University Press of Kansas, 1999), p. 5.

11. Anyon, *Ghetto Schooling*, p. 7.

12. Jennifer L. Hochschild, *Facing Up to the American Dream: Race, Class, and the Soul of the Nation* (Princeton, N.J.: Princeton University Press, 1995).

13. Richard M. Battistoni, *Public Schooling and the Education of Democratic Citizens* (Jackson, Miss.: University of Mississippi Press, 1985).

14. Lawrence Cremin, *American Education: The Colonial Experience, 1607–1783* (New York: Harper & Row, 1970).

15. Martin Carnoy and Henry M. Levin, *Schooling and Work in the Democratic State* (Stanford, Calif.: Stanford University Press, 1985).

16. Carl F. Kaestle, *Pillars of the Republic: Common Schools and American Society, 1780–1860* (New York: Hill and Wang, 1983).

17. Quoted in David L. Angus, "Common School Politics in a Frontier City: Detroit, 1836–1842," in *Schools in Cities: Consensus and Conflict in American Educational History*, eds. Ronald K. Goodenow and Diane Ravitch (New York: Holmes & Meier, 1983).

18. To illustrate, the percentage of students in private schools in New York City declined from 62 percent in 1829 to 18 percent in 1850 and in Salem, Massachusetts, from 58 percent in 1827 to 24 percent in 1846. Kaestle, p. 116, 220–222.

19. C.f. Samuel Bowles and Herbert Gintis, *Schooling in Capitalist America: Educational Reform and the Contradictions of Economic Life* (New York: Basic Books, Inc., 1976).

20. Michael Katz, "Education and Inequality: An Historical Perspective," in David J. Roth and Santon Wheeler, eds., *Social History and Social Policy* (New York: Academic Press, 1981), p. 57.

21. Ira Katznelson and Margaret Weir, *Schooling for All: Class, Race, and the Decline of the Democratic Ideal* (New York: Basic Books, 1985).

22. David B. Tyack, *The One Best System: A History of American Urban Education* (Cambridge, Mass. Harvard University Press, 1974).

23. For example, in 1991, after decades of controversy, Boston gave the mayor power to appoint its school committee. The previous elected school committee had been riven by factional politics of race, class, and culture, and committee members used their seats as stepping stones to higher office. New York's Mayor Michael Bloomberg won control of the city's board of education in 2002.

24. Carnoy, p. 94.

25. Jon C. Teaford, *The Unheralded Triumph: City Government in America, 1870–1900* (Baltimore, Md.: Johns Hopkins University Press, 1984), p. 263.

26. James B. Conant, *The American High School Today: A First Report to Interested Citizens* (New York: McGraw-Hill, 1959).

27. Anna Quindlen, "The Problem of the Megaschool," *Newsweek*, March 26, 2001, p. 68.

28. Michael Rutter et al., *Fifteen Thousand Hours: Secondary Schools and Their Effects on Children* (Cambridge, Mass.: Harvard University Press, 1979).

29. Patrick Welsh, *Tales Out of School: A Teacher's Candid Account from the Front Line of the American High School Today* (New York: Penguin, 1986), p. 66.

30. Thomas Toch, *In the Name of Excellence: The Struggle to Reform the Nation's Schools, Why It's Failing, and What Should Be Done.* (New York: Oxford University Press, 1991), p. 121.

31. Carnoy, p. 96.

32. Ann Bastian et al., *Choosing Equality: The Case for Democratic Schooling* (Philadelphia, Penn.: Temple University Press, 1986), ch. 3.

33. Mark V. Tushnet, *The NAACP's Legal Strategy against Segregated Education, 1925–1950* (Chapel Hill, N.C.: University of North Carolina Press, 1987); Richard Kluger, *Simple Justice: The History of Brown v. Board of Education and Black America's Struggle for Equality* (New York: Vintage Books, 1975).

34. Gary Orfield, "Turning Back to Segregation," in *Dismantling Desegregation: The Quiet Reversal of Brown v. Board of Education*, eds. Gary Orfield, Susan E. Eaton, and the Harvard Project on School Desegregation (New York: The New Press, 1996), pp. 7–8.

35. 391 U.S. 430 at 437–8.

36. 402 U.S. 1 (1971).

37. *Keyes v. School District No. 1, Denver,* 93 S.Ct. 2686 (1973). More specifically, the Supreme Court ruled that once it had been demonstrated that a school district had deliberately acted to promote racial segregation "in a meaningful portion of a school system" through, for example, new school sitings or attendance zone decisions, the burden of proof switches to the school district to show it is not responsible for all aspects of racial segregation throughout the entire school system. Ibid., at 2697.

38. J. Anthony Lukas, *Common Ground: A Turbulent Decade in the Lives of Three American Families* (New York: Alfred A. Knopf, 1985).

39. C.f. Leslie Inniss, "School Desegregation: Too High a Price?" *Social Policy* (Winter 1993): 6–16. Although Inniss participated in one of the earliest desegregation cases in the South, the trauma she experienced was representative of that endured by thousands of other students of color who later integrated all-white schools.

40. David J. Armor, *Forced Justice: School Desegregation and the Law* (New York: Oxford University Press, 1995).

41. Dennis R. Judd and Todd Swanstrom, *City Politics: Private Power and Public Policy* (New York: HarperCollins, 1994), pp. 200–7; W. Dennis Keating, *The Suburban Racial Dilemma: Housing and Neighborhoods* (Philadelphia: Temple University Press, 1994).

42. *Milliken* 418 U.S. 717 (1974) marked the first time civil rights organizations had suffered a defeat in a school desegregation case before the Supreme Court since *Brown* two decades earlier. The most likely explanation for the Court's change of direction was a transformation in the Court's personnel during the early 1970s. President Richard Nixon, an avowed opponent of mandatory busing, had succeeded in getting four of his conservative nominees appointed to the Court, all of whom voted with the 5-to-4 majority in *Milliken*.

43. Mandatory interdistrict busing became unlikely in light of *Milliken*, but not impossible. The U.S. Justice Department subsequently found enough evidence of prior intentional discrimination to file cases seeking interdistrict busing remedies in Louisville, Indianapolis, and Wilmington.

44. Orfield, "Turning Back to Segregation," p. 13.

45. C.f. Frye Gaillard, *The Dream Long Deferred* (Chapel Hill, N.C.: University of North Carolina Press, 1988).

46. Alison Morantz, "Desegregation at Risk: Threat and Reaffirmation in Charlotte," in *Dismantling Desegregation*, eds. Orfield, Eaton, and the Harvard Project.

47. Christine H. Rossell, *The Carrot or the Stick for Desegregation Policy* (Philadelphia, Penn.: Temple University Press, 1990).

48. Alison Morantz, "Money and Choice in Kansas City: Major Investments with Modest Returns," in *Dismantling Desegregation*, eds. Orfield, Eaton, and the Harvard Project.

49. Dirk Johnson, " 'F' for Kansas City Schools Adds to the District's Woes," *New York Times*, May 3, 2000, p. A16.

50. Susan E. Eaton, Joseph Feldman, and Edward Kirby, "Still Separate, Still Unequal: The Limits of *Milliken II's* Monetary Compensation to Segregated Schools," in *Dismantling Desegregation*, eds. Orfield, Eaton, and the Harvard Project.

51. Richard Fossey, "Desegregation Is Not Enough: Facing the Truth about Urban Schools," in *Race, the Courts, and Equal Education: The Limits of the Law*, ed. Richard Fossey (New York: AMS Press, 1998), p. 8.

52. Orfield, "Turning Back to Segregation," p. 18.

53. Under *Board of Education of Oklahoma v. Dowell*, 498 U.S. 237 (1991) and *Freeman v. Pitts* 503 U.S. 467 (1992), once "unitary status" has been attained, any official actions that result in greater racial segregation, such as the adoption of neighborhood-based school assignments, are presumed innocent unless it can be shown that such actions were motivated by intentional racial discrimination. Since such intent is always difficult to prove, the effect of these Supreme Court decisions is to pave the way toward widespread resegregation of public schools that had succeeded in producing significant racial balance.

54. Sue Anne Pressley, "Charlotte Schools Are Scrambling," *Washington Post*, November 8, 1999, p. A03.

55. Bastian et al., *Choosing Equality*, p. 43.

56. Julie Roy Jeffrey, *Education for Children of the Poor: A Study of the Origins and Implementation of the Elementary and Secondary Education Act of 1965* (Columbus, Ohio: Ohio State University Press, 1978), p. 12.

57. Janet Currie and Duncan Thomas, "School Quality and the Long-Term Effects of Head Start," Working Paper 6362, National Bureau of Economic Research, January 1998.

58. Geoffrey D. Borman and Jerome V. D'Agostino, "Title I and Student Achievement: A Meta-Analysis of Federal Evaluation Results," *Educational Evaluation and Policy Analysis* 18 (1996), p. 25.

59. C.f. Diane Ravitch, *Left Back: A Century of Failed School Reforms* (New York: Simon & Schuster, 2000).

60. Borman and D'Agostino, "Title I," p. 25.

61. In 1902, property taxes provided 89 percent of all local revenues, and that figure remained relatively stable for decades. In 1978, the year that California passed a statewide limit on the levy, property taxes still accounted for 80 percent of local revenues.

62. Eric A. Hanushek, "The Impact of Differential Expenditures on School Performance," *Educational Researcher* 18; 4 (1989): 47. See also Eric A. Hanushek, "The Economics of Schooling: Production and Efficiency in Public Schools," *Journal of Economic Literature* 24 (Sept. 1986): 1141–77; John E. Chubb and Eric A. Hanushek, "Reforming Education Reform," in *Setting National Priorities: Policy for the Nineties*, ed. Henry J. Aaron (Washington, D.C.: Brookings Institute, 1990), pp. 213–48.

63. Richard Murname, "Interpreting the Evidence on Does Money Matter?" *Harvard Journal on Legislation* 28 (1991): 457–464; Ronald F. Ferguson and Helen F. Ladd, "How and Why Money Matters: An Analysis of Alabama Schools," in *Holding Schools Accountable: Performance-Based Reform in Education*, ed. Helen F. Ladd (Washington, D.C.: Brookings Institute, 1996); Ken Ellinger, David E. Wright III, and Michael W. Hirlinger, "Brains for the Bucks? School Revenue and Student Achievement in Oklahoma," *Social Science Journal* 32; 3 (1995): 299–308.

64. Jonathan Kozol, *Savage Inequalities: Children in America's Schools* (New York: HarperCollins Publishers, 1992), pp. 138–140.

65. Ibid., pp. 100, 145.

66. Arthur Wise, *Rich Schools, Poor Schools: The Promise of Equal Educational Opportunity* (Chicago: University of Chicago Press, 1968); Kirk Vandersall, "Post-*Brown* School Finance Reform," in *Strategies for School Equity: Creating Productive Schools in a Just Society*, ed. Marilyn J. Gittell (New Haven, Conn.: Yale University Press, 1998), p. 14.

67. Vandersall, "Post-Brown," pp. 13–4.
68. Minorini and Sugarman, p. 43.
69. Ibid., pp. 53–4.
70. Clarence Y. H. Lo, *Small Property Versus Big Government: Social Origins of the Property Tax Revolt* (Berkeley: University of California Press, 1990).
71. Paul A. Minorini and Stephen D. Sugarman, "Educational Adequacy and the Courts: The Promise and Problems of Moving to a New Paradigm," in Janet S. Hansen and Rosemary Chalk, editors, *Education and Adequacy Issues in Education Finance: Issues and Perspectives* (Washington, D.C.: National Academy Press, 1999), pp. 34–71.
72. Diane Ravitch, *National Standards in American Education: A Citizen's Guide* (Washington, D.C.: The Brookings Institution, 1995), p. 64. See also Annegret Harnischfeger and David E. Wiley, *Achievement Test Score Decline: Do We Need to Worry?* (Chicago: CEMREL, 1975).
73. For example, a 40-point gap between white and black seventeen-year-old students in mathematics declined to 26 points in 1992, while a 53-point difference between the same groups in reading was reduced to 37 points. Similar differentials were reported for white and Latino students. Ravitch, *National Standards*, p. 72.
74. Ibid., pp. 84–5.
75. National Commission on Excellence in Education, *A Nation at Risk: The Imperative for Educational Reform* (Washington, D.C.: 1983), p. 5.
76. Ravitch, *National Standards*, pp. 50–1, 67–8.
77. John E. Chubb and Terry M. Moe, *Politics, Markets, and America's Schools* (Washington, D.C.: Brookings Institution, 1990).
78. Diane Ravitch, *The Schools We Deserve: Reflections on the Educational Crises of Our Times* (New York: Basic Books, 1985).
79. Marc S. Tucker and Judy B. Codding, *Standards for Our Schools* (San Francisco: Jossey-Bass, 1998).
80. Donald B. Gratz, "High Standards for Whom?" *Phi Delta Kappan* (May 2000): 685–6.
81. Diane Ravitch, *National Standards in American Education*.
82. Quoted in Richard W. Clark and Patricia A. Wasley, "Renewing Schools and Smarter Kids: Promises for Democracy," *Phi Delta Kappan* (April 1999): 592; Nel Noddings, "Renewing Democracy in Schools," *Phi Delta Kappan* (April 1999).
83. Gratz, "High Standards," p. 686; Linda M. McNeil, *Contradictions of School Reform: Educational Costs of Standardized Testing* (New York: Routledge, 2000).
84. Louann A. Bierlein, *Controversial Issues in Educational Policy* (Newbury Park, Calif.: Sage Publications, 1993), p. 77.
85. C.f. Steven Greenhouse, "City and Teachers Remain Far Apart on a New Contract," *New York Times*, November 13, 2000, p. A1.
86. Toch, pp. 156–7.
87. The National Center for Education Information tracks alternative teacher preparation and certification strategies in the states. The organization's Internet site (www.ncei.com) regularly updates information about how states and districts respond to teacher shortages.
88. Kate Walsh, "Positive Spin," *Education Next*, Spring 2002, p. 84.
89. James W. Fraser, "A Tenuous Hold," *Education Next*, Spring 2002, p. 20.
90. Bierlein, p. 78.
91. Maria Newman, "New Jersey Finds No Simple Solutions in School Takeovers," *New York Times*, March 21, 1999, p. 37.
92. Ravitch, *National Standards in American Education*, pp. 94–5.
93. Ibid., pp. 75, 97.
94. David J. Kearns and James Harvey, *A Legacy of Learning: Your Stake in Standards and New Kinds of Public Schools* (Washington, D.C.: Brookings Institution Press, 2000), p. 28. Another recent study by the Brookings Institution reached similar conclusions regarding the lack of student progress on reading and math tests. See Jodi Wilgoren, "Students Show Few Gains in Reading Skills," *New York Times*, September 6, 2000, p. A16.
95. Ibid., p. 34.
96. Kate Zernicke, "Gap Widens Again on Tests Given to Blacks and Whites," *New York Times*, August 25, 2000, p. A14.
97. Bierlein, p. 41; Richard D. Kahlenberg, *All Together Now: Creating Middle-Class Schools through Public School Choice* (Washington, D.C.: Brookings Institution Press, 2001).

98. Terry M. Moe, "Teachers Unions and the Public Schools," *A Primer on America's Schools*, ed. Terry M. Moe (Stanford, Calif.: Hoover Institution Press, 2001).

99. Bierlein, p. 43.

100. Chubb and Moe, *Politics, Markets, and America's Schools*.

101. Gerald Grant, *The World We Created at Hamilton High* (Cambridge, Mass.: Harvard University Press, 1988), p. 221.

102. "Financing Elementary and Secondary Education in the States: 1997–98," National Center for Education Statistics: Research and Development Report (Washington, D.C.: U.S. Department of Education, 2002), p. 49.

103. Grant, p. 151.

104. Chubb and Moe, pp. 31–2.

105. Milton Friedman, "The Role of Government in Education" in *Economics and the Public Interest*, ed. R. A. Solo (New Brunswick, N.J.: Rutgers University Press, 1955); see also Milton Friedman, *Capitalism and Freedom* (Chicago: University of Chicago Press, 1962).

106. The notion of giving parents broader choices in selecting public schools for their children gained legitimacy among many urban residents in the 1970s with the rise of alternative and magnet schools to advance social goals such as school desegregation. Robert C. Bulman and David L. Kirp, "The Shifting Politics of School Choice," in *School Choice and Social Controversy: Politics, Policy, and Law*, eds. Stephen D. Sugarman and Frank R. Kemerer (Washington, D.C.: Brookings Institution Press, 1999), p. 39.

107. Paul Taylor, "Milwaukee's Controversial Private School Choice Plan Off to Shaky Start," *Washington Post*, May 25, 1991, p. A3; Jill Leovy, "School Voucher Program Teaches Hard Lesson," *Los Angeles Times*, October 9, 2000, p. A1, available at http://www.schoolchoiceinfo.org/what/milwaukee.jsp.

108. http://www.schoolchoiceinfo.org/what/cleveland.jsp; Mike Clary, "Florida to Be First to Launch Statewide School Vouchers," *Los Angeles Times*, April 29, 1999, p. A1.

109. *Zelman v. Simmons-Harris*, 534 U.S. 1111 (2002).

110. Terry M. Moe, *Schools, Vouchers, and the American Public* (Washington, D.C.: Brookings Institution Press, 2001), see Chapter 2: "Satisfaction with Public Schools." Also, in November 2000, citizens initiatives to establish taxpayer-supported voucher programs in California and Michigan were resoundingly defeated by 70 percent of the voters in each state. The California initiative would have expanded the availability of vouchers far beyond any existing voucher program by providing $4,000 each to all of California's 6.6 million students in kindergarten through twelfth grade wishing to attend a private school. Such a universal voucher program was widely criticized as a burden on the state treasury and a threat to the public schools. Aaron Zitner, "Decision 2000: Vouchers Lose as Voters Decide Ballot Measures," *Los Angeles Times*, November 8, 2000, p. A22.

111. Laurie Goodstein, "The Nation: In States, Hurdles Loom," *New York Times*, June 30, 2002, section 4, p. 3; Anemona Hartocollis, "Best Chances for Vouchers Lie in the Cities," *New York Times*, June 29, 2002, p. B1; Michael Leo Owens, "Why Blacks Support Vouchers," *New York Times*, February 26, 2002, p. A25.

112. John F. Witte, *The Market Approach to Education: An Analysis of America's First Voucher Program* (Princeton, N.J.: Princeton University Press, 2000), p. 149.

113. Ibid., p. 150.

114. William G. Howell, Patrick J. Wolf, Paul E. Peterson, and David E. Campbell, "Effects of School Vouchers on Student Test Scores," in *Charters, Vouchers and Public Education*, Paul E. Peterson and David E. Campbell, eds. (Washington, D.C.: Brookings Institution Press, 2001); Jay P. Greene, "The Surprising Consensus on School Choice," *Public Interest* (Summer 2001). But see Martin Carnoy, *School Vouchers: Examining the Evidence* (Washington, D.C.: Economic Policy Institute, 2001).

115. Brian P. Gill et al., *Rhetoric Versus Reality: What We Know and What We Need to Know about Vouchers and Charter Schools* (Santa Monica, Calif.: RAND, 2001), p. 114.

116. Jeffrey R. Henig, "School Choice Outcomes" in *School Choice and Social Controversy: Politics, Policy, and Law* (Washington, D.C.: Brookings Institution Press, 1999), pp. 74–5. Furthermore, anecdotal evidence suggests that some parents who are initially frustrated by an unsuccessful lottery outcome still find ways to enroll their children in a desired school by tapping "connections" that they may have with school personnel. It is difficult to assess how pervasive this problem is, since it has attracted little if any scholarly attention, but as a

policy matter, poorly administered lottery systems have important implications for the question of who stands to benefit from school choice programs.

117. Amy Stuart Wells, "African-American Students' Views of School Choice," in *Who Chooses? Who Loses? Culture, Institutions, and the Unequal Effects of School Choice*, eds. Bruce Fuller and Richard F. Elmore (New York: Teachers College Press, 1996), pp. 28–31.

118. Amy Wells et al., "Charter Schools as Postmodern Paradox: Rethinking Social Stratification in an Age of Deregulated School Choice," *Harvard Educational Review* 69 (Summer 1999): 198.

119. Gill et al., p. 156.

120. Ibid., p. 183.

121. Jodi Wilgoren, "Young Blacks Turn to School Vouchers as Civil Rights Issue," *New York Times*, October 9, 2000, p. A1.

122. Chester E. Finn, Jr., Bruno V. Manno, and Gregg Vanourek, *Charter Schools in Action: Renewing Public Education* (Princeton, N.J.: Princeton University Press, 2000), p. 15.

123. "Charter Schools to Receive Aid; Clinton Lauds Idea, Grants $95 Million," *Washington Post*, August 29, 1999, p. A12.

124. Ray Budde, "Education by Charter," *Phi Delta Kappan* 70 (March 1989); *The State of Charter Schools, 2000: National Study of Charter Schools*, U.S. Department of Education (Washington, D.C.: U.S. Government Printing Office, 2000), pp. 10–11, 18; *National Charter School Directory, 2001–2002*, 7th ed., Center for Education Reform, 2002.

125. Finn et al., pp. 152, 157.

126. Ibid., p. 102.

127. See *The State of Charter Schools, 2000*, pp. 44–5, for a summary of implementation problems, including a lack of start-up funds, inadequate planning time, and hiring staff during a period of teacher shortages.

128. April Gresham et al., "Desert Bloom: Arizona's Free Market in Education," *Phi Delta Kappan* (June 2000), p. 756.

129. Robert Maranto, Scott Milliman, Frederick Hess, April Gresham, "In Lieu of Conclusions: Tentative Lessons from a Contested Frontier," in *School Choice in the Real World: Lessons from Arizona's Charter Schools*, eds. Robert Maranto, Scott Milliman, Frederick Hess, and April Gresham (Boulder, Colo.: Westview Press, 1999), pp. 243–4.

130. Finn et al., p. 155.

131. Maranto et al., p. 242.

132. Even with unexpectedly lax bureaucratic monitoring, in Arizona nineteen of 272 charter schools had been shut down by April 1999 either because of inadequate enrollments or revocation of the charter. This contrasts with the fact that no district schools in Arizona have been closed because of poor performance. Ibid.

133. Gary Miron and Christopher Nelson, *Student Academic Achievement in Charter Schools: What We Know and Why We Know So Little*, Occasional Paper No. 41, National Center for the Study of Privatization in Education, Teachers College, Columbia University, 2001; Gresham et al., p. 756.

134. Wells et al., "Charter Schools," pp. 174–5, 195; Finn et al., p. 157; and Maranto et al., pp. 244–5.

135. Wells et al., "Charter Schools," pp. 194, 175; Frank Brown, "North Carolina's Charter School Law: Flexibility versus Accountability," *Education and Urban Society* 31; 4 (August 1999): 483; see also Wong and Shen, p. 26.

136. Robert Maranto and April Gresham, "The Wild West of Education Reform: Arizona Charter Schools," in *School Choice in the Real World*, p. 106.

137. Maranto et al., p. 245.

138. Wells et al., "Charter Schools," p. 196.

139. Frederick M. Hess, *Revolution at the Margins: The Impact of Competition on Urban School Systems* (Washington, D.C.: Brookings Institution Press, 2002).

140. This conception of government adhered to by advocates of charter schools is derived from the reinventing government movement that started in the 1980s as an alternative to the Reagan administration's push for a massive downsizing of government. Advocates of reinventing government agreed with the Reaganites that significant efficiency and productivity gains would be realized by delegating the delivery of at least some services to private entities through a competitive bidding process, but they also emphasized that public authorities

still had a vital role to play in setting society's goals and then monitoring service delivery to ensure those goals were being met. The philosophy was neatly captured by the metaphor of a government steering but not rowing the boat. David Osborne and Ted Gaebler, *Reinventing Government: How the Entrepreneurial Spirit Is Transforming the Public Sector* (Reading, Mass.: Addison-Wesley, 1992).

141. Jeffrey R. Henig, *Rethinking School Choice*, p. 178; Robert B. Reich, "The Case for 'Progressive' Vouchers," *Wall Street Journal*, September 6, 2000, p. A26.
142. Charles V. Willie and Michael Alves, *Controlled Choice: A New Approach to Desegregated Education and School Improvement* (Providence, R.I.: Education Alliance Press, 1996).
143. There are increasing constitutional questions about using race in school admissions decisions. Also, some object to the possible implication that predominantly white schools are presumptively superior to predominantly nonwhite schools.
144. Richard D. Kahlenberg, *All Together Now*. The seminal study on the relationship between socioeconomic status and academic achievement is James S. Coleman, et al., *Equality of Educational Opportunity* (Washington, D.C.: Government Printing Office, 1966). Kahlenberg discusses and cites numerous subsequent studies establishing the link as well; see chapter 3, "The Case for Economic School Desegregation."
145. Kahlenberg, p. 1. The author defines middle-class status as an annual income higher than $32,000 for a family of four, which is the eligibility level for the subsidized school lunch program.
146. Ibid., pp. 137–41.
147. Ibid., p. 202.
148. Ibid., pp. 23–4.
149. Marilyn J. Gittell, ed., *Strategies for School Equity: Creating Productive Schools in a Just Society* (New Haven, Conn.: Yale University Press, 1998); *Equity and Adequacy in Education Finance*, ed. Helen F. Ladd, Rosemary Chalk, and Janet S. Hansen (Washington, D.C.: National Academy Press, 1999).
150. *Sheff v. O'Neill*, 238 Conn. 1, 678 A.2d 1267 (1996).
151. Memorandum of Decision, *Sheff v. O'Neill*, *Connecticut Law Tribune*, March 15, 1999.
152. Rick Green, "Magnet Schools Send an S.O.S.," *Hartford Courant*, May 30, 2001, p. A1; Robert A. Frahm, "*Sheff* Plaintiffs Back to Prod Desegregation," *Hartford Courant*, December 29, 2000, p. A1.
153. Jeffrey R. Henig, Richard C. Hula, Marion Orr, and Desiree S. Pedescleaux, *The Color of School Reform: Race, Politics, and the Challenge of Urban Education* (Princeton, N.J.: Princeton University Press, 1999).
154. Melissa C. Carr and Susan H. Fuhrman, "The Politics of School Finance in the 1990s," in *Equity and Adequacy in Education Finance*, ed. Ladd, Chalk, and Hansen.

Chapter 6

1. Emile Durkheim, *The Rules of Sociological Method* (New York: Free Press, 1982), Book 3.
2. Patrick F. Fagan and Robert E. Moffit, "Crime," in *Issues '96: The Candidate's Briefing Book* (The Heritage Foundation), available at http://crime-free.org/chpt8.html.
3. Robert J. Waste, *Independent Cities: Rethinking U.S. Urban Policy* (New York: Oxford University Press, 1998), p. 124.
4. Mark Mauer, *The Race to Incarcerate* (New York: New Press, 1999), p. 28.
5. "America's Cities: They Can Yet Be Resurrected," *The Economist*, January 10, 1998, p. 17.
6. Pat Mayhew and Jan J. M. Can Dijk, *Crime Victimisation in Eleven Industrialized Countries* (Ministry of Justice; The Netherlands, 1999), p. 27.
7. Marvin E. Wolfgang, Robert M. Figlio, and Thorsten M Sellen, *Delinquency in a Birth Cohort* (Chicago: University of Chicago Press, 1987).
8. Ted R. Miller, Mark A. Cohen, and Brian Wiersema, "The Extent and Costs of Crime Victimization: A New Look," *National Institute of Justice Research Review* (January 1996).
9. R. T. Naylor, *Wages of Crime: Black Markets, Illegal Finance, and the Underworld Economy* (Ithaca, N.Y.: Cornell University Press, 2002), p. 28.
10. Malcolm W. Klein, "Street Gang Cycles," in James Q. Wilson and Joan Petersilia, eds., *Crime* (San Francisco: Institute for Contemporary Studies, 1995), p. 231.
11. U.S. Newswire, briefing by Vice President Albert A. Gore, Jr., March 7, 1994.

12. Patrick J. Ryan, *Organized Crime: A Reference Handbook* (Santa Barbara: Contemporary World Issues, 1995), p. 159.
13. Jim Yardley, "The Client of a Lifetime, with One Drawback," *New York Times*, February 15, 1998.
14. Brendon K. Applegate et al., "Assessing Public Support for Three-Strikes-and-You're-Out Laws: Global Versus Specific Attitudes," *Crime and Delinquency* 42 (October 1996), pp. 522 and 529.
15. Katherine Beckett, *Making Crime Pay: Law and Order in Contemporary American Politics* (New York: Oxford University Press, 1997), pp. 14–27.
16. Edward Donnerstein and Daniel Linz, "The Media," in Wilson and Petersilia, eds., *Crime*, pp. 248–9.
17. Christopher Jencks, *Rethinking Social Policy: Race, Poverty, and the Underclass* (New York: Basic Books, 1992), p. 93.
18. Ann L. Pastore and Kathleen Maguire, eds., *Sourcebook of Criminal Justice Statistics*, Washington, D.C.: National Criminal Justice Reference Service (2000), available at http://www.albany.edu/sourcebook.
19. Paula D. McClain, "Urban Crime in the USA and Western Europe: A Comparison," in Ronan Paddison, ed., *The Handbook of Urban Studies* (London: Sage Publications, 2001), pp. 222–223.
20. Joel Best, *Random Crime: How We Talk about New Crimes and New Victims* (Berkeley: University of California Press, 1999), pp. 21–22.
21. Jeff Cohen and Norman Solomon, "On Local TV News, If It Bleeds It (Still) Leads," *Media Beat*, December 13, 1995, available at http://www.fair.org/media-beat/951213.html.
22. For the seminal discussion of the free-rider problem, see Mancur Olson, *The Logic of Collective Action: Public Goods and the Theory of Groups* (Cambridge, Mass.: Harvard University Press, 1965).
23. Mancur Olson, *The Logic of Collective Action*.
24. William Julius Wilson *When Work Disappears: The World of the New Urban Poor* (New York: Alfred A. Knopf, 1996), p. 21.
25. George Kelling and Catherine Coles, *Fixing Broken Windows: Restoring Order and Reducing Crime in Our Communities* (New York: Free Press, 1996), p. 30.
26. Peter W. Greenwood, "Juvenile Crime and Juvenile Justice," in Wilson and Petersilia, p. 51.
27. Franklin E. Zimring and Gordon Hawkins, *Crime Is Not the Problem: Lethal Violence in America* (New York: Oxford University Press, 1997), p. 64.
28. See Sourcebook of Criminal Justice Statistics online, available at http://www.albany.edu/sourcebook/1995/pdf/t44.pdf.
29. Michael Schumacher and Gwen A. Kurz, *The 8 Percent Solution: Preventing Serious, Repeat Juvenile Crime* (Thousand Oaks, Calif.: Sage, 1999).
30. Martin Sanchez Jankowski, *Islands in the Street: Gangs and American Urban Society* (Berkeley: University of California Press, 1994).
31. See Jeffrey Butts and Jeremy Travis, *The Rise and Fall of American Youth Violence, 1980 to 2000*, The Urban Institute, Justice Policy Center Research Report, March 2002. See also *Challenging the Myths*, Juvenile Justice Bulletin, U.S. Department of Justice, February 2000.
32. Zimring and Hawkins, *Crime Is Not the Problem*, p. 65.
33. Ibid., p. 66.
34. Quoted in Robert Wright, "The Biology of Violence," *New Yorker*, March 13, 1995, p. 72.
35. Man's chemistry actually changes when the environment presents disorder and threats. Low levels of serotonin, which make men more prone to violent behavior, are one good indicator of this interplay between biology and environment.
36. Christopher Jencks, *Rethinking Social Policy*, p. 110.
37. "Prison Literacy Programs," ERIC Digest No. 159, available at http://www.ed.gov/databases/ERIC_Digests/ed383859.html.
38. *Education as Crime Prevention: Providing Education to Prisoners*, Soros Foundation, Research Brief for the Center on Crime, Communities, and Culture, September 1997.
39. Michael S. Brunner, *Retarding America* (Portland, Oreg.: Halcyon House, 1993), pp. 29–30.
40. Christopher Lasch, *Haven in a Heartless World: The Family Besieged* (New York: W.W. Norton, 1995).
41. National Institute of Justice, "Extent, Nature, and Consequences of Intimate Partner Violence," July 2000, available at http://www.ncjrs.org/pdffiles1/nij/181867.pdf.

42. Joan McCord, "A Forty Year Perspective on the Effects of Child Abuse and Neglect," *Child Abuse and Neglect* 7 (1983), pp. 265–70.
43. Currie, 212–3.
44. Currie, p. 209.
45. Malcolm Gladwell, "Damaged," *New Yorker*, February 24 and March 3, 1997, p. 140.
46. See Malcolm Gladwell's discussion in *The Tipping Point: How Little Things Can Make a Big Difference* (Boston: Little, Brown, 2000), ch. 4.
47. James Q. Wilson and George L. Kelling, Jr., "Broken Windows," *The Atlantic Monthly*, March 1982, available at http://www.theatlantic.com/politics/crime/windows/htm.
48. Wilson and Kelling, "Broken Windows."
49. Malcolm Gladwell, *The Tipping Point*.
50. Bernard E. Harcourt, *Illusion of Order: The False Promise of Broken Windows Policing* (Cambridge, Mass.: Harvard University Press, 2001), p. 103.
51. Geoffrey Canada, *Fish Stick Knife Gun: A Personal History of Violence in America* (Boston: Beacon Press, 1996).
52. Zimring and Hawkins, *Crime Is Not the Problem*, p. 109.
53. Stephen Raphael and Rudolf Winter-Ebmer, *Identifying the Effects of Unemployment on Crime*, Centre for Economic Policy Research, Paper No. 2129, available at http://www.cepr.org.
54. Bruce A. Weinberg, Eric Gould, and David B. Mustard, "Crime Rates and Local Labor Market Opportunities in the United States: 1979–1997," *Review of Economics and Statistics* 84; 1 (February 2002), pp. 45–61.
55. Weinberg is quoted in Ohio State Research, "Higher Crime Rate Linked to Low Wages and Unemployment, Study Finds," available at http://www.acs.ohio-state.edu/researchnews/archive/crimwage.htm.
56. See, for example, George Winslow, "Capital Crimes: The Political Economy of Crime in America," *Monthly Review* (November 2000), available at http://www.monthlyreview.org/1100wins.htm.
57. For a complete profile of the prison population, see National Institute for Literacy, "Correctional Education Facts," http://www.nifl.gov/nifl/facts/correctional.html.
58. Edward C. Banfield, *The Unheavenly City Revisited* (Prospect Heights, Ill.: Waveland Press, 1974), pp. 185–6.
59. Jens Ludwig, Greg J. Duncan, and Paul Hirschfield, "Urban Poverty and Juvenile Crime: Evidence from a Randomized Housing Mobility Experiment," draft of paper prepared for publication in *Quarterly Journal of Economics*, available at http://www.wws.princeton.edu/~kling/mto/mto_balt_delinquency.pdf.
60. National Center for Policy Analysis, "Month in Review," March 1996.
61. Gary T. Marx, "Ironies of Social Control: Authorities as Contributors to Deviance Through Escalation, Nonenforcement, and Covert Facilitation," *Social Problems* 28 (February 1981), pp. 221–246.
62. For a fascinating portrait of this story, see Dick Lehr, and Gerard O'Neill, *Black Mass: The Irish Mob, the FBI, and A Devil's Deal* (New York: Thorndike Press, 2001).
63. Human Rights Watch, "Shielded from Justice: Police Brutality and Accountability in the United States," 1998, available at http://www.hrw.org/reports98/police/uspo14.htm.
64. David A. Harris, "Driving While Black: Racial Profiling on Our Nation's Highways," A Special Report for the American Civil Liberties Union, June 1999, available at http://www.aclu.org/profiling/report/.
65. Kenneth Adams et al., "Use of Force by Police: Overview of Local and National Data," National Institute of Justice, U.S. Department of Justice, pp. vii and viii, available at http://www.ncjrs.org/pdffiles1/nij/176330–1.pdf.
66. Hans H. Chen, "A Police Brutality Study's Surprising Find," *APB News*, January 6, 2000, available at http://www.apbnews.com/cjprofessionals/behindthebadge/2000/01/06/force0106_01.html?s=emil. See also Edwin J. Delattro, *Character and Cops: Ethics and Policing* (Washington: AEI Press, 1994).
67. For a psychological examination of stress on the job, see Hans Toch, *Stress in Policing* (Washington, D.C.: American Psychological Association, 2002).
68. David Remnick, "The Crime Buster," *The New Yorker*, February 24 and March 3, 1997, p. 103.
69. Remnick, "Crime Buster," p. 107.

70. John Hopkins and Mark Braykovich, "Police-Racial Issues 'Can Be Worked Out,'" *Cincinnati Enquirer*, June 24, 1997.

71. Brian Forst, "Prosecution and Sentencing," in Wilson and Petersilia, pp. 363 and 365.

72. Lara James and John Caher, "Draconian Drug Laws No Panacea," *Albany Times-Union*, May 9, 1999.

73. Alfred Blumstein, "Prisons," in Wilson and Petersilia, eds., *Crime*, p. 417.

74. Tom R. Tyler and Robert J. Boechmann, "Three Strikes And You're Out, But Why? The Psychology of Public Support For Punishing Rule Breakers," *Law and Society Review* 31 (1997), pp. 237–265.

75. National Center for Policy Analysis, "Month in Review," March 1996.

76. "Three Cheers for Three Strikes: California Enjoys a Record Drop in Crime," *Policy Review*, 80 (November-December 1996).

77. Neil Steinberg, "The Law of Unintended Consequences," *Rolling Stone*, May 5, 1994, p. 33.

78. Norval Morris and Michael Tonry, *Between Prison and Probation: Intermediate Punishments in a Rational Sentencing System* (New York: Oxford University Press, 1991).

79. Malcolm Gladwell, "Damaged," p. 71.

80. For a summary, see "Prisons in the United States of America," Human Rights Watch Prison Project, available at http://www.hrw.org/advocacy/prisons/u-s.htm.

81. See Morgan Reynolds and Knut Rostad, "Creating Factories Behind Bars," National Center for Policy Analysis, available at http://www.ncpa.org/pub/ba/ba354. For a larger discussion of how prison employment can reduce recidivism, see Stephen Duguid and Ray Pawson, "Education, Change, and Transformation: The Prison Experience," *Evaluation Review* (August 1998): 470–495.

82. Fox Butterfield, "Idle Hands within the Devil's Own Playground," *New York Times*, July 16, 1995.

83. W. Reed Benedict and Lin Huff-Corzine, "Return to the Scene of the Punishment: Recidivism of Adult Male Property Offenders on Felony Probation, 1986–1989," *Journal of Research in Crime and Delinquency* 34 (May 1997), p. 237.

84. Paul van Slambrouck, "U.S. Prisons—under Pressure—Show Increase in Violence," *Christian Science Monitor*, August 6, 2000.

85. National Center on Addiction and Substance Abuse, Columbia University, "Behind Bars: Substance Abuse and America's Prison Population," January 1998, available at http://www.casacolumbia.org/usr_doc/5745.pdf.

86. Fran Lexcen and Richard E. Redding, "Mental Health Needs of Juvenile Offenders," Juvenile Forensic Evaluation Resource Center, University of Virginia School of Law, available at http://www.ilppp.virginia.edu/Juvenile_Forensic_Fact_Sheets/MHNeedsJuroff.html.

87. James Q. Wilson, *The Varieties of Police Behavior: The Management of Law and Order in Eight Communities* (Cambridge, Mass.: Harvard University Press, 1968).

88. Max Weber, "Bureaucracy," in Hans Gerth and C. Wright Mills, ed., *From Max Weber: Essays in Sociology* (New York: Oxford University Press, 1990).

89. Wilson, *Varieties of Police Behavior*, p. 178.

90. "Media Release," Metropolitan Nashville Police Department, January 22, 2001. See http://www.police.nashville.org/news/media/2001/january/01222001.htm.

91. "This is 911 . . . Please Hold," *U.S. News and World Report*, June 17, 1996.

92. Quoted in Kelling and Coles, *Fixing Broken Windows*, p. 41.

93. See Wesley G. Skogan, *Disorder and Decline: Crime and the Spiral of Decay in American Neighborhoods* (Berkeley: University of California Press, 1990).

94. Kelling and Coles, p. 25. *Fixing Broken Windows*.

95. "CompStat: A Crime Reduction Management Tool," available at http://www.excelgov.org/innovations/innov96/compstat.htm.

96. Raymond Dussault, "Jack Maple: Betting on Intelligence," *Government Technology*, April 1999, available at http://www.govtech.net/publications/gt/1999/apr/maple/maple.phtml.

97. Heather MacDonald, "America's Best Police Force," *City Journal* (Summer 2000): 17.

98. Kelling and Coles, pp. 119–120.

99. Robert J. Waste, *Independent Cities: Rethinking U.S. Urban Policy* (New York: Oxford University Press, 1998), p. 101.

100. Human Rights Watch, "Shielded from Justice: Police Brutality and Accountability in the United States," available at http://www.hrw.org/reports98/police/index.htm.

101. James Q. Wilson, "Thinking about Crime," *Atlantic Monthly* (September 1983), available at http://www.theatlantic.com/politics/crime/wilson.htm.
102. Peter Maas, "Who Is the Mob Today?" *Parade*, February 25, 1996.
103. National Narcotics Intelligence Consumers Committee, "The Supply of Illicit Drugs to the United States," August 1995, available at http://www.mninter.net/~publish/dea1.htm.
104. Richard Sennett, *The Uses of Disorder: Personal Identity and City Life* (New York: W.W. Norton, 1992), p. 164.
105. Matthew A. Crenson, *Neighborhood Politics* (Cambridge, Mass.: Harvard University Press, 1983), p. 165.
106. Richard Sennett, *The Corrosion of Character: The Personal Consequences of Work in the New Capitalism* (New York: W.W. Norton, 1998), p. 143.

Chapter 7

1. See Jane Jacobs, *Cities and the Wealth of Nations: Principles of Economic Life* (New York: Random House, 1985).
2. Paul E. Peterson, *City Limits* (Chicago: University of Chicago Press, 1981).
3. Paul E. Peterson, *The Price of Federalism* (Washington, D.C.: Brookings Institution Press, 1995). This logic also explains why Peterson and like-minded scholars are critical of efforts to devolve authority over welfare policy from the national government to the state and local governments. The fear is that, given the intense competition among state and local governments for capital investment, devolution will unleash a "race to the bottom" in which subnational governments will try to outdo one another in cutting back on welfare benefits in order to minimize upward pressure on tax rates on business and upper-income residents. C.f. John D. Donahue, *Hazardous Crosscurrents: Confronting Inequality in an Era of Devolution* (New York: Century Foundation Press, 1999).
4. Peter Dreier, John Mollenkopf, and Todd Swanstrom, *Place Matters: Metropolitics for the Twenty-First Century* (Lawrence, Kans.: University Press of Kansas, 2001).
5. David Rusk, *Cities without Suburbs* (Washington, D.C.: Woodrow Wilson Center Press, 1995).
6. Myron Orfield, *Metropolitics: A Regional Agenda for Community and Stability* (Washington, D.C.: Brookings Institution, 1997).
7. Steven Johnson, *Emergence: The Connected Lives of Ants, Brains, Cities, and Software* (New York: Scribner, 2001).
8. For a brief overview of this approach applied to cities and regions, see Charles C. Euchner, "Where Is Greater Boston? Framing Regional Issues," in Charles C. Euchner, ed., *Governing Greater Boston: The Politics and Policy of Place* (Cambridge, Mass.: Rappaport Institute for Greater Boston, 2002), available at http://www.ksg.harvard.edu/rappaport/research/GGB-Chapter%201.pdf.
9. See Stephen Goldsmith, *The 21st Century City: Resurrecting Urban America* (Lanham, Md.: Rowman and Littlefield, 1997). For critical assessments of other privatization strategies, see Paul Starr, *The Limits of Privatization* (Washington, D.C.: Economic Policy Institute, 1987); and John D. Donahue, *The Privatization Decision: Public Ends, Private Means* (New York: Basic Books, 1991).
10. This section was based on the author's interviews with state and local officials in Minnesota in the summer of 2001. For more information, see http://www.bgic.state.mn.us.
11. William Julius Wilson, *Bridge over the Racial Divide: Rising Inequality and Coalition Politics* (Berkeley: University of California Press, 1999).
12. Quoted in Mickey Kaus, *The End of Equality* (New York: Basic Books, 1992), p. 162.
13. Matthew A. Crenson and Benjamin Ginsberg, *Downsizing Democracy: How America Sidelined Its Citizens and Privatized Its Public* (Baltimore, Md.: Johns Hopkins University Press, 2002), p. 104.
14. Alexis de Tocqueville, *Democracy in America*, ed. and abridged by Richard Heffner (New York: Signet Classics, 2001), pp. 200, 201.
15. Charles C. Euchner, *Extraordinary Politics: How Protest and Dissent Are Changing America* (Boulder, Colo.: Westview Press, 1996).
16. Of course, these movements were thoroughly infused with anti-immigrant bias. Even the most benign reforms were intended to control the behavior of the less-well-off classes. It's a

funny thing about reformers. Sometimes their very best values are wrapped up in a will to power and control. Every great reform movement has an underbelly that undermines the empowerment of someone. To elevate one cause necessarily means reducing others.

17. Ironically, this populist tool can become the instrument of well-heeled interests. Successful ballot measures tend to have an upper-class bias; note, for example, the tax-limitation and rent-control measures passed in California, Massachusetts, and other states. Ballot issues are often so complex that only policy wonks can hope to understand them. Mounting a referendum campaign can cost millions of dollars; fund-raising is subject to the same kind of elite influence as ordinary political strategies. The complexity does not end with the balloting. The constitutionality of many initiatives is contested in court for years, as attested by California's continuing controversies over votes concerning automobile insurance and affirmative action. To work, the referendum process needs a vetting process to ensure clear and authoritative questions allowed on the ballot and to finance campaigns so that all sides—not just the pro and con sides—can contribute to the debate. A body with members appointed by all three branches of government could rule on whether ballot questions are sufficiently fundamental and clear; the standards for quality would depend on whether a ballot would be binding or advisory. Referenda can promote sophisticated deliberation or reckless and biased plebiscites. It depends on the process for putting questions to the people.

18. Theodore J. Lowi, "American Business, Public Policy, Case Studies and Political Theory," *World Politics* 16 (July 1964).

19. Robert D. Putnam, *Making Democracy Work: Civic Traditions in Modern Italy* (Princeton, N.J.: Princeton University Press, 1993); and Robert D. Putnam, *Bowling Alone: The Collapse and Revival of American Community* (New York: Touchstone Books, 2000).

20. Richard Moe and Carter Wilkie, *Changing Places: Rebuilding Community in the Age of Sprawl* (New York: Henry Holt and Company, 1997), p. 138.

Index